"OBSCENE" LITERATURE
AND CONSTITUTIONAL LAW

"OBSCENE" LITERATURE
AND
CONSTITUTIONAL LAW

A Forensic Defense of Freedom of the Press

By Theodore Schroeder

New Introduction by Jerold S. Auerbach
Wellesley College

DA CAPO PRESS · NEW YORK · 1972

Library of Congress Cataloging in Publication Data

Schroeder, Theodore Albert, 1864-1953.
  "Obscene" literature and constitutional law.

  Includes bibliographical references.
  1. Obscenity (Law) — U. S.   2. Liberty of the
press — U. S.   I.   Title.
KF4774.S3 1972   342'.73'085   72-116913
ISBN 0-306-70156-1

First published by the author, New York, 1911;
republished 1972 with a new introduction.

Copyright © 1972 by Da Capo Press

A Subsidiary of Plenum Publishing Corporation
227 West 17th Street, New York, New York 10011

All Rights Reserved

Manufactured in the United States of America

INTRODUCTION

Description by superlative is an enduring American trait. As a people we derive comfort from periodic enumerations of our greatest Presidents, wealthiest businessmen, and best-dressed women. Amid the welter of adjectives there occasionally lurks a neglected subject deserving of the accolades. Theodore Schroeder (1864–1953), lawyer and author, was such an individual. Described by journalist Harold L. Nelson as "probably the most prolific champion of free speech and press in American history," by historian Paul S. Boyer as "the man who did the most to advance [the] pre-World War One censorship debate," and by a publisher's blurb as "the world's leading authority on the legal aspects of freedom," Schroeder nonetheless languishes in obscurity. Little of his work is in print, and it is unlikely that many of his nearly two hundred articles are read in any of the six languages in which they were published. If superlatives are necessary to rekindle interest in him, it surely may be said that Schroeder, a maverick radical, ventured further than any of his contemporaries in exploring the meaning of literary and political freedom of expression.[1]

Schroeder's prodigious literary output reached its peak during the Progressive era between the turn of the century and World War I, years of reform ferment when Americans first attempted to confront the problems that accompanied industrialization and urbanization. Crusades to conserve natural resources and arrest political corruption, to purify food and humanize factory conditions, to eradicate slums and abolish prostitution, and to liberalize divorce and extend literary freedom, however disparate they seemed, arose from deeply-shared convictions regarding the thwarted promise of American life. Reformers infused each issue

---

[1] Harold L. Nelson, ed., *Freedom of the Press from Hamilton to the Warren Court* (Indianapolis: Bobbs-Merrill Co., 1967), p. 279; Paul S. Boyer, *Purity in Print: The Vice-Society Movement and Book Censorship in America* (New York: Charles Scribner's Sons, 1968), p. 41; Amicus Curiae [pseud.], *May It Please the Court* (New Jersey: Sunshine Book Co., 1945). For an insightful study of Schroeder's life and work, see David Brudnoy, "Liberty's Bugler: The Seven Ages of Theodore Schroeder" (Ph.D. diss., Brandeis University, 1971).

v

with a moral urgency which testified to their conviction that the very soul of the nation was in jeopardy. Schroeder's ceaseless campaign to halt censorship of allegedly obscene literature seemed superficially to place him on the barricades against the moralists, rather than on their side. But the appearance was deceptive. Schroeder knew, as so many of our own contemporaries now understand, that the problem of obscenity (in the words of a current scholar) "involves far-reaching questions about the nature of our community — the ends and values by which this civil society shall be governed. . . ."[2] Schroeder, no less than his archenemy Anthony Comstock, the self-appointed censor for the nation, fought so tenaciously because the moral stakes were so high.

The problem of obscenity, which simultaneously cuts across individual freedom of expression and the role of government in relation to public morality, presents momentous legal and social issues. During the 1960's, in the wake of the first Supreme Court decisions on the subject, venturesome publishers and film directors once again forced Americans to confront the very issue that galvanized Theodore Schroeder more than half a century ago: where shall the line be drawn between individual expression and social restraint? If the law of obscenity, in the judgment of one expert, has become "a constitutional disaster area," this is but a reflection of disagreements in society so fundamental that any compromise is viewed as a defeat, and every defeat seems to portend disaster. "Moralists" fight to preserve fundamental values; "libertarians" seek escape from oppressive constraints. On the Court as in the country, the protagonists move back and forth across the same battlefield with neither side able to eradicate, nor live without, the other. There is agreement only on the questions — "Should the line be drawn as close as possible to hard-core pornography in order to insure that no serious work of literature will ever come within the cognizance of the law? Or, should we be willing to tolerate some restraints on some forms of serious literature in order to restrain sensuality and indecency which falls short of the worst extremes?"[3] What, in other words, is the role of government in the realm of morality?

2 Harry M. Clor, *Obscenity and Public Morality: Censorship in a Liberal Society* (Chicago: University of Chicago Press, 1969), p. 3.
3 The phrase "constitutional disaster area" is from C. Peter Magrath, "The Obscenity Cases: Grapes of Roth" in Philip B. Kurland, ed., *The Supreme Court Review* (Chicago: University of Chicago Press, 1966), p. 59. This paragraph draws liberally upon the perceptive analysis in Clor, *Obscenity and Public Morality*, especially pp. 1–11.

Schroeder's was the first generation of Americans to confront this issue in its modern setting. During the last quarter of the nineteenth century, Americans whose values were rooted in a pre-urban, pre-industrial nation sought to preserve their culture against the ominous currents of social change that swept across the countryside. These defenders of rural Protestant values in an increasingly heterogeneous urban society battled for purity on many fronts. Purity in print, in Paul S. Boyer's felicitous phrase, was especially critical at a time when new techniques of mass communication portended mass literacy on an unprecedented scale. American custodians of Victorian culture joined hands in the vice-society movement, "a response to deep-seated fears about the drift of urban life in the post-Civil War years."[4] In an era which was "perhaps the last in which adults had a fair chance to impose their judgments on young people," censorship of obscene literature became for many Americans a compelling social obligation.[5]

So thought Anthony Comstock, a native of rural Connecticut who spent months lobbying for federal anti-obscenity legislation (enacted in 1873) and forty years enforcing it. According to his own proud boast, he bravely stationed himself "in a swamp at the mouth of a sewer," where, during his lifetime, he destroyed 160 tons of obscene literature. Comstock's obsession with obscenity was not without its rewards. As his biographers noted, he "could have his cake and suppress it, too." Anything that Comstock found personally objectionable was obscene. He gladly conceded that the language of the 1873 statute, prohibiting the mailing of "every obscene, lewd, lascivious, indecent, filthy or vile article, matter, thing, device, or substance," opened a "wide-mouthed trap for evil-doers" — but that was as it should be. Comstock's moral values were widely shared, of course; otherwise, his name and cause would have been doomed to obscurity. "What set him apart was not his ideas, but his compulsion to put them into action."[6] As special agent for the Post Office Department, and as founder of the New York Society for the Suppression of Vice, Comstock searched unremittingly to find evildoers for his trap. There was no shortage.

If time was Comstock's ally in the nineteenth century, it loomed as his enemy by the beginning of the twentieth. The older Victorian

---

[4] Boyer, *Purity in Print*, pp. 3, 6–7.

[5] Anthony Comstock, *Traps for the Young*, ed. Robert Bremner (Cambridge: Harvard University Press, 1967), p. viii.

[6] *Ibid.*, pp. vii–viii, xiii, xvii, xxix; Heywood Broun and Margaret Leech, *Anthony Comstock: Roundsman of the Lord* (New York: Albert & Charles Boni, 1927), pp. 12, 16, 19.

synthesis began to fragment; cracks appeared in the fortress of traditional culture. As William O'Neill observes, "the shift from delicacy and evasion to realism and candor in the treatment of sexual themes took place with remarkable speed, and the shock that this new frankness produced can hardly be appreciated. . . ."[7] Certainly Comstock must have been shocked by the explicitness of the literary realists, by the popularity of yellow journalism, and by the public debates over divorce, prostitution, and birth control. Although actions for obscenity, most frequently instigated by Comstock, still "plagued the world of books and magazines," the censors no longer enjoyed the support of an overwhelming moral consensus for purity.[8] Yet it is the final measure of Comstock's influence that "those who hated him were no less shaped by his career than the many who respected his principles."[9] Many Progressives, in their struggles for freedom, displayed the very moral absolutism so characteristic of their opponents.

Theodore Schroeder personified this paradox. His was an intolerant crusade for tolerance, an authoritarian struggle for liberty, an emotional pursuit of reasoned truth. His shocked perception of obscenity drove him to the declaration that nothing was obscene. Nemesis of the vice societies, he nonetheless could call upon "enlightened public opinion" to obliterate the "sanctified lust" of the Mormons. His fear of sexual perversion led him to advocate freer divorce. And his horror of promiscuity and venereal disease propelled him into a holy war against the censors who shared his horror — but not his tactics for exorcising its causes. Bitter substantive disagreements made Schroeder and Comstock appear as polar opposites, but they shared more than they ever realized.

Schroeder was born on a Wisconsin farm in 1864, the son of a German Catholic mother and a stern German Lutheran father. Little is known of his early years; with the exception of a solitary incident, one can search in vain through his voluminous writings for autobiographical revelations. But that exception is crucial to an understanding of Schroeder's career. When he was fifteen, he recounted, he had left home to find work in Chicago — perhaps to escape his father's strict discipline. There he worked as an errand boy and then as a salesman of women's hosiery and underwear in a Halstead Street department store. One day he wandered into a

---

7 William L. O'Neill, *Divorce in the Progressive Era* (New Haven: Yale University Press, 1967), pp. 142–43, 257.
8 Nelson, ed., *Freedom of the Press*, p. xxxi.
9 Broun and Leech, *Anthony Comstock*, p. 15.

museum of anatomy, where, as he remembered the visit twenty-five years later, he

> saw perfect imitations in wax of all the indescrib-
> able horrors, consequent upon venereal infection.
> Of course the exhibition was obscene and indecent
> beyond description, but it was something more as
> well. It was an object lesson giving occular demon-
> stration of the terrible consequences of promis-
> cuity and could not do otherwise than to inspire
> a wholesome fear of which I have not rid myself
> to this day.[10]

Here the paradox of Theodore Schroeder began: his lifelong insistence that censorship of the obscene was unjustifiable because
obscenity was nothing more than a subjective state of mind, was
itself a product of an encounter with something so "obscene and
indecent" as to produce "a wholesome fear" from which Schroeder
never escaped.

After studying intermittently at the University of Wisconsin during the 1880's, earning an undergraduate degree in civil engineering
and, in 1889, an LL.B., he left Wisconsin for Salt Lake City, where
he launched both his law practice and his unceasing warfare against
Mormonism. In Utah, Schroeder published a series of pamphlets entitled "Lucifer's Lantern." In one, he asked "Was Joseph Smith an
Abortionist?" and answered unequivocally in the affirmative. Smith,
he maintained, had presided over an abortion mill in the Mormon
temple at Nauvoo, Illinois. The Mormons, no doubt with unin-
tended irony, sued Schroeder for sending obscene literature through
the mails. Undaunted, he fought vigorously and successfully for
the exclusion of polygamist Congressman Brigham Roberts from
the House of Representatives. Schroeder, according to a friend,
viewed polygamy as "a special manifestation of the over-sexed condition which . . . was a phase of emotionalism that usually accom-
panies intense religious enthusiasm."[11] Shortly before departing

---

[10] Schroeder's account of the visit appears in *Freedom of the Press and "Obscene" Literature* (New York: Free Speech League, 1906), p. 25, and in
"Obscene" Literature and Constitutional Law, (New York: The Author,
1911), *infra* pp. 56–57. Additional biographical information is drawn largely
from Joseph Ishill, "Theodore Schroeder," in Ishill, *A New Concept of
Liberty from an Evolutionary Psychologist: Theodore Schroeder* (New
Jersey: Oriole Press, 1940), pp. ix–lxxx.

[11] Editorial note by Benjamin O. Flower to Schroeder, "The Impurity of
Divorce Suppression," *Arena* XXXIII (February 1905): 142.

Utah for New York City in 1901, he referred to Mormonism as a "degrading and damning social system. . . . Social vice elsewhere is held under the ban of enlightened public sentiment. In [Mormonism] it changes its name and adds the mumblings of a priest — and lust is sanctified."[12]

Schroeder discovered new enemies in the East. Vituperative outcries against "prurient prudes," "quack reformers with diseased nerves," and "social purists" began to punctuate his writings. From the Mormon issue Schroeder moved easily into the debate over liberalization of divorce. At the time it was not uncommon for Americans to perceive divorce as a stage of consecutive polygamy; they could, therefore, oppose divorce and Mormonism with equal intensity. Schroeder, always *sui generis,* favored one and fought the other. He not only challenged the notion, promoted by conservatives, that liberalized divorce laws would foster immorality, but he stood the claim on its head and asserted that strict divorce laws would be "likely to increase the number of moral perverts." To deny opportunity for divorce and remarriage meant the likelihood of "increased sex-irregularity, usually with the countenancy of concubinage, and especially on the part of women sex-inversion and other perversions. . . ."[13] For Schroeder, divorce represented an exit from sin, not an entrance into it.[14] And again, once a vision of moral perversion possessed him, it drove him relentlessly — drove him, paradoxically, to the very frontiers of liberalism and libertarianism. He never stopped to consider that his allegation of "erotophobia" against the "purists" could be hurled back to him as a *tu quoque,* that his monomania was no less intense than theirs. Like them, Schroeder did indeed protest too much.[15]

Schroeder's odyssey from the museum of anatomy to obscenity, polygamy, and divorce brought him finally to the issue of censorship and free expression. "A decent regard for the moral welfare of the community," he insisted, "compels us to demand for the general public such liberty of the press, and other means of publicity, as will protect each in his right to learn and to know. . . ."[16]

---

[12] Schroeder, "Polygamy in Congress: The Mormon Breach of Faith," *Arena* XXIII (February 1900): 114.

[13] Schroeder, "Impurity of Divorce Suppression," pp. 142, 146.

[14] See the suggestive analysis in O'Neill, *Divorce in the Progressive Era*, pp. 50n, 209–10.

[15] Just as Schroeder crossed the bridge of Mormonism to divorce, so the divorce issue, in turn, brought him to the problem of prostitution. He argued that to compel unhappily married couples to remain married was enforced prostitution. *Ibid.*, p. 224.

[16] Schroeder, *Freedom of the Press and "Obscene" Literature*, pp. 26–27.

In 1911, in pursuit of this goal, Schroeder established the Free Speech League, an organization which attracted Progressives like Lincoln Steffens and Brand Whitlock. The League, an incorporated extension of Schroeder's own personality and an outlet for his publications, opposed all forms of government censorship of expression. Schroeder's prolific campaign against "the infamous and ignorant conspiracy of silence" regarding sexual matters led him to reexamine the meaning of liberty, the boundaries of free expression, and the precepts on which sumptuary laws rested.[17] In book after book — including *Freedom of the Press and "Obscene" Literature* (1906), *Free Press Anthology* (1909), *Free Speech for Radicals* (1916), *Constitutional Free Speech* (1919), and *Free Speech Bibliography* (1922) — Schroeder played variations on the theme of liberty of expression. His magnum opus, *"Obscene" Literature and Constitutional Law* (1911), rooted though it surely was in Schroeder's uneasy assimilation of his own experiences, was described by a contemporary lawyer as "unanswered and unanswerable," and by an historian as a "remorselessly logical statement of the anticensorship position — a position totally at variance with the prevailing consensus."[18]

In a postscript to chapter XIV of the book, Schroeder confessed that "I tried hastily to make a book by the use of a paste pot and some magazine articles, where I should have rewritten the whole." Few readers will wish to quarrel with the author's judgment. Many of the chapters had been published previously as articles — some in obscure medical journals, others in prominent law reviews, a number in popular magazines. As a result, the style is uneven and occasionally turgid, and Schroeder's argument is frequently repetitive.

Schroeder declared his intention "to address an argument to the members of the bar generally and to others interested." But this was an overly modest conception, for his subject, then as now, was too important to be left to lawyers and scattered laymen. His book deserves a wide audience not merely because the author was a daring eccentric, but because he alone in his time ventured to explore so much uncharted terrain: the relationship between obscenity and guarantees of free speech (chap. I–VII); the historical background of freedom of expression (chaps. VIII–XII); the psychological components of obscenity (chaps. XIII–XVII); and the difficulty

---

[17] *Ibid.*, p. 24.
[18] James F. Morton, Jr., "Our Foolish Obscenity Laws," *Publisher's Weekly* XC (July 8, 1916): 97; Boyer, *Purity in Print*, p. 42.

of reconciling prosecutions for obscenity with due process of law
(chaps. XVIII–XXIII).

Schroeder's brief against censorship of allegedly obscene literature contained three major propositions: first, obscenity statutes
were unconstitutional because they violated the First Amendment,
the due process clause, and the ex post facto provision of the Constitution, as well as various state bills of rights; second, censorship
contributed to ignorance, which, in turn, produced serious mental
and emotional disorders; finally, obscenity, a subjective state of
mind devoid of objective reality, reflected a personal pathology and
would disappear when people ceased to believe in its existence. But
however eclectic his approach, Schroeder's goal remained fixed:
"the judicial annulment of all present State and Federal laws
against 'obscene' literature."[19]

At the core of Schroeder's legal-constitutional argument was the
assertion that obscenity statutes were void because of vagueness.
Terms like "lewd," "indecent," "filthy," and "disgusting" were,
Schroeder properly insisted, "outrageously undefinable." The ordinary citizen could never know in advance whether his actions were
criminal; nor were there criteria by which judge or jury could determine guilt. As a result, enforcement officials were vested with
enormous discretion and "obscenity" was transformed into a constructive offense whose limits were as capacious as Anthony Comstock's imagination. Therefore, Schroeder argued, every obscenity
statute "is void, because 'where the law is uncertain there is no
law,' and no 'due process of law.' "[20]

Schroeder vigorously (and presciently) rejected the notion of
punishment based on the alleged bad tendency of expression. "It is
time enough to punish dangerous opinions when the 'danger' has
ceased to be merely speculative and hypothetical," he argued. "Let
us then put ourselves firmly on the side of those who would never
punish any opinion, until it had resulted in an overt act. . . ."[21]
These striking passages, which alone entitle Schroeder to recogni-

[19] *"Obscene" Literature and Constitutional Law, infra* p. 11.
[20] *Ibid.*, pp. 45, 361, 364, 402. The careful reader will observe that Schroeder
tends to weaken his own argument by insisting upon the existence of something called *"the law."* Constructive offenses arose because "not one lawyer
in ten thousand has a truly scientific conception of *the law,* or of its essential nature." *Ibid.*, p. 344. The function of the judiciary, he wrote elsewhere, "is to discover, declare and enforce the prior existing law, and never
to construct or create law." Schroeder, "The Scientific Aspect of Due Process of Law and Constructive Crimes," *American Law Review* XLII (May-
June 1908): 373. Paradoxically, Schroeder managed to transform his legal
fundamentalism into a substantive position antithetical to legal orthodoxy.
[21] *"Obscene" Literature and Constitutional Law, infra* pp. 92–93.

tion as a libertarian of shining magnitude, simultaneously looked backward to the most advanced libertarian thought of the eighteenth century and forward to the ringing opinions of Justice Holmes, whose clear and present danger test shortly would become the libertarian substitute for bad tendency. As firm a believer as Holmes in the marketplace of ideas, Schroeder capped his legal argument with a highly pragmatic rationale for freedom:

> If our conceptions of sexual morality have a rational foundation, then they are capable of adequate rational defense, and there is no need for legislative suppression of discussion. If our sex ethics will not bear critical scrutiny and discussion, then to suppress such discussion is infamous, because it is a legalized support of error. In either case the freest possible discussion is a necessary condition of the progressive elimination of error.[22]

Schroeder was equally daring, although perhaps less convincing, when he turned from the constitutional to the psychological implications of sex censorship. In passages which seem to harken directly back to his shocking experience in the Chicago Museum of Anatomy, Schroeder tied freedom of expression to freedom from disease. Censorship prevented "the innocent sufferers of venereal infection [from learning] just how terrible are the ravages of these diseases — how their presence may be detected — and that they can be cured, and their spread prevented." Furthermore, suppression of discussion about sexual matters promoted "morbid curiosity," which left its victims "easy prey to the wiles of the designing." As a result of censorship and ignorance, "thousands of people are in asylums who would not be there but for our legalized prudery."[23] Schroeder admitted no legitimacy whatever to the arguments supporting *some* regulation of obscene literature. Judgments in support of obscenity laws were not only developed out of ignorance, but were "re-inforced by emotions which often owe their intensity to diseased nerves." To favor regulation of obscenity was to manifest "diseased sex-sensitiveness," which, Schroeder confessed, "arouses in me the most profound contempt of which my phlegmatic nature is capable."[24]

At this juncture, however, Schroeder's argument gave signs of unraveling. Modesty and prudery, Schroeder claimed (not without

22 *Ibid.*, p. 87.
23 *Ibid.*, pp. 8, 66.
24 *Ibid.*, pp. 7, 27.

some measure of truth in some instances), "are founded on excessive sensuality"; prudery was nothing but a manifestation of "perverted sexuality."[25] If, however, Comstockery was nothing more than hypersensitive sensualism, then by analogy what is one to make of Schroeder's obsession with sex and disease, and his evident fear of sex as a destructive force? It is at least open to conjecture that his advocacy of sexual literary freedom concealed as prim a personality as characterized the most proper Victorian — even though some of his opponents may have seen in Schroeder a resemblance to those "other Victorians" about whom Steven Marcus has written.[26]

The third string in Schroeder's bow was his insistence that "the 'immorality' resulting from reading a book depends, not upon its 'obscenity,' but upon the abnormality of the reading mind, which the book does not create, but simply reveals."[27] Obscenity, in other words, was devoid of objective reality. Therefore, just as witches vanished when men ceased to believe in them, "so when men shall cease to believe in the 'obscene' they will also cease to find that."[28] Schroeder exhaustively documented divergent cultural definitions of obscenity, but his reasoning from the evidence was flawed. It does not necessarily follow, as Schroeder argued, that because norms regarding obscenity were culturally subjective, no regulation was permissible. The furthest that one can reasonably extend Schroeder's argument is that the high subjectivity component in obscenity dictates *prudent* regulation or proscription. Indeed, even this assertion requires careful hedging, which Schroeder, in his righteous fury, never provided. First, not everything labeled obscene may fairly be assessed as the reader's projection into the text. Definitions, within some fairly narrow limits, are possible — and the fact that they are cultural definitions hardly negates them.[29]

---

25 *Ibid.*, pp. 324, 325.
26 See Steven Marcus, *The Other Victorians: A Study of Sexuality and Pornography in Mid-Nineteenth-Century England* (New York: Basic Books, 1966). As late as 1945, Schroeder, who lived until the age of eighty-eight, still insisted that "obscenity is always and exclusively in the shame-psychology of the accusing and contemplating persons. Their sensitiveness is a product of their own past 'guilty' experience." Amicus Curiae, *May It Please the Court*, p. 35.
27 *"Obscene" Literature and Constitutional Law*, *infra* p. 103. See also pp. 13–14.
28 *Ibid.*, p. 254.
29 See, for example, Clor, *Obscenity and Public Morality*, pp. 158–59, *passim*; Richard H. Kuh, *Foolish Figleaves? Pornography in — and out of — Court* (New York: Macmillan Co., 1967).

Furthermore, disagreement over a definition does not cause the concept itself to vanish. Truth, beauty, and sin, like obscenity, cannot be wished away because reasonable men find it difficult to formulate precise definitions which can win wide acquiescence. Finally, as Harry M. Clor inquires, "Is it not the case that writers of pornography intend to produce a prurient effect and that readers in fact experience this effect?"[30] Notwithstanding the definitional circularity in this question, it still suggests the possibility of a social evil that the state may have a right to prevent. No matter how frequently Schroeder reiterated his conviction that if obscenity "had any existence outside the mere mind and feelings of the obscenity-seeing humans, then the standard of 'obscenity' would be uniform," his analysis on this point begged important questions.[31]

Schroeder, however, was quite convinced. Toward the end of *"Obscene" Literature and Constitutional Law* he declared that "it has been exhaustively shown that, whether studied from the viewpoint of abstract psychology, sexual psychology, abnormal psychology, ethnography, juridical history, ethics or moral sentimentalism," obscenity statutes were unjustified. "Accordingly," he concluded in his final sentence, "all laws against 'obscene' literature or art are . . . void."[32] Schroeder may well have claimed credit for more than he had proven, but his sensitivity to the manifold dimensions of the obscenity problem, his application, however flawed, of the social sciences to legal issues, and his dedication "to the liberation of mankind from the tyrannies of governments, of fears and superstitions" more than entitle him and his work to serious consideration and to libertarian acclaim.[33]

In our own time we can easily discern the altered contours of the obscenity issue. The total freedom for which Schroeder contended has not been won, but the pendulum has swung further in the direc-

[30] Clor, *Obscenity and Public Morality*, pp. 158–59.
[31] Schroeder, "Our Prudish Censorship," *Forum* LIII (January 1915): 87. Schroeder was by no means the sole defender of this position. Obscenity, maintained civil liberties lawyer Morris Ernst, "is only a superstition of the day — the modern counterpart of ancient witchcraft." Morris L. Ernst and William Seagle, *To the Pure . . . A Study of Obscenity and the Censor* (New York: Viking Press, 1928), p. x. And at least as late as 1948 an Ohio judge wrote in an opinion: "Obscenity is very much a figment of the imagination — an indefinable something in the minds of some and not in the minds of others. . . ." Quoted in Clor, *Obscenity and Public Morality*, p. 210. However simplistic this position may seem, it should be remembered that it defined the libertarian stance toward obscenity for many decades.
[32] *"Obscene" Literature and Constitutional Law, infra* pp. 414, 424.
[33] Ishill, *A New Concept of Liberty*, p. lvii.

rection of broad latitude for literary expression than most of Schroeder's contemporaries would have contemplated — or tolerated. Nonetheless, the Comstock law — the 1873 statute for which Comstock had successfully lobbied — was upheld by the Supreme Court by a one-vote margin in 1957, and the crusading zeal that once suffused its enforcement has not entirely subsided.[34] Indeed, recent scholarly analyses of obscenity defend an active governmental role in the promulgation and enforcement of moral norms. "It must be a task of modern government and law," Harry Clor maintains, "to support and promote the public morality on which a good social life depends." And attorney Richard Kuh insists that antipornography measures "should be available to protect 'established morality'. . . . "[35]

These writers reject Comstock's zeal and Schroeder's absolutism. But Schroeder, like Comstock, can be ignored only at peril of ignorance by those who seek to understand the social history of the United States as it entered the urban-industrial age. The pre-World War I years witnessed heightened tension between rival American cultures whose antagonisms often were so intense because the protagonists still shared so much in common. Schroeder and Comstock both stepped outside their rural Protestant heritage to confront modern America. Both were so frightened by their observations that the direction of their lives was permanently altered. Comstock fought tenaciously to preserve the old order; Schroeder struggled courageously to understand the new. Neither was entirely successful. Comstock could not prevent change; Schroeder could not hasten it.[36] But the careers of both shed light on murky corners of

---

[34] The federal anti-obscenity statute, popularly known as the Comstock law, was upheld in *Roth* v. *United States*, 354 U.S. 476 (1957).

[35] Clor, *Obscenity and Public Morality*, pp. 182–94; Kuh, *Foolish Figleaves?*, p. 282.

[36] A final irony, and indignity, occurred after Schroeder's death in 1953. In his will Schroeder had left his property to two friends for the purpose of collecting and publishing his writings. But two female first cousins successfully brought suit to break the will. The Supreme Court of Connecticut ruled that for a public charity to be upheld, it must be consistent with public policy. Referring to Schroeder's work, the Court declared: "The law will not declare a trust valid when the object of the trust . . . is to distribute articles which reek of the sewer." The Court explained that reading one of his articles was "a truly nauseating experience in the field of pornography." *The Fidelity Title and Trust Co., Executor (Estate of Theodore Schroeder)* v. *Ethel Clyde et al.*, 143 Conn. 247, 255 (1956).

our national history. The issue, after all, went deeper than obscenity; it cut to the very core of our moral standards and national
values in an era of sweeping social change.

Wellesley College
Wellesley, Massachusetts

JEROLD S. AUERBACH

"OBSCENE" LITERATURE
AND CONSTITUTIONAL LAW

" He that would make his own liberty secure, must guard even his enemy from oppression, for if he violates this duty he establishes a precedent that will reach to himself."

—*Thomas Paine.*

" Those powers of the people which are reserved as a check upon the sovereign can be effectual only so far as they are brought into action by private individuals. Sometimes a citizen by the force and perseverance of his complaints, opens the eyes of a nation."

—*De Lolme.*

" I will be harsh as truth and as uncompromising as justice. I am in earnest; I will not equivocate; I will not excuse; I will not retreat a single inch; and I will be heard."

Garrison.

CONTENTS

3

CONTENTS

ERRATA.

Page 31 : Westermarck, Finnish scholar, not Swedish.

P. 71 : Foot-note 20 probably refers to whole article, as no refer-ence figure appears in the text.

P. 308 : Foot-note corresponding to Reference 91 (Ohio Decameron case, U. S. Court) is missing.

P. 318 : Foot-note, *Wollstonecraft*, not "Woolstonecraft."

P. 320 : Foot-note 113 should refer to Prof. W. I. Thomas, not to "Fables for the Female Sex."

P. 392 : Foot-note corresponding to Reference 63 is missing.

P. 401 : Foot-note 86, quoted from memory, is State *vs.* Holland, 37 Mont., 393." Also, a decision from Oregon or Washington holding invalid an anti-cigarette ordinance for want of a definition of what con-stitutes a cigarette.

P. 401 : The foot-note here, McJunkins *vs.* State, 10 Ind., 145 (A. D. 1858,) should go to page 406 as foot-note 87.

P. 406 : Foot-note now numbered 87 should be numbered 88, Cook *vs.* State, 59 N. E. Ind. 489-90 (1901).

P. 407 : Foot-note 89 should be, "Requoted from Heywood's Defense, p. 29."

P. 407 : Foot-note 90 should be, Ex parte Andrew Jackson, 45 Ark. 164 (1885).

P. 407 : Foot-note 91 should be, U. S, *vs.* Commerford, 25 Fed. Rep. 904, West. Dist. of Texas.

P. 407 : Foot-note now numbered 91 is astray, there being no corresponding reference in text.

There are quite a number of breaks in the continuity of several series of the foot-notes and the corresponding reference figures in the text, due to the transference of parts of the text to other places in the book after the citations and the foot-notes were linotyped.

PROLEGOMENA

I understand a preface to be the place used by authors for explaining the reason of the existence and the character of their performance, and sometimes to aid the reader to some advance appreciation of the author's purpose and viewpoint. To these ends I will devote this introduction.

My numerous smug friends, who pride themselves on their "eminent respectability," often reproach me gently for my extensive advocacy of freedom of speech and press, and of uncensored mails and express. To defend the right of all humans to an opportunity to know all there is to know, even about the subject of sex, to the polluted minds of my "pure" friends, is to defend an "uncleanness"—not at all unclean so far as it relates to their own bodies, but "unclean" to talk and read about —not "unclean" as to any acts or facts in their own lives, but "unclean" only to admit a consciousness of those facts. I reluctantly confess that all such hypocritical moral cant, or diseased sex-sensitiveness, arouses in me the most profound contempt of which my phlegmatic nature is capable. Perhaps that is ONE reason why I was impelled to do this uncompensated and unpopular work and sometimes to do it in a manner that is devoid of tact, according to the judgment of those who dare not countenance robust frankness.

They say to me, "What do you care? You know all you wish to upon the tabooed subject; what do you care, even though the general public is kept in ignorance, and a few [thousand] go insane as the result? That doesn't harm you any, and may be the public is benefited, in that, together with serious and searching sex-discussion, much real smut is also suppressed." Such has always been the specious plea of the shortsighted and the cowardly, during the whole period of the agitation for a secular state and freedom of speech.

The answers to such specious "arguments" have been often made in the contests of past centuries, and I can do no better than to quote the answer of Dr. Priestly: "A tax of a penny is a trifle, but a power imposing that tax is never considered as a trifle, because *it may imply absolute servitude in all who submit to it.* In like manner the enjoining of the posture of kneeling at the Lord's supper is not a thing worth disputing about in itself, but *the authority of enjoining it is;* because it is in fact a power of making the Christian religion as burdensome as the Jewish, and a power that hath actually been carried to that length in the church of Rome. * * * Our ancestors, the old Puritans, had the same merit in opposing the imposition of the surplice that Hampden had in opposing the levying of ship money. In neither case was it the thing itself they objected to, so much *as the authority* that enjoined it *and the danger of the precedent.* And it appears to us that the man who is as tenacious of his religious as he is of his civil liberty will oppose them both with equal firmness. * * * The man of a strong and enlarged mind will always oppose these things when only in the beginning, when only the resistance can have any effect; but the weak and the timid, and short-sighted, will attempt nothing till the chains are riveted and resistance is too late. In civil matters the former will take his stand at the levying of the first penny by improper authority, and in matters of religion, at the first, though the most trifling, ceremony that is without reason made necessary, whereas the latter will wait till the load, in both cases, is become too heavy to be either supported or thrown off."

In itself it may not be of great importance that by unconstitutional statutes, much disagreeable literary and inartistic matter about sex is suppressed, nor even that the best scientific literature about sex is withheld from the laity, and to some extent even from physicians; it may not even be of importance that, as a result of this general compulsory ignorance about sex, thousands of people are in asylums who would not be there but for our legalized prudery, and compulsory ignorance, but it is of infinite importance to destroy a precedent which implies the admission of a power to wipe out any literature upon any subject, which, through popular hysteria or party passion, may be declared "against the public welfare."

So long as the present laws against "obscene" literature stand unchallenged as to their constitutionality, we admit that here, as in Russia, liberty of the press is liberty only by permission, not liberty as a matter of right. With the "obscenity" laws as a precedent, our censorship has grown until now (and I say this deliberately and later may furnish the proof of it), liberty of the press in the United States is more perniciously and more extensively curtailed than it was in England at the time of our revolution. That sounds strange to the American dullards who on the Fourth of July *talk* about liberty without knowing its meaning, but a comparison of the laws then and now will justify my conclusion.

Most of the following essays have already appeared in various popular, radical, medical and legal journals. My intention was primarily to address an argument to the members of the bar generally and to others interested. I have not thought it best to change any of the substance of my argument or the manner of stating it on account of the fact that it may be presented to a judicial tribunal. I hope I do not over-estimate the intellectual hospitality of our appellate courts, by not having taken into account those little tricks of intellectual expediency which lawyers often feel compelled to resort to when addressing judges of smaller mental caliber. I have bluntly stated what to me seemed to be the truth and I wish to remind the judges who may do me the honor to read this, that no litigant whose interests may be involved can be justly held accountable for my indiscretions or want of tact. I am almost glad that I did not have time thoroughly to revise these essays after their publication in the magazines, lest I should have been tempted to withdraw the compliment to our courts, which is implied in my robust frankness.

At the very outset, I feel an urgent necessity for expressing some misgivings which I entertain, as to the arguments that follow, and thus incidentally I express my apologies therefor if such are deemed to be due from me. In many places, it seems to me that I have unnecessarily elaborated what perhaps is so elementary that I should have assumed every lawyer's familiarity with it. If I fail to make this assumption, it is because I remember that thousands of lawyers, in as many cases, have had opportunity, and courts have had the duty, to make a practical application of these fundamental principles, without giving a hint that they knew of their existence. Many of these cases have gone to appellate courts, including the Supreme Court of the United States.

Am I in error in thinking these principles elementary? Or is it error to assume that innumerable distinguished lawyers and courts are familiar with elementary principles? These are the questions which perplex. It seems to me that others have unconsciously taken too much for granted; shall I then deliberately repeat their error? In this perplexing situation, I must resolve all doubts against myself. In view of all the facts relating to innumerable prosecutions where the principles herein-to-be contended for should have been applied, I feel myself unqualified to determine what is safe to take for granted. If I am wrong in that which I will claim, the courts will correct me, when this argument reaches them, as it ultimately will. If I am right, I dare not take for granted that others know it as axiomatic, for I must heed the warning given me by the recorded experience of others.

In closing, I must again ask that judges to whom this argument may be presented will not hold either the lawyers who may refer to it or their clients responsible for my indiscretions, if I am deemed guilty of such. This argument has been prepared, as also all possible revised editions of it will be, without reference to any particular case, or any particular court. Had a thorough revision been possible before book-publication, I should have eliminated many repetitions of thought, which seemed necessary in preparing the separate magazine articles.

New York City.   THEODORE SCHROEDER.

CHAPTER I.

A STATEMENT OF THE CONTENTIONS

Revised from *The Albany Law Journal,* Nov., 1907.

I am now making a statement of the questions to be hereafter discussed.   I will briefly outline them, giving references to a few preliminary discussions in professional periodicals and pamphlets.   These contentions, when adequately
presented, I believe must result in the judicial annulment of all
present State and Federal laws against "obscene" literature.
That such laws have been enforced vigorously for nearly half
a century without having their constitutionality seriously questioned, is as unusual as are the factors to which the Constitution must be applied in order to reach the result herein contended for.   Many of the problems here involved are difficult
of solution to those who are not trained specialists in psychology and especially in sexual psychology.   Later on, in the completed argument, when we come to study the nature and psychology of modesty, we will find the explanation of this long
acquiescence to be of the very essence of our emotional life,
which, coupled with the general absence of psycho-sexual intelligence, have so befogged the critical capacity of the members of
the profession as even to preclude a search for the discovery of
such questions as I am about to raise.   My contention is that
the postal and other laws against "obscene and indecent" literature are unconstitutional for the following reasons:

I.   Because not within any expressed or implied power of
the Congress to enact.

Syllabus of the Argument: The power to create a postal
system implies ,the power to pass all laws "necessary and
proper" to the end of executing the power to establish post
offices and post roads, but it does not authorize Congress,
under the pretext of creating and maintaining post offices, to
make the postal system a means to the accomplishment of
ends not entrusted to the care of Congress.   The very creation
of a postal system necessarily involves a determination of the

gross physical characteristics of that which is to be carried or excluded and therefore implies the power to determine such qualities. A like implication cannot be made in favor of a power to determine what are mailable ideas, because a differential test of mail matter, based upon the opinions transmitted through the mails, or the psychological tendencies of such opinions upon the addressee of the mails, or a differential test based upon an idea which is not actually transmitted, but is suggested by one that is transmitted, bears no conceivable relation to the establishment or maintenance of post offices or post roads for the transmission of physical matter only.

It may be admitted that the power granted implies the power to preclude the use of the mails as an essential element in the commission of a crime otherwise committable, and over which the Congress has jurisdiction (such as fraud and gambling), within the geographical limits of its power. But it is claimed that the power of Congress is limited to the use of means which are a direct mode of executing the power to establish post offices and post roads, or some other power expressly granted, and it cannot, under the pretense of regulating the mails, accomplish objects which the Constitution does not commit to the care of Congress. Such an unconstitutional object is the effort of Congress, under the pretext of regulating the mails, to try to use the mails as a means to control the psycho-sexual condition of postal patrons.[1]

Neither can the exercise of the present power be justified as an incident to the power to regulate interstate commerce, because the censorship is not limited thereto. It includes Intrastate transmission as well as that of private letters, or gifts, which are not at all matters of commerce either Inter-state or otherwise, and so cannot be upheld as a regulation of Interstate commerce.[2]

For these reasons the power exercised is not vested in the Congress at all.

2. The postal laws against "obscene" literature are void under the constitutional prohibition against the abridgment of freedom of speech and of the press. Likewise all similar State legislation is void under State Constitutions.

Syllabus of the argument: This constitutional guarantee of

---

[1]"ON THE IMPLIED POWER TO EXCLUDE 'OBSCENE' IDEAS FROM THE MAILS." *Central Law Journal,* V. 65, p. 177. (Sept. 6, 1907.)
[2]Howard vs. Ill. Cent. R. R., 28 Sup. Ct. Rep. 141.

freedom of the press is violated whenever there is an artificial legislative destruction or abridgment of the greatest liberty consistent with an equality of liberty, in the use of the printed page as a means of disseminating ideas of conflicting tendency. The use of printing is but an extended form of speech. Freedom of speech and press is abridged whenever natural opportunity is in any respect denied, or its exercise punished, merely as such; that is, in the absence of actual injury, or when by legislative enactment there is created an artificial inequality of opportunity, by a discrimination according to the subject-matter discussed, or a discrimination as between different tendencies in the different treatment of the same subject-matter, or according to differences of literary style in expressing the same thought. All this is now accomplished under obscenity laws as at present administered, and therefore our laws upon the subject are unconstitutional.

This contention involves the establishment of a new definition of "freedom of the press," based upon the viewpoint that the framers of the Constitution intended by that clause to enlarge the intellectual liberty of the citizen beyond what it had theretofore been under the English system. Some State courts have erroneously assumed that the only purpose was to exchange a censorship before publication for criminal punishment after publication, without the least enlargement of the right to publish with impunity so long as no one is injured. The contention will be that the Constitution changed liberty of the press by permission, to Liberty as a right, because thus only can all citizens be protected in their proper opportunity to hear and read all that others have to offer, and without which freedom unrestricted there is no intellectual liberty at all as a matter of right.[*]

3. The "obscenity" laws violate the constitutional guarantee of "due process of law."

Syllabus of the argument: The statute furnishes no standard or test by which to differentiate the book that is obscene from that which is not, because of which fact the definition of the crime is uncertain. Furthermore, it is a demonstrable fact of science that obscenity and indecency are not sense-perceived

[*]"THE JUDICIAL DESTRUCTION OF FREEDOM OF THE PRESS," in *Government,* for Dec., 1908; *Albany Law Journal,* Nov., 1908.
"THE SCIENTIFIC ASPECT OF 'DUE PROCESS OF LAW,'" in *American Law Review,* for June, 1908.
"LIBERTY OF CONSCIENCE, SPEECH AND PRESS," in *The Liberal Review,* for August and Sept., 1906.
"FREEDOM OF THE PRESS AND 'OBSCENE' LITERATURE," N. Y., 1907.

qualities of a book, but are solely and exclusively a condition or effect in the reading mind. This is evidenced in the result that it has been, and always will be, impossible to state a definition or test of obscenity in terms of the qualities of a book, or such a one that, solely by applying the test to any given book, accuracy and uniformity of result must follow, no matter who applies the test, nor such that when there is no dispute about any physical fact of present or past existence, any man may know in advance of a trial and a verdict, solely from reading the statute, what the verdict must be as to the obscenity, and consequent criminality, of every given book. Neither the statute, nor the judicially created tests of obscenity or indecency, furnish any certain advance information as to what must be the verdict of a jury upon the speculative problem of the psychological effect of a given book upon an undescribed hypothetical reader. Their verdict is, therefore, not according to the letter of any general law, but according to their whim, caprice and prejudices, or varying personal experiences and different degrees of sexual hyperæstheticism and varying kinds and quality of intelligence upon the subject of sexual psychology, or moral idiosyncracies. In consequence, every such verdict is according to a test of obscenity personal to the court or jury in such a case, and binding upon no other court or jury and not according to any general law or uniform rule. One of the reasons underlying this uncertainty is the fact that "obscenity" is not a quality inherent in a book or picture, but wholly and exclusively a contribution of the contemplating mind, and hence cannot be defined in terms of the qualities of a book or picture, but is read into them.[4]

(a) The first result of this uncertainty is that the statute of Congress herein involved creates no certain or general rule of conduct for the guidance of citizens, and does not enable them to know if their proposed act is in violation of the statute, and therefore every indictment and conviction under said statute is without due process of law. Unless the statute so defines the crime that by the application of its letter alone every person of ordinary intelligence must always draw the same line of

---

[4]"WHAT IS CRIMINALLY 'OBSCENE.'" Proceedings XV. International Medical Congress, Lisbon, Portugal, April, 1906; *Albany Law Journal*, for July, 1906.

"LEGAL OBSCENITY AND SEXUAL PSYCHOLOGY," in *The Medico-Legal Journal*, for Sept., 1907, and *The Alienist and Neurologist*, for Aug., 1908.

"VARIETIES OF OFFICIAL MODESTY," in the *American Journal of Eugenics*, for Dec., 1907; *Albany Law Journal*, Aug., 1908.

"FREEDOM OF THE PRESS AND 'OBSCENE' LITERATURE," N. Y., 1906.

demarkation between the books or pictures which are prohibited and those which are not, then the statute is void for uncertainty under the old maxim, "Where the law is uncertain there is no law," and consequently there is no "due process of law."

(b) Furthermore: "The doctrine is fundamental in English and American law that there can be no constructive offenses." These are of four kinds. First, where the act to be punished is by judicial construction brought within a statute whose plain and literal meaning does not cover it. In this case the statutory criteria of guilt are assumed to be certain as to meaning. The second class of constructive offenses arises where the statutory criteria of guilt are ambiguous, and the courts presume, by judicial legislation, to penalize an act which is not clearly within every possible, plain and certain meaning of the statute. Here the courts make a legislative choice as to which meaning is to be enforced. The third class of constructive offenses arises from an uncertainty (as distinguished from an ambiguity) in the statutory criteria of guilt. Here, there is a total absence of criteria of guilt, and these become wholly a matter of judicial creation (as distinguished from selection when the statute is only ambiguous). Because of the uncertainty—that is, of a total absence of definite statutory criteria of guilt—under all of the "obscenity" laws, nothing is ever unavoidably certain within the letter of the statute. It is necessary in order to secure conviction that judicial, so-called, construction, or, more accurately speaking, judicial legislation, be enacted which *creates the* criteria of guilt not furnished by the statute, from which it follows that all guilt hereunder is but constructive guilt, and the crime only a constructive, that is, a judicially created crime, and not due process of law.

The fourth class of constructive crimes are those which do come within the actual and literal definition of the criminal statute, but where that predicates crime upon conduct which is only a constructive, and not a real and actually achieved material injury, to any living being, nor conditioned upon any imminent danger thereof, the existence of which is determinable by any known law of the physical universe. In such a case, the reality and materiality of the injury, which is an indispensable foundation of all criminal statutes, is entirely absent, except as a matter of legal fiction, and not as a material actuality described in the letter of the law. The same propo‹ tion may be thus stated: One is being punished for a constructive crime whenever the alleged crime consists only in the dissemination of ideas, if under the statute the penalty attaches upon conditions other than that the ideas have actually resulted in material injury to some one. Every psychologic crime, so long as it remains a mere psychological offense whose injury is constructive only, can never become anything except a constructive crime. Such purely constructive wrong and constructive crime cannot be penalized in any country whose constitution was ordained to promote liberty, and therefore such a statute cannot constitute "due process of law."[5]

4. The statute in practical operation violates the constitutional guarantee against *ex post facto* laws.

Syllabus of the argument: The second result of this uncertainty of the statute is that every indictment and conviction under said statute is always according to an *ex post facto* law or standard of judgment, specially created by the court or jury for each particular case. The Congress of the United States has no power to authorize a jury to determine guilt or crime according to varying personal standards, such as must control the opinion of a jury on the psychological tendency of a book upon an undescribed hypothetical reader, and which standard, because it is personal to the juror, in the nature of things cannot be known at the time the alleged act was committed, nor before the rendition of a verdict thereon.

A conviction and punishment under such circumstances is always by virtue of *ex post facto* legislation on the part of the court or jury, and is none the less unconstitutional because the attempted delegation of power to enact it was made before the conduct to be punished. All criteria of guilt must be found in a prior statute.[6]

[5]"THE SCIENTIFIC ASPECT OF 'DUE PROCESS OF LAW,'" in *The American Law Review*, for June, 1908.
"STATUTORY UNCERTAINTY AND 'DUE PROCESS OF LAW,'" in *The Central Law Journal*, for Jan. 3, 1908.
"THE HISTORICAL INTERPRETATION OF 'LAW,'" in *The Albany Law Journal*, for April, 1908.
"'DUE PROCESS OF LAW,' IN RELATION TO STATUTORY UNCERTAINTY AND CONSTRUCTIVE OFFENSES," N. Y., 1908.
"CONSTRUCTIVE OFFENSES DEFINED," in *The Central Law Journal*, Dec. 18, 1908.
[6]"THE SCIENTIFIC ASPECT OF 'DUE PROCESS OF LAW,'" in *The American Law Review*, for June, 1908.
"STATUTORY UNCERTAINTY AND 'DUE PROCESS OF LAW,'" in *The Central Law Journal*, for Jan. 3, 1908.
"THE HISTORICAL INTERPRETATION OF 'LAW,'" in *The Albany Law Journal*, for April, 1908.
"'DUE PROCESS OF LAW' IN RELATION TO STATUTORY UNCERTAINTY AND CONSTRUCTIVE OFFENSES," N. Y., 1908.

-ia~45. The statute in its practical operation violates the seventh amendment to the Constitution in this: By reason of the want of definition of the crime, by a statutory statement of the criteria of guilt, the courts submit to the jury a determination of the question of law as to what shall constitute "obscenity." Congress has no power to make juries the judge of the law, especially not in cases wherein they were not authorized to be such judges under the common law of England. No such acts as are now punished under "obscene" literature were ever included under the common law crime of "obscene libel."[7]

Furthermore, Fox's libel act, which made English juries in libel cases the judges of the law, as well as of the facts, did not pass the English Parliament until 1792.

ARE THE FOREGOING OPEN QUESTIONS?

Is the constitutionality of our moral censorship of literature by the post office department still an open question? An answer to this problem can be satisfactorily reached only by analyzing all the judicial mention of the subject, in the light of the foregoing assignable reasons for asserting the unconstitutionality of these laws, and in the light of the following words from Chief Justice MARSHALL:

"It is a maxim not to be disregarded that general expressions in every opinion are to be taken in connection with the case in which these expressions are used. If they go beyond the case they may be respected, but ought not to control the judgment in a subsequent suit when the very point is presented for decision. The question actually before the court is investigated with care and considered in its full extent. Other principles which may serve to illustrate it are considered in their relation to the case decided, but their possible bearing in all other cases is seldom investigated."[8]

The first case to make reference to the postal censorship of the mails is Ex Parte Jackson, 96 U. S. 727.

This was an application for a writ of habeas corpus and certiorari, after conviction, for mailing lottery matter. The only question raised in the argument for the petitioner is summed up in these words:

"So long as the duty of carrying the mails is imposed upon Congress, a letter or packet *which was confessedly mailable matter at the time of the adoption of the Constitution cannot*

[7] "OBSCENE LITERATURE UNDER THE COMMON-LAW," *Albany Law Journal*, May, 1907.
[8] Cohens v. Virginia, 6 Wheat. 398. See, also, Corn Exchange Bank v. Peabody, 111 App. Div. 553, 98 N. Y. Sup. 78.

be excluded from them, provided the postage be paid and other regulations be observed. Whatever else has been declared to be mailable matter * * * all of which were unknown to the postal system when the convention concluded its labor in 1787, may in the discretion of Congress be abolished."

No other question was raised and no argument based upon the construction of the expressed or implied power of Congress was presented. To enforce the above argument and reduce the contrary position to an absurdity, as it was believed, counsel for the convict said: "If Congress can exclude from the mail a letter concerning lotteries which have been authorized by State legislation, and refuse to carry it by reason of their asserted injurious tendency, it may refuse to carry any other business letter." No arguments of any nature as to the correctness of such suggestion of power, or the limitations, if any, by which the Constitution does or does not hedge about this alleged arbitrary power, were even mentioned, much less discussed. The Attorney-General rested the contrary view solely upon the dogmatic and very doubtful assertion that "if there is a right to exclude any matter from the mails, the extent of its exercise is one of legislative discretion."

The court did not have before it any question except as to lotteries, and *then only in so far* as it related to the power of Congress *to declare non-mailable what custom had sanctioned to be mailable at the time of the adoption of the Constitution.* The court indulged in some dictum based upon the loose talk of counsel concerning side issues. In that dictum, however, the court distinctly negatives the idea suggested by the United States attorney, that there are no limits to the power of regulating the mails, and some such limitations are pointed out by the decision without negativing the existence of other limitations.

The court among other things said: "The validity of legislation prescribing what should be carried and its weight and form and the charges to which it should be subjected has never been questioned. What shall be mailable has varied at different times, changing with the facility of transportation over the post roads. At one time only letters, newspapers, magazines, pamphlets and other printed matter, not exceeding eight ounces in weight were carried; afterwards books were added to the list, and now small packages of merchandise, not exceeding a prescribed weight, as well as books and printed matter of all kinds, are transported in the mail.

"The power possessed by Congress embraces the regulation of the entire postal system of the country. The right to designate what shall be carried necessarily involves the right to determine what shall be excluded. *The difficulty attending the subject arises not from the want of regulations as to what shall constitute mail matter, but from the necessity of enforcing them consistently with rights reserved to the people, of far greater importance than the transportation of mail."* Then some limitations of the regulative power are pointed out. Without claiming to enumerate them all, the court continues in part:

"The constitutional guaranty of the right of the people to be secure in their papers against unreasonable searches and seizures extends to their papers thus closed against inspection, wherever they may be. Whilst in the mail they can be opened and examined under like warrant issued upon similar oath or affirmation as is required when papers are subjected to search in one's own household. All regulations adopted as to mail matter of this kind must be in subordination to the great principle embodied in the fourth amendment to the Constitution.

"Nor can any regulation be enforced against the transportation of printed matter in the mail, which is open to examination, so as to *interfere in any manner with the freedom of the press.* [*What might constitute such interference is not indicated.*] *Liberty of circulating is as essential to that freedom as liberty of publishing;* indeed, without the circulation the publishing would be of little value. If, therefore, printed matter be excluded from the mails, its transportation in any other way cannot be forbidden by Congress." [Since then, and in spite of this dictum, Congress has attempted to forbid other means of transmission, in addition to post office suppression.]

"In excluding various articles from the mail, the object of Congress *has not been to interfere with the freedom of the press,* or with any other rights of the people, but to refuse its facilities for the distribution of matters deemed injurious to the public morals.

"All that Congress meant by that act was that the mail would not be used to transport such corrupting publications and articles, and that any one who attempted to use it for that purpose should be punished."[9]

[9] Ex parte Jackson, 96 U. S. 727 to 736.

Several propositions are made clear from the reading of this dictum. The first is, there are some limitations upon the congressional power to regulate the mails. Second, that the court was not called upon, nor attempted, to enumerate all of those limitations. Third, that what was said about freedom of press and postal regulations excluding obscene literature was not at all necessary to a decision of the question before the court, nor was this dictum based upon any argument attempting to construe the meaning of "freedom of the press." Fourth, the court admitted that Congress could not make a regulation such as would abridge the freedom of the press, but the decision does not attempt to point out the kind of postal regulation which would constitute such an abridgment, nor the test by which such regulation may be judged an abridgment of the freedom of the press.

Applying the test of Cohens v. Virginia,[10] it follows that nothing in this case is conclusive upon any feature of the constitutionality of postal laws against "obscene" literature.

The next two cases in which this subject is mentioned are in re Dupre,[11] and in re Rapier.[12] These two cases were argued together and decided together, and in both the precise matter under discussion, as in the former case, was lotteries and the mail.

Counsel for Dupre says: "We are not at this moment objecting to the statute as invalid because aimed to accomplish an object beyond the power of the Congress, or because forbidden by some express prohibition of the Constitution," but because the means employed were not legitimate to the end of maintaining the mail service. However, counsel for the accused did not meet the real issue, which may be thus stated: Congress has power to prohibit gambling on premises over which it has jurisdiction, as in post offices owned by the government, and in the Territories and District of Columbia, and, as an incident to that power, might prohibit gambling through the mails. It was argued that absence of right to exclude lottery advertisements *did not involve absence of right to exclude obscenity,* because the latter was "undoubtedly" *mala in se* and the former only *mala prohibita.* Again the attorney says: "Our argument in no manner involves the consequence that existing legislation of Congress, excluding obscene books and pictures

---

[10]6 Wheat. 398.
[11]143 U. S. 110.
[12]143 U. S. 110.

from the mails, is invalid, as abridging the freedom of speech."

Furthermore, it was not claimed that the matter constituting the content of lottery advertisements and tickets alone involved an exercise of the freedom of the press, but only that they incidentally affected the press by denying pulishers the revenue to be derived from advertising, etc.

The court in Dupre case (same opinion as Rapier case), after denying a distinction between *mala in se* and *mala prohibita* as urged, continues thus:

"*Nor are we able to see that Congress can be held in an enactment to have abridged the freedom of the press.* The circulation of newspapers is not prohibited, but the government declines itself to become an agent in the circulation of printed matter [to wit, lottery advertisements and tickets] which it regards as injurious to the people. The freedom of communication is not abridged within the intent and meaning of the constitutional provision, unless Congress is absolutely destitute of any discretion as to what shall or shall not be carried in the mails and compelled arbitrarily to assist in the dissemination of matters condemned by its judgment, through the governmental agencies which it controls." Then the court reaffirms the Jackson case.

I may admit the right of Congress to exclude dynamite from the mails, or any other actual instrument whose transmission is a material element in the commission of an actual crime, over which Congress has jurisdiction, but it does not yet follow that Congress has the power to exclude "incendiary" opinions from the mails, nor unpopular opinions about the ethics of lotteries or of sex.

So Congress, within its geographical jurisdiction, which includes, among other places, the post office buildings owned by the government, may make gambling a crime, and, as an incident to that power, Congress may punish or prohibit the actual commission of gambling through the use of the postal system. It does not follow that it can also punish the constructive crime of sending through the mail matter which merely expresses or suggests the idea of gambling, entirely separate from any particular scheme for accomplishing gambling. There is all the difference in the world between punishing the use of the mails for disseminating opinions advocating the morality of gambling and punishing the use of mails to accomplish the crime of gambling. To decide that Congress has the power to do the latter, does not in the remotest degree imply that it has the power to do the former. Admitting that Congress has power in some places to punish certain sexual misconduct, it does not follow that it may punish purely intellectual crimes predicated merely upon sex discussions through the mails. It follows that nothing which has been directly or necessarily decided in any of the lottery cases has any bearing whatever upon the present controversy, as set forth in the foregoing statement of contentions.

Admitting for the sake of the argument that courts have rightfully decided that Congress has the power to prohibit the use of the mails for the accomplishment of the actual crimes of fraud and gambling, it does not follow, and has not been decided, that the Congress has also power to make a *constructive crime* of such an act as using the mails for the dissemination of a truthful scientific book on the physiology, psychology or hygiene of sex, or of spreading through the mails legislatively unapproved ideas about sex-ethics. It may still be true, notwithstanding all that courts have thus far said, and even including the most rash dictum, that Congress has not the power, implied from its authority to established post offices, of creating a constructive crime out of the dissemination of unpopular ideas, under the pretense of regulating the mails.

In School of Magnetic Healing v. McAnnulty[18] the court says this: *"Conceding, for the purpose of this case,* that Congress has full and absolute jurisdiction over the mails, and that it may provide who may and who may not use the mails, and that its action is not subject to review by the courts, and also conceding the conclusive character of the determination of the Postmaster-General,"* etc. (p. 107). Then the court goes on to hold that even conceding all that, "for the purposes of this case," the postmaster had transcended his power. Here again it is clear that nothing was either directly involved or decided which bears upon the extent or limitations of the implied power of Congress to regulate the mails, or the constitutional questions hereinbefore suggested.

The next case is Public Clearing House v. Coyne[14].

This was an application for an injunction against the postmaster of Chicago for relief against a fraud order. After restating and reaffirming, by way of dictum, the case of Ex Parte Jackson, the court continues its dictum thus: *"While it*

[18]187 U. S. 107.
[14]194 U. S. 507.

may be assumed for the purpose of this case that Congress would have no right to extend to one the benefits of its postal service and deny it to another person in the same class and standing in the same relation to the government, it does not follow that under its power to classify mailable matter, applying different rates of postage to different articles, and prohibiting some altogether, it may not also classify the recipients of such matter, and forbid the delivery of letters to such persons or corporations as in its judgment are making use of the mails for the purpose of fraud or deception or the dissemination among its citizens of information of a character calculated to debauch the public morality."[15]

Again nothing was before the court which elicited argument or involved a decision upon the power of Congress to differentiate between mail matter according to its approval or disapproval of the opinion transmitted, or the psycho-sexual states of the postal patrons. The only direct bearing of this decision upon the question as to the extent of the implied power to regulate mails is that the judicial dictum suggests a limitation upon that power not heretofore suggested. It also leaves the whole matter of other limitations on the implication of absolute power over mails an open question.

No case directly involving the constitutionality of the postal law against obscene literature has ever gone to the Supreme Court for decision, nor does it appear from the reported cases in the lower courts that any serious contention has ever been there made against their constitutionality. The foregoing analysis already shows that, in so far as the logic of the dictum in the Jackson case has been taken to mean that there were no limitations upon congressional control over the mails, even that dictum has been clearly misconstrued, as is shown by the numerous judicial suggestions to the effect that there are some limitations.

We conclude, therefore, that every objection to be hereinafter urged against the constitutionality of these laws, as herein-above suggested, *is not only undecided, but free from the embarrassment of even an adverse dictum.* If there is any doubt as to this conclusion it must be dissipated by the declaration of the Supreme Court itself, where it says: "The constitutionality of this law [against obscene literature] we believe has never been attacked."[16]

[15]Public Clearing House v. Coyne, 194 U. S. 507.
[16]Public Clearing House v. Coyne, 194 U. S. 507.

CHAPTER II.

ON THE ADVERSE EMOTIONAL PREDISPOSITION

The worst insult I ever heard charged against any court was an assertion that its judge was without prejudice upon any question of law. Our laws against obscenity in literature have been upon the Federal statute books about thirty-five years and elsewhere have existed even longer. After this lapse of time, one who presumes to raise new objections for the annullment of those laws, without assuming the existence of an adverse judicial, as well as popular, predisposition might have his conduct construed as an insult to judicial intelligence, or at least as a serious reflection upon his own.

Long public acquiescence, the force of inumerable precedents, and an "eminently respectable" indorsement of these laws, combined with the natural and proper conservatism of the judiciary, all conduce necessarily to create a popular and judicial predisposition against my contentions. The special emotional intensity, which is almost certain to accompany a discussion of such laws as are here under consideration, impairs the human capacity for a dispassionate rational weighing of argument. The practical importance of that mental attitude, in creating a general, strong and perhaps a passionate hope that my contention will fail, would be very much and very foolishly underestimated by me if I omitted all direct effort to re-establish an open-minded hospitality toward the arguments to be advanced later on.

Furthermore, I have read all the officially reported decisions in "obscenity" cases, and I have read many unofficial reports of instructions to juries and other accounts of the conduct of courts in such trials. According to many of these reports, even the seemings of judicial calm have been abandoned, and that which is false as a matter of science has been dogmatically asserted in language which suggests a substitution of passionate vituperation for logical processes. From the information thus acquired, from my acquaintance with the psychology of modesty and my knowledge of human nature, I know how easy it is to transform a proper and necessary conservatism into a passionate "will to believe," when, as in this class of cases, conservatism is associated with the sensitive emotions having their origin in our sex-natures. I believe it is precisely this intellect-befogging combination which has precluded the prior presentation of the contentions now to be urged.

I am well aware that, in theory, our courts have nothing to do with the expediency of the laws, when passing upon their constitutionality. But I also know that the interests of the litigant have very much to do with the judicial opinion about their expediency, because too often that unconsciously determines whether the judge will be impelled to exercise his greatest ingenuity toward a discovery of reasons which will tend to uphold or to annul the statutes under investigation. Those who disbelieve in freedom of the press naturally and unavoidably will see at once all or many of those considerations which conduce to such a "construction" of the Constitution as will make an accomplished fact of that curtailment of liberty which they desire. If this mental predisposition is accompanied by intense emotional approval, as in this class of cases it is almost certain to be, a restoration of such open mindedness as leaves the individual amenable to accurate weighing of argument is all but impossible except to the most highly developed intellect.

As to the legislation against "obscene" literature, the public conscience feels the same passionate "moral" necessity which once impelled judges to exercise their wits and their might in a crusade against witchcraft and verbal treason. In Harper's Magazine, for Sept., 1907, we have a graphic portrayal of the prejudiced zealous federal judge who upheld the constitutionality of the sedition laws. Some more recent decisions upon a kindred question, if they evince less display of passion, yet show an equally deficient intellectual vision in the upholding of similar laws. All this comes from the fact that we erroneously ascribe to a "moral" cause that emotional aversion whose remote source is usually unknown to us, but whose immediate reason for being is laid deeply hidden in our subjective (emotional) states.

And here again I am compelled to express regret at my inability in a masterful single terse sentence to present an instantaneous and complete picture of all the related co-ordina-

25

tions, as I see them. Yet such is the limitation of human thought and its expression that it cannot be done. My regret in the matter lies in this: To state some of my conclusions about emotional predispositions, before having argued out the psychology of modesty and obscenity, may intensify the very emotional aversion which I seek to obviate. And to elaborate the psychology first and at this stage of the discussion, is likely to secure me unmerited condemnation for its immateriality and impertinence. So, then, if I am to be condemned by emotional processes, my case is hopeless. If I cannot secure a patient attention to the very end of my presentation, then my very effort to attack the adverse emotional predisposition may intensify it, and it is sure to do so if I have overestimated the reader's healthy-mindedness and his capacity for subjecting his so-called "moral" emotions to a severe critical introspection.

That there is an adverse predisposition concerning my contentions seems unavoidably and unmistakably certain. The relation of the subject-matter to our emotional life makes it quite probable that there exists in most minds an *intense* "will to believe"—a passionate hope—that I am wrong. If our human natures have that uniformity which is usually ascribed to them, it is highly probable that in such a case as this a judicial conservatism, otherwise commendable, may evolve into a one-sided zealous quest for means to uphold the laws in question, rather than a scientist's dispassionate search for truth, and in proportion as this zeal is great the capacity to weigh the relative merit of arguments will be impaired.

Of course this argument is prepared with the thought that sometime, somewhere, before some judicial tribunal, it will be a subject for examination. To the end, therefore, that there will be a minimum of unconscious emotional bias to cloud the vision, I must devote myself to efforts at weakening that adverse mental predisposition, which is sure to exist in most minds. In so far as the approval of "obscenity" laws is a matter of emotions, the situation is very difficult to meet adequately. Feelings are seldom successfully displaced by calm logical processes. However, the most efficient means must still be an analysis of our "moral" emotions, to show the impropriety of making them the basis of ethical judgment, and to make a rational attack upon the expediency of maintaining the laws in question, and this will now be proceeded with. When I have done what I am able to do to weaken the potency of that "moral" sentimentalizing which creates the mental attitude that will more diligently and energetically concern itself with verbalisms which lend only a seeming support to the feeling-conviction, than with discovering the logical necessities of constitutional right, then I will proceed with the more direct argument of the constitutional merits of the case.

When later on we come to study the psychology of modesty, we will find explanations for this very general acquiescence by the members of the bar and the laity. It will, then, be found that the strong emotional approval of these laws by the general public, ignorant of all scientific knowledge of psychology, and especially of sexual psychology, has been due to the fundamental and all but universal error by which we objectivize our emotional appraisment of moral values. Thus the masses think they know because they feel and are firmly convinced in proportion as they are strongly agitated.

The judgment of the righteousness of these laws, thus founded upon an error of ignorance, and re-inforced by emotions which often owe their intensity to diseased nerves, associated in the same person with a nasty-mindedness, characteristics of prurient prudes, has, by a process of suggestive contagion, become obsessive, even with more intelligent and healthy-minded persons. This process is easily understood by those who know the psychology of modesty. The few intelligent ones know that the emotional state underlying modesty and shame arises simply from a fear-induced application to ourselves of judgments primarily passed upon others. Upon this practically all psychologists are agreed, and it is this emotional aversion and fear, with the blurred vision coming from psychologic ignorance, which has produced such tremendous success for the vehemence of our moralists-from-diseased-nerves.

The same emotional and psychologic factors which make it all but impossible for a jury to doubt the obscenity of a book alleged to be so, will make it nearly as difficult to secure an open-minded judge upon the same question or that of the unconstitutionality of these laws. We have an abundance of emotional associations with unpopular words and ideas and we have ethical sentimentalizing without limit, but these cannot furnish us with any objective facts, or standards for a rational judgment. What is the result of a prosecution for obscenity before a jury thus totally lacking in every element for deter--

27

mining the issue of obscenity with even moderate precision? The pretentious agents of vice-societies, the prosecuting attorney and the judge, in impassioned tones vent their emotional disapproval in vigorous epithetic argument against the offending book. In the nature of things, they cannot furnish the jury with anything else. If they could, the question of obscenity would be a question of law determinable by the court according to mathematically accurate standards and not a question of fact for the jury, to be determined according to whim, caprice, and moral sentimentalizing. Even when courts have treated it as a matter of law, their decisions have still been only decisions reached by the same uncertain and personal standards. In these matters it is true of all of us that we know only because we feel, and are firmly convinced because strongly agitated.

The jury, of course, wish to be thought respectable, and a similar feeling will more or less unconsciously influence judges who have not been warned against this dangerous tendency. It may be that the book offends their own emotional sense of propriety. The changes are rung on the necessity for protecting the home, the women, the family and the children, until the avalanche of righteous vituperation creates such a mist of emotional disapproval that the juror forgets or loses what little capacity he may have had for looking behind the question-begging epithets. In the face of this condition the defense is helpless. It also is unable to furnish a scientifically exact yardstick, such as enables the juror in other cases to check his emotional predispositions. In the absence of a clear and over-mastering vision to the contrary, every juror's vanity of respectability, unavoidably and unconsciously compels him unthinkingly to condemn everything which is vigorously denounced as "impure," by anyone connected with the prosecution or by popular ignorance, prejudice, superstitition, or passion. In the face of a question-begging epithetic argument, made in such a case and under such circumstances of ignorance and want of experience, no juror is able to reason upon the question at issue, which, according to the usual judicial legislation is: Does this particular book really tend to deprave and how, why, and by what code of morality is depravity to be determined? If compelled to answer these questions without promptings from the court or prosecution, the juror must confess his inability to state *how* and *why*. The result is that just as in the witchcraft prosecutions, so here, in practically every case, to be accused is equivalent to a conviction, yet not according to the letter of any statute. but according to the whim, caprice, prejudice or superstition of those who shape the emotions of a jury, wholly reasonless, as to this particular subject. The professional vice-hunters can and do boast that practically they never fail to convict. They ascribe this to the inerrancy of their judgments, and point to the uniformity of convictions as an evidence that they exercise a wise discretion in the enforcement of a law which they admit is uncertain und therefore permits of abuses. In fact, this result is a product of ignorance and prejudice and is to be explained by the uncertainty of the statute and the fact that modesty is but fear of the judgment of others (the respectable prosecutors). When the verdict of the jury reaches an appellate tribunal, the uncertainty of the law makes impossible a reversal on the question of obscenity. There being no exact standard, no thermometer of obscenity, by which its relative degrees can be measured, and the precise freezing point of modesty determined, the appellate court in its helplessness practically never can reverse the judgment, because, their own emotional proprieties being in the least offended, the conviction of obscenity never seems to be without *some* "evidence" to support it.

This uniform affirmance of every verdict, like the original uniformity of conviction, is made unavoidable by the psychologic nature of modesty and the uncertainty of the statute and not in either case by the letter of the law. And so it may be even when we come to a discussion of the constitutional questions involved. If the emotional predisposition of the judge is but properly enlisted on the side of the "moralists," of hysteria, we may expect to find that mere figures of speech will be mistaken for analogies, question-begging epithets will take the place of fact and argument, and mere empty verbalisms, born of self-righteous emotions, will have the probative force of a mathematical demonstration to the mind of an average judge, who has not been warned against this dangerous source of error. Even some who have been warned, as I am now trying to warn them, will still lack that high intellectual development which alone makes possible a subordination of the emotions to the cold-logic processes.

Because men are ignorant of sexual psychology, they lack insight to discover the valuelessness of the "moral" emotions of others, and being without that clarity of vision which could frame a satisfactory defense against the personal application to self of such unreasoned "moral judgments" by others, it usually follows that they have not the intelligent disposition or courage to attack these laws. Even the attorneys employed to defend such cases have quite uniformily found their intellectual acumen paralyzed in the conflict with their own emotional approval of these laws. In the half-conscious fear of the like unreasoned and more intense emotions of their prudish neighbors, who perhaps are the unconscious victims of sexual hyperaestheticism, these attorneys quite unavoidably apologize for defending such a client. By his very demeanor the defendant's attorney insinuates a verdict of guilty into the mind of the judge and juror. The same intellect-benumbing influence has thus far made it impossible for any attorney employed in over 5000 of such cases to even discover that there are constitutional questions which it was his duty to present in defense of his client. Where such conditions prevail, no lawyer is doing his duty if he does not open a discussion of the constitutional problems by an attack upon this adverse mental predisposition—by a plea for open-mindedness.

In the past ten years, sexual psychology has made long initial strides. A few besides the specialist are beginning to see that, like witches, obscenity exists only in the minds of those who believe in it. Of this more will be said hereafter. Knowing this, these few are ceasing to fear the emotional judgment of salacious ascetics, because they are now accounted for by a diseased sex-sensitiveness and are seen not to be entitled to any moral valuation. When lawyers are so clean-minded as to believe, and be firmly and *scientifically* convinced, as later on we expect to convince them, that "unto the pure all things are pure," then, and not till then, can there be any open-minded and fearless inquiry into the constitutionality of these laws.

Only in such confident clean-mindedness can we hope for the moral courage to resist the suggestive intimidation of prurient prudes, and replace the befogging intensity of emotional aversion to my contention with the lucidity of scientific evidence and logical argument. When the completed presentation of the case is made to such a court, our present laws against obscenity must disappear, perhaps to be replaced by others which will be more intelligible and consonant with a decent and enlightened conception of constitutional liberty.

Prof. Wm. James, of Harvard University,[1] wrote this:

[1]Varieties of Religious Experiences, p. 74.

"The truth is that in the metaphysical and religious sphere, articulate reasons are cogent for us only when our inarticulate feelings of reality have already been impressed in favor of the same conclusion." In the very nature of our being, in its present state of evolution, the whole matter of sex is so inseparably involved with mystical religious and other emotions, that in all discussion of sex subjects, even more so than in the field of metaphysics and religion, we assume to "know because we feel and are firmly convinced because strongly agitated." Out of this very exceptional condition comes the fact that, no matter how highly the critical faculty of his mind may be developed in its application to other subjects, when it comes to matters of sexual topics scarcely one man in a million can reason calmly; for his "moral" emotions will dethrone his reason, and mere verbalisms, and righteous vituperation will take the place of logical facts of experience, and thus articulate *seemings* of reason will be cogent enough to confirm any conclusion which the inarticulate "moral" feelings have already predisposed us to believe. This will usually be so notwithstanding these feelings are based upon mere unreasoned sympathetic imitation and emotional association, imposed by the mere thoughtless reiteration of customs, which often have their source and derive their special character from the vehemence of those who are afflicted with psycho-sexual abnormity, (erotophobia) often claiming religious indorsement, and which the rest of us, without rationally well defined ethical convictions, will adopt, though ourselves healthy-minded. Upon this subject we shall yet have much to say, especially when later in its relation to "Due Process of Law" we come to discuss the psychology of modesty more in detail.

The practical problem is to discover how we are to insure in ourselves that open-mindedness to the realities of reasoning which the importance of the situation imposes, and the peculiar psychologic factors of the problem make so difficult? Simply by remembering and submitting ourselves to the control of a very few maxims of ethical science as contra-distinguished from "ethical" sentimentalism. Wordsworth Donisthorpe, M.P., puts it thus: "No man has ever yet succeeded in defining virtue a priori."[2] To bear that in mind and always act upon it would all but destroy moral sentimentalism. Dr. Edward Westermarck, a very distinguished Swedish scholar, implies a similar truth when he is writing of "the error we

[2] A Plea for Liberty, p. 73-74.

commit by attributing objectivity to our moral estimates," the folly of which he points out in the following words: "The quantity of moral estimate is determined by the intensity of the emotions which their object tends to evoke under exactly similar circumstances."[3]   Prof. Munsterburg, of Harvard, expresses it thus: "No subjective feeling of certainty can be an objective criterion for the desired truth."[4]   More will be said upon this subject when we come to study the uncertainty of the "moral" test of "obscenity."

If, then, the reader desires to avoid moral sentimentalizing in favor of the rational ethics, and further desires to approach the constitutional questions herein involved with that open-mindedness which can come only as an accompaniment to subjugated emotions, we must first of all resolve to be guided only by objective criteria for the desired truth.   Having resolved to be thus guided, let us make a little preliminary inquiry as to what may be and has been suppressed under these laws, and determine, by such tests as we have now agreed to use, whether any real question of morality is involved.   This discussion, and more of a kindred nature which is to follow, has for its objects: First, to increase the intellectual hospitality for the constitutional argument to follow; second, to exhibit some of the general considerations upon which our constitutional guarantee of freedom of the press was adopted, and thus furnish us helpful clues to the interpretation of that clause of the Constitution.   To this end will be exhibited some of the evils which come from such laws, and this will be followed by a general vindication of the right of every adult citizen to know all that can be known even about the subject of sex.

[3]Origin and Development of Moral Ideas, v. 1, p. 13.
[4]*Times Magazine,* March, 1907, p. 428.

CHAPTER III.

NO "OBSCENE" LITERATURE AT COMMON LAW

Revised from *The Albany Law Journal,* May, 1907

For nearly a century unintelligent reformers have asserted, and unindustrious attorneys have repeated the statement, and courts, made credulous by a passionate hope that it might be true, have, by way of dictum, affirmed that obscenity, as we now understand the term, in the light of our modern puritanism, was an offense at common law.

The truth or error of the statement has several important bearings. When we come to a discussion of the meaning of "freedom of the press" it may be of importance to know just how much liberty of the press was enjoyed at the time of the adoption of our Constitution.

In studying the present outrageous suppression of medical and controversial literature under the pretense of suppressing "obscenity," I am reminded of this cynical statement of Sergeant Hill: "When judges are about to do an unjust act, they seek for a precedent in order to justify their conduct by the faults of others." But there is another reason for destroying the professional illusion about obscenity at the common law, because by destroying the veneration, often superstitious, which lawyers and courts give to supposed precedent, we may also increase their intellectual hospitality for the constitutional argument which follows:

Going back to the sixteenth century, we find no such general prudish sentimentalizing as is now current over the "obscene" of the nude human, nor over a robust frankness in the discussion of sex-problems. Of course, even before this, we find ascetics of unbalanced mind, who declaimed against all that stimulated their unhealthy sex-sensibilities, but no law as yet had made their diseased condition the standard of virtue. Not being able to suppress the more healthy naturalness of others, they usually fled to some mountain or desert retreat, to escape the temptations which endangered their "spiritual" welfare.

Among those who did not thus flee, we find Christian sects who esteemed it a special virtue to parade the highways, and more privately worshiped, in Adamic costume. From such habits these sects have come to be known as "Adamites." No law was invoked to suppress their "obscenity," though they suffered persecution for their heresies. The obscene in nature not having received legal recognition, of course an "obscene libel" was then unknown.

In March's "Action for Slander and Arbitrement"[1] published in 1648, and revised in 1674, it is said concerning libelous letters: "Yet the star Chamber of the King did take knowledge of such cases and punish them; the reason is for that such quarrellous letters tend to a breach of the peace." Numerous refinements were indulged in to exclude from suppressive measures what did not directly tend to violence. Thus it was held that a general charge of criminality was not slanderous, since only a very specific accusation would tend to a breach of the peace. So long as such tendency to violence was the test of the criminality of a publication, nothing could be punished merely because it was generally "obscene," though a specific charge of obscenity against a living person, who would be tempted to resent it, might be indictable.

Since England had an established church, naturally anything (including the so-called obscene publications) which discredited the official religion would also be held libelous. We shall presently see how, from the suppression of "obscene impiety," has erroneously grown the notion that all so-called "obscene" literature was suppressed at common law.

The oldest case of conviction for obscenity, found in the law reports, was decided in 1663. The printed record, handed down, only informs us that on "confession of information against him for showing himself naked in a balcony and throwing down bottles (piss in) vi & armis among the people in Covent Garden," he was fined 200 marks.[2] It seems that in addition to actual violence, in throwing the bottle, Sedley was guilty of blasphemy. Stephens tells us that Sedley "Stripped himself naked and with eloquence preached blasphemy to the people."[2a]

The next reported decision was rendered in 1708, by Lord

[1] p. 139.
[2] King v. Sedley, Kebble, 620, Siderfins R. 168, 10 State Trials Ass. 93.
[2a] Criminal Law of England, V. 2, p. 70.

34

Holt, who, more than other judges, stood out against the tyrannies of the crown. The decision uses these words: "A crime that shakes religion, as profaneness on the stage, etc., is indictable, but writing an obscene book, as that entitled 'The fifteen plagues of a maidenhead,' is not indictable, but punishable only in the spiritual courts."[3]

The next reported decision is of the date of 1727. This case is of importance to us, because it is the one case which is relied upon to show that the circulation of "obscene" literature was a crime at common law, and, as we shall see later, it is erroneously assumed that "obscenity" then meant what "obscenity" now means, according to puritan standards.

Information against the defendant was "for that he *existens homo iniquus et celeratus ac nequiter machinans et intendens bonos mores subditorum hujus regni corrumpere, et eos ad nequitiam inducere, quendam turpem iniquum et obscaenum libellum intitulat* (Venus in the cloister, or the nun in her smock) *impio et nequiter impresset et publicavit ac imprimit et publicari causavit* (setting out the several lewd passages) *in malum exemplum,"* etc.

The defendant was found guilty, and a motion made in arrest of judgment. For the motion Mr. Marsh argued: "The defendant may be punishable for this in the spiritual court as an offense *contra bonos mores,* yet it cannot be libel for which he is punishable in the temporal courts. In the case *de libellis famosis* my Lord Coke says that it must be against the public, or some private person, to be a libel; and I don't remember ever to have heard this opinion contradicted. Whatever tends to corrupt the morals of the people, ought to be censored in the spiritual court, to which, properly, all such causes belong. I don't find any case wherein they were prohibited in such a cause; in the reign of King Charles the Second there was a filthy run of obscene writings, for which we meet with no prosecution in the temporal courts."

The Attorney-General admitted that there was no precedent for this conviction. He argued: "Peace includes good order and government, and that peace may be broken in many instances without actual force: 1, if it be an act against the constitution or civil order; 2, if it be against religion; 3, if it be against morality."

Under the third head the Attorney-General argued as follows: "As to Morality, destroying that is destroying the peace or government, for government is no more than public order,
[3]Qeen v. Read. 11 Modern Reports, case No. 205.

which is morality. My Lord Chief Justice Hale used to say Christianity is a part of the law, and why not morality, too?

"I do not insist that every immoral act is indictable—but if it is destructive of morality in general, if it does or may effect the king's subjects, it then is an offense of a public nature. And upon this distinction it is that particular acts of fornication are not punishable in the temporal courts and bawdy houses are. In Sir Charles Sedley's case it wàs said, that this court is the *custos morum* of the king's subjects, and upon this foundation there have been many prosecutions against the players for obscene plays, though they have had interest enough to have the proceedings stayed before judgment."

The chief justice said he would convict were it not for the decision in Queen v. Read. "If it tends to disturb the civil order of society I think it is a temporal offense." Justice Fortesque said: "I own it is a great offense, but I know of no law by which we can punish it. Common law is common usage, and where there is no law there can be no transgression. At the common law drunkenness, or cursing and swearing, were not punishable; and yet I do not find the spiritual courts took notice of it. This is but a general solicitation of chastity and not indictable. Lady Purbeck's case was for procuring men and women to meet at her house, and held not indictable unless there had been particular facts to make it a bawdy house. To make it indictable there should be a breach of the peace or something tending to it, of which there is nothing in this case. Libel is a technical word at common law, and I must own the case of the Queen v. Read sticks with me, for there was a rule to arrest the judgment *nisi.* And in Sir Charles Sedley's case there was a force in throwing out bottles upon the people's heads."

After the second continuance, Chief Justice Fortesque having in the meantime retired from the bench, the reporter adds:

"In two or three days they gave it as a unanimous opinion that this was a temporal offense. . . . They said if Read's case was to be adjudged they should rule it otherwise." No reasoning is given or precedent cited.[4]

In the earlier report of this same case we find a different and better statement of the reasons for the decision. It is in these words:

"After solemn deliberation, the court held it to be an offense properly within its jurisdiction; for they said that reli-

4 Rex v Curl, 2 Strange Rep. 789.

gion was part of the common law; and therefore whatever is an offense against that is evidently an offense against the common law. Now morality is the fundamental part of religion, and therefore whatever strikes against that, must, for the same reason, be an offense against the common law. The case of King and Taylor, 1 Ventris, 293, is to this very point."[5]

The case of King and Taylor, cited by the court, was a case of obscene blasphemy for calling Jesus Christ a bastard, and a whore-master, and declaring all religion a cheat. It is evident, therefore, morality is used only in the sense of religious morality, especially since no scientific ethics had yet come into existence.

It is evident from the authority cited, and from the judicial language, "morality is the fundamental part of religion," and from the title of the book, "Venus in the cloister or the Nun in her smock," that the court had no occasion or thought to penalize obscenity in literature *as obscenity,* and when it did not discredit the established religion or its servants, nor was of a seditious nature, nor concerning an individual so as to provoke a breach of the peace.

Subsequent authorities show that the foregoing analysis is correct, since no other interpretation of King v. Curl can be made to harmonize with subsequent judicial action.

The next reported case was decided in 1733. This decision clearly shows a healthy mindedness which now is scarce among us, and confirms the conclusion that Curl's case was decided on the *impiety* of the offending book, and not because of its obscenity as such. The report in the Gallard case reads as follows:

"Indictment *contra bona mores,* for running in the common way, naked down to the waist, the defendant being a woman. S. moved to quash, because the fact is not indictable. F. *contra*: Indictment will lie *contra bonas mores* as against Curl for publishing an obscene book, 1 Sid. 168, Sir Chas. Sedley's (Sedley's) case, 1 Keb. 620. *Quia immodests* and *irreverentas,* behaved himself in church. Another indictment was for printing Rochester's poems: *Sed. per Curl.* The indictment must be quashed, for nothing appears immodest or unlawful."[6]

The next case of "obscene and impious libel" was against the notorious and stormy John Wilkes in 1768. He fled the country and was outlawed without contest, and in the subse-

5King v. Curl, Barnardiston's Report 29 (A. D. 1744).
6King v. Gallard, W. Kelynge, p. 163.

quent proceedings only technical questions of procedure were considered. It seems that several of his publications gave offense, though the name of but one is furnished us, "An Essay on Woman." This is a bawdy poem, in which the name of the deity is impiously interwoven with its description of lascivious joys. The pamphlet closed with another bawdy entitled "The Maid's Prayer," and addressed to "The propitious God of Love."

The report informs us that "Mr. Wilke's counsel and agent making no objection thereto—declining to enter into his defense, verdicts were found against him," and he was outlawed. Later he came into court, and, on technical grounds, moved to vacate the judgment, and "with a written speech to justify the crimes." The outlawry was reversed upon technical defects in the papers, but the conviction was undisturbed, only technical questions of procedure being considered by the King's bench. In the record of Wilke's sentence only these few words enlighten us as to the reason for the conviction: "Being convicted of certain trespasses, contempts and grand misdemeanors, in printing and publishing an obscene and *impious* libel, entitled 'An Essay on Woman' *and other impious libels, etc.*"[1]

Especially in view of Wilke's turbulent career and the stormy times which surrounded this trial, the judgment entered by default can not properly be said to be of much weight as an authority. Yet it was designated an "impious libel," as well as obscene, and therefore is in harmony with our theory that it required something more than mere obscenity to make a publication criminal at common law.

These are the only decisions on obscenity prior to the separation of the American colonies, and therefore the only ones which became a part of the common law of America. Furthermore they demonstrate that "obscenity," merely as such, was not a criminal offense. To make it punishable it must be of that personal and specific character (against a living person) such as tended to disturb the peace, or else it must be interwoven with impiety such as tended to discredit the established religion or government.

To make it still more clear that the English common law, before the Revolution, never punished "obscene libels," as such, that is, where unconnected with blasphemy or seditious tendencies, we may profitably review a few of the English

[1]Rex v. John Wilkes, 4 Burrows, 2527-2575.

authorities immediately following the American Revolution.

The first of such cases, King v. Tophan, decided January, 1791, was a case of libel on the memory of Earl Cowper, which had been published in a newspaper. The indictment charged that defendant had accused the Earl of having "led a wicked and profligate course of life, and had addicted himself to the practice and use of the most criminal and unmanly vices and debaucheries on," etc., "at," etc., "to the evil example," etc., "and against the peace."

Now, to publish accounts of such "unmanly vices" would almost certainly be adjudged "obscene " and had it been so considered in 179. the defendant would in this case have been convicted. Lord Kenyon, in his opinion, quoted with approval 1 Hawkins Pleas of the Crown as follows: "The chief cause for which the law so severely punishes all offenses of this nature [libels] is the direct tendency of them to a breach of the public peace, by provoking the parties injured, and their friends and families to acts of revenge." (Citing 1 Haw. P. C., chap. 73, sec. 3.) The court continues: "Now to say, in general, that the conduct of a dead person can at no time be canvassed; to hold that even after ages are passed, the conduct of bad men cannot be contrasted with the good, would be to exclude the most useful part of history." It was accordingly held that the indictment stated no offense, or, in other words, to publish of a dead person accounts of "unmanly vices and debaucheries" was not a libel, either obscene or otherwise.[8]

The analysis of all the cases on obscenity that were reported in England before the American Revolution, as well as those authorities that came into existence immediately after, are conclusive upon the point, that mere "obscenity," as such, was not a common law crime before the Revolution, and, therefore, never became a common law crime in America, although I believe some courts, on a superficial and uncritical view, have held otherwise.

That in the Curl case it was the irreligious tendency of the book which made it criminal and not the bawdy character thereof, is further shown by the law writers of the time.

"The mere speculative wantonness of a licentious imagination, however dangerous, or even sanguinary, in its object, can in no case amount to a crime. It is a passion inseparable from the essence of the human mind to delight in the fiction of that the actual existence of which would please."[9]

[8]Rex v. Topham, 4 Term Rep. 129.
[9]Lord Auckland's Principles of Penal Law, p. 84, Lond., 1771.

With knowledge of, and in spite of the decision in King v. Curl, Hawkins, in his "Pleas of the Crown," thus states the common law on the subject: "However, it seems clear, that no writing whatsoever is to be esteemed a libel, unless it reflects upon some particular person; and it seems that a writing full of obscene ribaldry, without any kind of reflection upon anyone, is not punishable, *as I have heard it agreed in the court of King's bench.*"[10]

In 1809 we come to the first English case wherein our modern puritanical conception of modesty finds recognition. The indictment was for exposing the naked person by bathing in the sight of homes. A verdict of guilty was followed by an appeal, and the Court of King's Bench left this report of its conclusion: "As this is the first prosecution of this sort in modern times, they [the judges] consented to his being discharged."[11]

As a further confirmation of our conclusion that the common law of England and America knew of no such crime as circulating obscene literature except when it was of the particular kind which directly discredited religion, we may point to the law-book writers of the time, who uniformly classified it as an offense against God, not at all as one of any other *direct* consequences to the civil order.

With the creation of our secular commonwealths, wherein a union of church and state is forbidden, our constitutions have repealed all common law offenses against God. Writers such as Blackstone make no mention of such an offense except as an offense against God.

This little review, which I think covers all the reported cases bearing upon the common law against obscenity, shows conclusively that it is an error to claim, as often is done, that obscenity in our modern sense was an offense at common law.

If any further proof was necessary to show the relative indifference to so-called obscenity as such, we may find it in the statement of Erskine in his argument in the case of Thomas Carnau. He said: "I should really have been glad to have cited some sentences from the one hundred and thirteenth edition of Poor Robin's Almanack, *published under the revision of the Archbishop of Canterbury, and the Bishop of London,* but I am prevented from doing it by a just respect for the house. Indeed, I know of no house—but a brothel—that could suffer

[10]Hawkins' Pleas of the Crown, vol. 2, p. 130, Seventh Ed. 1795.
[11]Rex v. Cruden, 2 Campbell, 89.

the quotation. The worst of Rochester is ladies' reading when compared with them. . . . When ignorance, nonsense and obscenity, are thus fostered under the protection of a royal patent, how must they thrive under the wide spreading fostering wings of an act of Parliament."[12]

If still more proof is desired we have it in the literature of pre-revolutionary times. When, in 1888, Vizetelly, a celebrated English publisher, was arrested for "obscenity" in the vending of Zola's novels, he published a unique defense. After exposing and denouncing the falsehood published to arouse public opinion, he re-published "EXTRACTS PRINCIPALLY FROM ENGLISH CLASSICS, SHOWING THAT THE LEGAL SUPPRESSION OF M. ZOLA'S NOVELS WOULD LOGICALLY INVOLVE THE BOWDLERIZING OF SOME OF THE GREATEST WORKS OF ENGLISH LITERATURE." These extracts made a good sized volume, and included Shakespeare, Beaumont and Fletcher, Massinger, Defoe, Dryden, Swift, Prior, Sterne, Fielding, Smollet, and scores of others. I am informed that these passages were deemed so "obscene" that the court punished him for contempt for having even presented them in argument. And yet, not one of these was ever the subject of prosecution at common law.

For each and all of these reasons, I assert that "obscenity" merely as such, (that is, dissociated from blasphemy and sedition or a tendency to provoke a breach of the peace in private revenge) was not punishable at common law, and that at the adoption of our constitutions and prior, the circulation of such matter was a part of the freedom of the press, although such freedom was only a matter of permission.

However, under the judicial amendments of our constitutionally guaranteed freedom of the press as an unabridgable right, we have fewer privileges for sexual discussion than were enjoyed before the American constitutions or revolution. So much has our constitutional right been judicially annulled. The question is: Shall our constitutional freedom be restored?

[12]Erskine's Speeches, vol. 1, pp. 51-52.

CHAPTER IV.

THE ETIOLOGY and DEVELOPMENT

OF OUR

CENSORSHIP of SEX-LITERATURE.

The etiology of depotism is always quite the same. The absence of understanding, or appreciation, of liberty on the part of the masses and the natural lust for power, which makes every human a potential tyrant; makes him indifferent to all tyranny which does not directly effect him; and makes him submissive to even that tyranny which is exercised injuriously over himself if only in his turn he can tyrannize over others—it is these conditions, now combined with the prevalence of a prurient prudery, which have produced the present result. The initial exercise of tyrannical power always has to do with subjects as to which there is great public indifference, or a quite general approval, at least of a sentimental sort. The populace thus accustomed to the exercise of tyrannous authority, doze on with the delusion of liberty secure, while the lust for power induces officials to extend their authoritarian blight from one subject to another, until in the end the stupid masses awake to find that they possess all their liberties only as tenants at will of masters whom they thought servants of their own creation. I cannot believe these "obscenity" laws would ever have passed any American legislative body, had it been previously announced that the result would be such as it now is, within and beyond the domain of sex-discussion.

Here I must limit myself to an exhibition of the forces behind this censorship and of its development from the suppression of "obscene blasphemy" to "blasphemous obscenity"; from the suppression of mere pornographic filth to the nude in legitimate art; from medical prudery to the suppression of popular medical books, thence to serious and more pretentious sexual science and finally including "purity books" and perhaps

42

the Bible. The extension of the censorship into the realm of politics and economics I cannot discuss, though it has been astonishingly wide.

When, from the vantage ground of an age of true enlightenment, future generations shall look back on our vaunted age of (contemptible?) civilization, they will be moved by mingled feelings of pity and scorn, even as we are so moved when looking back upon the "Dark Ages". As now we see the monstrosities of the witch-craft superstition, so some future generation will look back in wonderment at our present sex-superstition.[1] While in the "dark ages" men were punished for doubting some tenet of the creed of dogmatic theology, we in this "age of civilization" punish men for expressing doubt as to some tenet of the creed of our dogmatic sex-morals; where formerly humanity was by law compelled to accept inspired geology, we of to-day are by law compelled to accept inspired sexology. For centuries the astrologers made it a crime to teach the common people astronomy, just as in this twentieth century it is a crime to teach the common people real sexual science. The general dissemination of information about geology and astronomy was prohibited *because* they discredited the fables of Genesis about the creation of the earth; to-day the general dissemination of information about the sexual sciences (physiology, anatomy, psychology, and ethics) is prohibited because these sciences discredit the fables of ascetic priests about the reproductive function of man. Formerly it was thought extremely dangerous to allow common people to read the Bible because of the awful consequences of erroneous private judgment, just as now sexual discussion and sciences must be withheld on account of the same stupid fear.

We are so intoxicated with unenlightened emotions over the *word* "liberty" that we have not the capacity to find out its meaning, nor to discover that we have less liberty of speech and press to-day than existed in England a century ago. There would be grim humor in most of what I am going to record, if only we could relieve ourselves of foolish apprehensions based upon our popular superstitions and egomania, and view ourselves and our fellows, as thesophists say we may view our present activities, from the eminence of some future incarnation.

[1]See "OBSCENITY AND WITCHCRAFT, TWIN SUPERSTITIONS," in *Physical Culture* for June, 1907; "WHAT IS CRIMINALLY OBSCENE?" *Albany Law Journal*, July, 1906.

KNEELAND BLASPHEMY TRIAL.

When the descendants and the successors of the puritan witch-hunters came to framing their fundamental law for the State of Massachusetts, they thought it necessary to God's vanity that his existence be given official recognition in the Constitution. This seems to have operated as a limitation, or the creation of an exception, to other clauses of the Constitution, such as the guarantee of freedom of speech.

But in the blasphemy trial of Abner Kneeland, which occurred in Massachusetts in 1834, the charge of blasphemy was reinforced by the prosecutor with this quotation from a work sold at the office of Kneeland's paper, *The Investigator*: "We have now, perhaps, sufficiently matured the subject, so as to be prepared to propose and answer the question, 'what laws would you have in relation to matrimony?' To which I answer—Marriage is a civil contract between the parties which stands upon the same basis of all other civil contracts, which are binding as long as the parties mutually agree, and no longer. The parties who make the contract, can dissolve it at pleasure, or by mutual consent. But if the parties cannot agree to separate by mutual consent, then it is necessary to call in a third party, one or more, as referee or arbitrators, not to bind the parties together—for in relation to matrimony, where the ties of affection do not bind them, this is impossible —but to say on what terms they shall separate, not only in regard to the property, but also to the maintenance and the education of the children, if there be any;***** I would have no one therefore marry for life, in the first instance nor for any certain period of time.*****But be not alarmed, the above principles are not intended for the present state of society at all, and not until all children are provided for by the public (who are not sufficiently provided for by their parents), both as regards their maintenance and education." For circulating this "blasphemous" statement the defendant was vigorously denounced before the jury, and after reading the foregoing extract these questions were asked of the jurors as answering themselves: "Who will say that courts of justice ought not to enforce the law against disseminating the moral and political poison of Atheism, and blasphemy? and proclaim their disgust at a system combining blasphemy, atheism, infidelity, adultery, lewdness, removing all moral and religious and legal checks

44

upon human depravity, and *leading to a community of property,* and striking directly at the foundation of civil society? *Prosecutions against blasphemy at this time, in this country, are not merely the causes in which God and Religion only are concerned"*[2]. A verdict of guilty was rendered and affirmed on appeal.

Later the word "blasphemy" became unpopular and lost its sting as an epithet of criminality, and, notwithstanding the law, those who desired to blaspheme could do so with practical impunity. The high-priests of fanaticism therefore felt compelled to secure laws which, under less archaic names, would enable them more successfully to punish what theretofore had been called "blasphemy"; and they are about to succeed. I am informed that in 1872 the original draft of the "obscenity" statutes included "blasphemous" literature among the unmailable postal matters. In 1878 the N. Y. Society for the Suppression of Vice,[3] boasted that a "class of publications issued by freelovers and free-thinkers is in a fair way of being stamped out." Since then many of the statutes against "obscene" literature have been amended by the addition of several other epithets, such as *indecent, filthy,* and *disgusting,* which are even more outrageously indefinable than the original "obscene." Under the vague statutory words "indecent, filthy, disgusting," several attempts have been made to secure conviction for circulating merely anti-religious literature. Such cases were the arrest of Bennett for circulating "An Open Letter to Jesus Christ"; the arrest of Moore, in Kentucky, for circulating irreligious literature, and the arrest of Vanni, a news dealer, for vending foreign anti-clerical papers. Up to this time, the courts have not indulged in the necessary judicial legislation to make the indefinable statutory epithets cover cases of mere theologic heresy. However, judging by the progress being made, and the increasing ease with which postal authorities and courts, by usurped power, interpolate into such uncertain statutes their own *ex post facto* criteria of unmailability and guilt, the time is not far off when the just stated hope of the N. Y. "Society for the Suppression of Vice" will be a realized fact. Thus, without "blasphemy" in the Statute, the persecutors of unpopular opinions will accomplish all the inequity formerly achieved by the laws against blasphemy.

FROM "OBSCENE BLASPHEMY" TO "BLASPHEMOUS OBSCENITY."

I have shown that at Common Law "obscenity," *merely as*

[2]Argument of the Attorney of the Commonwealth in the trials of Abner Kneeland, p. 89.
[3]See p. 7 of its Report for that year.

such, was not an offense. However, there was a kind of blasphemy which was distinguished from other sorts of blasphemy by the adjective "obscene."[4] "Obscene blasphemy," as known at Common Law, seems, under the determining influence of puritanism, to have evolved into the notion that all heresy as to sex-morals and ideals was in itself a blasphemy. With the growth of religious liberality, and the consequent odiousness of prosecutions for "blasphemy", there came a change of name, and a modification of sentiment, which resulted in the first penalization of all "obscenity" merely as such, and, as in all blasphemy laws, the creation of psychologic crimes, by making the penalty attach without proof of actual injury, or the imminent danger thereof according to any *known* laws of our physical universe. Unfortunately, these statutes never furnish the criteria of guilt, but leave that to the whim, caprice and "moral" idiosyncracy of judges and jurors, and this in spite of our constitutional guarantee of "due process of law."

The earliest "obscenity" prosecutions to attract widespread attention were for the sale of "Cupid's Yokes." This pamphlet, although not written with an eye single to politeness of style, yet manifestly is a serious and bona fide attempt to discuss the difficult sociologic problem of sex, and evidences more thought and study in its preparation than is usual in such productions. The author was an Infidel, and the vendors of it were most often persons who, having seen the utility of encouraging heresy in matters of theology, were willing also to encourage a dissent from religious sex-morals. So these culprits were apt to be Infidels, as also were those who were willing to defend the right of men to advocate even disapproved sex-heresy. The doctrines advocated in this pamphlet were similar to those quoted in the foregoing comment on the Kneeland blasphemy case. The chief of our moralists for revenue called it "blasphemous obscenity."

To the unreflecting crowd the difference between "obscene blasphemy" and "blasphemous obscenity" is not very great, and to our sex-worshiping moral sentimentalists there is no difference at all. To the latter, all frank discussion of sex is blasphemy because it unveils their sacred idol, and all other blasphemy is immoral chiefly because it tends to discredit the divine guarantee of their *a priori* sex-morality. Thoughtful persons saw in all this a new departure. Formerly the criterion of guilt was theologic heresy while now there was to be an

[4]*Albany Law Journal,* May, 1907.

extension of the censorship into purely sociologic realms which once had been recognized as secular domains, beyond the province of Religio-State control.

ON THE MANUFACTURE OF PRECEDENTS.

Before proceeding to the exposition of the evolutionary process and achievements of our censorship, I think it well to indicate how designing men can manufacture judicial precedents gradually enlarging a dangerous undefined power. Those who practise a lucrative morality, by regulating the intellectual food-supply of others, are much more far-seeing than the friends of freedom, and in their manufacture of precedents our moralists for revenue exercise a considerable ingenuity. If a book they wish to suppress is published by an influential firm, they may think it unwise to attack the publisher, but go after some obscure or unpopular and impecunious retailer of the book. If he shows fight and the book is one which might find many friends to champion it, the culprit is invited to plead guilty and pay a nominal fine. Usually he is quite willing to assist in establishing a pernicious precedent if only it saves his purse. By citing precedents thus manufactured, others are cowed into submission, and courts are finally lead to adopt them in extension of the censorship. In a recent case an employee was arrested for distributing an alleged "obscene" pamphlet. A nominal fine was suggested if he would plead guilty. Upon refusing to accept the offer, his employer was threatened with arrest. Still refusing, the court held the pamphlet no violation of the law. At other times, when, in all probability, indictment and conviction cannot be had, appeal is made to the Postal Department to exercise its power, made arbitrary by uncertainty of the statute, to refuse the transmission of the offending book, and all advertisements of it. If the courts are resorted to, they deny relief because the same statutory uncertainty makes it impossible to say that the postal authorities have abused their discretion, which discretion, however, is conferred only by implications arising from the same uncertainty of the same statute. Thus are our liberties frittered away by piece-meal construction. Then, too, our professional purists often are very wise in the choice of jurisdiction in which they seek to make a precedent. They soon learn that some judges will construe books to be criminal which other judges, perhaps more clean-minded, would probably hold to be no violation of this uncertain statute. We all know where they would seek to create their precedent. Because these statutes do not furnish the criteria of guilt, all this is possible and easy. The public must be content with dogmatism and question-begging epithets. No one dares republish the "obscene" matter, even for the purpose of convincing the voting public that the law which condemned it should be repealed.

"SEXUAL HYGIENE."

The chief force behind these "obscenity" laws is the waning influence of the ascetic ideal. Very generally, Christians had accepted the views of Origen and St. Hieronymos that "Marriage is always a vice; all we can do is to excuse and to cleanse it." Quite logically it followed from such premises that to produce the most virgins and Christian soldiers should come to be estimated as the least offensive life for those who claimed a "sacramental authority to live unchaste." Of course, to such minds the artificial sterilization of marriage was the greatest possible offense and akin to blasphemy, in that it was the frustration of the "divine plan."

As the ascetic ideal was losing its influence over sane minds its apostles most naturally resorted to the usual legalized violence to enforce it upon the increasing number inclined to repudiate it. Sometimes an effort was made to stretch the Common-law crime of "obscene blasphemy" so as to provide punishment for those who disseminated information as to the prevention of conception. Later, when the "obscenity" statutes had been passed, it was contended that such information was "obscene." Courts and juries did not always lend themselves to the enforcement of this view. Then our moralists for revenue secured statutes which specifically penalized such information.

A most practical book for physicians and intelligent laymen is entitled, "Sexual Hygiene, Compiled from Books, Articles, and Documents, Many not Heretofore Published, by the Editorial Staff of — — —."[5] Both sides of many controverted questions are presented. Among other things, there is a short chapter discussing methods for the prevention of

---

[5] I heard of this suppression quite accidentally. The publishers declined to furnish any information and requested that I do not mention it. This attitude, which is very general among publishers, makes it almost impossible to find out what our censors are suppressing.

conception. This book was recently suppressed by threat of prosecution, and doubtless because it was "obscene," if allowed to get into the hands of laymen, as well as because of its discussion of preventives. So it has come to this that it is a crime to assist in preventing the prolific propagation of the unfit, and, so far as the law can promote such ends, we have compulsory breeding, breeding enforced by statute. This, too, in a land where it is declared that the maintainance of liberty is the end of government.

FROM BAWDRY PICTURES TO NUDITY IN ART AND SEXUAL ANATOMY.

In the beginning it seems as though people thought that only bawdry portrayals were to be suppressed. "Filthy" was the characterization of Congressman Merriam when in 1873 he made a statement in favor of the suppression of the "obscene." Such question-begging epithets of course preclude a thoughtless public from the weighing of human liberty against moral sentimentalism, or of considering the evolution of precedents, or even asking for statutory critera of guilt. A dull and unconcerned populace did not see that the precedents which they applauded would lead to the suppression of all nudity in art, and ultimately to the suppression of all contradiction of the theology of sex. The transition was swift from suppressing what disgusted most people to the suppression of that which could offend only the extreme ascetic, or prude. Boston banished its bronze Bacchante. A copy of "The Triumph of Charles V," by Hans Makart, was ordered out of the window of a New York candy-store. A Fifth Avenue art dealer had to conceal a landscape portraying some children discreetly walking away from the beholders. That these pictures had the saving grace of high art did not protect their owners, and these owners, not caring to indulge in the expense of defending human liberty, succumbed to the threat.

Emboldened by similar successes, the Art Students League catalogue was attacked because of its drawings of nude men. Washington postal authorities had declared it mailable, so an arrest was made under State laws. The defendant was induced to plead guilty on assurance that no appreciable penalty would be inflicted. This also was cheaper than to defend human rights, and thus the seemings of another judicial precedent were established. However, this doubtful victory and the great publicity given it did not yet give courage for attacking a popular magazine which soon after adorned its title page with the posterior view of nude children. The result might have been different had it been a periodical more generally disapproved, or which had previously and for other reasons excited official condemnation.

From art to literature was not a far reach. First of course the censors suppressed the purely bawdry literature, as for example, "Fanny Hill" and "Memoirs of a Woman of Pleasure." Thence the extension to "The Yoke" and "Three Weeks"; Zola, Boccaccio and Rabelais also have been attacked with varying success, and even lately a woman was arrested in New Jersey for sending to her husband, by mail, a copy of Burn's "Merry Muses." In New York a woman, having qarreled with her husband, had him arrested for having mailed her a lascivious letter. Tolstoi's "Kreutzer Sonata" was suppressed by Postmaster General Wanamaker. Bills have already been introduced to penalize advertisements of liquors and cigarettes, and descriptions of drinking and smoking scenes. Soon we will have a literature that is not only sexless but also drinkless and smokeless. But what good will have come to humanity when all this is achieved? Will sexual and other irregularities really cease in fact because they cannot openly exist in type? Will justice be more certain and liberty more secure?

Dr. R. W. Shufeldt, Major U. S. Army (retired), is internationally one of the best known among American Scientists. He has published a number of books and over 1,100 essays making many valuable contributions of original research and of great scientific value. One of his latest is a handsome volume, which in the cheapest edition sells for $15.00, and is entitled "Studies of the Human Form."

The author says: "The aim in writing it has been to make a contribution to the subject which may prove to be of use to students of art; to professional artists and sculptors; to craftsman requiring a knowledge of the human figure; to medical men of all classes * * *; and finally to quicken the cause for the good of the national and individual morals and ethics of the race, to the death of all prudery, superstition, and vice."

This last was the unpardonable sin, to those of whom it may be said: Unto the lewd all is lewd. Although the book had received the highest praise from many scientists and artists, one of our moralists for revenue, armed with the authority of a postal inspector, threatened the publishers with immediate arrest unless they would suppress the entire edition. They promised, but at the same time began preparing for an appeal to those higher up in the Postal Department. As a result, the inspector's decision was reversed, with a string on the reversal. The postal authorities prescribed limitations as to the manner of sale and persons to whom alone the sales are to be made. None of these limitations is found in, nor derived from, the Statutes, but the officials decided that, so long as the departmental legislation is complied with, the book is not "obscene" and its transmission through the mail would not be prosecuted as a crime. Always remember that this did not occur in Russia but in the United States, where it is thought that the Constitution vests all Federal legislative power in the Congress of the United States, where alone the criteria of guilt and legal rights should be defined. However, the postal authorities at Washington, in the light of what they might have done, are to be praised for allowing us at least this much liberty.

The purists' battle against all nude in art is not wholly won. However, our postal laws have just been amended by adding the indefinable epithet "filthy" to the description of what is non-mailable. No doubt this additional statutory vagueness will accomplish much in the progress of tyranny over literature and art. It can mean anything or nothing according to the tastes of the postal censor.

Having desired to suppress bawdry pictures, and the nude in legitimate art, it became necessary that courts and moralists for revenue should legislate into existance criteria of "obscenity" adequate to accomplish the ends. Again, the judicial legislation thus brought into existence was capable of application to books with illustrations of sexual anatomy, thus leading up to a censorship over scientific sex-literature. When the portrayal of all human nudity has been penalized, consistancy requires the suppression of all portrayals of sexual anatomy. Soon we may have the complete suppression of both.

PRUDERY IN THE MEDICAL PROFESSION.

In order properly to understand the growth of this new legalized prudery and its intrusion into other realms of medical science, we must appreciate to the full the influence of past centuries of dominant ascetic ideals as evidenced by the manifestations of prudery even in the medical profession. When we realize how much of it is to be found even there, we will better appreciate the greater quantity to be found in the less educated and more sentimental masses.

Of course, the mere study of medicine, in and of itself, does not necessarily relieve the physician of his superstitions, either professional, moral, or religious. Because of this, we find within the medical profession quite as much sentimental opposition to unpopular allegations of truth and approval of persecution for professional or other heresy as are found elsewhere.

At the meeting of the American Medical Association, held at Columbus in 1899, a paper was read on the "The Gynecologic Consideration of the Sexual Act," by Denslow Lewis, M. D., Professor of Gynecology in the Chicago Polyclinic: President of the Attending Staff of the Cook County Hospital, Chicago; President of the Chicago Medical Examiners' Association; Vice President of the Illinois State Medical Society; Ex-President of the Physicians' Club, of Chicago; Late Special Commissioner from the Illinois State Board of Health and the Health Department of Chicago for the investigation of Municipal Sanitation in European Cities. Later Dr. Denslow Lewis was the Chairman of the section on Hygiene and Sanitary Science of the American Medical Association. I mention these things to show that Dr. Lewis was a man of prominence in his profession. The before-named paper was discussed some. Dr. Howard Kelly of Baltimore, who assumed the role of chief advocate for mystery and ignorance, among other things, said: "I do not believe in the current teaching of the day, that is, talking freely about these things to children. * * * * * * Its discussion [before this association] is attended with more or less filth, and we *besmirch ourselves* by discussing it *in public.*"

Later the article was denied publication in the *Journal of the American Medical Association,* where papers read at the national meeting usually appear. The editor of that *Journal,* in a letter to Dr. Lewis refusing to publish the paper, said: "There is nothing in it [the paper] that is not true and possibly it ought to appear in the *Journal,* but with my personal views in reference to this class of literature, I hardly think so." A member of the publication committee of the American Medical Association, justifying his conduct in voting against the publication of Dr. Lewis' essay, said: "The publication of the article will lay the Board of Trustees open to the charge of sending 'obscene' matter through the mails."

At the next meeting of the Association, held at Atlantic City, Dr. Lewis decided, if possible, to have the Association over-rule the publication committee. In order that members might have an enlightened judgment as to the character of the paper whose publication they were to pass upon, Dr. Lewis had his address printed in pamphlet form and distributed among the members. After all sorts of interference with the distribution of the pamphlet, the matter finally came before a general session of the Association. Dr. Howard Kelly stated that he had remained over a day longer than he intended so he might take part in the controversy to make sure that the pages of the *Journal* were not "polluted" by the publication of the essay in question. After a vociferous meeting the committee was sustained in its refusal to publish. Later on Dr. Lewis was forced to resign his position as professor of Gynecology in the Chicago Polyclinic, and Dr. Fernand Henrotin, who forced this result, asserted as a reason that Dr. Lewis' action at the Atlantic City meeting had excited unfavorable comment.

In 1901, at the St. Paul meeting of the American Medical Association, Dr. Lewis presented a paper before the section on Hygiene on the subject, "The Limitation of Venereal Diseases." Although such conspicuous prudes as Dr. Howard Kelly consented to discuss the paper, it also was refused publication in the official organ of the Association.[6] It was about this time that the American Public Health Association considered Gonorrhea too loathsome to be tolerated for discussion.

I have it upon the authority of one of the most widely known scientists of America, that many medical journals hold substantially the same attitude toward the discussion of sexual topics. No wonder, then, that such periodicals deplore the physicians' ignorance of sexual science, and the consequent unprevented, but preventable, social ills.[7] With such superstition and prudery even in the Medical profession, it is not strange that the populace should protest but little because of facts presently to be recited. Farther on I shall quote something showing the attitude of medical editors toward sex-discussion.

THE EVOLUTION TOWARD MEDICAL BOOKS.

Besides its prudes, the medical profession has its regular

[6] It was subsequently published in the *Medico-Legal Journal* for June and September, 1903. For recital of facts, see Poe. Med. Journ. about 1907.
[7] See *Am. Jour. of Clinical Medicine*, January, 1909, p. 134.

quota of "moral" snobs. As the result, many physicians, and nearly all hospitals, refuse to treat venereal diseases. As a necessary consequence of this silly sentimentalism, those who are willing to treat such cases are quite generally ostracized and called disagreeable names. Naturally, they adjust themselves by seeking greater financial returns for their efforts so as to compensate them for the odium they invite. So through the prudery of some, we develop out of others the "lost manhood" specialist. Judged by any code of rational ethics, much of the advertising of venereal specialists is perfectly legitimate. Of course, it is not to be expected that "professionl ethics" is rational, and to emphasize the fact that it has nothing to do with ethical science it assumes a distinctive qualifying name, just as "Christian Science," by the qualification attached to "science," announces that it bears no necessary relation to any real science. So it comes that physicians indiscriminately call all advertising doctors bad names, and are willing to invoke any bad law to punish a "bad" man. From such motives the obscenity laws have been frequently invoked against the man who advertises his profession in an unconventional way, and "regular" physicians have applauded the effort because they lacked the foresight to see that the very precedents they were helping to establish would later be used to plague them.

Quite a number of physicians have been arrested and convicted for sending through the mails information as to venereal diseases. One of these books, which serves as a type, has been thus described by a former assistant attorney-general of the post office department. He says the book "consisted mainly of a description of the causes and effects of venereal diseases, and secondly, two circulars, one of which described in separate paragraphs the symptome of various venereal diseases." That was held to be criminally "obscene." The courts, however, occasionally take a different view of it.[8]

Easy was the transition from this outlawing of the warfare against the venereal peril to the suppression of popular medical books, which, though a little more "legitimate," also cut down the "regular" practitioners' earnings. The judicial legislation, creating criteria of guilt in one class of cases, was soon found applicable to the other.

Having now exhibited the forces behind this legislation, and something of the evolutionary processes by which this

[8]Hansen v. U. S., 157 Fed. Rep. 749.

modern censorship has developed, we will examine a little into its achievements.

THE CASE OF HICKLIN.

The first reported English decision[9], which attempted to state a test of obscenity, was decided in 1868, and furnished the precedent for practically all American decisions. The facts were as follows: Hicklin, the accused, had sold a pamphlet entitled, "The Confessional Unmasked: Showing the Depravity of the Romish Priesthood, the Iniquity of the Confessional, and the Questions put to Females in Confession." The pamphlet consisted of extracts from Catholic theologians, one page giving the exact original Latin quotations and the adjoining page furnishing a correct translation thereof. Much of the pamphlet admittedly was not at all obscene. It was not sold for gain, nor with any intention to deprave morality, but, as the defendant believed, to improve morality. It was sold by him as a member of the "Protestant Electoral Union," formed "to protest against those teachings and practices which are un-English, immoral, and blasphemous, to maintain the Protestantism of the Bible and the liberty of England. * * * To promote the return to Parliament of men who will assist them in these objects and particularly will expose and defeat the deep-laid machinations of the Jesuits, and resist grants of money for Romish purposes."

Notwithstanding all these admitted facts the court held the pamphlet to be obscene and laid down this test: "Whether the tendency of the matter charged as obscenity is to deprave and corrupt those whose minds are open to such immoral influences, and into whose hands a publication of this sort may fall." It will be observed that it was criminal, if in the hands of any one imaginary person it might be speculatively believed to be injurious, no matter how much it tended to improve the morals of all the rest of mankind, nor how lofty were the motives of those accused, nor how true was that which they wrote. This is still the test of obscenity under our laws, and it has worked some results which could hardly have been in contemplation by our legislators in passing our laws against indecent literature.

This prosecution, altho' not designated blasphemy, was yet more nearly allied to that than is apparent on superficial view. The main purpose of the book was to discredit the

[9]Reg. vs. Hicklin, L. R. 3 Q. B. 360.

largest and most influential section of Christian priests. In Germany, where practically no attention is given to "obscenity," merely as such, a novel entitled "The Sinful Bishop," written by a Catholic priest, and which "in no sense offends morals," was suppressed. In New York City, though no attention is given to ordinary plays, yet, when "Mrs. Warren's Profession" presented a plot wherein a priest in his boyhood had fathered an illigitimate child, *that,* in the opinion of Police Commissioner Bingham, made it "obscene." Mark you, because it was a priest and tended to discredit clergymen and the church. No play in which non-clericals are guilty of illicit love ever excited the police commissioner. In California a book substantially like that in the Hicklin case was also suppressed.[10]

THE MUSEUM OF ANATOMY.

Connected with this subject of publicity about venereal infection, and its relation to purity, I shall presume to relate a personal experience. When a boy of 15 years, I left the parental home to find work in Chicago.

I soon discovered here a Museum of Anatomy conducted by one of those persons whom we contemptuously call "quacks," because they advertise their willingness to treat diseases which many compassionless moral snobs in the medical profession refuse to treat, which refusal results in so much suffering to the innocent.

In this Museum, for a trifling admission fee, I saw perfect imitations in wax of all the indescribable horrors consequent upon venereal infection. Of course the exhibition was obscene and indecent beyond description, but it was something more as well. It was an object lesson giving ocular demonstration of the terrible consequence of promiscuity and could not do otherwise than to inspire a wholesome fear of which I have not rid myself to this day. The vividness of the impression produced by one such sight would far surpass all the moral and religious sermons that could be preached from now till doomsday, because the innuendos or even the direct statements can mean nothing to the child-mind, before it is possessed of the experience which enables it to translate the words into corresponding mental pictures.

Nowadays such museums are suppressed because of their obscenity. It is deserving of consideration whether such forces for good had not better be encouraged by their attach-

[10]Price v. U. S., 165 U. S. 311, I believe was the case.

ment to our public schools, in preference to their suppression because shocking.

STRATTON'S "THE SEXUAL LIFE."

Recently a book agent was arrested in Boston for selling "obscence" literature. The following is the title of the book which gave offense: *"The Sexual Life, Including Anatomical Illustrations and Obstetric Observations, also a series of engravings illustrating the Formation of Life, Growth of the Embryo, Development of the Fœtus, and the Cæsarean Operation, by Prof. Benjamin Franklin Stratton. Sixth edition revised and enlarged."*

A conviction was secured, perhaps made possible largely by other associated charges.

"CLARK'S MARRIAGE GUIDE."

In Massachusetts one Jones was arrested for sending through the mails "Clark's Marriage Guide." It must already be apparent that under the laws in question no one can tell in advance what is or is not criminal, because no one can predetermine what will be the opinion of a judge or jury upon the speculative problem of the book's psychological tendency upon some hypothetical reader suffering from sexual hyperaestheticism. Unfortunately, Mr. Jones went for advice to a lawyer who must have been a good deal of a prude, and who therefore advised his client to plead guilty, which he did. Later, when Judge Lowell was called upon to impose the sentence, he is reported as having said that the book "is not immoral or indecent at all," and imposed only a very light fine. In Chicago, the same book was suppressed by heavy fines; aggregating over $5,000.00.

"THE LIFE SEXUAL."

Edgar C. Beall, M.D., wrote a little book entitled "The Life Sexual, a Study of the Philosophy, Physiology, Science, Art and Hygiene of Love," which was suppressed in 1906 by threat of prosecution. The book was written for the general reader and differs from the ordinary "purity" book in that the theology of sex in supplanted by a more enlightened view, and much very wholesome and needed advice, in spite of its slight element of "phrenophysics." However, this had nothing to do with its "obscenity." I have read much of this book and can not for the life of me conceive why it should be deemed offensive, because the book is written in a refined style and is instructive. The opening chapter is devoted to a strong criticism of "The Ban upon Sexual Science," and maybe therein lies the cause of complaint. Another explanation was offered by a minor official, and it was that this matter, coming to the attention of the post office department immediately after the suppression of Professor Malchow's book, the similarity of title suggested a necessary similarity in treatment of the subject and therefore a like "obscenity."

"VICE: ITS FRIENDS AND ITS FOES"; "UP-TO-DATE FABLES."

In a letter dated Nov. 15, 1907, an assistant Attorney General of the U. S., who really is the master of our intellectual food supply, pronounced a magazine unmailable for advertising "Vice: Its Friends and its Foes," and "Up-to-Date Fables," of which he says—"both of which, from the table of contents set forth in each advertisement, are obscene, lewd, lascivious, or indecent." The first of these booklets I have seen and in the main it is an attack on Comstockery, and an argument for sexual intelligence. Even Mr. Comstock would not have found this booklet to be obscene, though of course he would disagree with its conclusions. The table of contents is too long to reproduce here, but I will reproduce the table of contents of the "Up-to-Date Fables" just to show how little information is necessary to discover "obscenity" when one has a "pure" mind. Here it is: "Contents: the Male Amazons, The Strassburg Geese, Bread Eaten in Secret, The One Tune, A Tale about Noses, The Women and the Wells, Mrs. Grundy's Two Boarding Schools, The Emancipated Horses." Now, then, from that, and that alone, a pee-wee clerk in the government employ is able to decide and does decide, that this booklet is degrading to our morals, an advertisement telling us where it may be had is unmailable, and to send any of these through the mails entitles the sender to five years in jail.

CRADDOCK AND STOCKHAM CASES.

As illustrating how our fears are often but the product of ignorance, I am going to relate to you how and why I changed my mind about two booklets pronounced "the most obscene" that ever came to the criminal court. If these really are the most offensive of condemned literature then I am prepared to stand all the rest. Both were entitled "The Wedding Night," and dealt with their subject in a very detailed manner. One was by an unfortunate woman named Ida Craddock, who styled herself a "purity lecturer." Mr. Comstock denounced her book as "the science of seduction." It could have been more accurately described as advice for the best means of consummating the marriage. The judge who denounced the author called it "indescribably obscene." To one who, from diseased sex-sentiveness, is incapable of reading a discussion of sex functioning with the same equanimity as would accompany a discussion of lung functioning, or to one who would apply the absurd judicial "tests" of obscenity, this booklet must appear just as these men described it. Of course she was found guilty. Later she committed suicide to escape the penalty of the law.

For the book Mrs. Craddock claimed to have the endorsement of several prominent members of the Woman's Christian Temperance Union, and published a letter from the Rev. W. S. Rainsford, the very distinguished rector of the fashionable St. George's Episcopal Church of New York City, in which he said: "This much I will say, I am sure if all young people read carefully 'The Wedding Night,' much misery, sorrow, and disappointment could be avoided."

The other booklet was by Dr. Alice Stockham, the well known author of Tokology and similar books, and in name and substance, I believe, it was very much like the Craddock book. A Post-Office Inspector pronounced it the most obscene book he had ever read. She was convicted and heavily fined, though with many friends she vigorously defended the propriety and necessity for her booklet of instructions. Of course neither of these books nor any like them are now anywhere to be had.

The question is what good could be done by such books, so unquestionably obscene if judged by present judicial standards? I confess that when first I heard of these cases I knew of no excuse for the existence of this unpleasant literature.

I had read in medical literature statements like this: "The shock and suffering endured by the young wife, in the nuptial bed, is too frequently prolonged into after-life, and may seriously mar the connubial bliss."[11] Such generalizations, however, meant nothing to me until a strange set of circumstances came to my notice, which I will relate to you in the order of their occurrence.

Not long since I learned of the marriage of persons in a

[11]The Sexual Life, p. 127.

most conservative social set. The couple had been chums since childhood and engaged lovers for many years. After this long waiting, came the joyously anticipated wedding, and the bride was the ideal picture of radiant love. The day after her marriage she acted strangely, and by evening her husband and relatives concluded that her reason had been dethroned, and ever since she has been confined in a sanitarium. Through her incoherent speech, only one thing is sure and constant, and that is that she never again wants to see her husband. More information is not given to the conservative circle of her friends. All profess ignorance as to the immediate cause of this strange mania, which reverses the ambition, hope, and love of a lifetime.

Strangely enough, within two days after hearing this painful story, a friend handed me the *Pacific Medical Journal,* for January, 1906.[12] Therein I read the following paragraphs and to me the mystery had been solved. Now I thought I knew why one bride had her love turned to hate, her mind ruined, and why her relatives were so shamefacedly silent, lest some should learn a useful lesson from their affliction.

The material portion of the article reads as follows: "While upon this point I would say that under the so-called sanctity of the Christian marriage, untold thousands of the most brutal rapes have been perpetrated, more brutal and fiendish indeed, than many a so-named criminal rape. So outrageous has been the defloration of many a young girl-wife by her husband, that she has been invalided and made unhappy for the balance of her natural life. There are cases on record where so violently has the act of copulation been performed that the hymen, being thick and but slightly perforated, death has followed its forcible rupture, and the nervous shock associated with the infamous proceeding. Here the criminally ignorant young husband and the ravisher are at par, and no censure that the world can mete out to them can be too great."

And now I thought I had received new light on those strange and not infrequent accounts one reads in the newspapers of young women who commit suicide during their "honeymoon."

Here another strange chance led me upon Dr. Mary Walker's book, "Unmasked, or the Science of Immorality,"

[12] Article by R. W. Shufeldt, M. D., Major Medical Department of U. S. Army, and Trustee of the Medico-Legal Society of New York.

where I read the following paragraph: "There are instances of barrenness, where the only cause has been the harshness of husbands on wedding nights. The nerves of the vagina were so shocked and partially paralyzed that they never recovered the magnetic power to foster the life of the spermatozoa until the conception was perfected."

With this much I went to a physician friend, and he promptly confirmed all that had been said by the others and handed me "Hygiene of the Sexual Functions, a lecture delivered in the regular course at Jefferson Medical College of Philadelphia, by Theophilus Parvin, A. D., M. D., Professor of Obstetrics and Diseases of Women and Children." On page two I read the following: "Occasionally you read in the newspapers that the bride of a night or of a few days, or of a few weeks, has gone home to her parents, and never to return to her husband; but there is a Chicago divorce concluding the history. One of the most distinguished French physicians, Bertillon, has recently said that every year, in France, he knows of thirty to forty applications for divorce within the first year of marriage, and he has reason to believe that a majority of these are from the brutalities of the husband in the first sexual intercourse."

After reading these statements from highly reputable physicians, I could no longer doubt that these "most obscene books ever published," were really most humanitarian efforts on the part of those who perhaps had a wider knowledge than I possessed. If this is the worst, I am prepared to take chances on lesser "obscenity."

"CONJUGIAL LOVE."

The two books now about to be mentioned are not medical books in any sense, and yet mark a sort of transition state toward the more scientific discussion of sex-problems.

The heading is the title of one of the best known books of that conspicuous philosopher and dreamer, Emanuel Swedenborg. Of course this book was written about a century and a half ago. The Swedenborg Society of London was organized in 1810, since which time it has been promoting the circulation of the more important works of Swedenborg. It is probable, therefore, that the English rendition of "Conjugial Love" has been on the market for over half a century. In the year 1909, in the City of Philadelphia, a magistrate judicially declared it to be obscene. Thus, again, not only was an "obscene" book suppressed, but also a heretical sect was discredited. [13]

"LOVE AND ITS AFFINITIES."

This is the title of a very interesting little book by Dr. George F. Butler, of Chicago, who is well known to the medical profession.

In the preface, the author describes his effort as one to present "a physiological study of love and its relationship to phychical as well as physiological phenomena. * * * * * The grosser features of the sexual instinct, of itself ideally pure—revolting as they may appear, have, therefore, not been disguised. * * * * * The motive of the present monograph is an ascent from the lower to a higher, purer phase of passion, an aspiration whose heavenward struggle and stately floresence are the crown and glory of mortal love."

And such a book by such a man cannot go through the mails, nor be so advertised, because a postal clerk says it can't and is backed by a statute so uncertain that it neither affirms nor contradicts his authority.

It used to be thought that ours was not a bureaucracy and that, because of our Constitution, departmental legislation could never supersede congressional enactment. It was even judicially declared that all "is purely legislative which defines rights, permits things to be done or prohibits the doing thereof."[14] But what does a stupid public, or its official masters, care for such old judicial opinions as to constitutional rights, when these interfere with the masters' lust for power, and moral sentimentalism?

"PURITY" BOOKS SUPPRESSED.

Recently a distinguished "purity" worker issued a wholesome little pamphlet entitled "Not a Toothache or a Bad Cold," which was suppressed by threat of arrest, though the Post-Office authorities had declared it mailable.

"The Social Peril" is a book dealing with venereal infection, and is by one of the best known professional moralists in America. Mr. Comstock threatened him with arrest for "obscenity," partly for a fifteen page quotation from a book by Rev. Henry Ward Beecher. The "Social Peril" is suppressed, through fear of a criminal prosecution, though other elements finally culminated to accomplish the same end.

It seems part of the irony of fate that those who are more

---

[13]The Public, Mch. 26, 1909.
[14]U. S. v. Mathew, 146 Fed. Rep. 308; U. S. v. Eaton, 144 U. S. 687.

or less consciously fostering this absurd legislation in support of the ascetic ideal, should be caught in their own traps. There are other examples of the same kind to which we will direct attention.

"FROM THE BALL-ROOM TO HELL."

This book has the endorsement of practically all opponents of dancing. It furnished the suggestions for thousands of sermons; it had the commendation of innumerable clergymen, including several bishops; it went through the mails unchallenged for 12 years. A Chicago postal official now declares it criminally "obscene" and the book is suppressed. Again it is not a rule of general law which makes this book criminal, but the whim or caprice of a postal subordinate.

"ALMOST FOURTEEN."

In 1892, Dodd, Mead & Co., published a little book entitled "Almost Fourteen," written by Mortimer A. Warren, a public school teacher. Before publishing it, Mr. Mead submitted the manuscript to his wife and to the pastor of the Broadway Tabernacle, and of the Church of the Heavenly Rest, and to Dr. Lyman Abbott. All these endorsed its aim and tone.

After publication, there were of course prudes who criticised, but such papers as the Christian Union gave it a favorable review. The Rev. L. A. Pope, then pastor of the Baptist church of Newburyport, Mass., placed the book in the Sunday School library of his church, and purchased a large number at a reduced price, selling them at cost, simply that the young might read and learn, so well did he think of the book. In my own view it would be impossible to deal properly with the subject of sex and do it in a more delicate, inoffensive manner.

No question was raised about the book until 1897, when Albert F. Hunt, of Newburyport, Mass., was arrested for selling obscene literature. Mr. Hunt had made himself very unpopular as an aggressive reformer. He had attacked the police force, exhibited the iniquity of the city administration, exposed the sins of the city, such as the practice of taking nude photographs, the aggressions of the saloonkeepers, and exposed the owners of buildings leased for prostitution. He had many influential enemies. In this condition he secured permission to republish "Almost Fourteen" in his paper, was arrested, convicted, and fined.

I have no doubt in my mind that, judged by the scientifically absurd tests of obscenity as applied by the courts, this innocent book was criminal under the law against obscene literature, because no doubt somewhere there existed some sexually hyperaesthetic person into whose hands it might come, and in whose mind it might induce lewd thoughts. The legislative "obscenity" takes no account of the thousands who might be benefited by such a book; it only asks if there may be one so weak that it might injure him.

After this conviction for circulating humanitarian literature of a most useful kind, the author of this good book was driven from his place as principal of the public schools, by the prudish bigotry of his fellow townsmen and employers. The book can now be had only with much of its most useful matter eliminated. We need liberty of the press for persons like Warren, Hunt, and Dodd, Mead & Co.

MRS. CARRIE NATION ARRESTED.

Most of the literature intended to promote personal purity is so veiled in a fog of verbiage as to be utterly meaningless to the young, because they lack the intelligence which alone could make it possible to translate the innuendoes into the mental pictures which the words are supposed to symbolize. Recently Mrs. Carrie Nation in her paper published some wholesome advice to small boys. She used scientifically chaste English and took the trouble to define the meaning of her words. She wrote so plainly that there was actually a possibility that boys might understand what she was trying to teach them. She wrote with greater plainness than some of those books which have been adjudged criminally obscene.

A warrant was issued for her in Oklahoma, for sending obscene matter through the mails. She being then in Texas on a lecture tour, was there arrested and taken to Dallas before a U. S. Commissioner. Fortunately she found there a U. S. Attorney with some sense, who, though he did not approve of her taste, consented to the discharge of the prisoner. Mrs. Nation is to be congratulated upon having discovered one spot in this country not dominated by the prurient prudery of New England and New York. Unfortunately none can know when and where another healthy-minded prosecutor will be found. However, the postal authorities, disagreeing with the courts, still exclude the article from the mails.[15]

[15]*The Hatchet,* Dec., 1906.

THE BIBLE JUDICIALLY DECLARED OBSCENE.

One of the early American prosecutions of note was that of the distinguished eccentric, George Francis Train, in 1872. He was arrested for circulating obscenity, which it turned out consisted of quotations from the Bible. Train and his attorneys sought to have him released upon the ground that the matter was not obscene, and demanded a decision on that issue. The prosecutor, in his perplexity, and in spite of the protest of the defendant, insisted that Train was insane. If the matter was not obscene, his mental condition was immaterial, because there was no crime. The court refused to discharge the prisoner as one not having circulated obscenity, but directed the jury, against their own judgment, to find him not guilty, on the ground of insanity, thus, by necessary implication, deciding the Bible to be criminally obscene.

Upon a hearing on a writ of habeas corpus, Train was adjudged sane, and discharged. Thus an expressed decision on the obscenity of the Bible was evaded, though the unavoidable inference was for its criminality.

In his autobiography, Train informs us that a Cleveland paper was seized and destroyed for republishing the same Bible quotations which had caused his arrest in New York. Here then was a direct adjudication that parts of the Bible are indecent, and therefore unmailable.[16]

In 1895, John B. Wise of Clay Center, Kansas, was arrested for sending obscene matter through the mails which again consisted wholly of a quotation from the Bible. In the United States Court, after a contest, he was found guilty and fined.

Just keep in mind a moment these court precedents where portions of the Bible have been judicially condemned as criminally obscene, while I connect it with another rule of law. The courts have often decided that a book to be obscene need not be obscene throughout, the whole of it, but if the book is obscene in any part it is an obscene book, within the meaning of the statutes.[17]

You will see at once that under the present laws and relying wholly on precedents already established, juries of irreligious men could wholly suppress the circulation of the Bible, and in some states the laws would authorize its seizure and destruction and all this because the words "Indecent and ob-

[16]Here I think Train must be referring to the conviction of John A. Lant, publisher of the Toledo Sun, and later other papers.
[17]U. S. v. Bennett, 6 Blatchford 838, F. C. No. 14571.

scene" are not definable in qualities of a book or picture. In other words, all this iniquity is possible under present laws because courts did not heed the maxim, now scientifically demonstrable, viz.: "Unto the pure all things are pure."

Of course, the Old Testament in common with all books that are valuable for moral instruction, contains many unpleasant recitals, but that is no reason for suppressing any of them. I prefer to put myself on the side of that English judge who said: "To say in general that the conduct of a dead person can at no time be canvassed; to hold that even after ages are passed the conduct of bad men cannot be contrasted with the good, would be to exclude the most useful part of history."[18]

I therefore denounce this law because under it may be destroyed books containing records of human folly and error from which we may learn valuable lessons, for avoiding the blight from violating nature's moral laws. Under our present statutes some of the writings of the greatest historians and literary masterpieces have been suppressed and practically all would be suppressed if the courts should apply to them impartially the present judicial test of obscenity.

SUPPRESSED BECAUSE NOT "OBSCENE."

Every evil, real or imaginary, which we endeavor to avoid by wrong methods seem necessarily to involve other evils as a consequence. By suppressing all sex discussion we make it impossible for people to satisfy their natural and healthy inquisitiveness. Thus we unintentionally promote morbid curiosity, in view of which those who are its victims become an easy prey to the wiles of the designing. I will illustrate by one concrete example. One of the suppressed books of fiction which has been much discussed is called "Fanny Hill." Because it is believed to be extremely racy and because of the great risk in selling it the real "Fanny Hill" commands from collectors a very fancy price; copies have been reported sold for as high as forty ($40.00) dollars. Knowing this, some unscrupulous book dealers will take any ordinary conventional novel, clothe it in a new cover and title page which will give it the name of "Fanny Hill," and thus sell it to the gullible seekers after pornography for from ten to twenty dollars. Of course the purchasers only fool themselves. It is not of such a case, however, that I am going to write, tho', manifestly, the postal authorities could not see the difference

[18]Rex vs. Topham, 4 T. R. 129.

between such a case as the one described and the following one.

A publisher has been getting out a little series of pamphlets that contain well written and pleasing short stories, with not a single improper suggestion, word or thought, even tho' judged by the most conservative of conventional standards. Therefore, to attract attention and promote sales, catchy titles were given to these pamphlets; some of the titles seem to have been chosen with the view to induce young people to read what would give them some very wholesome, conventional and, I fear, necessary though commonplace, advice. The following are the titles of such pamphlets: *Advice To Young Husbands, Only A Boy, A Siege In The Dark, Only A Girl, A Young Girl's Book Of Experience, Eaten Alive* and *Sham Religion, Revelations Of A Model, A Country Boy's First Night's Experience, History of Kissing,* and *The Confessions of Two Old Maids.* Unto the lewd all things are lewd. There are some people in official life, as well as out of it, to whom such titles as the foregoing could suggest nothing but lasciviousness,

Such minds are incapable of imagining non-sexual "Advice to Young Husbands," or non-sexual "Confessions of Two Old Maids," and solely because of their own degenerate condition these titles would create anticipations of psycho-salacious joys. But the fact remains that the titles were as accurately descriptive of the contents of the books as book-titles usually are. Under these circumstances, no man learned in the law would dream that these titles were a misrepresentation of essential fact such as would entitle the purchaser of a lot of these books to recover back the purchase price on the ground of fraud because the books were not in fact obscene. Although the book-titles in question do not amount to a representation that the contents are obscene, and altho' the contents were not in fact obscene, nor claimed by any one to be so, yet the Postal Department concluded that the excessively lewd, whose unreasonable sensual anticipations might be disappointed, must be protected against the misleading effects of these titles upon their own psycho-sexual abnormity. Accordingly, the authorities threatened to stop the vendor's mail by a fraud order if he did not cease selling these booklets. Of course he suppressed the books. If this is fraud then all the "purity" sex-books which are being sold by many professional moralists also are frauds. These books are all advertised to help one solve his personal sex-problems, but very, very seldom give the least bit of enlightenment or assistance. But we must not complain. Like the King, the Postal Department can do no wrong.

"HISTORY OF PROSTITUTION."

Dr. Sanger's "History of Prostitution" is one of the best, if not *the* most learned disquisition in the English language, which deals with that important problem. It was first published in 1858, and in numerous editions has been on the market ever since. I am advised that it has been publicly endorsed even by an extremely puritanical postal inspector and has been widely advertised and sold through the "Purity" journals. No one ever dreamed that it was an obscene book until November 15th, 1907, when the post office authorities for sentimental reasons desired to suppress *The American Journal of Eugenics* and were looking for an excuse to give to the editor and the public. R. M. Webster, Acting Assistant Attorney General for the Post Office Department, on the date last above given, wrote an opinion excluding said magazine from the mails, in part for advertising the book under discussion. He wrote: "On page 50 is advertised a book entitled 'The History of Prostitution,' which *from its very name* is clearly indecent and unfit for circulation through the mail." Evidently he had not read the book, but simply decided that the subject was one, no matter how it was treated, which could not be discussed through the mail, and his arbitrary will and not statutory criteria determined the issue. Yet, some continue to assert that ours is a government by law. The people may make—*must make*—laws upon the subject of prostitution, but cannot get enlightenment upon it, because their servant, a Government employee, says they cannot be entrusted with knowledge.

DR. MALCHOW AND "THE SEXUAL LIFE."

Connected with the Methodist Episcopal Church schools is Hamline University College of Physicians and Surgeons. C. W. Malchow was there the Professor of Proctology and Associate in Clinical Medicine. He was also the President of the Physicians' and Surgeons' Club of Minneapolis, and a member of the Hennepin County Medical Society, the Minnesota State Medical Society, and the American Medical Association.

He wrote a book on "The Sexual Life" which received strong praise from educational and medical journals and from professional persons. I have seen commendatory reviews from ten professional magazines. While in press, he read a most preplexing chapter from the book to a meeting of Methodist Ministers and its delicate treatment of a difficult subject was strongly commended.

Yet under the absurd tests prescribed by the courts and in spite of the protests of the Minneapolis *Times* and *Tribune,* Dr. Malchow and his publisher are (1907) both serving a jail sentence, for selling through the mail a high class scientific discussion of sex to the laity.[19]

During the trial the court refused the defendants the right to prove that all in the book was true, holding, with all the judicial decisions, that their being true was immaterial in fixing guilt. An unsuccessful effort was make to prove the need for such a book because of the great ignorance of the public upon sex matters, and the "learned" judge remarked that he hoped it was true that the public was ignorant of such matters, and excluded the evidence. President Roosevelt being asked by members of Congress to pardon the convict because of the propriety of his book, is reported to have expressed an amazing regret that he could not prolong the sentence.

This case received a little attention in the medical journals, but, let it be said to their everlasting disgrace, the great medical organizations of this country were either too indifferent or too prudish or too cowardly to come as an organized body to the rescue of Dr. Malchow or to demand a repeal or amendment of the law which made this outrage possible.

DR. KIME AND THE IOWA MEDICAL JOURNAL.

A very few years ago, Dr. Kime, the editor of the *Iowa Medical Journal,* was convicted of obscenity. He was a physician of high standing and a trustee of a medical college, in which a few young rowdy students were apparently endeavoring to drive out the women students. A protest to the college authorities resulted only in a two weeks' suspension. On further complaint, instead of protecting the women in their equal right to study medicine under decent conditions, the authorities excluded women altogether from the medical school. Filled with indignation, Dr. Kime reiterated his protest, and gave publicity to some of the methods of persecution, includ-

[19]U. S. v. Burton, 142 F. R. 57, C. C. A.

ing an insulting prescription which appeared on the blackboard where all the class could see it. In his *Medical Journal* he wrote: "We had thought to withhold this prescription, owing to its extreme vulgarity, but we believe it our duty to show the condition exactly as it exists, and let each physician judge for himself as to the justness of the protest filed." Then followed the " obscene " prescription, the obscenity of which consisted wholly in the use of one word of double meaning.

For this he was arrested, and although supported by all four daily papers of his home city, by the clergy of all denominations, the presidents of the Y. M. C. A., the W. C. T. U., and the Western Society for the Suppression of Vice, and the Society for the Promotion of Social Purity, he was convicted, branded as a criminal and fined. Judged by the absurd judicial tests of obscenity which are always applied, the conviction was unquestionably correct.

"STUDIES IN THE PSYCHOLOGY OF SEX."

In England, under a law just like our own in its description of what is prohibited, Dr. Havelock Ellis' "Studies in the Psychology of Sex," I believe have been wholly suppressed as obscene. These studies are so exhaustive and collect so much original and unusual information that they mark an entirely new epoch in the study of sexual science. The German edition of this very superior treatise is denied admission into the United States, to protect the morals and perpetuate the ignorance of the German-American physicians. Futhermore, no one can doubt that their exclusion is in strict accord with the letter of the law, as the word "obscene" is now interpreted, *or interpolated, through the judical "tests" of obscenity.*

That scientifically absurd test is decisive even though applied to a scholarly treatise upon sex, circulated only within the medical profession, for the statute makes no exception in favor of medical men. An impartial enforcement of the letter of the law, as the word "obscene" is now interpreted, would entirely extirpate the scientific literature of sex. So deeply have the judges been impressed with this possible iniquity, that by dictum, quite in excess of their proper power, they have made a judicial amendment of the statute, excepting from its operation books circulated only among physicians. Such judicial legislation of course is made under the pretense of "statutory interpretation" and involves the ridiculous proposition that a book which is criminally obscene if handed to a layman, changes its character if handed to a physician. It assumes that a scientific knowledge of sex is dangerous to the morals of all those who do not use the knowledge as a means of making money in the practice of medicine, and that it becomes a moral force, when, and only when, thus employed for pecuniary gain. To send to "purity workers" the standard scientific literature of sex is a crime. Even such persons cannot be trusted to have accurate information. Public morals demand their ignorance. The suppression of the American edition of "Studies of the Psychology of Sex" only awaits the concurrence of caprice between some fool reformer and a stupid jury and judge. The same statutory words which furnished a conviction in England, and here are adequate to exclude the German edition, will sooner or later determine the suppression of the American edition.

Thus far we have exhibited a few of the matters which can be and have been suppressed under our present mysterious criminal law against "obscene" literature. More will be said upon this matter when we come to study the relation of our compulsory sex-ignorance to insanity and when we come to study the varieties of official modesty.

"HUMAN SEXUALITY."

An attempt was made to suppress another most useful book, which bears this title page: "Human Sexuality—A Medico-Literary Treatise, on the Laws, Anomalies, and Relations of Sex, with Especial Referance to Contrary Sexual Desire. By J. Richardson Parke, Sc. B., Ph. G., M. D., late Acting Assistant Surgeon, U. S. Army." In Aug., 1909, in Philadelphia the author of this valuable book was arrested for having sent it through the mails. The book is a large volume of nearly 500 pages of useful scientific matter. It received very high praise from medical journals and prominent physicians.

An author, writing upon the pathology of the lungs, may properly and advantageously lighten up his text by a few humorous anecdotes about the "one lungers." Dr. Parke thought he had a similar privilege, although writing about sex, and because he related a few stories, such as he believed any physician might properly tell another, he furnished the official prudes a pretext for trying to put him in jail. He was arrested and bound over to await the action of the Grand Jury. Fortunately, the matter seems to have come before reasonably

[20]*Albany Law Journal*, Aug., 1908; Freedom of the Press and "Obscene" Literature.

sane jurors, who refused to find an indictment. The distinguished author received much unpleasant notoriety, was put to much personal inconvienience and expense, only to get a "vindication" which is not necessarily binding upon either the Post Office Department or any other Grand Jury, or Court, and all because ours has ceased to be a Government according to "Law," when it comes to determining what are the criteria of guilt if the question of "obscenity" is involved.

SUGGESTIONS OF THE DEPEW BOARD OF HEALTH

Dr. George N. Jack is the Health Physician of the Board of Health for Depew. Like many another more foolish person, Dr. Jack and the Board of Health thought this a free country in which a man not intending to deceive but meaning to help mankind might proclaim that which he believed to be the truth. Accordingly, Dr. Jack prepared a paper which was read and adopted at a meeting of the Depew Board of Health, Feb. 3rd, 1909. This paper was published for free distribution under the title: "'Suggestions adopted by the Depew Board of Health for the Prevention of Sickness, Corruption, or Crime, and as an Evolutionary aid to Humanity." Of course, this paper dealt largely with sexual vices. Since unto the lewd all is lewd, Dr. Jack was promptly arrested for circulating "obscene" literature, through the mails. At the time of writing this his case has not been disposed of.

FIELD-MUSEUM IMPORTATIONS

About April 11, 1909, the newspapers announced that pictures and manuscripts collected in China by Professor Berthold Laufer of Columbia University, and for the Field Museum of Chicago, had been seized by Collector of Customs Ames, because of their obscenity. It seems the seizure was made in Oct. 1908, and the fact kept from the public. The news item continues thus: "At that time, United States District Judge Landis listened to arguments in chambers. It was admitted that the importation of the collection constituted a technical violation of the law, but it was likewise admitted that the collection formed an essential basis for scientific investigation. Judge Landis stated that he had no doubt the photographs, paintings, manuscripts, etc., were brought into this country for a perfectly proper purpose, but he saw no way, without a technical violation of the law, of releasing them."

Subsequently the judge decided to permit the entry of

this valuable material. Thus we have arrived at the stage where the dissemination of any of the material of sexual science is a crime, and it is the function of a Federal Judge, not to enforce the law impartially, but to say arbitrarily who shall go unscathed.

It is so long ago that we have both forgotten and neglected the truth expressed by the Federal Supreme Court in these words: "It would certainly be dangerous if the legislature could set a net large enough to catch all possible offenders and leave it to the courts to step inside and say who could be rightly detained, and who should be set at large. This would to some extent substitute the judicial for the legislative branch the government." [21]

This then, is a partial record of useful things coming under the ban of our censorship of literature. Some other books as valuable as the best of those which have been herein mentioned, I can not speak of, because the authors and publishers prefer that no mention should be made of the fact. The most injurious part of this censorship, however, lies not in the things that have been suppressed, as against the venturesome few who dare to take a chance on the censorship, but rather on the innumerable books that have remained unwritten because modest and wise scientists do not care to spend their time in taking even a little chance of coming into conflict with an uncertain statute, arbitrarily administered by laymen to the medical profession, in which profession are many not over-wise and sometimes fanatical zealots in the interest of that ascetism which is the crowning evil of the theology of sex.

[21] U. S. v. Reese, 92 U. S. 291-221.

CHAPTER V.

THE REASONS UNDERLYING OUR CONSTITUTIONAL GUARANTEE OF A FREE PRESS, APPLIED TO SEX-DISCUSSION.[1]

Arguments which deal with the inexpediency of abridging freedom of speech and of the press necessarily restate the considerations which moved the framers of our constitutions to prohibit such abridgment and therefore exhibit to us that conception of freedom which they intended to perpetuate. It follows from this that all argument which concerns itself with a consideration of the inexpediency of abridging intellectual freedom, unavoidably illuminates the whole problem of a judicial interpretation of our constitutional guarantee of an unabridged freedom of speech and of the press.

Only a few decades ago, the mighty governed the many, through cunning, strategy, and compulsory ignorance. A lay citizen was punished by law, if he presumed critically to discuss politics, officials, slave emancipation, astronomy, geology, or religion. To teach our African slaves to read, or to circulate abolitionist literature, was in some States a crime, because such intelligence conduced to an "immoral tendency" toward insurrection. To have the Bible in one's possession has also been prohibited by law, because of the "immoral tendency" toward private judgments, which general reading of it might induce.

One by one the advocates of mystery and blind force have surrendered to the angels of enlightenment, and every enlargement of opportunity for knowledge has been followed by the moral elevation of humanity. Only in one field of thought do we still habitually assume that ignorance is a virtue, and enlightenment a crime. Only upon the subject of sex do we by statute declare that artificial fear is a safer guide than intelligent self-reliance, that purity can thrive only in conceal-

[1]Revised from *Liberal Review,* Aug. and Sept., 1906.

ment and ignorance, and that to know all of one's self is dangerous and immoral. Here only are we afraid to allow truth to be contrasted with error. The issue is, shall we continue thus to fear full and free discussion of sex facts and sex problems? Does the constitution permit the suppression of such discussion? Later this will be thoroughly discussed.

The first question to be answered is, why discuss the subject of sex at all? There are those who advise us to ignore it entirely, upon the theory that the natural impulse is a sufficient guide. To this it may be answered that all our sex activities cannot be subjected to the constant and immediate control of the will. We cannot ignore sex by merely willing to do so. Our attention is unavoidably forced upon the subject, by conditions both within and without ourselves. That we may deceive ourselves in this particular is possible; that we all can and many do lie about it is certain.

Without sexual education, we cannot know whether we are acting under a healthy or a diseased impulse. It is known to the psychologist that many are guilty of vicious and injurious sexual practices, without being in the least conscious of the significance of what they are doing. Everywhere we see human wrecks because of a failure to understand their impulses, or to impose intelligent restraints upon them. Many become sexually impotent, hyperaesthetic, or perverted by gradual processes the meaning of which they do not understand, and whose baneful consequences intelligence would enable them to foresee and easily avoid. Since individuals will not go to a physician until the injury is accomplished and apparent, it follows that there is no possible preventive except general intelligence upon the subject. At present the spread of that knowledge is impeded by laws and by a prurient prudery, which together are responsible for the sentimental taboo which attaches to the whole subject. The educated man of to-day measures our different degrees of human progress by the quantity of intelligence which is used in regulating our bodily functioning. No reason exists for making sex an exception.

THE PHYSICAL FOUNDATION FOR MORAL HEALTH.

To those who accept a scientific ethics, moral health is measured by the relative degree to which their conduct achieves physical and mental health for the race. To the religious moralist, who has other ends in view, pathologic sexuality is probably the greatest impediment to the practical realization of his ideal of sexual morality. Everywhere we see that disease is the greatest obstacle to moral health. From either point of view, it follows that one of the most important considerations in all purity propaganda must be the diffusion of such knowledge as will best conduce to the highest physical and mental perfection. This seems so self evident that we necessarily ask, Why is our conduct so contrary?

The Desire to Persecute.

The desire to persecute, even for mere opinion's sake, seems to be an eternal inheritance of humans. We naturally and as a matter of course encourage others in doing and believing whatever for any reason, or without reason, we deem proper. Even though we have a mind fairly well disciplined in the duty of toleration, we quite naturally discourage others, and feel a sense of outraged propriety, whenever they believe and act in a manner radically different from ourselves. Our resentment becomes vehement just in proportion as our reason is impotent, and our nerves diseasedly sensitive. That is why it is said that "Man is naturally, instinctively intolerant and a persecutor."

From this necessity of our undisciplined nature comes the stealthy but inevitable recurrence of legalized bigotry, and its rehabilitation of successive inquisitions. From the days of pagan antiquity to the present hour, there has never been a time or country wherein mankind could claim immunity from all persecution for intellectual differences. This cruel intolerance has always appealed to a "sacred and patriotic duty," and masked behind an ignorantly made and unwarranted pretense of "morality."

"Persecution has not been the outgrowth of any one age, nationality or creed; it has been the ill-favored progeny of all." Thus, under the disguise of new names and new pretensions, again and again we punish unpopular, though wholly self-regarding, non-moral conduct; imprison men for expressing honest intellectual differences; deny the duty of toleration; destroy a proper liberty of thought and conduct; and always under the same old false pretenses of "morality," and "law and order."

Whenever our natural tendency toward intolerance is reinforced by abnormally intense feelings, such as diseased nerves produce, persecution follows quite unavoidably, because the intensity of associated emotions is transformed into a conviction of inerrancy. Such a victim of diseased emotions, even more than others, "knows because he feels, and is firmly convinced because strongly agitated." Unable to answer logically the contention of his friend, he ends by desiring to punish him as his enemy. Because of the close interdependence of the emotional and the generative mechanism, it is probable that unreasoned moral sentimentalizing inducing superstitious opinions about the relation of men and women will be the last superstition to disappear.

The concurrence of many in like emotions, associated with and centered upon the same focus of irritation, makes the effective majority of the state view the toleration of intellectual opponents as a crime, and their heresy, whether political, religious, ethical or sexual, is denounced as a danger to civil order, and the heretic must be judicially silenced. Thus all bigots have reasoned in all past ages. Thus do those afflicted with our present sex-superstition again defend their moral censorship of literature and art.

These are the processes by which we always become incapable of deriving profit from the lessons of history. That all the greatest minds of every age believed in something now known to be false, and in the utility of what is now deemed injurious or immoral, never suggests to petty intellects that the future generations will also pity us for having entertained our most cherished opinions.

The presence of these designated natural defects, which so very few have outgrown, makes it quite probable that the battle for intellectual freedom will never reach an end. The few, trained in the duty of toleration, owe it to humanity to re-state, with great frequency, the arguments for mental hospitality. Only by this process can we contribute directly toward the mental discipline of the relatively unevolved masses, and prepare the way for those new and therefore unpopular truths by which the race will progress. The absolute liberty of thought, with opportunity, unlimited as between adults, for its oral or printed expression is a condition precedent to the highest development of our progressive morality.

Men of strong passions and weak intellects seldom see the expediency of encouraging others to disagree. Thence came all of those terrible persecutions for heresy, witchcraft, sedition, etc., which have prolonged the midnight of superstition into "dark ages." The passionate zeal of a masterful few has always made them assume that they only could be trusted to have a personal judgment upon moral questions, while all others must be coerced, unquestioningly, to accept them upon authority, "with pious awe and trembling solicitude."

THE DANGERS OF PRIVATE JUDGMENT.

Such egomania always resulted in the persecution of those who furnished the common people with the materials upon which they might base a different opinion, or outgrow their slave-virtues.

One of Queen Mary's first acts was an inhibition against reading or teaching the Bible in churches, and against printing books. In 1530, the king, pursuant to a memorial of the House of Commons, issued a proclamation requiring every person "which hath a New Testament or the Old, translated into English or any other boke of Holy Scripture, so translated, being in printe, to surrender them within fifteen days, as he will avoyde the Kynge's high indignation and displeasure," which meant death.

Another and similar proclamation was issued, covering the New Testament and writings of many theologians. The act passed in the 3rd and 4th Edward VI., repeated this folly. So thousands of Bibles were burned under the personal supervision and benediction of priests and bishops, because of the immoral tendency toward private judgment involved in reading the "Divine Record."[2]

Poor William Tyndale, who took the infinite trouble of translating the scriptures into English, found that "his New Testament was forthwith burnt in London;" and he himself, after some years, was strangled and burnt at Antwerp. (1536).[3]

So now we have many who likewise esteem it to be of immoral tendency, for others than themselves, to secure such information as may lead to a personal and different opinion about the physiology, psychology, hygiene, or ethics of sex, and by law we make it a crime to distribute any specific and detailed information upon these subjects, especially if it be unprudish in its verbiage or advocate unorthodox opinions about marriage or sexual ethics. This is repeating the old folly that

[2]Vickers' Martyrdom of Literature, pp. 190, 225 to 227. See also Paterson's Liberty of the Press, p. 50.
[3]Books Condemned to be Burnt, page 9.

the adult masses cannot be trusted to form an opinion of their
own.

The "free" people of the United States cannot be allowed to have the information which might lead to a change
of their own statute laws upon sex.

SUPPRESSING TRUTH FOR EXPEDIENCY.

There will always be those thoughtless enough to believe that truth may be properly suppressed for considerations
of expediency. I prefer to believe with Professor Max Müller,
that "The truth is always safe, and nothing else is safe";
and with Drummond that "He that will not reason, is a bigot;
he that cannot reason, is a fool, and he that dares not reason,
is a slave"; and with Thomas Jefferson when in his inaugural address he wrote, "Error of opinion may be tolerated, when
reason is left free to combat it"; and I believe these are still
truisms even though the subject is sex.

We have only to go back a few centuries to find an influential clique of pious men trying to maintain a monopoly
of "truth." Those who disputed their affirmations, whether
about geology or theology, were promptly beheaded or burnt.
The clerical monopolists denied common people the right, not
only of having an independent judgment as to the significance,
or value, or truth of "holy writ," but even denied them the
right to read the book itself, because it would tempt them to
independent judgment, which might be erroneous, and thus
make them "immoral."

The contents and the interpretation of the Bible, together
with the political tyranny founded on these, must, "with
humble prostration of intellect," be unquestioningly accepted.
Those who disputed the self-constituted mouthpieces of God
were promptly killed. And now, those who, without "humble
prostration of intellect," dispute any of the ready-made ignorance on the physiology, hygiene and psychology or ethics of
sex, are promptly sent to jail. Yet we call this a "free" country, and our age a "civilized" one.

By the same appeal to a misguided expediency, we find
that only a few years ago it was a crime to teach a negro
slave how to read or write. Education would make him doubt
his slave-virtues, and with a consciousness of the injustice
being inflicted upon him, he might disturb the public order
to secure redress. So, imparting education became immoral,

and was made a crime. An effort was made to make it a crime to send anti-slavery literature through the mails because of its immoral tendency, and southern postmasters often destroyed it without warrant of law, thus refusing delivery to those to whom it was addressed.

Within the past century, married women had no rights which their husbands need respect, and education of women was made impossible, though the imparting of it was not penalized. Now they may acquire an education about everything, except what ought to be the most important to them, namely: A scientific knowledge of the ethics, physiology, hygiene, and psychology of sex. To furnish them with literature of the highest scientific order, even though true and distributed from good motives, or in print to argue for their "natural right and necessity for sexual self-government," is now a crime, and we call it "obscenity" and "indecency."

Formerly, when bigots were rampant and openly dominant, the old superstition punished the psychological crime of "immoral thinking," because it was irreligious, and it was called "sedition," "blasphemy," etc. Under the present verbal disguise, the same old superstition punishes the psychological crime of immoral thinking, because it may discredit the ethical claims of religious asceticism, and now we call it "obscenity" and "indecency." What is the difference between the old and the new superstition and persecution?

Strange to say, there are hundreds of thousands of the unchurched, who, for want of clear mental vision or adequate moral courage, are fostering the suppression of unconventional thinking, and justify it, upon considerations of expediency.

The argument against the expediency of truth is ever the last refuge of retreating error, a weak subterfuge to conceal a dawning consciousness of ignorance. In all history, one cannot find a single instance in which an enlargement of opportunity for the propagation of unpopular allegations of truth has not resulted in increased good.

"If I were asked, 'What opinion, from the commencement of history to the present hour, had been productive of the most injury to mankind?' I should answer, without hesitation: 'The inexpediency of publishing sentiments of supposed bad tendency.'" It is this infamous opinion which has made the world a vale of tears, and drenched it with the blood of martyrs.

THE ABUSE OF FREEDOM.

I am fully mindful of the fact that an unrestricted press means that some abuse of the freedom of the press will result. However, I also remember that no man can tell *a priori* what opinion is of immoral tendency. I am furthermore mindful that we cannot argue against the use of a thing, from the possibility of its abuse, since this objection can be urged against every good thing, and I am not willing to destroy all that makes life pleasant. Lord Littleton aptly said: "To argue against any breach of liberty, from the i'* use that may be made of it, is to argue against liberty itself, since all is capable of being abused."

Everyone who believes in the relative and progressive morality of scientific ethics, must logically believe in the immorality of a code which preaches absolutism in morals upon the authority of inspired texts, instead of deriving moral precepts from natural, physical law. But that is no warrant for the scientific moralist suppressing the teaching of religious morality, as inexpedient, even if he believed it to be so and had the power. Neither can the religious moralist justify himself in the suppression of the opinions of his scientific opponents. It is alone by comparison and contrast that each perfects his own system, and in the end all are better off for having permitted the disputation.

No argument for the suppression of "obscene" literature has ever been offered which, by unavoidable implication, will not justify, and which has not already justified, every other limitation that has ever been put upon mental freedom. No argument was ever made to justify intolerance, whether political, theological, or scientific, which has not been restated in support of our present sex superstitions and made to do duty toward the suppressing of information as to the physiology, psychology, or ethics of sex. All this class of arguments that have ever been made, have always started with the false assumption that such qualities as morality or immorality could belong to opinions, or to a static fact.

Because violence is deemed necessary to prevent a change, or the acquisition of an opinion concerning the hygiene, physiology or ethics of sex, we must infer that those who defend the press censorship are unconsciously claiming omniscient infallibility for the present sexual intelligence. If their sex opinions were a product of mere fallible reason,

they would not feel the desirability, the need or duty to suppress rational criticism. By denying others the right of publishing either confirmation or criticism, they admit that their present opinions are a matter of superstition and indefensible as a matter of reason. To support a sex superstition by law is just as reprehensible as, in the past, it was to support the, now partially exploded, governmental, scientific and theological superstitions, by the same process. This, be it remembered, was always done in the name of "morality," "law and order," etc.

Will Truth, Crushed, Rise Again?

There may still be those who argue that the persecutors of Christians were right, because the persecution of an advocate is a necessary ordeal through which his truth always passes successfully; legal penalties, in the end, being powerless against the truth, though sometimes beneficially effective against mischievous error.

It may be a historical fact that all known truths, for a time, have been crushed by the bigot's heel, but this should not make us applaud his iniquity. It is an aphorism of unbalanced optimists, that truth crushed to earth will always rise. Even if this were true, it must always remain an unprovable proposition, because it postulates that at every particular moment we are ignorant of all those suppressed truths, not then resurrected, and since we do not know them, we cannot prove that they ever will be resurrected. It would be interesting to know how one could prove that an unknown truth of past suppression is going to be rediscovered, or that the conditions which alone once made it a cognizable fact will ever again come into being. And yet a knowledge of it might have a very important bearing on some present controversy of moment.

Surely, many dogmas have been wholly suppressed which were once just as earnestly believed to be as infallibly true as some that are now accepted as inspired writ. Just a little more strenuosity in persecution would have wiped out all Christians, if not Christianity itself. How can we prove that all the suppressed, and now unknown, dogmas were false? If mere survival after persecution is deemed evidence of the inerrancy of an opinion, then which of the many conflicting opinions, each a survivor of persecution, are unquestionably true, and how is the choice to be made from the mass? Is it not clear that neither a rediscovery, nor a survival after persecution, can have any special relation to truth as such? If it is, then let us unite to denounce as an unprovable hallucination the statement that truth crushed to earth will rise again.

The abettors of persecution are more damaged than those whom they deter from expressing and defending unpopular opinions, since, as between these, only the former are depriving themselves of the chief means of correcting their own errors. But the great mass of people belong neither to the intellectual innovators, nor to their persecutors. The great multitude might be quite willing to listen to or read unconventional thoughts if ever permitted, amid opportunity, to exercise an uncoerced choice

FALSE ANALOGY.

Much of the justification for intolerance derives its authority from false analogies, wrongfully carried over from physical relations into the realm of the psychic.

Thus some argue that because, by laws, we protect the incompetent against being (unconsciously) infected with contagious disease, therefore the state should also protect them (even though mature and able to protect themselves by mere inattention) against the literature of infectious moral poison. Here a figure of speech is mistaken for an analogy. "Moral poison" exists only figuratively and not literally in any such sense as strychnine is a poison.

Ethics is not one of the exact sciences. Probably it never will be. Until we are at least approximately as certain of the existence and tests of "moral poison," as we are of the physical characteristics and consequences of carbolic acid, it is folly to talk of "moral poison" except as a matter of poetic license.

In the realm of morals no age has ever shown an agreement, even among its wisest and best men, either as to what is morally poisonous, or by what test it is to be judged as morally deadly. Moral concepts are a matter of geography and evolution. The morality of one country or age is viewed as the moral poison of another country or age. The defended morality of one social or business circle is deemed the immorality of another. The ideals which attach to one man's God, are those of another man's devil. Furthermore, our best scientific thinkers concur in the belief that all morality is relative and progressive, whereas numerous other men deem a part or all of our conduct to be *per se* moral or immoral. Some deem the source of authority in matters of morals to be God, as his will is manifested through the revelations or prophets of his particular church, or that interpretation of them which some particular branch of some particular church promulgates. Others find morality only in the most health-giving adjustment to natural law, and still others find their authority in a conscience, unburdened either with supernatural light or worldly wisdom. Only the generous exercise of the most free discussion can help us out of this chaos.

PROGRESS BY KNOWLEDGE OF NATURAL LAW.

Philosophers tell us that life is "the continuous adjustment of internal relations to external relations." The use of conscious effort toward the achievement of the fullest life, through our most harmonious conformity to natural laws, is the essential distinction between the human and other animals.

Observance of natural law is the unavoidable condition of all life, and a knowledge of those laws is a condition precedent to all effort for securing well-being, through conscious adjustment to them. It follows that an opportunity for an acquaintance with nature's processes, unlimited by human coercion, is the equal and inalienable right of every human being, because essential to his life, liberty, and pursuit of happiness. No exception can be made for the law of our sex nature.

It also follows that in formulating our conception of what is the law of nature, and in its adjustment or application by us to our infinitely varied personal constitutions, each sane adult human is the sovereign of his own destiny and never properly within the control of any other person, until some one, not an undeceived voluntary participant, is directly affected thereby to his injury.

The laws for the suppression of "obscene" literature, as administered, deny to adults the access to part of the alleged facts and arguments concerning our sex nature, and therefore are a violation of the above rules of right and conduct.

MORAL ADVANCE THROUGH CRITICISM.

We all believe in intellectual and moral progress. Therefore, whatever may be the character or subject of a man's opinions, others have the right to express their judgments upon them, to censure them, if deemed censurable or turn them to ridicule, if deemed ridiculous. If such right is not protected by law, we should have no security against the exposition or perpetuity of error, and therefore we should hamper progress.

It follows that the believer in a personal God or in the Trinity, the Mormon with his "Adam-God," the Agnostic with his "Unknowable," the Christian-scientist with his impersonal "All mind and all love" God, the Unitarian with his "Purposeful Divine Immanence," the Theosophist with his godless "Nirvana," and the Atheist, all have an equal right to vie with one another for public favor and, incidentally, to censure or ridicule any crudities which they may believe they see in any or all rival conceptions.

It is only by recognition and exercise of such a liberty that humanity has evolved from the primal sex-worship through the innumerable phases of nature worship to our present relatively exalted religious opinion. Even though we reject all, or all but one, of the numerous modern anthropomorphic and deistic conceptions of God, we must still admit that each of these is based upon a more enlightened and enlarged conception of the Universe and man's relation to it, than can possibly be implied in the worship of the phallus. Thus liberty of thought and of its expression has been and will continue to be the one indispensable condition to the improvement of religions.

If we are not thus far agreed as to the equal moral rights of each, then which one has less right than the rest? It is beyond question that the solitary man has an unlimited right of expressing his opinion, since there is no one to deny him the right. With the advent of the second man surely he still has the same right with the consent of that second man. How many more persons must join the community before they acquire the moral warrant for denying the second man the right and the opportunity to listen to, or to read, anything the other may speak or write, even though the subject be theology or sex-morality? By what impersonal standard (not one based merely upon individual preferences) shall we adjudge the forfeiture of such individual rights, if forfeiture is to be enforced by a limitation?

If such impersonal standard cannot be furnished then the argument must proceed as follows: If all disputants have the equal right to question and deride the conceptions of all the rest as to the existence, nature or knowableness of their respective God, then they have an equal right to question the

85

divine origin or interpretation of that which others believe to be divine revelation.

If men have a right to cast doubt upon the source and fact of divine revelation, then, of course, they must have an equal right to discredit that which others believe to have been taught by such divine revelation, even though the subject be the relation of the sexes.

More specifically, that means this: The Catholic priest may advocate, as others deny, the superior morality of his celibacy; the one may argue for, and the other against, the compatibility of the best health and life-long continence, and to this end either may adduce all the evidence, historical, experimental or scientific, which is deemed material; the marriage purists may argue for, and others against, the superior morality of having sexual relation only for the purpose of procreation; the Bible Communist of Oneida may advocate, as others deny, the superior morality of "free love"; the Episcopalians and Ethical Culturists, may advocate, as others deny, the superior morality of indissoluble monogamy; the Agnostic or Liberal Religionist may advocate, and others may deny, the superior morality of easy divorce; the Utilitarian may advocate, as others deny, the superior morality of stirpiculture with or without monogamic marriage; the Mormon may advocate, as others deny, the superior morality of polygamy, etc., etc.

I assume for the present, and for the sake of the present argument only, that they do not advocate the violation of existing marriage laws, but limit their demand and argument to a repeal or amendment of those laws, so as to make them conformable to their respective ideals. Under present laws numerous persons have been arrested for making arguments in favor of some of the foregoing propositions, while advocates of the contrary view have gone on unmolested.

Those who hold to any one of these ideals necessarily believe all others to be of immoral tendency; and it seems to me that ridicule, fact and argument, unrestricted as to adults, are the only means by which the race can secure that progressive clarification of moral vision which is essential to higher moral development.

The vaunted morality of one age is the despised superstition and barbarism of succeeding ages. Thus we have proceeded, as far as our sexual morality is concerned, through irresponsible, indiscriminate promiscuity, group marriage, female slavery, the sacred debauchery of sex-worship, polyandry, polygamy, the abhorrent ideals of ascetics and sex-perverts, to our present standards, and the course of moral evolution is not yet ended.

Since, then, the very superiority of our present morality is due to the liberty of thinking and of exchanging thoughts, how absurd and outrageous it is now to impair or destroy the very basis upon which it rests, and upon which must depend the further development of our progressive morality!

Since advancement in the refining of our ethical conceptions is conditioned upon experimentation and the dissemination of its observed results, it follows that the most immoral of present tendencies is that which arrests moral progress by limiting the freedom of speech and press. When viewed in long perspective, it also follows that we must conclude that the most immoral persons of our time are those who are now successfully stifling discussion, and restricting the spread of sexual intelligence, because they are most responsible for impeding moral progress, as to the relations of men and women.

Those who in these particulars deny a freedom of speech and press and the correlative right to hear, unlimited as to all sane adults, by their very act of denial exercise a right which they would suppress in others. The true believer in equality of liberty allows others the right to speak against free speech, though he may not be so hospitable as to its actual suppression. No man truly believes in liberty who is unwilling to defend the right of others to disagree with him, even about free-love, polygamy or stirpiculture.

If our conceptions of sexual morality have a rational foundation, then they are capable of adequate rational defense, and there is no need for legislative suppression of discussion. If our sex ethics will not bear critical scrutiny and discussion, then to suppress such discussion is infamous, because it is a legalized support of error. In either case the freest possible discussion is a necessary condition of the progressive elimination of error.

OUR OPINIONS ARE INVOLUNTARY.

No man can help believing that which he believes. Belief is not a matter of volition. No man, by an act of will, can make himself believe that twice two are six. He may say it, but he cannot believe it, that is, he cannot acquire a corresponding concept. No man, solely by an act of will, can stop thinking. No man can tell what he will think tomorrow, nor arbitrarily determine what he will think next year.

If there still remain any believers in the free-will super-stition, as applied to matters of belief, each of them can, by a simple test, demonstrate to himself the impossibility of ar-bitrarily controlling his conviction. Let him, solely by an *uncaused* exercise of his "free-will," abolish his belief in its existence, and substitute the conviction that a man in his men-tal life is a mere irresponsible automaton. Then, having firmly held this latter conviction for just ten days, let him, by another *uncaused* act of the "free-will" (which then he does not be-lieve in), restore his belief in its existence. Not until I find a sane man who honestly believes that he has performed this, to me impossible feat, can I admit that the existence of a "free-will" as applied to our thought-products, is even a debatable question.

"Free will" in the determination of one's opinion is but a special phase of the general "free-will" doctrine. Those who, in spite of the foregoing suggestions, continue to be-lieve in the lawlessness of the intellect and their own ability to believe doctrines without evidence or against what to them-selves seems a preponderance of the evidence, must be re-ferred to the scientific literature upon the subject.[4]

Professor Fiske, in his Cosmic Philosophy, fully considers and answers all the arguments for a "lawlessness of volition" and concludes his discussion with these paragraphs:

"From whatever scientific standpoint we contemplate the doctrine of lawlessness of volition, we find that its plausible-ness depends solely on tricks of language. The first trick is the personification of will as an entity distinct from all acts of volition; the second trick is the ascription to this entity of 'freedom,' a word which is meaningless as applied to the process whereby feeling initiates action; the third trick is the assumption that desires or motives are entities outside of a person, so that if his acts of volition were influenced by them he would be robbed of his freedom.

"Whatever may be our official theories, we all practically ignore and discredit the doctrine that volition is lawless. Whatever voice of tradition we may be in the habit of echo-ing, we do equally, from the earliest to the latest day of our self-conscious existence, act and calculate upon the supposi-tion that volition, alike in ourselves and in others, follows invariably the strongest motive.

[4]Maudsley, "Body and Mind," Part I; Herbert Spencer, "Principles of Psy-chology," Vol. I, pp. 495 to 613; Ribot, "Diseases of the Will"; John Fiske, "Cosmic Philosophy," Vol. II, chap. 17; "Universal Illusion of Free Will," by A. Hamon.

"Finally, in turning our attention to history, we have found that the aggregate of thoughts, desires and volitions in any epoch is so manifestly dependent upon the aggregate of thoughts, desires and volitions in the preceding epoch, that even the assertors of the lawlessness of volition are forced to commit logical suicide by recognizing the sequence. Thus, whether we contemplate volitions themselves, or compare their effects, whether we resort to the testimony of psychology or to the testimony of history, we are equally compelled to admit that law is co-extensive with all orders of phenomena and with every species of change.

"It is hardly creditable to the character of the present age of scientific enlightenment that such a statement should need to be made, or that twenty-six pages of critical argument should be required to illustrate it.

"To many, this chapter will no doubt seem an elaborate attempt to prove the multiplication table. Nevertheless, where such blinding metaphysical dust has been raised, a few drops of the cold water of common sense may be not only harmless but useful."

OPINIONS ARE NON-MORAL.

Since our beliefs are not a matter of uncaused choice, but an unavoidable consequence, man cannot properly be held morally responsible for what he believes. Moral responsibility or guilt cannot attach itself to our thoughts, and no man should be punished for holding or expressing unpopular or unconventional or miscalled "immoral" opinions, at least until it is shown that actual material and direct injury has resulted to some one, not an adult who invited the damage or was himself an immediate participating cause.

An abstract opinion, or its verbal expression, cannot be either moral or immoral, though conduct based thereon may be. Those who advocate a moral censorship of literature are confounding the consequences of opinion with those of conduct. The evil consequences of the latter flow from the acts alone, while opinions in themselves can have no evil consequences. To produce such the published opinion must first be assimilated by the receiving mind, and then transformed into injurious non-selfregarding action. Therefore it is the conduct and never directly the opinion which is immoral.

Some who justify intolerance admit this, and think they evade its consequences by saying that they believe in punishing difference of opinion only in its expression, which is acting, not thinking. "Thinking is free," they say, "but speech is so only by tolerance, not as a matter of right. No man may injure us by his speech, any more than with his club. The spoken or printed word may be an act as guilty, as inexcusable and as painful as a knife-thrust." This is all true, but, rightly interpreted, is no answer to the doctrine of the freedom of speech, rightly understood.

Save in palliating exceptions, well recognized in the law of libel and slander, you may not talk *about* one person to another, so as wantonly to injure the former in his good name, credit, property, etc. This, however, cannot be made to justify the proposition that you may not, with the consent of the listeners or readers, express to them any speculative conviction, upon any subject, even sex, which is not directly invasive of anyone's rights or equality of liberty. That speech is free only by tolerance is also an acceptable maxim, if we understand the tolerance of the sane adult listener, or reader, and not the tolerance of others. No one should, or can, be compelled to read anything or to assimilate what he reads. Consequently nobody needs the help of the state to protect him against compulsory intellectual exercise.

The Right to Hear and Read.

The right of expression of opinion is inseparable from the right to hear and weigh arguments. The state can have no property right in the unchangeableness of anyone's opinions, even about sexual ethics, such as to warrant it in prohibiting him to alter such opinions. If the state has no warrant to prohibit a change of view, it has no moral right to compel attendance at church or elsewhere, for the purpose of unifying thought, nor to prohibit any person to supply the facts and arguments which may be the means of producing a changed view. This conclusion is not to be altered according to whether the ideas are woven into poetry, fiction, painting, music or science. No one can compel another to read; no one can rightfully deny him the privilege of reading, or another the opportunity of preparing or furnishing him the reading matter upon request; none but an insufferable tyrant would attempt such a thing, even upon the subject of sex. To deny one the right to come into possession of part of the evidence is just as objectionable as to compel attendance where only the rest of the evidence will be related.

A change of opinion, through added knowledge and its rational assimilation, only means intellectual development which can seldom injure anyone. But if injury shall ever come to us by our acquisition of new facts, or the achievement of new opinions, then, unlike the injury of another's knife-thrust, it comes only by our active co-operation toward the accomplishment of that injury.

Usually the "injury," resulting directly from an acceptance of unpopular beliefs, exists only in the imagination of those holding contrary opinions, and they should never be entrusted with the always dangerous power of forcing upon sane adults, against their protest, any unappreciated and undesired, ready-made, intellectual blessing. Of necessity, minorities must have the same right and opportunity to express their opinions and to try to secure the majority endorsement, as the majority have to express contrary ones. To deny this is to destroy all possibility for intellectual advancement, since new truths are at first revealed only to the few, and these innovators, and their advanced ideas, are invariably denounced by the stupidity of an unreasoning conservatism. This is just as true about the hygiene, physiology, psychology and ethics of sex, as about anything else. In support of this contention for a liberty of speech and press regardless of dreaded hypothetical consequences, we may well quote the unanswerable logic of Professor Cooper. He wrote:

THIS IS DEMONSTRATION.

"Indeed, no opinion or doctrine, of whatever nature it be, or whatever be its tendency, ought to be suppressed. For it is either manifestly true or it is manifestly false, or its truth or falsehood is dubious. Its tendency is manifestly good, or manifestly bad, or it is dubious and concealed. There are no other assignable conditions, no other factors of the problem.

"In the case of its being manifestly true and of good tendency, there can be no dispute. Nor in the case of its being manifestly otherwise; for by the terms it can mislead nobody. If its truth or its tendency be dubious, it is clear that nothing can bring the good to light, or expose the evil, but full and free discussion. Until this takes place, a plausible fallacy may do harm; but discussion is sure to elicit the truth and fix public opinion on a proper basis; and nothing else can do it."

Again, let me also quote from Vol. 6 of Westminster Review:

"It is obvious there is no certain and universal rule for determining, *a priori*, whether an opinion be useful or pernicious, and that if any person be authorized to decide, unfettered by such a rule, that person is a despot. To decide what opinions shall be permitted and what prohibited, is to choose opinions for the people; since they cannot adopt opinions which are not suffered to be presented to their minds. Whoever chooses opinions for the people possesses absolute control over their actions, and may wield them for his own purposes with perfect security, and for evil as well as for good unless infallible."

If there exists an opinion, the truth or falsity of which is unanimously conceded to be of no consequence to humanity, either for good or evil, then no excuse can be given for suppressing it, and indeed, no one would be interested to prohibit its discussion or to discuss it. If the truth of an opinion is by any deemed to be of consequence to humanity, then there exist only reasons for encouraging the greatest freedom of discussion and experimentation, since these are the only avenues to the correction of any opinions, even upon the subject of sexual physiology, psychology, hygiene, or ethics.

So long as there is, among sane adults, difference of opinion about anything, our race has not as to that subject matter attained to certain knowledge, and only freedom in the interchange of opinion and experimentation can help us onward. When our knowledge of sex, religion, etc., has been established to a mathematical certainty there will be no difference of opinion, and to suppress or abridge discussion upon these subjects before we have reached mathematical certainty for our conclusions, is an outrage because it is the most effective bar to our attainment of such certitude.

"Dangerous" Opinions.

But, it is said, this justifies the spread of "dangerous" opinions. Yes, it does. It is time enough to punish dangerous opinions when the "danger" has ceased to be merely speculative and hypothetical; that is when it is shown to have actually resulted in the violent or fraudulent invasion of nature's rule of justice.

If the advocate of a "dangerous" opinion has not himself been induced by it to commit an unjust interference with the largest equal liberty of others, it is *improbable* that it will induce his hearers or readers to become invaders. If the opinion is dangerous in those who might hear or read it, it is presumably equally dangerous in the mind of him who would express it verbally, if permitted. If we are warranted in excluding the opinion from the minds of others because it

92

tends towards "dangerous" acts, then we are also warranted in making such dangerous acts impossible to those who already entertain such "dangerous" opinions. Furthermore, we cannot then be logically compelled to await the realization of that danger from those already convinced, any more than from those about to be convinced. Such premises bring us unavoidably to the result that society would be justified in engaging in inquisitions for the discovery of every man's opinions, with the purpose of incarcerating him for life, or until a change of conviction, as a means of preventing the "danger" which his opinions are supposed to threaten. Thus the denial of an unlimited liberty of speech and press leads us by unavoidable logic back to a total denial of both liberty and secrecy of conscience.

Since these speculative and hypothetically "dangerous" opinions are to have their dangerousness determined wholly by *a priori* methods, no limitation by way of general rule can possibly be put upon the whim, caprice, or superstitious fears of the mob. It follows that if we are to admit the power or justify any suppression whatever, of the expression of any opinion whatever, we by necessary inference admit the existence of a rightful authority for every inquisition, and the punishment of every unpopular opinion, though silently and harmlessly entertained. There is no line which can be drawn between admitting the jurisdiction of the State to incarcerate any man for any opinion whatever, even those secretly entertained, and the liberty of conscience, speech and press unrestricted even in the very slightest degree. The initial act of tyranny by which we now justify our present abridgments of the liberty of speech and press, thus furnishes the precedent and justification for a total denial of the liberty of conscience.

If we would preserve any semblance of liberty of opinion, it must be liberty for the entertainment and expression of any opinion whatever. Let us then put ourselves firmly on the side of those who would never punish any opinion, until it had resulted in an overt act of invasion, and then punish the holder of the "dangerous" opinion only for his real participation in that act, as a proven accessory, and not otherwise.

Foundation of Liberty.

This then brings us back to that firm foundation of liberty which was expressed by Holt,[5] in these words: "Private immorality or vice without public example [of invasion], and

[5] Law of Libel," p. 72, 1816.

93

terminating in the individual, is left to a more solemn reckoning."

The same thought is found in Herbert Spencer's definition of liberty, expressed by him in these words: "Every man has freedom to do all that he wills, provided he infringes not the equal freedom of any other man." No opinion, even though it advocates such infringement of another's equal freedom, can by the mere verbal expression of it constitute such infringement. It follows that, no matter how slight, every abridgment of the liberty of conscience, speech or press is itself an unpardonable tyranny and necessarily implies a justification for every form of inquisition, and for every form of lawless absolutism, in the constituted tyrannical power.

RIGHT AND WRONG METHODS.

The methods and evil consequences of the intellectual activity of all superstitious or bigoted persons are the same. Instead of leading others to an acceptance of their conclusions by encouraging an examination of all possible pertinent evidence, they inculcate their convictions by dogmatic reiteration and a cultivation of associated emotions of approval. Thus they instil into the minds of the weak and immature a forceful habit of unfairness, of imbecility, and of mental corruption, which unfits all affected ones for honest inquiry or the love of truth, or a desire to weigh opposing evidence. The bigot always attempts to frighten others from honestly or thoroughly investigating his convictions, by denouncing disagreement as dangerous, wickedly heretical, and therefore "immoral." By such superstitious, ethical sentimentalizing, the benighted, in the name of the social good, deny others the right or the means of examining their boasted "morality."

The small mind is incapable of seeing the distinction between indifference to the truth of one's opinions and indifference as to which of conflicting opinions shall prove to be true. The former is the attitude of the bigot and persecutor, otherwise he could not justify the limitation of discussion, and the suppression of evidence. The latter proposition presents the temper of the scientists, who therefore desire to consider all the material evidence adducible.

The man of rational mind considers all evidence, for the love of truth, but never loves any statement of alleged truth before it is fairly demonstrated to be true, and even then, he accepts it as only a conditional truth, for the correction of which all new evidence will ever be welcomed.

Purists of literature confound the attributes of belief with those of the behavior toward evidence. They ascribe to mere belief the praise or blame which can only be due to one's mode of dealing with evidence. Thus they make a virtue of unfairness, by forcibly suppressing a part, or punishing an honest weighing of all the evidence. They bribe men's intellect to the suicide of logic, by withholding praise or reward from the only mental activity which merits praise or blame, viz., the presence or absence of a full and impartial inquiry by every individual for himself. Since instilling opinions into others, without evidence, engenders an habitual neglect of evidence, the dogmatist of morals is the only man who can be guilty of intellectual immorality, because he nurtures the essence of all depravity.

"The habit of forming opinions and acting upon them without evidence, is one of the most immoral habits of mind. As our opinions are the fathers of our actions, to be indifferent about the evidence of our opinions is to be indifferent about the consequences of our actions. But the consequences of our actions are the good and evil of our fellow creatures. The habit of neglect of evidence, therefore, is the habit of disregarding the good or evil of our fellow creatures." This is the foundation of all evil, and it follows that the moral censors of literature, being guilty of this habit, it must be a rare accident if, from a more enlightened view, and in long perspective, they be not judged deep in vice.

It is the disregard for and misuse of evidence by the masses which explains the existence of all pernicious institutions, and the mischievous opinions which support them and furnish their hateful durability.

If there can be any intellectual crime, it must consist of the voluntary neglect of evidence within reasonable access, and the highest degree of this criminality must attach to those who deliberately suppress this evidence which otherwise might be accessible to others prepared to make a right use of it. No man can be held responsible, nor should he be punished, for the effect which may be produced on his understanding by the partial evidence to which alone he had access. From this it follows that errors of the understanding must be corrected by an appeal to the understanding. Fines and imprisonment are bad forms of syllogism, which may suppress truth, but can never elicit it.

"The public interest requires that every difficult question [even questions of the hygiene, the psychology and the ethics of sex] should be patiently and deliberately examined on all sides, under every view in which it presents itself; that no light should be excluded, but evidence and argument of every kind should have their full hearing. It is thus that the doubtful truths of one generation become the axioms of the next; and that the painful results of laborious investigation and deep thinking gradually descend from the closet of the learned and pervade the mass of the community, for the common improvement of mankind."

It must be axiomatic that upon every question of importance to any human being it is the right of each individual to have the most intelligent opinion of which his capacity for understanding will permit. That being true, it is his inalienable right to have access to all the arguments and evidences which any other human would be willing to supply, if permitted to do so. The denial of this right, through the moral censorship of literature for sane adults, is an infamous tyranny.

"All benefit of having evidence is lost if it comes into a mind prepared to make bad use of it. The habit of attaching one's self to one side of a question is a habit of confirmed selfishness, of low order, and immoral. By the habit of believing whatever a man [under perverse associations of his emotions of approval] wishes to believe, he becomes in proportion to the strength of the habit, a bad neighbor, a bad trustee, a bad politician, a bad judge, a shameless advocate. A man whose intellect is always at the command of his sinister interest, is a man whose conscience is always at the command of it."

INTELLECTUAL IMMORALITY.

It irresistibly follows from these considerations that the only intellectual "immorality" which any man can commit, is that committed by those who systematically procure the suppression of evidence, and in this regard, no exception can be made because the subject matter of the suppression is sexual. I therefore charge that the most "immoral" persons on earth are those responsible for the suppression of miscalled "impure literature." If error and knowledge are incompatible, then error and ignorance must be inseparable and the censors of literature must be the chief perpetuators of mental and moral stagnation.

"It is a truth that men ought no longer to be led, and it

would be a joyful truth, if truth it were, that they are resolved no longer to be led blindfold in ignorance. It is a
truth that the principle which leads men to judge and treat
each other, not according to the intrinsic merit of their action,
but according to the accidental and involuntary coincidence
of their opinions, is a vile principle. It is a truth that man
should not render account to man for his beliefs"—even on
the subject of sex.

Authority Destroying Liberty.

All those who love liberty more than power, and have the
intelligence to see in the present and future the development
of tyranny by our rapid growth of arbitrary power as manifested in our growing censorship of the mails and press; the
spread and development of "constructive contempt" of court;
the progress of executive legislation at Washington; the assertion through government by injunction that the justice of employers, or our economic system, is to be criticized only at the
times and places, and to the persons who have the court's permission; the laws creating a censorship over the opinions of
all immigrants, and prohibiting the advocacy within some of
our states of violent resistance of tyranny abroad; the punishment of a Philippine editor for publishing our Declaration
of Independence as conducing to insurrection; the suppression
of an American paper in Porto Rico for criticizing public officials and denying the rightful opportunity to prove the
truth of its allegation; the official destruction by the New
York postal officials of several hundred thousand post-cards,
which reflected on a candidate for public office; the demand of
the beef packers that magazines criticizing their busniess be denied the use of the mails; the arrest in Idaho of an editor for
publishing questions asking a petty militia-despot where under
the Constitution he found the warrant for his acts during a
strike-disorder—all these developments of recent years show in
our country a condition, which, with many other circumstances,
tends to the downfall of our liberties. Unless these tendencies
are checked, and checked effectively, the time may come
when the descendants of those who now will not defend the
liberties of others may have to defend their own under the
added difficulty of multiple precedents.

The best way to prevent this is to re-establish, as the foundation of all liberties, all that freedom of speech and press,
which is now in various ways abridged upon a half dozen subjects, and soon may be abridged upon still other subjects.

97

ON THE RIGHT TO KNOW

All life is an adjustment of constitution to environment. The seed dies, or has a stunted or thrifty growth, according to the degree of harmonious relationship it effects with soil, moisture and sunlight. So it is with man: He lives a long, happy and useful life, just to the degree that his own organism functions in accord with natural law operating under the best conditions. It follows that a growing perfection in the knowledge of those laws is essential to a progressive harmony in the individual's conscious adjustment to his physical and social environment, and every one of us has the same right as every other to know all that is to be known upon the subject of sex, even though that other is a physician.

Since a comparative fullness of life depends upon the relative perfection of the individual's adjustment to the natural order, and since the greatest knowledge of nature's rule of life is essential to the most perfect conscious adjustment (which is the most perfect life), it follows that our equality of right to life, liberty, and the pursuit of happiness entitles every sane adult person to know for himself, to the limit of his desire and understanding, all that can be known of nature's processes, not excluding sex.

Every sane adult person, if he or she desires it, is equally entitled to a judgment of his or her own as to what is the natural law of sex as applied to self, and to that end is personally entitled to all the evidence that any might be willing to submit if permitted. It is only when all shall have access to all the evidence and each shall have thus acquired intelligent reasoned opinions about the physiology, psychology, hygiene, and ethics of sex, that we can hope for a wise social judgment upon the problems which these present. The greatest freedom of discussion is therefore essential as a condition for the improvement of our knowledge of what is nature's moral law of sex, and is indispensable to the preservation of our right to know.

It was precisely this right to know that the framers of our Constitution intended to guarantee to us by those provisions against the abridgment of our freedom of speech and of the press. Prior to our American Constitutions, the English subject had a liberty to hear, but it was an abridgable liberty, existing as a matter of permission. The makers of our Constitution intended to guarantee to us an unabridgable liberty to hear and to read, that is, they intended to insure us an unlimited intellectual liberty as a matter of constitutionally guaranteed right.

A Suggestion For The Timid.

Those who reason sanely it seems must conclude that when any persons are old enough by law to enter matrimony, when any person is old enough by law to enter matrimony, which involves actual sex experience, then they should be conclusively presumed competent to choose for themselves the quantity and quality of psychic sex stimuli they wish to have, and whether it shall come through the means of good or bad art, literature, drama, or music. It is not clear to me why we should seek by law to control the sexual imaginings of those persons to whom it accords a perfect right to sexual relations. I can even see force in the methods of the ancient Greeks who believed that dancing and athletics in nudity conduced to health and honored marriage.

Those who esteem mere psychic lasciviousness a more serious offense than the corresponding physical actuality, lay themselves open to be justly accused of erotomania. How can we expect even married people to live wholesome lives so long as we deny them the opportunity for any detailed discussion as to what tends toward wholesomeness?

By giving the widest possible scope for the dissemination, among adults, of the scientific literature of sex, and by furnishing appropriate instruction in our public schools, the present morbid curiosity would soon be dissipated and within a generation practically all parents could be made competent and judicious instructors and guides for their own children. With this accomplished, you need never again fear the ills which are now dreaded, and the present sexual intelligence would have been so much improved as to insure a very general progress in public morals. Thus through the greatest liberty of speech and press, at least for the instruction of all over 18 years of age, we may reasonably hope to secure for the next generation an enlightened conscience as to all questions of sexual health and morals. Since minors bear a different relation to the government than do adults, it is probable that Congress and the States would have power to pass appropriate laws applicable only to such minors, even though present laws were held unconstitutional. However that may be, our present laws cannot be upheld without repudiating all those considerations which underlie our constitutional guarantees for unabridged liberty of speech and of the press, nor without the judicial destruction of those guarantees themselves.

CHAPTER VI.

OBSCENITY, PRUDERY AND MORALS.*

The advocates of our present censorship of literature believe that their work is justified by the claim of its moralizing tendency. It is my contrary opinion that to-day there is no organized force in American life which is more pernicious or more productive of moral evil in the domain of sex, than the very work which has come to be known as Comstockery. Of course this judgment is based upon the broadest possible outlook, including both the remote and immediate consequences of that prudery which finds its main stay in the legalized portion of it. This "moral" claim needs closer scrutiny.

I assume that no healthy person, under perfectly natural conditions, ever intentionally inflicts injury except in the anticipation of a compensating benefit. If then every one possessed health, infinite wisdom, and power to control those external conditions which now often determine our conduct, no one would be vicious. If under such possibilities any one deliberately injured self or another, it must be a mere matter of wantonness unexplainable by any normal motive, and hence would conclusively evidence a diseased mind. Thus viewed intelligence and vice are incompatible in healthy people, and ignorance is the efficient handmaid of vice, and the parent of vice-promoting. Every man who is adequately informed as to the consequence of his act, and having a mind sufficiently well trained to enable him accurately to see the remote painful consequence of his conduct and weigh this against its immediate pleasures, will never be vicious if being virtuous is within his power. If all possessed such intelligence, it would follow that the few remaining vicious ones must be either diseased or acting under external compulsions which make them vicious in spite of their judgment and desire to be otherwise. Therefore, general sexual intelligence must be the most efficient means of minimizing sexual vice in the healthy ones, and likewise operate as the most efficient preventive of much of the

*Revised from *Am. Journal of Eugenics* and *To-morrow.*

disease which results from, and in turn increases vice. It follows that every hindrance to sexual intelligence must be an aid to sexual vice, and all the sexual vices and diseases are chargeable to ignorance, and all of the latter is practically compulsory, and most of it is chargeable to prudery legalized and unlegalized—that is Comstockery.

The crowd, with its sensitive vanity and incapacity for critical thinking, so long as no personal material interests are involved, readily indorses whatever is labeled "moral" and claims an "eminently respectable" rating.

An organization devoted to promoting the seemings of virtue and the substance of vice, and strong in the pietism of diseased nerves as well as political influence, is now asking the public to follow our present nonsensical legislation to its logical conclusion. If these unintelligent "dearies" have their way, we shall soon have not only a sexless, but also a "smokeless literature." This means that public libraries are to exclude, and ultimately legislation is to suppress, all books wherein smoking or drinking is described. Soon all publications which use the words *tobacco* or *alcohol* will be excluded from the mails, and just as logically and "morally" as what is now excluded. "Moral" sentimentalizing is naturally expressed in righteous vituperation. Unenlightened minds readily mistake question-begging epithets for reasoning, and cowardly political adventurers enact its sentiments into law, thus bargaining away the liberties they are sworn to protect.

WHERE ARE THE IMMORAL CONSEQUENCES?

To the end that the unreason of our purists' claim of moral motive may be shown to be untrue, let us make a searching inquiry into the relationship of morals, literary fashion and our aversion to "obscene" literature.

I never have met a purist nor any one else who would admit that his own sex-morality had ever been the least impaired as the result of reading "obscene" books. I never have found any one even endeavoring to prove that a single case of sexual depravity would not have been *except for* "obscene" literature or art. In my boyhood, and since, I have seen pictures of lewdness and have read some so-called "obscene" books, and I cannot discover that it has injured me any, unless it be injury to have my sex-sensibilities considerably blunted, which I suspect may have come partly as a result of my study of sexual psychology.

102

Mr. Comstock is also an unconscious witness to the harm-lessness of obscenities. In a recent report he informs us that for thirty years he has "stood at the mouth of a sewer," search-ing for and devouring "obscenity" for a salary; and yet he claims that this lucrative delving in "filth" has left him, or made him, so much purer than all the rest of humanity that they cannot be trusted to choose their own literature and art until it has been expurgated by him. Why is Mr. Comstock immune? It may be because he is an abnormal man, upon whom, for that reason, sensual ideas do not produce their nor-mal reaction—in which case it is an outrage to make his abnormity a standard by which, under an uncertain statute, to fix what must be withheld from others. On the other hand, Mr. Comstock may be an average normal man, who has seen more "obscene" pictures and read more "obscene" books, and retained a larger collection of these, than any other living man. If it is true that his morality is still unimpaired, then it would seem to follow that "obscenity" cannot injure the ordinary normal human.

There are no other conditions to the problem than the two above stated, and this proves that "obscene" literature and art are morally harmless upon all normal persons, and that if undesired results shall anywhere manifest them-selves these are primarily due to abnormity in the individual and not to any evil inherent in the particular stimulation, which only brought the evidence of the abnormity to light. This is illustrated by the fact that reading *Uncle Tom's Cabin* was the starting-point in making one man a sex-pervert, and a book on surgery not connected with sex, as well as much religious exhortation to "love God," has proved to operate as an aphro-disiac. Of this more will be said later. The "immorality" re-sulting from reading a book depends, not upon its "obscenity," but upon the abnormity of the reading mind, which the book does not create, but simply reveals.

The girl-child who stimulates into activity the defloration mania of some old roué is not responsible for his assault upon her, and the child should not be suppressed or punished upon any such theory. A small boy, the sight of whom operates as an aphrodisiac upon a pervert, should not on that account be suppressed or punished. If a book or a picture does the same for a nymphomaniac or a satyr, the book is not to blame; and for the same reason that we do not punish the children in the above cases, so we should not punish the publisher in the last case. The desire for pornographic literature is but the evidence that healthy and natural curiosity has grown morbid through the purist's success in suppressing the proper information, which would satisfy it in 'the normal state and would be a most important factor in keeping it healthy. More voluminous and more free sex-discussion is therefore essential as a prophylactic.

The public welfare and morality are concerned to discover and cure social diseases and are not in the least concerned in the mere concealment of their symptoms, and that is all the purist's present efforts amount to.

LITERARY FASHION AND MORALS

There are still other means of proving the falsity of the claim that social utility and public morals are concerned in the suppression of obscene literature. I will now show that in another large number of instances it is a mere matter of unreasoned moral sentimentalizing over words,—that is, over literary style, and not over the ideas expressed or suggested nor their moral consequences, but over the manner in which it is done.

Even the United States Courts in their varied intellectual wabblings sometimes agree with me in asserting that the obscenity test of literature is purely a matter of literary style. Read this decision:

"The problem of population, and other questions of social ethics and the sexual relations, may be publicly discussed upon such a high plane of philosophy, thought, *and fitness of language* as to make it legally unexceptionable. They may be discussed so as to be plain yet chaste, so as to be instructive and corrective *without being coarse, vulgar, or seductive.* But when such publication descends to a low plane of *indecent illustrations and grossness of expression it loses all claim to respectability,*"[1] and therefore is criminal. But the "intelligent" moralists of hysteria are still so certain that it is ethics and not literary style which is in issue during most "obscenity" prosecutions, that I must make a more careful analysis of the moral claim, or pretense, put forth in justification.

Those exemplary moralists, the newspaper-scribblers and their purist adherents, think, or pretend, that they are conserving morality by mentioning sexual irregularity only by well-veiled but effectively pointed insinuations. These verbal mor-

[1] U. S. vs. Harman, 45 Federal Reporter, p. 423.

alists will announce that a divorce has been "granted upon biblical grounds," when they mean "adultery," but for "moral" reasons would not use the word. Let us study the question a little and see if morality is really concerned, or if this is a mere matter of expediency in politeness of style, and based upon moral sentimentalizing, instead of rational ethics. Perhaps I can best show the absurdity of the former contention by a series of different expressions, all conveying precisely the same thought—which shall be one that is generally considered as unquestionably moral—and then inquire where the immorrality begins in the course of several successive changes in the mode of presenting, without changing the idea itself.

I think I may assume that there is no one so silly as to object even slightly to such a phrase as this: "Thou shalt not forsake thy spouse and permit thyself to become a participant with another in the initial act for the investiture of a human life." Perhaps no one would object as yet if I became a little more specific and wrote: "Thou shalt not disobey the seventh commandment." From the fact that all journals for general circulation so studiously avoid the exact words of the commandment, I judge that many must deem it objectionable to print "Thou shalt not commit adultery."

Now then, I ask, how is morality differently concerned in these different modes of expressing the same idea? Only the same identical thought is suggested to the mind in each case, and that same idea, no matter by what words symbolized, must present the same *moral command* notwithstanding different emotions are evoked by the different words in whichever mode of expression is used. That the one set of word-symbols is associated with emotions of approval and another with emotions of disapproval, concerns exclusively the style of expression and has nothing whatever to do with morality.

Let me carry this method a little further and see if it must not lead us always to the same result, even though it may become more difficult to keep our "moral" sentimentalism subordinate to our reasoning faculties. Having now resolved that reason shall be your only guide, I will suggest a few other ways of expressing the seventh commandment.

Let us suppose that some publisher should replace the last word of the commandment by others, still presenting the same idea and nothing else, and to that end let us suppose that he should use the stable-boy's mode of expression. Thus from sheer poverty in vocabulary one might use that word which we all learned and used during our youth, "the most objectionable word in the English language." The idea which the commandment seeks to implant is unchanged and the morality of it is not in the least altered, and yet most people would now demand a prosecution for "obscenity." Then isn't it a mere matter of literary style?

I might even carry this transition in modes of conveying the thought still further and suggest the possibility that some one might take the ten commandments and replace the verbal symbol of that which is condemned by a pictorial presentation. The morality of the idea and the idea itself are unchanged in every instance, and yet for thus expressing the prohibition of one of the commandments every one (that is, almost every one who has come under the influence of puritan "civilization") would rise to demand the severest punishment of the publisher. Although the idea of the seventh commandment would still be accurately expressed, but simply because it is done in an unusual and unprudish manner, it would be declared criminal. But why?

Again I ask, how is morality differently concerned in these different modes of expressing the same idea? Only the same identical thought is suggested to the mind in each case, and that same idea probably would have and produce the same moral consequences whichever of the foregoing modes of expression is used, notwithstanding the difference in the emotions evoked by the different thought-symbols. All this only proves over again that "obscenity" is not in the idea conveyed, nor in differences as to the moral consequences of variously expressing the seventh commandment, but wholly and exclusively in the emotions associated with particular methods of symbolizing the thought.

It is all but a special illustration of the rule stated by Professor Thomas when he says: "When once a habit is fixed, interference with its smooth running causes an emotion. The nature of the habit broken is of no importance. If it were habitual for *grandes dames* to go barefoot on our boulevards or to wear sleeveless dresses at high noon, the contrary would be embarrassing."[2] So it is in literary fashion as well. "The most objectionable word in the English language" has become so only in recent times. It is found in the unexpurgated editions of Shakespeare, and was the word in polite use at his time.

[2] Sex and Society, p. 207.

In that edition of the Bible published in London in 1615, known as the "Breeches" edition (because of the use of that word in Genesis iii, 7), we find "the most objectionable word in the English language" at I Corinthians, chap. vi, verse 9. In N. Bailey's dictionary, that same "most objectionable word in the English language" has only a figurative application to the procreative act and its meaning is "to plant." By reason of its coming into general use, those who wished to be different from the common people invented new words to express the same fact. When these new words cease to operate as a veil, because their former figurative meaning has become literal, and they have come into general use among the vulgar, emotions of disapproval will come to be associated with the new words. Other words are then coined by the polite, and what formerly was "good form" now becomes obsolete and is denounced as "obscene," but rational morality is not in the least concerned with this change of literary fashion. No! It is only a matter of ethical sentimentalizing—of the morals of hysteria—and has to do only with modes of expression—that is, with literary style, and not moral consequences. The claim that the latter is its motive comes as a result of that very ancient and still very popular error of trying to objectivize our emotional (subjective) moral estimates. Persons with trained minds recognize some difference between a literary style which is offensive to chaste people and so may reinforce the chastity of their lives, and that literary style which, without the coarseness which excites aversion, seduces to libidinous conduct. Our literary purists usually fail to distinguish between an offense to modesty and the endangerment of chastity, which are two very different conditions, as different as vexation and temptation, or aversion and desire So it comes that their opposition is too often the most vehement where the question of morals is least real.

LITERARY VULGARITY AND MORALS.

This is not a new thought, for it was expressed over 300 years ago by the erudite Peter Bayle, and he furnished many illustrations in support, some of which will be reproduced. He says: "Such is the nice taste of our Purists, they blame one expression and approve another, though they equally offer the same obscenity to the mind. * * * The new whims of those, who, as I am told, begin to reckon the words glister and physic among the obscene terms, and use the general word remedy in their room, would be less unreasonable. The word glistere (Glister) was laid aside, as including too many circumstances of the operation, and the word lavement took its place, having a more general signification. But because the idea of the word lavement is become specific, and takes in too many circumstances, it will be quickly laid aside for fear of sullying the imagination, and none but general phrases will be used, such as J'etois dans les remedes, un remede lui sut ardonne, &c., which do not more particularly denote a glister or a purge, than a bag of herbs hung about the neck. These are certainly very strange whims."

Furthermore I believe it can easily be demonstrated that if there is any ethical effect at all that then vulgarity of literary style in dealing with sex subjects must be more conducive to puritan morality than are the refined insinuations of veiled phraseology.

Upon this question I am also fortunate to be able to quote judicial decisions in support of my contention. Here is the language of a United States Judge. "The most debasing topic may be presented in the choicest language. In this garb it is the more dangerous. Impure suggestions clothed in pleasing attire allure and corrupt, when bald filth would disgust and repel."[3]

I want to elaborate this thought and in doing so vindicate my assertion that an equally strong case can be made to prove that superior moral consequences may be expected from using vulgar phrasing in discussing sex. First let us get at the reason for this and later illustrate it by application to sex subjects.

Suppose I publish of a man the statement that he values his political principles so lightly that they are easily outweighed by small material advantage. That is so very delicate a way of saying that he will sell his convictions that one would scarcely feel any indignation over his moral turpitude. If on the other hand I denounce the same conduct of the same man by calling him "a political prostitute" we at once feel more profound resentment, because of the emotions of aversion which are usually associated with the last word of the phrase and consequently felt for everything to which it can be applied. It is the same in discussing matters of sex. To do so in coarse and vulgar language is to arouse an aversion never experienced in the polite phraseology of the unobscene. If then morality is

[3]U. S. vs. Smith, 45 Fed. Rep. 477.

at all involved it must follow that vulgarity of style is more adapted to promote aversion to sensualism than is the unobjectionable form of sex discussion.

PETER BAYLE ON OBSCENITY.

Here too, I could quote elaborately from learned authority in support, but since I cannot take the space to reproduce all of Mr. Bayle's erudite discourse entitled, "An Explanation Concerning Obscenities," I must content myself with quoting only a few more paragraphs. Writing of those who use the veiled phrase to picture their nudities, he says:

"The delicacy of their touches has only this effect, that the people look upon their pictures the more boldly, because they are not afraid of meeting with nudities. Modesty would not suffer them to cast their eyes upon them, if they were naked obscenities; but when they are dressed up in a transparent cloth, they do not scruple to take a full view of them, without any manner of shame, or indignation against the Painter: and thus the object insinuates itself more easily into the imagination, and is more at liberty to pour its malignant influence into the heart, than if the soul was struck with shame and anger. * * * * *

"Add to this, that when an obscenity is expressed only by halves, but in such a manner that one may easily supply what is wanting, they who see it finish themselves the picture which sullies the imagination; and therefore they have a greater share in the production of that image, than if the thing had been fully explained. In this last case they had only been passive, and consequently the admission of the obscenic image would have been very innocent; but in the other case they are an active principle, and consequently are not so innocent, and have more reason to fear the contagious effects of that object, which is partly their work. Thus this pretended regard to modesty, is really a more dangerous snare; it makes one dwell upon an obscene matter, in order to find out what was not clearly expressed. * * * * *

"This is of still greater force against the writers who seek for covers and reserves. Had they used the first word they met with in a Dictionary, they had only touched upon an obscene thing, and gone presently over that place; but the covers they have sought out with great art, and the periods they have corrected and abridged, till they were satisfied with the fineness of their pencil, made them dwell several hours upon an obscenity. They have turned it all manner of ways; they have been winding about it, as if they had been unwilling to leave such a charming place. Is not this ad sirenum scopulos consenescere, to cast anchor within reach of the syren's voice, and the way to spoil and infect the heart? It is certain, that excepting those who are truly devout, most of our other Purists are not in the least concerned for modesty, when they avoid so carefully the expressions of our ancestors; they are professed gallants, who cajole all sorts of women, and have frequently two mistresses, one whom they keep, and another who keeps them. Truly it becomes such men very well to exclaim against a word that offends modesty, and to be so nice when something is not left to be supplied by the reader's imagination! We may apply to them what Moliere said of a pretended prude: 'Believe me, those women who are so very formal, are not accounted more virtuous for it. On the contrary, their mysterious severity, and affected grimaces, provoke all the world to censure their actions. People delight to find out something to blame in their conduct. And to give an instance of it, there were the other day some women at this play opposite to our box, who by their affected grimaces during the whole representation, and turning aside their heads, and hiding their faces, made people tell many ridiculous stories of them, which had never been mentioned if they had not behaved so; nay, a footman cried out, that their ears were chaster than all the rest of their body.' The men I speak of, think only of making themselves admired for the delicacy of their pen. * * * * *

"This cannot be denied: Nay, women of an imperfect virtue would run less danger among brutish men, who should sing filthy songs, and talk rudely like soldiers, than among polite men who express themselves in respectful terms. They would think themselves indispensably obliged to be angry with those brutes, and to quit the company, and go out of the room with rage and indignation. But soft and flattering compliments, or at most such as are intermixed with ambiguous words, and some freedoms nicely expressed, would not startle them; they would listen to them, and gently receive the poison. A man who courts a maid would immediately destroy all his hopes, should he grossly and filthily propose his ill design; he is a perfect stranger to the Art of Love, if he has no regard to modesty in the choice of his expressions. There is no father, but would rather have his daughters blush than laugh at some stories told in their presence. If they blush they are safe; shame prevents the ill effect of the obscenity; but if they laugh, it makes an impression, and nothing diverts the stroke. If they laugh, it is doubtless because the obscenity was artfully wrapped up, and seasoned with an apparent modesty. Had it been grossly expressed, it would have excited shame and indignation. Farces in our days are more dangerous than those of our ancestors; in former times they were so obscene, that virtuous women durst not appear at them; but now they do not scruple to see them under pretence that obscenities are wrapped up, though not in impenetrable covers. Are there any such? They would bore them through, were they made up of seven hides like Ajax's shield.

"If anything could make La Fontaine's Tales very pernicious, it is their being generally free from obscene expressions.

"Some ingenious men, much given to debauchery, will tell you that the satires of Juvenal are incomparably more apt to put one out of conceit with lewdness, than the most modest and most chaste discourses that can be made against that vice. They will tell you that Petronius is not so dangerous, with all his gross obscenities, as he is in the nice dress of Count de Rabutin; and that the reading of the book entitled, Les Amours des Gaules, will make gallantry much more amiable than the reading of Petronius. * * * *

"I know the Stoics laughed at the distinction of words, and maintained that every thing ought to be called by its proper name, and that there being nothing dishonest in the conjugal duty, it could not be denoted by any immodest word, and that therefore the word used by clowns to denote it is as good as any other. * * * *

"If chastity was inconsistent with impure ideas, we should never go to church, where impurity is censured, and so many banns of matrimony are bid: we should never hear that office of the Liturgy that is read before the whole congregation on a wedding-day: we should never read the most excellent of all books, I mean the Holy Scriptures; and we should avoid, as so many infectious places, all the conversations where people talk of pregnancies, childbirths, and christenings. Imagination is a rambler which runs in a moment from the effect to the cause, and finds the way so well beaten, that it goes from one end to the other, before reason has time to stop it."[4]

[4]Bayle's Historical and Critical Dictionary, pp. 845 to 850, edition of 1837.

All these considerations prove again that literary vulgarity and immorality are not at all related to each other as Purists assert.

ON MORAL SENTIMENTALIZING.[6]

No habit of human thought is more universal and more pernicious than that by which the social utility, or evil, of conduct is measured by the intensity and kind of the emotional states which we associate with it. Most of humanity still approves all human conduct which induces agreeable emotions and likewise assumes that the degree of badness may be accurately measured by the intensity of the resentment which is felt towards those whose act is to be judged. This is moral sentimentalizing, though often it is characterized by more pretentious names. Scientific or rational ethics is the very antithesis of this. Instead of measuring moral values by "moral" emotions, the scientific mind limits moral emotions by moral values which are measured according to objective standards.

Where the emotions are most concerned there the check of right reason is least effective, and moral sentimentalism, for that very reason, is most potent and most misleading. Thence it comes that in determining statute laws and ethical creeds, regulative of sex-conduct, we are more often controlled by the vehemence of hysteria, than by calm judgments derived by the scientific method. Even those who live natural lives with sound bodies, and therefore have too healthy minds to indulge themselves in frantic moral sentimentalizing, yet readily succumb to the maniacal persistence and vehemence of the moralists-of-diseased-nerves. This is so because even the healthy minded ones lack clear insight to a rational ethics, and therefore they cannot frame to their own satisfaction arguments sufficiently convincing to afford the courage of resistance.

Here do we also find the explanation for those conspicuous discrepancies between statute law and actual life, that is, between public pretense and a personally justified secret conduct. On the whole, in such matters as sex-ethics, our uncoerced behavior is quite as likely to be in accord with a harmless and healthy naturalness as are our pretensions. The latter are apt to be controlled in such manner as to avoid the censure of the most boisterous sentimentalizer of the community, who

[6]Condensed from *The Pacific Medical Journal* for Nov., 1907.

in turn are the least safe guides to a rational ethics. In the matter of sex-ethics this means that, as to their pretensions, those who possess only an ordinary healthy bodily mechanism and a healthy mind not highly trained will be cowed into an acquiescence with others who are possessed by abnormal sensualism.

The only time that the subject of sex becomes a matter of real controversy before the public is when the excessively sensual of different modes of thought are pitted against one another. As illustrations we may point to the past contests between the Mormon polygamists, or the Bible Communists of Oneida, on the one hand, and prurient prudes and sentimental monogamists on the other. Can any one recall a single real argument for social utility that has ever been advanced upon either side? It is all mere violent outbreaks of moral sentimentalizing, expressed in dogmatic verbalisms and question-begging epithets, all inspired by diseased nerves. And yet we allow these hysterical yelps upon both sides to be the only views that ever achieve public expression or reach the legislative and judicial ear. No wonder then that the few who can or try to reason, even about sex-ethics, stand aghast at the achieved results of such mania, and the general public remains densely ignorant in spite by the "arguments" of mere "righteous" vituperation. There is room for difference of opinion upon many problems arising from sex, and it is an outrage that these are never allowed to be publicly and fundamentally discussed by the clean-minded with superior capacity. The stupid and untrue dogmatism which is tolerated, and the passionate outbursts of salacious prudes and voluptuaries, which come upon us in spite of repression, only make bad matters worse.

The abnormal aversion to healthy sensualism is never founded upon sexual indifference, but always the reverse. Acute eroto-phobia differs but slightly in degree and not at all in its essence, from prudery. I remind the reader that I am writing of the real prudery, and not its ignorantly parroted imitation.

Thus understood, all genuine prudery is always the manifestation of excessive sensuality, coupled with a proportionately extravagant, fear-created, desire to conceal it, all inducing violent emotions of aversion, either simulated or real.

The kinship of the relation between insanity and health, on the one hand, and moral sentimentalizing and rational ethics

113

on the other, is far more real than apparent. From modesty, through prudery, to acute eroto-phobia, is but a difference of degrees in the intensity of emotional aversion. All these different degrees may be excited in different persons by the same objective stimulus, which, however, will leave one who is comparatively indifferent to sex, without any consciousness either of modesty or of shame.

Moderate modesty, like milder forms of mono-mania, is due to a lost perspective, imposed by perverse education. A sex-centered attention thus induced, easily destroys all capacity for seeing the obsessing subject-matter in its right proportion to related objects. When to this we add that emotional intensity and certitude, which are the product of diseased nerves, modesty becomes eroto-phobia. The degree of prudery is usually the exact measure of the individual's hypersensualism.

So then it comes to this, that modesty, like insanity, in the kind and degree of its sensitiveness, is dependent primarily upon subjective conditions. Each person's modesty is sensitive to lascivious suggestion, just to the degree that such individual is sensually obsessed, and the degree to which the sexual nerve centers are diseased. All prudery which is not a mere stupid mimicing of others, that is all genuine prudery, is therefore seen to be founded upon excessive lewdness.

Abnormal sex-sensitiveness always produces sex over-valuation, either of the beneficence or the sinfulness of the sensual appetite. Similarly we see that intense religious enthusiasm always conduces to the apotheoses of love, and sex, and to excessive venery, either of indulgence or suppression. Where religion seeks to spiritualize sex-passion, science rationalizes it. As against moral sentimentalizing, a scientific ethics traces causes and results and builds moral standards according to ascertained, material, social consequences.

All emotions, including those which are generally classified as "moral," have varieties of intensity according to one's environment, education and healthy or diseased condition of the nerves. Hence the same fact will produce more intense emotions of approval or aversion in a hysterical person than in a healthy one. Again, the intensity of the emotion evoked by an object is in inverse ratio to the duration of the stimulation. That to which we have become accustomed is not so shocking as it was when it first interfered with a fixed contrary habit of thought or of life. So it comes that moral sentimentalizing varies not only as between different individuals,

114

but also differs at different times in the same individual. From these facts arises the danger of submitting to the guidance of our "moral" feeling.

The "moral" emotions are intense as the nerves are diseased. The doctrine that men may rightfully claim to know because they feel and to be firmly convinced because strongly agitated, finds its extreme of absurdity in this, that the certitude of a feeling-conviction often reaches its highest degree in the obsessive illusions of the insane, and the absurd conduct of hystericals.

CONSCIENCE AN UNSAFE GUIDE.

Individually and racially, according to its pleasurable or painful effects on them, men come to associate some conduct with emotions of approval and other conduct with emotions of disapproval. In these matters each individual is a law unto himself, and only an unconscious sympathetic imitation induces the superficial appearance of similarity. As these emotional "moral judgments" become habitual by frequent repetition, the unreason of their origin becomes progressively less conspicuous, and when lost sight of humanity enthrones this moral sentimentalizing on an imaginary pedestal outside the brain, calls it "conscience," and now the emotional association, perhaps founded on diseased nerves, is believed to constitute an innate and therefore infallible moral guide. Then "good people," ever confident in the inerrancy of their feelings, begin to regulate their neighbors' conduct, especially their sex-conduct, because our emotional nature is more involved therein, and because upon the subject of sex-ethics we have, on that account, been less accustomed to reason than upon any other subject. Here moral sentimentalizing is most natural and most pernicious, precisely because it is here sure to be least "tainted" by right-reason.

The mistake in all this popular method of arriving at "moral truth" lies in the fact that, like the insane, we ascribe to conduct those qualities which are mere associated emotional states of the perceiving mind. To cease the objectivizing of our emotional "moral judgments" is the beginning of rational ethics, and the highest degree of it will have been reached when all moral sentimentalizing shall have been abolished and each individual, from his own perfect knowledge of natural law, in which I include natural justice, shall no longer have the desire to live contrary to it.

We shall never be able to dispense with those mental processes which produce what we call conscience, but we will approach a higher and better humanity only in so far as we abolish from our own lives the authority of that conscience which is only moral sentimentalizing, and in lieu of that authority enthrone a pure cold logic machine which, without artificial human restraint, shall control our self-regarding action according to natural law, and our social conduct according to the nearest approximation to natural justice of which our minds are capable of conceiving. When we have abolished moral sentimentalizing, have acquired exact and complete information as to what is natural law, and what is required of us by exact natural justice and when we shall live in perfect accord with these requirements, the millennium will be at hand and government will cease to have any functions to perform. Until then we can only work with the view of approximating this unattainable ideal view, each of us striving to promote it in others, while endeavoring to realize it in our own lives.

It is unreasoned moral sentimentalism and not ethics which upholds the laws under discussion. It was an unreasoned moral sentimentalism and not ethics which in the past ages upheld other literary censorship and abridged intellectual freedom. It was unquestionably the intention of the framers of our constitutions to make that impossible. Shall our constitutions be judicially amended so as to perpetuate and make possible the further extension of mere psychologic crimes? That is the all-important question.

The evil consequences of this moral sentimentalism, and prudish snobbery cannot be overestimated. Here I cannot adequately exhibit it but I can point to a few concrete facts to show how our compulsory ignorance through legalized prudery works for human ill.

IGNORANCE OF THE MEDICAL PROFESSION.

It is an unwarranted superstition that the members of the medical profession are safe and intelligent guides and instructors in matters of sex. They have adequate knowledge to give superficial instruction to children about the physiology and hygiene of sex, and they know a little about the most common forms of venereal infection. But when it comes to dealing with the intricate social problems involving sexual psychology most of them are in a wilderness of impenetrable darkness and ignorance, and the few specialists, who have gathered a few nuggets of truth from years of work with sexual psychopaths, are seldom given an opportunity to spread that

116

knowledge even among their professional brethren. The result is that upon the gravest social-sex-problems of the future the average physician is more ignorant than many laymen with a variety of "worldly" experience. I charge this ignorance to be a fact, and to be due almost entirely to prudery, and a potent cause of vice. The charge is a grave one, and I must adduce some proof.

I will begin by quoting from a recent Medical Journal showing the deliberate suppressing of sexual discussion even within the profession, and also showing their reason for it. These are the words of Prof. Wm. F. Waugh:

"We do not approve of making a feature of discussion and investigation of the sexual relations. We fully grant their importance and the need of their study. Men and women are cursing the day they were born, are fighting, going insane, driving others insane, making themselves devils and earth a hell, all for want of the knowledge that can only come from a free and untrammelled discussion of sexual physiology and pathology, by those who are competent. But this is exactly what is not to be had under present conditions. No such discussion is possible in any publication that circulates by post to a general public; hence any attempt in that direction is sure to be futile. It is not that the attempt to carry it on will surely bring trouble—to a man of the stuff before us, martyrdom holds out allurements not to be resisted—it is because of certain failure and wasted efforts sadly needed in directions where success is possible. Our objection is not prudent cowardice but calculating utilitarianism.

"There is this to be said about discussions of sexual matters: as one goes further into the topic, his viewpoint alters. *The limits he first set to what is permissible in the discussion recede, until things appear as a matter of course, that at first we would unhesitatingly have denounced as obscene. Then he is called to face a charge that is in itself a disgrace.* And we sympathize with a friend who asked for vaccination because he preferred to 'die of a clean disease.' Once there was a soldier, noted throughout his division for his many heroic exploits. Time and again he braved and escaped dangers that daunted the boldest, but he seemed ever to hold a charmed life. At last he was tremendously kicked by a big mule, and this time death was inevitable. When informed of his fate, to the amazement of all he burst into tears. Seeing the contempt on his comrades' faces, he exclaimed: 'It's not that,

117

boys; not that I am afraid to die; but after all the high and mighty chances of dying I've had, to be kicked to death by an infernal long-eared heehawing son of a jackass!' Same as to Comstock."[7]

I have had it upon the authority of one of the most widely known scientists of America, that many other Medical Journals hold substantially the same attitude to the discussion of sexual topics. The silence is the natural result of an uncertain statute, conferring arbitrary power upon stupid humans by the uncertainty of its criteria of guilt. Being ignorant himself, the physician, like our moralist for revenue, profits by the general ignorance and so joins in the opposition to sexual intelligence by a postal censorship.

In the *Medical Council* for October, 1908, is an article on "How shall we advise our boys on the question of sexual and moral prophylaxis?" by Prof. Frederic R. Sturgis. He is the author of "Sexual Debility in Man." other books and numerous essays in medical journals. He was formerly Clinical Professor of Venereal diseases in the Medical department of the University of the City of New York and of the Post Graduate Medical College; sometime visiting surgeon of the venereal division of the city hospital, Blackwell's Island, and has attained great distinction in his profession. (See Physicians and Surgeons of America, Edition of 1906, p. 326) When the manuscript was first submitted to the editor he was in doubt as to its availability, because the uncertainty of the statute made it impossible for him to find out if it were mail able. In this perplexity he submitted the manuscript to the Post Office authorities, and was told that it was not mailable. After expurgation it was published as above indicated. So it has now come to pass that a layman to the medical profession occupying a clerical position in the Post Office Department decides what the doctors may be permitted to publish or read upon sexual subjects. Future generations will look back with amazement at the cowardice and stupidity of a profession and of a general public which submitted without protest of such a censorship over the literary output of one of the most distinguished specialists in the United States. Had Dr. Sturgis told the lie that no sexual irregularities exist, or had he advised every one to lie to their sons about the subject of sex, so as not to run counter to the moral sentimentalizing of our ascetical theologasters, his falsehoods would have passed

[7]Am. Journal of Clinical Medicine, May, 1907. Prof. Wm. F. Waugh.

118

the censorship. But having a wide experience in such matters he preferred to portray our human sexuality as he found it, and to tell parents to tell the whole truth about it to their sons. This is the unpardonable sin in the code of our moral tinkers for revenue, and so one physician may not even advise another to tell his son the whole truth as it is conceived in the mind of the specialist. Thus our purism most efficiently promotes the vices, the suppression of which brings prosperity to our moralists for coin.

POPULAR IGNORANCE.

Reform organizations such as the Woman Christian Temperance Union, and the National Purity Federation, have been for years agitating the question of giving instruction in the public schools as to the hygiene and physiology (also theology) of sex, because they believe such instruction a moralizing force. Some members of the medical profession are falling into line as is shown by the organization of the American Society of Sanitary and Moral Prophylaxis, and kindred societies, and by such action as was recently taken by the Illinois Medical Association.[8] But here again prudery makes the accomplishment of this plan impossible, first because prudish public sentiment won't tolerate such instruction, and secondly, even if it did, thanks (?) be to prudery, there are none willing or competent to teach. Dr. Helen C. Putman, of Providence, R. I., quotes two leading educators, in sympathy with sexual education, as saying: "I know no men in the schools of my city and but few women, whom I would be willing to have talk on sex matters to my boy and girl." Dr. Putman adds: "I could quote others." She calls attention also to the fact that prudery has excluded the subject of sex hygiene from text books, and from the curriculum of the normal school, and consequently from the teacher's mind. She then shows by other investigations how the legalized and unlegalized prudery have produced a condition of affairs where none are competent to instruct.[9]

The literature upon the subject of sex which is prepared for general consumption is practically all either useless or pernicious, and always from prudish causes. On the one hand, because prudery compels general ignorance, we have developed a class of physicians who thrive by misinformation which scares the ignorami, systematically created by us, into the net of the quack.

[8]Medical Record, Oct. 12th, 1906, pp. 594 to 600.
[9]Boston Medical and Surgical Journal, Sept. 31st, 1907, p. 132.

Another class, who are almost as culpable, systematically obtain money under false pretences by advertising and selling sex-books. This class of books are sold on false representation, more or less definitely made, that they will give some helpful and detailed information upon one's concrete personal problems. Instead of answering the questions, which as young men and women we wanted answered and had a right to know about, the purchaser receives a little moral sentimentalism, some stupid and often truthless dogmas, which, together with some that is really true, is promptly disregarded, because no convincing reasons accompany the information. After the reading of such "purity" books, so well filled with vague and mystifying phrases, which mean absolutely nothing to those who do not already know what is sought to be hinted at, one is convinced that he has been robbed of his money without being enlightened, and the young come from the reading of these books feeling more mystified and helpless than ever before, over the personal problem.

Of another class of books, Pres. G. Stanley Hall, of Clark University, has this to say: "Realizing that God and nature have wrought an indissoluble bond between love and religion, these writers rely upon conversion, confirmation, prayer, or new resolutions, while some add an appeal to the sense of honor. There can be no doubt of the good intention of the writers of this class, nor that they have done good, but to me they all seem to have more zeal than knowledge." The absence of knowledge is again due to the prudery which makes the acquisition of satisfying knowledge difficult or impossible. He might also have quoted Jonathan Edwards, Bishop Lavington, Rev. S. Baring Gould, Dr. Spurgeon, and innumerable other clergymen to the effect that many of this class of reformers are ignorantly and unconsciously developing in others an abnormal lewdness, by the very excesses of emotional enthusiasms which they work into their methods of religious reform.[10]

Dr. Hall continues thus: "The last class of books that stand out clearly are writings that appear to be by mothers or aunts, for boys, and which are pervaded by sentiment, poetic, religious, and æsthetic, the interests of posterity and the chivalry which the true gentleman should feel for those of the other sex. Such appeals may effect girls, but the boy, at the callow, pin-feather age of fourteen, is rarely æsthetic, and if at this

[10]"Religion and Sensualism" in vol. 3, p. 16, of *Amer. Jour. of Religious Psychology.*

age he can be truly called a perfect gentleman there is something wrong with him."

Thus far I approve of Dr. Hall's criticism of purity literature, made almost useless by prudishness. Now let me show you how the same cause has also impaired the moral good which he designed by his article.[11]

He is trying to enlighten parents about what they must tell their children. The boy must be told of "the fact that not one, but both, of the most prevalent diseases due to impurity of life are of the gravest danger." Parents already familiar with these diseases did not need to be told of their danger. His article was written for that great mass who know nothing about them and who on reading Dr. Hall's article might wonder whether he meant the croup, scarlet fever or small-pox. Had he expressed his thought in the homely words we probably all heard in our youth, the uninformed reader whom he was trying to reach might have understood what he meant. But if he had found a publisher at all, legalized prudery would have sent him to jail. Had he used the scientific words gonorrhea and syphilis, the reader might at least have found out what he meant, by using a medical dictionary. But, as it is, prudery so dominated even this eminent scientist that he wrote a message designed to curtail vice, but which in large part was made useless by the avoidance of direct phrase and scientific exactness, such as he would have used in discussing every other subject. Thus again does prudery encourage vice.

Not long since I attended a meeting of the American Society of Sanitary and Moral Prophylaxis, where Professor Wilder, of Cornell Medical College, was announced to lecture upon the desirability of educating the young in matters of sex. He had prepared a discourse to show the great evils coming from ignorance. When he got to that portion where from medical journals and kindred sources he apparently was preparing to make concrete statements of facts about venereal infection and its result, he became visibly embarrassed, and scarcely having begun he announced that he hadn't the courage to proceed according to his original intention. Here then is a scientist of international prominence, so overawed by a consciousness of the general prudery which has developed with and from our legalized prudery, that he must withhold from an audience gathered to receive it information of the greatest

[11]Ladies' Home Journal, Sept., 1907, p. 26.

value. The resultant ignorance upholds these laws, promotes crime and disease, and these are a direct evil result of our legalized prudery.

The moral snobbery and legalized prudery of the professional vice-hunter and moralist for revenue is based wholly on stupid moral sentimentalizing, and not at all upon any rational or scientific ethics, and has made it impossible for parents to qualify themselves as instructors for their children, and those children are kept in ignorance upon a subject where ignorance is the most potent for evil, and yet that ignorance is lauded as a virtue, though it very often leads to ruin, as is shown by the records of our insane asylums.

These miscalled "purity" associations primarily destroy the opportunity of all for gratifying a healthy and natural curiosity and thus of necessity they aid in developing morbidity in relation to sex. Out of this morbidness, created mainly through their efforts, comes the market for that erotic and prurient literature which the salaried vice-hunters profess to deplore, and which they unconsciously foster and gladly profit by. With all restrictions removed and general opportunity for public-school education in sex matters, the second generation would be so healthy-minded as to destroy all market for the stuff which the "purists" profess so much to abhor.

In France, although general sexual education is wanting, it is openly asserted that the greater part of the demand for prurient literature and art comes from American and English tourists, and customers. I am aware that some of the "purists" profess to believe that there should be education about matters of sex, given to young people, but they invariably mean by this the theology of sex and not sexual science, which is a very different thing. In my view every human being should have an unlimited opportunity for knowing all that there is to be known about every part of the human anatomy, and that to preach against such intelligence, or impede its spread is always an outrage and always productive of evil.

Another way in which this evil manifests itself lies in this, that the "purists'" efforts, by their insane over-valuation of sex importance, always destroy people's perspective, much to the public injury. If there had been no attempted interference with "Mrs. Warren's Profession," most people would have seen in that play only the presentation of a social problem, by the consideration of which all of the visitors to the theater, and society at large, might have profited. After and by virtue of the stupid protest of morbid prudes, who were so obsessed by their own lewdness that they could see nothing but the sensual features of the play, it at once became impossible for the great mass of people to see any moral problem in it. From that time on they were induced by the very outcry of the "purists" to concentrate their attention on a watch for only its sensual stimuli. The same thing is true of their efforts to suppress the nude in art. By their very effort lewd moralists for revenue make it impossible for a great many people to see anything but the sensual features of a picture, whereas, if left alone without this interference from prurient prudes, which in such matters always misdirects the public attention, it would be possible for most people to see the beauties of form and of physical perfection.

Let me say right here that I am not devoting myself to criticising Mr. Comstock for any mistakes he may have made in the exercise of an arbitrary power, which an outrageously uncertain criminal statute seems to vest in him, and I have no patience with those critics of Comstockery who are devoting themselves to criticism of Mr. Comstock, instead of the conditions which he helps to perpetrate and which make him possible, and prosperous. My complaint is most with those stupid people who by their moral sentimentalizing are supporting the arbitrary power which authorizes his mistakes. I am not concerned in the least as to how that arbitrary power is exercised, whether wisely or unwisely. I am very much concerned that the arbitrary power itself should be destroyed, by making the law conform to the constitutional requirements of certainty in the statutory criteria of guilt. Mr. Comstock is simply exercising his ordinary right of being a moralist for revenue under the opportunities offered by a stupid public.

SEX IGNORANCE AND INSANITY.

This, then, brings me to the more unpleasant features, which relate to sexual insanities, and venereal infection. No one worthy to be counted a worker for improved morals can overlook these most important phases of the sex problem. I know only the use of the plain, direct, and scientifically chaste manner of speech. It is only by the use of such that I can proceed, while I briefly recapitulate some concrete facts known to the medical profession, and by me culled from standard medical authorities. By every known scientific code of ethics, the

123

morality of conduct is to be judged by its injurious consequences. Upon the record that follows, and much other kindred material, these damnable facts are all the consequences of
sexual ignorance, and this in turn is mainly the consequence of
our legalized suppression of sexual intelligence. Therefore I
charge our "moral" censorship of literature to be the most
pernicious influence in our American life, and our "highly
respected" prurient prudes the most immoral people in
America.

Picque found a proportion of 88% of gynocological affection among the insane, and some have found even more. It is
quite generally estimated that of all insanities 66% involve the
sexual mechanism or functioning. Where sex is the primary
cause of the ultimate derangement, sex-intelligence usually
could wholly preclude the evil consequences, or find an early
cure. In other cases where there is some sexual derangement
it is at first but a symptom of mental ailment, only in turn to
become an aggravating cause. Here a greater intelligence on
the part of friends and family, such as the general dissemination of the literature of sexual science would produce, will
enable them to understand what now seems dubious, and impel
them to apply much earlier for medical aid, when it would be
far more efficacious. Legislators and courts now treat the
sex-pervert as a criminal, thereby discrediting both our intelligence and our humanity. In an enlightened community
we will know that usually such are diseased, and thus be
prompted to restore them, rather than wreak vengeance upon
them.

SUFFERING OF THE VICIOUS TO SAFEGUARD VIRTUE.

A study of venereal infection gives us some appalling results. Every year in our country perhaps hundreds of thousands of persons become its victims. Owing to public ignorance and a mawkish sentimentalism, many of these persons
cannot secure treatment from the regular physician, nor will
be received in many hospitals. It is argued that to make them
suffer the penalty of vice is the best safeguard to virtue. Even
if the transgressors were the only sufferers, it would still be
an unpardonable inhumanity not to cure them if possible,
because in such cases they too often suffer in the inverse ratio
of their familiarity with the vicious. More general education conduces to more justice in fitting the natural punishment

to the crime. All disease is the result of some form of vicious living, and if we are to be guided by such irrational aphorisms we must abstain altogether from trying to relieve human suffering. The pains of dyspepsia or rheumatism must be endured lest by their cure we make vicious eating safe; dipsomania and delirium tremens must remain uncured lest we make alcoholic beverages safe.

VENEREAL INFECTION AND SUFFERING OF THE INNOCENT.[12]

When we come to consider the suffering which is unnecessarily inflicted on the ignorant innocent, by adherence to this absurd dogma, then the public's indifference toward the cure of venereal diseases becomes almost criminal. It is not infrequent that a syphilitic child will infect its uninformed nurse, or an infected wet nurse not knowing her own condition transmits the disease to the child under her care. Unnumbered persons become infected merely by a common use of eating, drinking, or toilet utensils.

That you may properly understand just how infamous is the taboo which we have placed upon this subject, let me go more into detail, and here I charge you specially to observe the suffering of the innocent. Eighty per cent. of the blindness of the new born, and twenty per cent. of this terrible affliction from all causes, is due to gonococcus infection, as also is a large proportion of vulvo-vaginitis and joint affections of children. Dr. Neisser estimates that at present there are in Germany about 30,000 blind persons who owe their affliction to his cause. In America no statistics are available.

Pinnard found that in 10,000 consecutive cases of miscarriage or abortions 42% were caused by syphilis, the remaining 58% were due to all other causes combined. The mortality from hereditary syphilis ranges from 60 to 80%, while those who survive are affected with degenerative changes which unfit them for the battle of life. Syphilis in France alone kills every year 20,000 children, producing $7\frac{1}{2}\%$ of the mortality form all causes combined. It is computed that 50% of all gonorrheal women are absolutely sterile, and gonorrheally infected men are responsible for 20% of involuntary sterile marriages. Sixty per cent. of the children gestated

[12]Practically all of this information about venereal infection is taken from "Social Diseases and Marriage," by Dr. Prince Morrow. and from the publications of the Am. Soc. for Sanitary and Moral Prophylaxis, of which he is President. The State Medical Board of Indiana has recently issued a pamphlet giving very similar statistics.

by syphilitic mothers die in utero, or soon after birth. Only two in five will survive even through a short life; 20 to 30% of gonorrheally infected women abort and from 45 to 50% are rendered irrevocably sterile.

Fournier's general statistics, embracing all classes of women, show that one in every five syphilitic women contracted syphilis from her husband soon after marriage. Among the married females in his private practice, in 75% of the cases the disease was unmistakably traced to the husband. D. Bulkley's statistics, in "Syphilis in the Innocent," state that in private practice fully 50% of all females with syphilis acquired it in a perfectly innocent manner, while in the married females 85% contracted it from their husbands. The report of a medical committee of seven gave it that in from 30 to 60% of the syphilitic women who had the disease it was communicated by the husband. Dr. Morrow in his experience in the New York Hospital found that 70% of the women who applied for treatment for syphilis were married and claimed to have received the disease from their husbands. 60% of all gynocologic surgical operations are chargeable to gonococcic infection.

To emphasize the danger which comes to the innocent from the infamous and ignorant conspiracy of silence, let me quote these awful words from a specialist of high authority. He says: "It may be a startling statement but nevertheless true, that there is more venereal infection among virtuous wives than among professional prostitutes in this country." The latter, being the more intelligent in such matters, use personal propylaxis, and secure treatment earlier after infection, while the ignorant virtuous wife continues to suffer in silence. In view of this appalling condition, what are you going to say to those moral sentimentalizers, who for fear of making vice safe, seek to penalize all announcements that venereal diseases can be cured? Will you by education help protect the innocent sufferers or will you through moral cowardice give silent support to the infamous taboo upon sexual education?

I have now shown the practical operation of the doctrine that to make men suffer the penalties of vice is the best safeguard to virtue, yet if you would issue general instructions for the detection of venereal infection, or for personal prophylaxis, all prurient sentimentalists would say you are making vice safe, you must go to jail for your "obscenity" and the "immoral tendency" of your book. Thus it is that the in-

126

nocent must continue to suffer, and the family physician continues to lie to the wronged wife, in order to protect her husband, and maintain the "sanctity" of such a home. Infected husbands must be screened at any cost of suffering to the innocent wife and children, simply because we are afraid that someone will say we are trying to safeguard vice.

In many states efforts have been made, and have almost succeeded, the success of which would have made it criminal, even in a hospital report or a professional treatise on venereal disease, to make it known where or how sexual ailments could be cured, and the excuse offered is that such information tends to make vice safe.

DEMAND OPPORTUNITY FOR KNOWLEDGE.

I have tried to point out the urgency for general education and the laws which preclude it. I cannot doubt that you are quite convinced that the situation is sufficiently grave to demand an immediate change if we would maintain a semblance of purity. I submit that a decent regard for the moral welfare of the community, or for the innocent sufferers of venereal infection, compels us to demand for the general public such liberty of the press, and other means of publicity, as will protect each in his right to learn and to know, just how terrible are the ravages of these diseases—how their presence may be detected—and that they can be cured, and their spread prevented. The practical legal question which all this presents is this: DOES THERE EXIST ANYWHERE UNDER OUR CONSTITUTIONS ANY AUTHORITY VESTED WITH POWER TO SUPPRESS SEXUAL INTELLIGENCE, AND THUS BY LEGALIZED COMPULSION INFLICT SUCH ILLS UPON HUMANITY?

ON THE DANGERS OF LIBERTY.

It is perhaps apparent now that our present tests of obscenity are grossly ridiculous in their results if impartially applied, and I am sorry to confess that I cannot furnish a better, because what is deemed objectionable is always a personal matter which cannot be defined in general terms. Furthermore, no man can tell a priori what is of bad tendency. If you have received the right training from your parents or preceptors, even the worst bawdy picture may produce a wholesome revulsion. Once open the door to all serious discussions of sex, and soon the healthy curiosity will be satisfied, which now becomes morbid only from the denial of satisfaction. No one thinks of caricaturing the reproductive mechanism of our domestic animals only because no one has any morbid curiosity about it, because there is no concealment. With the development of healthy mindedness through sexual education in our schools, all morbidity of curiosity would disappear in one generation. The demonstration of this is to be found among art students.

Years ago when it was proposed to prohibit the sending of abolition literature through the mails, because of its "immoral" tendency toward insurrection, the Hon. John P. King, a United States Senator from the South, protested and said: "I prefer the enjoyment of a rational liberty at the price of vigilance and at the risk of occasional trouble, by the error of misguided or bad citizens, to the repose which is enjoyed in the sleep of despotism." With this I concur. Liberty has dangers of its own, which we must overcome, or forego progress. If we have confidence that we have right on our side, we need not fear open discussion and warfare with error.

This then concludes the several preliminary discussions, which seemed necessary to clear away some of the mists of our moral sentimentalism, and brings us to the more direct discussion of the several constitutional questions involved.

CHAPTER VII.

ON THE IMPLIED POWER TO EXCLUDE "OBSCENE" IDEAS FROM THE MAILS.[1]

Syllabus of the Argument: *The Power to create a postal system implies the power to pass all laws "necessary and proper" to the end of executing the power to establish post offices and post roads, but it does not authorize Congress under the pretext of creating and maintaining post offices to make the postal system a means to the accomplishment of ends not entrusted to the care of Congress. The very creation of a postal system necessarily involves a determination of the gross physical characteristics of that which is to be carried or excluded and therefore implies the power to determine such qualities. A like implication cannot be made in favor of a power to determine what are mailable ideas, because a differential test of mail matter, based upon the opinions transmitted through the mails, or the psychological tendencies of such opinions upon the addressee of the mails, or a differential test based upon an idea which is not actually transmitted, but is suggested by one that is transmitted, bears no conceivable relation to the establishment of post offices or post roads for the transmission of physical matter only.*

It may be admitted that the power granted implies the power to preclude the use of the mails as an essential element in the commission of a crime otherwise committable, and over which Congress has jurisdiction (such as fraud and gambling), within the geographical limits of its power. But it is claimed that the power of Congress is limited to the use of means which are a direct mode of execution of the power to establish post offices and post roads, or some other power expressly granted, and it cannot, under the pretence of regulating the mails, accomplish objects which the Constitution does not commit to the care of Congress. Such an unconstitutional object is the

[1]*Central Law Journal*, V. 65, p. 177, Sept. 6, 1907.

effort of Congress, under the pretext of regulating the mails, to try to use the mails as a means to control the psycho-sexual condition of postal patrons.

The present postal laws against "obscene" literature, as the same are judicially administered, make the mailability of matter depend not only upon the so-called "obscenity" of that which is actually transmitted through the mails, but also upon ideas not actually transmitted, but according to their potential capacity for suggestiveness to the prurient, though the words and sentiments in themselves are free from objection. The question is, has Congress the implied power to make such regulations? Three thousand lawyers have been employed by the defendants in as many cases, and none of these have thought it worth while to question the existence of such a power.

This discussion involves only two clauses of the constitution, viz: The power "to establish post offices and post roads" and the authority "to make all laws necessary and proper" to the establishment of post offices and post roads. It has become the statement of an axiom to say that "the national government possesses no powers but such as have been delegated to it."[2] "Whenever, therefore, a question arises concerning the constitutionality of a particular power, the first question is, whether the power be expressed in the constitution. If it be, the question is decided. If it be not expressed, the next inquiry must be whether it is properly an incident to an express power and necessary to its execution. If it be, then it may be exercised by congress. If not, congress cannot exercise it."[3] The constitution nowhere expressly confers upon congress the power legislatively to discriminate between "moral" and "immoral" opinions.

IS THE IMPLIED POWER TO REGULATE UNLIMITED?

I now momentarily waive the contention that no such qualities belong to any opinions. The question then is, has congress the implied power to create a "moral" censorship over the opinions which may be transmitted through the mails, which implied power, if it exists, must arise wholly from the power to maintain post offices and post roads? The power to establish a postal system and to make all "necessary and proper" laws incident thereto, undoubtedly implies the unavoidable exercise

[2] Gilman v. Philadelphia, 70 U. S. 713-725; Martin v. Hunter's Lessee, 1 Wheat. 304-326; M'Culloch v. Maryland, 4 Wheat. 405; Pacific Ins. Co. v. Soule, 7 Wall. 444; United States v. Cruikshank, 92 U. S. 542.

[3] Story's Commentaries on the Constitution.

of the power to determine the gross physical characteristics of the matter to be transmitted and excluded. But does it follow that in other particulars there is any implied power to regulate the contents of the mails, and if so, is it unlimited? Has congress the power to say that nothing at all be carried which is not written or printed upon paper produced at a particular factory, and to penalize the transmission of otherwise undistinguishable paper coming from a rival factory? Clearly not. If the paper in all its physical characteristics is undistinguishable, a discriminating judgment based upon its different manufacturers, who themselves bear precisely the same relationship to the government and its postal system, cannot be a "necessary and proper" power impliedly existing in congress, because a decision upon that question is not necessary to either the establishment or maintenance of post offices and post roads, nor of any other power expressly delegated to the United States. To assert the contrary is to make the control of postal regulations a political prize, to be used in securing a monopoly in the manufacture of paper, and such an evil possibility is not to be tolerated, or called into being by any judicial process of unnecessarily creating implied power. When it is "necessary and proper" as an incident to any other expressed grant of power, it is possible that the postal system, and the mode of its regulation, by necessary implication, could be made subservient thereto. Thus congress has undoubted power to pass many criminal laws, and might, perhaps, prescribe deprivation of mail privileges as a penalty to be inflicted upon conviction, or it probably could prohibit the use of the mails as an instrument directly contributing an essential factor in the actual commission of such other actual crime, within the power of congress to create. But does it follow that therefore congress also has the power arbitrarily to deny the use of an established postal service to all citizens who bear the name of "Smith," or who do not believe in Christian science, or do not approve of a protective tariff? Clearly not. Because a decision based arbitrarily upon the name of the postal patron, or upon his characteristics of opinion merely, is not "necessary and proper" to the establishment of post offices and post roads, nor to the exercise of any other expressed power of the federal government. Admitting now the "necessary and proper" implied power in congress to determine the geographical extent and distribution of post offices and post roads, and the unavoidable, and therefore "necessary and proper" implied power to determine the gross physical characteristics of what may be transmitted, does it follow, all other conditions, including the physical characteristics, being the same, that congress has the power arbitrarily to make discriminations according to arbitrary standards, based upon the varying intellectual valuations of conflicting opinions, or opinions of suspected conflicting tendencies? Can the literature of Catholics, free-lovers, theists, and agnostics be excluded as unapproved by the law-making power, while the literature of evangelicals, polygamists and Christian scientists is transmitted because approved? May the literature of trades unionism be excluded and that of the employer's association transmitted? May the literature favoring the single tax, free trade, or state ownership of railroads be excluded, and those favoring an income tax, protective tariff and the repeal of anti-trust laws, be transmitted? Has congress the power to so regulate the mails as to transmit all literature "tending" to a centralization of power, progressive tyranny, moralization by force and that which "tends" to foster the ascetic ideal of sexual life, while it excludes all matter which "tends" toward decentralization and personal liberty, or "tends" to foster unconventional ideas of sex-life, all other conditions being the same? May the literature of prohibitionists be excluded, while that of their opponents is transmitted? Clearly, if congress has the implied power to do one of these things, it has the implied power to do them all, because they all bear the same relation, or more accurately, no relationship, to the establishment of post offices and post roads. We are not concerned with the question as to the likelihood of such a power being exercised to the fullest, nor are we concerned with the tremendous possibility for evil which might come from the abuse of so extraordinary a power, though that would make us hesitate to affirm its existence, unless the implication was an unavoidable one. Again we ask, has congress any such implied power? Clearly not, because its exercise bears no "necessary and proper" or conceivable relation to the establishment of post offices and post roads, nor to any other enumerated power of the federal government.

HOW IS THE IMPLIED POWER LIMITED?

Let us abandon the discussion from the standpoint of engrafting necessary exceptions upon an assumed unlimitedness of the implied power, and discuss the matter by developing the implications from the constitution itself. Congress is not expressly authorized by the constitution to determine even the gross physical qualities of mail matter, but that power is unavoidably implied from the authority to establish post offices and post roads, because the latter cannot be executed without the exercise of a discretion as to the physical characteristics of postal matter. Can the same be said about a discretion as to the psychologic tendencies of ideas expressed upon the transmitted matter? Congress is not expressly authorized to discriminate according to the intellectual or "moral" qualities of that which may be expressed upon, or suggested by that which is transmitted through the mails. Congress can have the implied power to make such differentiations according to psychologic standards only if post offices and post roads are impossible of establishment and maintenance without the implication of such power. But if on the contrary, it is essential to the establishment or maintenance of post offices and post roads, that congress exercise a legislative discrimination between mail matter, not only according to the opinions actually transmitted, but also according to the psychologic tendency of that which is only suggested by, but not expressed in the matter actually transmitted, then such power will be implied. A mere analytical statement of the question shows how absurd is the claim of such a power.

Every publication undoubtedly suggests different things to many different people. In each, that which it suggests depends upon what, by prior varying experiences, has become associated in his mind with that which has been written. That which I send through the mail is one element, but not at all the determining element in the resultant varying ideas suggested to the different readers. How ridiculous and monstrous it is to assert that a discrimination between mail matter, not according to its own inherent definable qualities, but according to its mental associations in the reader's mind, is a "necessary and proper" incident to, or "a direct mode of executing the power" to establish post offices and post roads! Yet according to such tests of obscenity are present laws executed. What has the reader's sensitiveness to the discovery of lewd suggestions, or the existence of an associated lascivious idea, or the jury's capacity for psycho-sexual receptivity, to do with establishing post roads? Plainly and unmistakably nothing at all. Here it is desirable to emphasize the fact that the incidental and implied powers of congress are required by the federal constitution to be both "necessary and proper." If this power under investigation is deemed only "proper," but not "necessary," in the sense of being unavoidable, then it does not exist. This does not mean that the particula. regulation must be indispensable, but the existence of a general power to choose between this particular regulation and some other, must be indispensable to the expressed power, as a "direct means of executing it." This is not a question of regulating the physical characteristics of mail matter, or postal charges, nor preventing the commission of another crime over which congress has been given authority, by another part of the constitution. This is an effort, by means of the postal system, to regulate, in the thoughts of the mail recipient, certain ideas which are not in themselves criminal. The theory is that these certain ideas tend to induce conduct which in itself is not necessarily either criminal or immoral, but sometimes becomes so, and which conduct, when it is criminal, is so by virtue of state laws, and is not within the power of congress to regulate, because that potential sexual conduct, if crime it be, when it has materialized into actuality, is never in any of its essential parts committed in the mails or on the post office's premises, where congress has jurisdiction over it. Unlike fraud and lottery-gambling, fornication and adultery cannot be committed by mail, and when otherwise committed in a place where congress has authority, it can be adequately punished without invoking the pretense of postal regulation, and when committed within the states is none of the concern of congress.

Our contention is that while congress may in its discretion use "any direct mode of executing" its expressed authority, it has no power to make the end authorized by the constitution a mere means to the accomplishment of an end that is not so authorized. Chief Justice Marshall expressed it thus: "Should congress, under the pretext of executing its powers, pass laws for the accomplishment of objects not entrusted to the government, it would become the painful duty of this tribunal * * * to say that such an act was not the law of the land."[4] Since Judge Marshall wrote the foregoing, numerous acts have been declared unconstitutional for coming within the foregoing

[4]M'Culloch v. Maryland, 17 U. S. 423.

prohibition.[5] That which Judge Marshall in M'Culloch v. Maryland said could not be done by congress is precisely what has been done in the legislation now under consideration. To control the psycho-sexual condition of the addressee of mail matter is not one of the expressed powers of congress; neither is the regulation of the psycho-sexual condition of the addressee of mail "a direct mode of executing" the power to establish post offices and post roads. In fact it bears no possible relation either to their establishment or maintenance. Therefore the act of congress now under consideration is not the law of the land, because the object to be accomplished is not one entrusted to congress. If regulating man's psycho-sexual conditions and the resultant sexual conduct, is an implied power, incident to a regulation of the mails, then it is within the discretion of congress to accomplish that same end by any other adequate means. Among such means would be the limitation of the use of the mails to the unsexed, or providing that all who willingly receive "obscene" mail, or any mail, shall submit to castration or ovariotomy. This would be as legitimate a power, implied from authority to regulate the postal system, as the other method of controlling the psycho-sexual condition of the mail addressee.

MAY CONGRESS USE POSTAL POWER AS A MEANS OF REGULATING TRADE?

Next we inquire if the foregoing conclusion can be avoided by the suggestion that the purpose to be achieved by this postal regulation was not to control the psycho-sexual states of postal patrons, but to withhold the aid of the postal system from a class of business which congress disapproves and desires to discourage, but which, within the states, it has not the expressed power to destroy by direct criminal legislation to that end. This again involves the same question as the last, namely: Can congress, under the pretext of regulating the mails, make that regulation avowedly subservient to objects with which it is not authorized to deal directly? In the exercise of an unavoidable duty to regulate the physical characteristics of mail matter, congress may transmit dry goods and

[5]Hepburn v. Griswold, 8 Wall. 603 (Legal Tender Act); Cummings v. Missouri, 71 U. S. 320 (Disloyal Clergyman); Ex parte Garland, 71 U. S. 333 (Disbarring Rebels); U. S. v. Reese, 92 U. S. 215 (Negro Suffrage); U. S. v. Steffens, 100 U. S. 82 (Trade Mark Cases); U. S. v. Stanley, 109 U. S. 3 (Civil Rights Cases); Pollock v. Farmers' L. & T. Co., 157 U. S. 429 (Income Tax); James v. Bowman, 190 U. S. 127 (Negro Suffrage); U. S. v. Matthews, 146 Fed. Rep. 308 (Com. Agric.); U. S. v. Scott, 148 Fed. Rep. 421 (Labor Union & Interstate Com.); Brooks v. So. Pac. Ry., 148 Fed. Rep. 996 (Emp. Liab. & Interstate Com.).

exclude printed matter. The incidental effect might be that the dry goods business would receive an appreciable impetus and the publishing business a relative set-back. Such an effect would not void the congressional enactment, so long as it is merely incidental to a discrimination based upon factors bearing such relation to the control of mail transportation as to be a direct mode of exercising the power to create post offices and post roads. However, the result is different when the avowed purpose is to make the establishment of the postal system a mere instrumentality for promoting approved trade, and to make the particular postal regulations therefor avowedly subservient to such other purpose, which congress cannot directly promote. If such other purpose of regulating trade, not authorized by any other expressed power, was by congress made the avowed object of postal regulations, the act would be a nullity, under the rule above quoted from M'Culloch v. Maryland. It follows that the law in question cannot be sustained by the process of judicially imputing to congress such an unconstitutional motive of trade regulation. That trade regulation was not the purpose is still further apparent from the fact that the act of congress does not make criminality depend upon a commercial transaction in "obscenity." Such matter sent as a gift, or in a private, sealed and personal letter, is as criminal under the act as if it were part of a commercial transaction.

To sustain this law, on the contention that congress may use the postal system as a means of regulating trade, would vest in congress the most dangerous power ever possessed by any tyrant. Congress might then say: "We wish to encourage the business of Jones. Jones may, and Smith may not, use the mails." Under the guise of regulating the mails congress might encourage the publication of literature favorable to a protective tariff and prohibit the transmission of that favoring tariff reform; it might transmit the books favoring Protestantism and exclude those favoring Catholicism; might deliver gratuitously literature commending its administration of the postal system and the political party in power, and penalize the posting of mail criticising the postal management and the political party in power. To establish such a power, is to make the post office a prize to be contended for by political machines and large industrial enterprises, for the destruction or curtailment of criticism and competition. The obvious answer to all such claims of power is that the sentiments expressed through the mails, or the speculations about the psychologic (moral) tendency of them, bears no possible relation to any possible factor in the establishment or maintenance of post offices and post roads, and therefore cannot be "a direct mode of executing" the power to create them, and is not an implied power of congress, and the law under consideration is therefore unconstitutional.

Furthermore, if it were contended that in excluding from the mails all "obscene" publications, congress had in view any other object than the single one of regulating the psycho-sexual states of postal patrons, the contention would be palpably false, as is readily seen by all the judicial decisions and the tests of "obscenity" prescribed by the courts as guides to jurors in the trial of these cases. It follows that here, by universal confession, we have just such a case as Chief Justice Marshall described, wherein "congress under the pretext of executing its power [did] pass laws for the accomplishment of objects not entrusted to the government," namely: the regulation of the intellectual food and mental states of its adult citizens.

HOW FAR CAN CONGRESS DIFFERENTIATE BETWEEN MAIL-RECIPIENTS?

One more question remains to be considered. May not congress, in the exercise of its implied power to regulate post offices, classify the recipients of mail matter, so as to exclude some from postal privileges which are granted to others? The answer of course is that it may do so, sometimes, but this, like all implied powers, is limited by the necessities which call the implication into existence. For example: Congress can have no power to exclude from postal privileges, on the same terms that it is granted to others, an adult citizen with red hair, simply because of his red hair, who in every respect bears the same relationship to the postal system and the government that do the citizens having different colored hair and who are permitted to use the postal facilities. The obvious reason is that a differential test, based solely on the postal patron's color of hair, bears no possible or conceivable relation to the establishment or maintenance of post offices and post roads. Neither does his psycho-sexual condition, either before or after using the mail, bear any such relation. But a classification of mail patrons according to their differing relations to the postal service, or to the government, would be a different matter. Thus, deprivation of mail service, might be imposed as a penalty upon conviction for any crime in the power of congress to create; or might be imposed to prevent the use of the mails as a material factor in the actual commission of crime over which congress has jurisdiction, and which crime is predicated upon an actual injury to some actual person. (Fraud and Gambling.) It is also quite certain that owing to the different relation of the government to lunatics and minors, congress would have the power to classify them separately from other citizens and make special regulations for them as a class. But all differentiation in the enjoyment of postal privileges, made between different classes of citizens must be based upon tests founded in their essentially different relations to the government itself, and not according to any arbitrary distinction based upon the color of their hair, or their psycho-sexual possibilities.

THE DANGER OF SUCH POWER.

We must not estimate lightly the dangers which are sure to be realized should a decision of the Supreme Court of the United States once affirm the unlimited power of congress to provide a censorship over the opinions, or over the psychologic tendency of opinions which are transmitted through the mails. It is fresh in our memory that when the agitation against the beef packers began, which agitation resulted in recent pure food laws, some packers demanded that the postmasters exclude from the mails all "muckrake" magazines which were criticising their business. Already a demand has been made to exclude from the mails everything tending to encourage the use of alcoholic liquors and tobacco, and in due time, no doubt, in the name of morality we will exclude everything which tends to encourage meat eating. This will come not alone from the scientific and sentimental vegetarians, but will have the endorsement of our sexual tinkers. In England the cry has already gone up from high church dignitaries that meat eating promotes lasciviousness. This warns us of the evil to come from unnecessarily enlarging by implication the congressional power to regulate the mental food of postal patrons.

If, prior to 1837, there had existed an authoritative judicial decision affirming the power over the mails, it would have been made a crime to send abolition literature through the post office. This again warns us that such a power is an insufferable menace to human progress. Its exercise at that time failed only because the great lawyers in the senate were united in the belief that no such power existed. About 1836, it was proposed by the postmaster-general and President Jackson to pass a bill penalizing the use of the mails for the transmission of abolition literature. I believe it was during that debate that Senator John P. King, a member from a slave-holding state, said this: "I prefer the enjoyment of rational liberty at the price of vigilance, and at the risk of occasional trouble by the error of misguided or bad citizens, to that repose which is enjoyed in the sleep of despotism. * * * No man was ever convinced of his error by refusing to hear him." Mr. Calhoun was made chairman of a special committee in the senate, and the subject received careful consideration. He evidently wished for the power to supervise the mails in the interest of slavery; but to his great honor, be it said, he plainly saw and declared that the constitution did not give congress the power, and he would not claim it. The most he could ask was that by the "comity of nations" the United States would restrain postmasters from delivering such matter in the states which had made its circulation illegal. The question was discussed fully in a senate of unequaled ability, and even this limited restraint, proposed by Mr. Calhoun, by a vote of twenty-five to nineteen was held to be impossible under the constitution.[6] In the debate Henry Clay said: "When I saw that the exercise of a most extraordinary and dangerous power had been announced by the head of the postoffice, and that it had been sustained by the President's message, I turned my attention to the subject and inquired whether it was necessary that the general government should under any circumstances exercise such a power, and whether they possessed it. After much reflection, I have come to the conclusion that they could not pass any law interfering with the subject in any shape or form whatever. The evil complained of was the circulation of papers having a certain tendency. The papers, unless circulated, and while in the postoffice, could do no harm. It is the circulation solely—the taking out of the mail and the use to be made of them—that constitutes the evil. Then it is perfectly competent for the state authorities to apply the remedy. The instant that a prohibited paper is handed out, whether to a citizen or sojourner, he is subject to the laws which compel him either to surrender or burn it." Mr. Clay then proceeded to demolish

[6]Con. Globe, 1836, pp. 36, 150, 288, 237, etc.

the claim that congress could legislate to carry into effect the laws of twenty-four different states or sovereignties, and said ironically: "I thought that the only authority of congress to pass laws was in pursuance of the constitution." To the question of Senator Buchanan, of Pennsylvania, to the effect that the postoffice power did give congress the right to regulate what shall be carried in the mails, he replied in the negative, saying: "If such a doctrine prevailed, the government may designate the persons, or parties, or classes who shall have the benefit of the mails, excluding all others." During the debate, one of the safest of senators, "Honest John" Davis, said: "It would be claiming on the part of government a monopoly, an exclusive right either to send such papers as it pleased, or to deny the privilege of sending them through the mail. Once establish the precedent, and where will it lead to? The government may take it into its head to prohibit the transmission of political, religious, or even moral or philosophical publications in which it might fancy there was something offensive, and under this reserved right, contended for in this report, it would be the duty of the government to carry it into effect." Mr. Davis also said he "denied the right of the government to exercise a power indirectly which it could not exercise directly; and if there was no direct power in the constitution, he would like to know how they would get the power of the states— legislative power at most." Mr. Webster expressed himself as "shocked" at the unconstitutional character of the whole proceeding. He said: "Any law distinguishing what shall or shall not go into the mails, founded on the sentiments of the paper, and making the deputy postmaster a judge, I should say is expressly unconstitutional."[7]

CONCLUSIONS.

Congress admittedly has no authority to regulate the sexual conduct of citizens within the states. Much less has it the power, as a means to that end, to control the mere psychosexual conditions of citizens of the states. It has never been claimed nor even imagined or dreamed, that the postal regulation against "obscene" literature is of the remotest consequence AS A MEANS to the maintenance of post roads, or that such regulation is of even the remotest conceivable use to the postal system as such. On the contrary, both judicially and other-

[7]Purity and Liberty, by Wakeman; Congressional Globe, 1836, pp. 36, 150, 288, 233, etc.; Von Holst's Life of Calhoun, p. 133.

wise, it has been stated, again and again, that the only purpose of that regulation was to control the psycho-sexual states of postal patrons, as a means of restraining their sexual activities. But this is an end the accomplishment of which is not entrusted to the congress of the United States. Confessedly then, we have here a case where congress, under the pretext of executing its powers to establish post offices and post roads, has passed a law for the accomplishment of objects not entrusted to the United States government, and this is exactly what Chief Justice Marshall said could not become the law of the land.[8] It can make no possible difference to the postal system as such whatever may be the psychologic effect of the opinions transmitted. Some physical factor of the postal system must be affected, making the postal system different from what it otherwise would be, or else the regulation is not an exercise of the power to establish and maintain it.

Neither can the exercise of the present power be justified as an incident to the power to regulate interstate commerce, because the censorship is not limited thereto. It includes Intrastate transmission as well as that of private letters, or gifts which are not at all matters of commerce either Inter-state or otherwise.[9]

For these reasons the power here under discussion is not vested in Congress at all, and the present laws creating a postal censorship over mail matter are unconstitutional.

[8]M'Culloch v. Maryland, 17 U. S. 438.
[9]Howard vs. Ill. Cent. R. R., 28 Supt. Ct. Rep. 141.

CHAPTER VIII.

CONCERNING THE MEANING OF "FREEDOM OF THE PRESS."*

The postal laws against "obscene" literature are void under the constitutional prohibition against the abridgment of freedom of speech and of the press. Likewise all similar State legislation is void under State Constitutions.

Syllabus of the argument: *This constitutional guarantee of freedom of the press is violated whenever there is an artificial legislative destruction or abridgment of the greatest liberty consistent with an equality of liberty, in the use of the printed page as a means of disseminating ideas of conflicting tendency. The use of printing is but an extended form of speech. Freedom of speech and press is abridged whenever natural opportunity is in any respect denied or its exercise punished, merely as such; that is, in the absence of actual injury, or when by legislative enactment there is created an artificial inequality of opportunity, by a discrimination according to the subject matter discussed, or a discrimination as between different tendencies in the different treatment of the same subject matter, or according to differences of literary style in expressing the same thought. All this is now accomplished under obscenity laws as at present administered, and therefore our laws upon the subject are unconstitutional.*

This contention involves the establishment of a new definition of "freedom of the press" based upon the viewpoint that the framers of the constitution intended by that clause to enlarge the intellectual liberty of the citizen beyond what it had theretofore been under the English system. Some State courts have erroneously assumed that the only purpose was to exchange a censorship before publication for criminal punishment after publication, without the least enlargement of the right to publish with impunity so long as no one is injured. The contention will be that the constitution changed liberty of the press by permission, to Liberty as a right because thus only

* Republished from *The Central Law Journal.*

can all citizens be protected in their proper opportunity to hear and read all that others have to offer, and without which freedom unrestricted there is no intellectual liberty at all as a matter of right.

Before proceeding with the more critical study of the meaning of "freedom of the press," it is well that we should point out, and so far as possible bar, the principal avenues of error, which have heretofore misled our courts.

THE DANGER OF PRECEDENTS.

Over a century ago Sargeant Hill cynically wrote this: "When judges are about to do an unjust act they seek for a precedent in order to justify their conduct by the faults of others." In matters of government, at least during the last few centuries, the evolution has been from despotism to liberty. It follows from this that the danger and iniquity of blindly following precedents is nowhere so great as in the attempts to define the limits of constitutional liberty by reverting to the ancient misconceptions of it, because the older precedents were all made by tyrants, or those not far evolved from their attitude of mind. As we evolve to a more refined sense of justice, and rational conception of liberty, the old precedents must be constantly overruled. It is this which marks the progress of our race in its evolution to a truer and final social liberty.

CRITICAL STUDY OF FUNDAMENTALS.

The utility of a brief historical review of the struggle for "freedom of the press" lies partly in this, that it shows how reluctant have been those in power to admit such freedom in practice, though seldom denying it in principle, and how shifty the powers of despotism have been in yielding up one form of repression as a concession to intellectual liberty, and at the same time creating a new method for effectually accomplishing the same impairment of intellectual opportunity. Such a study will also show how uniformly the moral sentimentalism of those in authority has prompted them to reinvent the same phrases in defence of each renewed attack upon freedom.

In order to understand the underlying impetus of all this, it must be remembered that when this problem first arose it was in every essence a religious one, and arose where there was a union of church and State. Those who governed

143

claimed to do so by divine right, and in their official acts represented the Deity. The King could do no wrong, and to criticize him or his acts was an insult to the Almighty for whom he acted, just as much as though legalized religion had been blasphemed. From the viewpoint of such a church-state it was inevitable that those in authority should affirm that: "To say that religion is a cheat is to dissolve all those obligations whereby civil societies are preserved; and Christianity being parcel of the laws of England, therefore to reproach the Christian is to speak in subversion of the law."[1] "It was the doctrine of Coke [1551-1632] and even so late as Holt, C. J. [1689-1710] and Treby [1692-1701] that any law, that is, any statute, made against any point of the Christian religion, or what they thought was the Christian religion, was void."[2]

Of course under the influence of such authority it necessarily followed that no one had any right to think or speak, upon matters of religion, rulers, or governments, who had not been thereunto authorized by those who were recognized as possessing some divine authority to give or withhold such permission. But religion and government, according to the views then prevailing, encompassed everything and so it followed inevitably that "Free speech was a species of gift by the Sovereign to the people."

Although we have all abandoned the original premises from which was drawn the conclusion that freedom of speech was a gift by the sovereign, yet most American judges seem to read the precedent so blindly that they adhere to the dogma that "freedom of the press" means a liberty by permission and not a natural right guaranteed by the constitution. This is self-evident from almost every judicial utterance upon the subject and in spite of the self-evident fact that our constitution-makers intended to perpetuate a different rule. This error, like many of the others, comes from the uncritical adoption of precedents and the consequent failure to realize that our very different theory of government has overturned the foundation which alone justified the older authorities, and failing to realize this change of base, our courts also fail to see the necessity for repudiating the precedents which had no other foundation.

THE TYRANTS "LOVE" OF LIBERTY.

Another matter to be guarded against is the false pretense

[1] Reg. v. Taylor, Ventris 293. The later view in England seems different. See 41 Fortnightly Review, 305.
[2] Patterson's Liberty of the Press, p. 67, citing 10 st. Tr. 75.

of a love of liberty which tyrants have always expressed, even in the very act of enforcing its destruction. Thus Lord Eskine tells us: "The public welfare was the burden of the preambles to the licensing acts; the most tyrannical laws in the most absolute governments speak a kind parental language to the abject wretches, who groan under the crushing and humiliating weights."[3] In France, October, 1803, an act was passed by which all booksellers were prohibited from vending any book without having submitted it to the censors, "and as if to add insult to injury the measure was introduced as one 'to secure the liberty of the press.'" * * * Napoleon the First did not consider liberty of the press as possible among Frenchmen, "who have a lively imagination," as it is in England where "the people being brutal are less likely to be influenced by writings, and are more easily kept in check by the throne and the aristocracy."[4]

In America we find a similar practice. Solemn judicial opinions sometimes reek with pharisaical eulogies of the judicial love of liberty, as a prelude to the arbitrary punishment of a man for contempt, without trial by jury or an opportunity to prove truth and justifiable motive before an impartial tribunal, and all because he had exercised his supposed right to express freely his opinion of a public servant, the court. Here is a sample:

"It is a well known fact, that the bench and the bar have been, in this and all other countries where the law has existed, as a distinct profession, the ablest and most zealous advocates of the liberal institutions, the freedom of conscience, and the liberty of the press; and none have guarded more watchfully the encroachments of power on the one hand, or deprecated more earnestly tendencies to lawless anarchy and licentiousness on the other. *The freedom of the press, therefore, has nothing to fear from the bench in this State.* No attempt has ever been made, and we may venture to say never will be, to interfere with its legitimate province, on the part of the judiciary, by the exercise of the power to punish contempts.

"The object of the clause in the Bill of Rights above quoted is known to every well informed man. Although the press is now almost as free in England as it is in this country, yet the time was in bygone ages when the ministers of the

[3]Vol. 1, p. 48, Edition of 1810.
[4]Vol. 15, Solicitors Journal & Reporter, 61 & 70.

crown possessed the power to lay their hand upon it, and hush its voice, when they deemed it necessary to subserve political purposes. A similar clause has been inserted in all the American constitutions, to guard the press against the trammels of political power, and secure to the whole people a full and free discussion of political affairs."[5]

This eulogy was followed by abridging freedom of the press through an affirmance of an arbitrary punishment for contempt. It is very dangerous to accept a tyrant's definition of liberty because he has the audacity to indulge in an extravagant praise of it.

THE DANGER OF PARTISAN DEFINITIONS.

Another misleading guide for the ascertainment of what is meant by "freedom of the press," is the definition of it framed by partisan defenders of it. These definitions nearly all have the defect that they generalize freedom to consist only in the absence of that particular abridgment of it which is then being specifically attacked. These defective generalizations are usually the combined product of defective intellectual vision and the dictates of expediency. It always seems as though those who have felt themselves called upon to defend against some particular abridgment of freedom, have been so overwhelmed by its importance that they have failed to define or defend freedom in general, possibly also influenced by the fear of including too much and thus overtaxing the moral courage of the judge or legislator.

A recent illustration of this is furnished by Mr. Gompers of the American Federation of Labor. He conceives himself to be making a great fight for freedom of speech and is fond of using the phrase as a shibboleth, but hastens into the public prints to explain that he neither contemplates nor desires such a thing as general "freedom of speech." He wants only freedom to advocate the boycott as against the restriction thereof by injunction. He deplores the havoc which would come from a general "Freedom of speech and the press." Just at the time when I am writing this, a large section of the American press is working itself into a white-heat of opposition to the indictment of the publishers of the *New York World* for a "libel on the government of the United States," consisting in that paper's attempt to discredit the dealings of the government in the matter of the Panama Canal. Yet not one of these same papers would likely dream of defending

[5]State vs. Morrill, 16 Ark., 402-403 (1855).

146

a like freedom for anarchists to discredit the government in the hope of ultimately securing its peaceable abolition. There is no doubt, either but that practically all these same newspapers can be relied upon to advocate the suppression of all searching and enlightening sex-discussion. So also I know an anarchist who, probably from fear of being wrongly suspected of believing in the forcible abolition of government, hastens to explain that though he esteems all government a nuisance he still thinks it proper for government to suppress even the fruitless advocacy of crime. Again, I know some radical and ardent sex-reformers who think it an outrage that plain spoken and searching sex-discussion is punishable, but see no objection to the suppression of an equally plain spoken and searching discussion by some of the more radical socialists and anarchists. So likewise we can find Protestants who desire unlimited liberty for themselves to criticise the religious tenets of their Catholic neighbors, and Catholics who desire to use a similar liberty against the theology of their Protestant neighbor, but both hasten to unite for the punishment of the atheist who would deride the tenets of both. Yet each and all of these will seriously tell you how ardently they love "freedom of speech," but they will always so define that freedom as to leave in full force the power to suppress those opinions of which they disapprove.

Let me illustrate still further. One reading a discussion of the licensing acts might easily conclude that freedom of the press meant only the absence of a licensor, all other forms of abridging free utterance being compatible with freedom. Another reading a definition of freedom of the press as these are sometimes formulated in relation to personal libel, would find himself in a rather hopeless situation if he should seek to apply that definition to a case where the abstract discussion of sex-ethics was involved, and the claim was made that it was obscene because it tended to deprave the morals. Likewise there might be difficulty in using a definition of freedom framed in relation to treason and seek to apply it to the case of a non-resistant anarchist. Errors of this sort have been frequently made in the misdirected effort to follow precedent, and have usually resulted in the definition of unabridgable freedom of speech so as to. permit abridgment.

Evidently the difficulty with most of these advocates of

freedom is that they have no conception of freedom in general, and erroneously conclude that everybody is enjoying the greatest possible freedom when they feel themselves unrestricted, though this seeming liberty for themselves may be wholly due to the fact that they are utterly devoid of anything like a serious, carefully reasoned opinion upon any subject whatever. If they had ever done any of the intellectual work which that presupposes, they would probably know something of the ease with which differences of opinion may arise upon every possible question and of the importance of maintaining the other fellow's right to disagree.

WHAT IS "INTERPRETATION"?

We are now to undertake a general discussion as to the interpretation of the constitutional phrase "Congress shall make no law abridging freedom of speech or of the press," and we must first endeavor to get a clear idea of what we mean by "interpretation." Manifestly "interpretation" does not mean that we may inject words, phrases, or exceptions, into the constitutional phraseology. On the contrary, by "interpretation" we can only mean that we are to arrive at the meaning of the constitution by deductions made exclusively from the words actually used therein, unless these are ambiguous. If there is any ambiguity, in the significance of the words which guarantee our freedom of utterance and the right to hear, then these words may be interpreted in the light of the historical controversy which supposedly was settled by the constitutional clause in question. On the other hand, if the words themselves do not of necessity involve any ambiguity, then the historical conditions at the time of their adoption can be of no consequence to us in the matter of determining their meaning, because if the meaning is plain the historical facts become immaterial and useless. If it can be done the significance of the constitutional phraseology must be determined wholly and exclusively by deductions made from the words themselves.

The words "speech" and "press" certainly are not ambiguous. They cover every idea expressed vocally or presented on a printed page. Although it is manifestly absurd, yet some courts in effect have said that speech is not speech, whether expressed orally or on the printed page, unless it can be fairly classed as serious and ladylike discussion. Others advise us that speech is not speech unless it was uttered "not intending to mislead but seeking to enlighten," and even then it is not speech at all if the other fellow happens to consider it to be "blasphemous, immoral or seditious"; some add "obscene, indecent, filthy, or disgusting." So in a variety of ways courts, under the false pretense of "construing" them, have amended our constitutional guarantees, of freedom of speech and of the press, so as to inject into them exception which the judges think ought to be there but which the framers of our constitutions neglected to insert.

When we say that speech isn't speech except when used in serious and lady-like discussion, such as does not irritate us, then we are indulging in sentimental nonsense, and I shall not be in the least inclined to change the epithet because in effect this has been often done by "learned" judges, and "distinguished" courts. I should be equally certain that the word "freedom," when used in connection with "speech and press," was entirely free of ambiguity, were it not for the extraordinary meanings assigned to it by the courts, under the pretense of construing "freedom." It appears to me that here the judges instead of interpreting the word "freedom" have interpolated into the constitution significations which are not at all implied in any of the words therein used. It seems to me that had our courts used common sense, instead of blindly following precedents established by those who never believed in free speech, and instead of adopting definitions of freedom framed by tyrants whose conception of it was repudiated by the American revolution, no embarrassing questions would ever have been raised.

If the constitution had said that "Congress shall make no law abridging man's freedom to breathe," no one would have any doubt as to what was meant and every one would instantly say that of course it precluded Congress from passing any law which should prohibit breathing contrary to the mandate of a licensor, before trial and conviction, and that it would equally preclude the passage or enforcement of any law which would punish breathing *merely as such* upon conviction after the fact. No sane man could be found who would say that such a guarantee, to breathe without any statutory abridgment, only precluded the appointment of Commissioners who should determine arbitrarily what persons might be licensed to breathe and who should not be so licensed, and that it would still permit Congress to penalize all those who do not breathe in the speci-

149

ally prescribed manner, even though such criminal breathing had not injured anyone, nor could possibly do so according to any of the known laws of our physical universe, by which I include the actual knowledge of our bacteriologists as to the transmission of infectious diseases.

There is not the slightest reason to be given why "freedom" in relation to speech and press should be differently interpreted. The only explanation for having interpreted it differently is that the people generally, and judges and others in authority in particular, believe in freedom to breathe but, emotionally at least, disbelieve in freedom of speech and of the press, and therefore they read into the constitution meanings and exceptions which are not represented there by a single syllable or word, and which are therefore interpolated to accomplish a Judicial amendment of the constitution, under the false pretense of "construing" it, only because the judges think, *or rather feel,* that the constitution *ought* not to guarantee freedom of speech and of the press in those matters which stimulate their emotional aversion, and so they dogmatically assert that "freedom" of utterance is not guaranteed, in the same sense in which we have spoken of freedom to breathe.

The ordinary and plain meaning of the word "freedom" should readily have solved all problems, if there ever really were any such, which were discoverable by reason uninfluenced by hysterical emotions. In common parlance, we all understand that a man is legally free to do an act whenever he may perform that act with impunity so far as the law is concerned. Thus no one would claim that another was legally free to commit larceny, so long as larceny involved liability of subsequent criminal punishment. No one would say that the law leaves a man free to commit murder, so long as there is a law punishing murder. Likewise no man *who is depending purely upon the phraseology of the constitution* will ever say that the laws leave speech and press free, so long as there is any law which prescribes a penalty for the mere utterance of any one's sentiments, merely as such utterance and independent of any actually accomplished injury to another.

THE ABUSE OF FREEDOM.

On the other hand, it would seem equally certain, to the ordinary understanding, that there exists no legal abridgment of a man's freedom to speak or write if he is punishable for the abuse of that freedom, provided we mean only by "abuse" an actual and not a mere constructive abuse: that is, provided he is punished only for an actual and not a constructive injury, resulting from his utterance. Manifestly in such a case he is not punished for the speech *as such*, but he is punished for an actual ascertained resultant injury to some one not a voluntary adult participant in the act.

His utterance in that case may be evidence of his complicity in, or contribution to that actual injury, and punishment for an actual resultant injury is not in the least an abridgment of the right to speak with impunity, since manifestly it is not a punishment for mere speaking *as such,* the essence of criminality—the criteria of guilt—being something other than the utterance of his sentiments. Manifestly, in this view, which is but the natural import of the words "freedom of speech and of press," the expression can only mean that a man shall have the right to utter any sentiment that he may please to utter and do so with impunity, *so long* as the mere utterance of his sentiments is the only factor in the case. It does not exempt him from punishment for murder, arson or other *actual and resultant injury,* but leaves it where he may be punished for his contribution toward and participation in bringing about these injuries. His utterances may be evidence tending to show his responsibility for the *actual injury* which is penalized, but the penalty attaches on account of that injury, and can never be predicated merely upon the sentiments uttered without, to that extent, abridging our freedom to utter. When the statute does this the constitutional right is violated.

ON THE MEANING OF WORDS.

Both the words "speech" and "press," as used in our constitutions, are limitations upon the word "freedom" as therein used. The purpose of this clause is to preclude the legislative abridgment, not of all liberty, but of liberty only in relation to two subjects, to wit: "speech" and "press." It is manifest therefore that the same word "freedom" cannot change its meaning according to whether the utterance is oral or printed. In other words, "freedom" must mean the same thing whether it relates to "speech" or "press." In the very nature of things "freedom of speech" cannot mean mere absence of a censor to whom an idea must be submitted before utterance, because the very act of submitting the idea to a censor implies its utterance. Furthermore, there never was a time when a censor assumed to pass upon oral speech, prior to its utterance. Unpopular oral speeches were punished only after utterance. The whole controversy over "freedom of speech" was a demand that speakers might be free from such subsequent punishment for those of their utterances which in fact had not actually injured anyone, and it was that controversy which the framers of our constitutions intended to decide for all time, by guaranteeing the right to speak one's sentiments upon any subject whatever, and with absolute impunity so long as no one was actually injured except by his voluntary and undeceived consent, as when the person is convinced to the changing of his opinion about some abstract doctrine of morals or theology the acceptance of which his neighbors might deem a deterioration, and the new convert esteem as a moral and intellectual advance. If, as I believe, this is the inevitable interpretation of "freedom" in relation to "speech," and the meaning of "freedom" in relation to "press" must be the same, then we are irresistibly forced to the conclusion that our courts have been wrong in asserting that "freedom" in relation to the press means only the absence of a censorship prior to publication, without enlarging those intellectual liberties which are beyond the reach of legislative abridgment.

The personal and psychologic cause of this judicial destruction of constitutional right is to be discovered in our defective human nature which almost unavoidably develops in judges, by reason of the very character of the function which they habitually perform, a growing lust for power, so strong that very, very few ever acquire sufficiently critical intellects to check it, so that they can officially acknowledge the right of an ordinary citizen at the bar of justice to damage the judge's vanity, or stimulate his emotions of aversion. Thus our judges, (especially through contempt proceedings and vague penal statutes, made certain by judicial legislation) have unconsciously demanded and secured for themselves the adulation usually given only to an inerrant pope or king, and have almost reduced the judicial bench to a sacrificial altar, the members of the bar to a kind of lesser priesthood, whose duty it is at least by silent acquiescence to keep the laity in ignorance of judicial incompetence and iniquity, and in an attitude of suppliant humility.

Shall this condition be accentuated and become definitely fixed by a continuing affirmance of the judicial destruction of our freedom of speech and of the press? Will the process of judically amending our constitutions by the interpolation of limitations upon freedom of press stop, or shall we have an ever increasing abridgment of such liberty? These are the serious questions which confront us.

When we come to make a historical study of the meaning of "freedom of the press" we will at once discover that the personal elements disappear, to be replaced by humanistic considerations. Now it is not merely a question of imprisonment or fines, but a question of intellectual opportunity, not only a question of the opportunity to speak, but of the more important opportunity of the whole public to hear and to read whatever they may choose when all are free to offer. Now it ceases to be a matter of the personal liberty of the speaker or writer, and must be viewed as a matter of racial intellectual development, by keeping open all the avenues for the greatest possible interchange of ideas. In this aspect the most important feature of the whole controversy simmers down to this proposition, namely: that every idea, no matter how unpopular shall, so far as the law is concerned, have the same opportunity as every other idea, no matter how popular, to secure the public favor. Of course only those ideas which were unpopular with the ruling classes were ever suppressed. The essence of the demand for free speech was that this discrimination should cease. In other words every inequality of intellectual opportunity, due to legislative enactment, was and is unwarranted abridgment of our natural liberty, when not required by the necessity for the preservation of another's right to be protected against actual material injury.

The contention stated at the head of this chapter will be amplified in statement, and will receive conclusive historical justification, when we come to the chapter on the scientific interpretation of freedom of speech. Before proceeding therewith we must, however, expose the mind-befogging judicial dogmatism upon this subject.

CHAPTER IX.

THE JUDICIAL DESTRUCTION OF FREEDOM OF THE PRESS.*

It seems to me that before proceeding to the direct task of interpreting "freedom of the press," it is desirable that we have some general discussion as to the judicial destruction of liberty of the press, and to indicate how this has been accomplished. By such a discussion we can best get a clear understanding as to the issue between the two conflicting viewpoints from which our task can be approached.

Some words and phrases become so associated with emotions of approval that we instantly avow them as a part of our creedal declaration of faith, though very often we have no very real belief in nor very definite conception of that which the words symbolize. This is often illustrated in religion, where men give avowed support to creeds, almost every detail of which they will repudiate under a searching cross-examination. So likewise is it with our constitutionally guaranteed "freedom of the press." As a general proposition every one professes belief in it and yet in the concrete apparently nobody upholds it, except for self, and almost everybody can be relied upon to indorse some abridgment of freedom of the press whenever others wish to use that freedom to express anything radically different from their own thoughts, especially if "moral" sentimentalism is involved. Thus it comes that men, trying to frame definitions of freedom, practically always leave a loop hole for at least their own pet tyranny and censorship over opinion.

As a result of this, all but universal, emotional disapproval of unlimited intellectual liberty, it has come to pass that our courts, in their efforts to make effective the judges' *disbelief* in freedom of the press though construing our constitutional guarantee of it, have by their authoritative dogmas amended our constitutions with the judicial interpolation of exceptions

*Republished from *The Albany Law Journal* and *Government*.

never even vaguely hinted at in our fundamental laws. The unintelligent mob, engrossed with its necessary sordid self-seeking, without even a whispered protest has acquiesced in these successive encroachments upon the liberty of the press, until to-day there is not a state in the union whose laws do not punish the mere psychologic crime of expressing unpopular ideas, even though no one is shown to have been hurt as the result. The remarkable thing is that the constitutionality of those laws is seldom questioned, and when the paper guarantee of liberty of the press is invoked, the courts have promptly and almost uniformly amended the constitutional guarantees of freedom of speech and press by dogmatically writing into them new exceptions and limitations, which are not represented by a single word in the constitution itself, but which find abundant justification in ancient precedents coming from courts whose judges were tyrants, or the minions of tyrants, or who, through woefully limited intellectual vision, sought to define liberty by generalizing a single fact, and thus made freedom mean only the absence of the one particular abridgment of it, which alone was then within contemplation, and occupied a place so near as to obscure the more remote but larger possibilities for the tyrannous invasion of liberty.

When moral sentimentalizing becomes focused about one or a few subjects, by being widely advertised by a fanatical and well organized band of zealots which lends its aid, the courts, with the concurrence of legislatures and in spite of constitutions, exercise a power to amend our charter of liberties and to enforce the abridgment of the freedom of the press. To this end it is only necessary to neglect one simple rule of constitutional construction. This done and under the guise of interpretation, meanings and exceptions, which are not expressed therein by a single word or syllable, will be, as they have been, dogmatically read into the constitutional phraseology, instead of developing the actual and literal signification of the words really used. English precedents, where only discretion tempers tyranny, can be easily misapplied to furnish a seeming justification for a judicial "interpretation" such as effectively accomplishes the judicial amendment of our constitutional guarantee for a free press. Many circumstances have combined to induce State courts, unconsciously, to interpolate exceptions into the free-press clause of State constitutions, and so precedents have already been made, which if

155

followed to their logical conclusion would vest all American legislative bodies with power to suppress every opinion upon every subject, should it choose to do so.

Too often legislators and judges have been afflicted with political myopia and so have seen only what seemed to them the beneficent immediate effect of their official destruction of the constitutionally guaranteed natural liberty of the citizen, and because of this shortsightedness have failed to see how every such additional liberty-invading precedent is related to the ultimate destruction of liberty and the unavoidable reaction through revolution by violence. Every invasive act, acquiring even a seeming acquiescence, contributes to the momentum by which we are increasingly inspiring thoughtful men with a contempt for the impotency of constitutional protection, and for governments, and simultaneously every such submission, even to a *popular* tyranny, inspires ambitious zealots with new hope for the realization of their lust for power. Thus by gradual stages we all thoughtlessly contribute to the development of that tyranny which in the end can be and is overthrown only by a violent revolution.

THE CONTEMPT FOR CONSTITUTIONS.

It is by such processes, for which the courts are largely responsible, that all constitutions have in the end come to be held in contempt, by thoughtful liberty-loving men as well as by the narrow-minded with autocratic ambitions. A few illustrations will suffice. "Ce n'est qu'en Angleterre, ou l'on pourroit faire ni avoir des livres sur des constitutions," said one of the most enlightened English ambassadors in Europe; and it is but a very few years since a French gentleman answered a foreigner who inquired for the best book upon the constitution of France, "Monsieur, c'est l'Almanach Royal."[1]

Likewise, in England, the wise and calm Herbert Spencer said: "Paper constitutions raise smiles on the faces of those who have observed their results," and in America General Trumbull is reported as having opined that, "The constitution has hardly any existence in this country except as rhetoric."

This sort of contempt for constitutional guarantees is based upon a real love of constitutional liberty and despair at finding its guarantee explained away by those whose contempt for the constitution is based upon a contempt for liberty itself—a lust for the power of an autocrat. Of that we also have an abund-

[1] John Adams in A Defence of the Constitutions of Government of the U. S.

156

ance in the United States. Years ago when the constitutionality of some anti-Morman legislation was under consideration, United States Senator Cullom is reported to have said that "in the United States there is no constitution but public opinion." Later, Congressman Timothy Sullivan inspired a nation with mirth, but not with resentment, under the following circumstances: He was urging President Cleveland to sign a bill which had passed the Congress, and the President objected because he believed it unconstitutional. Our earnest statesman broke in with this plea, "What's the constitution as between friends?" And so it is with our professional reformers. We can almost hear them say: "What's the constitution when our moral sentimentalism is involved?" We also find President Roosevelt and his Secretary of State boldly encouraging contempt for the constitution by publicly urging its judicial amendment. President Roosevelt in his Harrisburg speech said: "We need through executive action, through legislation, and *through judicial interpretation and construction to increase the power of the Federal Government.* If we fail *thus to increase it* we show our impotence." Again, read the foregoing in the light of Mr. Root's utterance. "The distinguished Secretary of State declared that it was useless for the advocates of State rights to inveigh against *the extension* of national authority, * * * and *that constructions of the constitution would be found to vest the power* in the national government." Here, then, we have the distinct admission by the highest officers of our nation that they desire to exercise a power which according to their own view the constitution does not confer, and that in spite of their official oath to uphold the constitution as it is they proposed to amend it, not by the method therein prescribed, but in contemptuous disregard of the constitution itself by "executive action, through legislation and judicial interpretation and construction" to accomplish a perjured usurpation of power and corresponding destruction of constitutional liberty.

When lust for power becomes so lawless as openly and deliberately to justify usurpation and official perjury, and when such conduct does not in the least impair the aspiring autocrat's popularity, our love and understanding of liberty has come to a very low ebb. Will our courts endorse such processes as applied to freedom of the press?

The purpose of this essay is primarily to protest against the judicial amendment of constitutional guarantee of liberty, and specially that liberty which underlies all others, the liberty to speak and to read. Only by way of contrast will we be concerned with the meaning of freedom of the press as we find it abridged in actual practice. Here it is intended only to exhibit the conflicting view-points, which will be very important in answering the question, What ought to be the practical effect and judicial significance of our constitutional guarantees of freedom of the press? With slight variations all our guarantees upon this subject are typified by these words of our federal constitution. "Congress shall make no law * * * abridging the freedom of speech or of the press." How, if at all, does this provision operate as a limitation upon the congressional power to regulate the mails, commerce, etc., etc.?

CONFLICTING VIEW-POINTS.

As the discussion progresses, it is important to keep in mind several conflicting view-points. It seems to me that, because of having neglected to consider these diversities of viewpoint, courts have been led strangely and far astray in their alleged "interpretations" of "freedom of the press." Is this language of the constitution to be interpreted as having been intended to protect or enlarge only the commercial opportunity of printing-press owners, or is it from the view-point of a protected and enlarged intellectual liberty that we are to proceed to the task of interpretation? Was it only to protect the personal privilege of the speaker or printer to utter his sentiments to himself in solitude, or are we to view the constitutional guarantee also from the view-point of protecting all the rest of humanity in an opportunity to hear and to read, if they choose, anything that anyone else would be willing to communicate if permitted?

Was it achievement of the first, or an enlargement of intellectual liberty, and the abolition of the mere psychologic crime of an unfruitful "immoral" thinking which was to be accomplished? Can it be that the only object of the framers of our constitution was the mere abolition of a censorship before publication, in favor of a censorship after publication, without any actual enlargement of intellectual liberty? Such censorship prior to publication had been abolished in England prior to the American revolution. Did the makers of our constitution believe the people before that revolution enjoyed adequate liberty of the press, or was it the intention by our constitutional guaranty to insure an enlargement of the liberty of the press above that which had been enjoyed?

Merely to ask these questions would seem to answer them and yet, strange to say, when the question of the freedom of the press has come up for judicial interpretation, courts have usually evaded the obvious answer, and have amended the constitution by "interpretations" which interpolate, and which leave our freedom just where it was in England before the revolution.

In order to interpret "freedom of the press" correctly, it seems to me that we must approach our problem in the light of the pre-revolutionary controversy over the question of intellectual liberty, which controversy our constitution-makers intended to settle for all time. Under the English system there was no controlling limitation upon the parliamentary power to abridge the liberty of the press, and such freedom was enjoyed only, according to parliamentary discretion, as *a privilege exercised by permission,* and not as a constitutionally protected right which could be exercised with impunity in spite of parliamentary enactments to the contrary. Under such a system as the English, liberty of the press could mean only such remnant of liberty as remained after parliamentary abridgment. Some American courts, erringly accepting the English judicial precedents, have defined our constitutional *freedom-as-a-right* to mean only what freedom had been declared by English courts to be under their different system, wherein was defined only the liberty which was a matter of permission by royal or parliamentary munificence. This suggests an issue as to whether we shall continue to misinterpret our *unabridgable* constitutional "freedom of the press" to mean only the same thing as that which, prior to the revolution, the English courts had described as their *abridgable* remnant of an unguaranteed freedom by permission? Or, on the other hand, must we assume that our constitution makers intended to enlarge our intellectual liberty in accord with views of "freedom of the press" entertained by those who were opposing the English (judicial) conception? If an *unabridged* intellectual liberty was *not* intended, then there was no need of any mention of the subject in our constitutions. According to the first view it has been held that, notwithstanding our constitutions, freedom of the press may be abridged by legislation just as much as it was, or can be, by the English parliament, the only difference being as to method, the constitution prohibiting only censorship prior to publication, but, as to subject-matter, having an equal power with the English parliament to suppress and punish after publication. Under this "interpretation," quite generally accepted in America, the constitution only changed the manner of censorship, somewhat for the worse, without protecting or guaranteeing any enlarged intellectual opportunity. According to the other view-point the constitution was designed to protect, beyond all possibility of abridgment, an enlarged intellectual opportunity, not by changing the manner of censoring, or the time of application of censorial methods, but by the destruction of all censorship by prohibiting forever any punishment of any sort, for any mere intellectual or psychological crime of any nature whatever, until it had ceased to be merely a psychological crime, by having become an actually realized material and proved injury to some actual living being, or the imminent menace of such injury, determined by the known laws of the physical universe, as applied to some overt act in consummation and execution of an expressed desire to inflict such injury. In such event no speech, merely as such, is punishable, and no crime can be predicated upon uncertain speculation about mere psychologic tendencies. The crime attaches to an actual injury *actually* attempted or inflicted. The speech is only the evidence of intent, not the essence of the offence. This view still awaits its first adequate presentation for judicial adoption in America.

There is another reason why the judicial statements of English courts, as to the meaning of freedom of the press, are of no possible value as precedents in the interpretation of our constitutional prohibition against the abridgment of freedom of the press. The reason will be manifest upon a moment's reflection. In England there are no restrictions upon the power of parliament to prevent its abridgment of the freedom of the press. It follows that declarations of English courts, therefore, are not the judicial interpretation of any constitutional clause or right, nor the declaration of any general principle which could control the validity of such laws either in England or America. On the contrary, there being no fundamental and binding restriction on parliament, or the English courts, against abridging freedom of the press, English judicial statements as to the meaning of such freedom as exists in England could not be a declaration of legal principle as to the constitutional limits of such liberty in the United States, but on the contrary English authorities state only a fact of observation, namely that under English conditions, freedom of the press means only such limited freedom as remains after its abridgment, in the parliamentary exercise of an unrestricted power to abridge. In other words, every judicial or polemical utterance coming from English sources is the declaration of what they mean by freedom of the press when such liberty is *liberty by permission* of parliament, and in the nature of things this can furnish no guide as to what is meant by American constitutions which were specifically designed to abolish English conditions upon the subject and which seek to establish *liberty of the press as a right* in spite of all legislative abridgments. American courts, by neglecting this distinction, have erringly followed English statements of their mere facts of practice, and because we mistook them for declarations of constitutional principles, and used them as guides in constitutional construction, our courts have almost reduced our liberty of press from liberty-as-a-right to mere liberty as a matter of permission, which is not liberty at all.

To accomplish the destruction of freedom of speech and of the press in America our courts dogmatically assert that the purpose of the constitution was, not to enlarge the intellectual liberty of the citizen, but simply to replace a censorship before printing to a criminal prosecution for having printed or published. This has been seemingly justified by the erroneous adoption of English precedents as a means of constitutional interpretation. Of course the judicial way of stating this proposition adroitly veils that direct avowal whose blunt absurdity my form of statement exposes. Here is the judicial formula: "The main purpose of such constitutional provisions is 'to prevent all such *previous restraints* upon publications as had been practiced by other governments' and they do not prevent the subsequent punishment of such as may be deemed contrary to public welfare."[2] There you have it! By judicial amendment our constitutional freedom of speech and of the press has been wholly explained away, and legislatures and courts now have the right to punish after utterance any opinion which "may be deemed against the public welfare," just as fully as such opinions may be punished in Russia or Turkey. Is this really freedom of speech and of press? The Supreme Court of the United States, the final arbiter and alleged "guardian" of our constitutional liberty, in the last above quoted sentence has said that the words "Congress shall make no law abridging the freedom of speech or of the press," means that within its

[2] Patterson v. People, 27 Sup. Ct. Rep. 556-558.

geographical jurisdiction the courts must enforce any law which congress chooses to make to punish the verbal utterance of any and every thought, by the congress "deemed contrary to public welfare."

The expression of opinions approved by those in power had never been abridged. Those who were waging the battle for intellectual liberty and suffered for having exercised freedom of speech and of press, thought by our constitution they had finally secured protection for the expression of those unpopular opinions the promulgation of which had theretofore been punished because "deemed against the public welfare"—that is, because unpopular. And now comes our Supreme Court and restores the pre-revolutionary tyranny over ideas, by saying in substance that "freedom of speech and of the press" means the right to be punished for speaking and publishing ideas which are deemed against the public welfare, because unpopular. Those who have thought a constitutionally guaranteed freedom to speak means freedom to speak with impunity, so long as no one is actually injured thereby, will hereafter understand that, as in Russia, our liberty is but a liberty by permission, to be punished whenever exercised without that permission of our masters, who have limitless power to punish the publication of unpopular opinions, "deemed against public welfare." When the question is fairly presented, will the court adhere to this pernicious dictum? The judicial opinion hereinabove quoted is not constitutional interpretation, but judicial constitutional amendment, by interpolation. The judicial language was never derived by deductions made from any words actually used in the constitution, but on the contrary they were judicially read into the constitutional phraseology, thus accomplishing the judicial amendment of our constitution by unconstitutional methods, and utterly destroying "freedom of the press" *as a right,* and creating instead a liberty by permission. Shall this be the permanent interpretation of our constitutional guarantee? This is the question to be decided, and is by far the most important question ever presented to the Supreme Court of the United States.

CHAPTER X.

JUDICIAL DOGMATISM ON "FREEDOM OF THE PRESS."

If we may determine the intellectual bankruptcy of our American judges by their utter incapacity for using logical processes in the presence of slight emotional irritation, then I fear that our courts must be adjudged to have assumed obligations largely in excess of their intellectual resources. This is a sweeping and a terrible indictment; but, is it true? To me it seems to be true, and largely upon the record made by the courts in their dogmatizing concerning "freedom of the press."

Where the constitutional guarantee of "freedom of speech and of the press" is involved before a court, unless the judge's emotions and unreasoned sentimentalism determined his "construction" of the constitution, he would find the constitutional meaning in the actual words of that instrument, from which the court would deduce a criterion of "freedom" for application to and decision of the case before it and all others as well. Not in a single case has this rational method ever been attempted. Instead the courts have drawn on their "inner consciousness," and by consulting only their temporary emotions have determined what, according to their feeling-convictions, the Constitution ought to be, and then dogmatically decreed this, their own personal will, to be the true intent and meaning of the Constitution—that is, they made their own personal wish to be the Constitution itself.

But my critics will say that maybe "freedom of speech" is so vague a phrase as not to permit of the above method of interpretation and therefore the courts should not be criticised for having failed to use it. In the first place, I do not believe the phrase in question to be so vague as to justify any other method of constitutional construction. Neither do the courts believe it; at any rate not one court has ever attempted to deduce a meaning—a criterion of freedom of the press—from

163

the words of the constitution, and thereupon decided that it couldn't be done; and, what is more important, no court has ever pursued the only rational alternative, which presents itself when the constitutional language leaves the matter in doubt.

What is that alternative? If the constitutional phrase "freedom of the press," does not in and of itself furnish the criteria of permissibility in intellectual output, the court should have said so, and accordingly pursued the historical method of interpretation. By the historical or scientific method, as applied to this problem, I understand a mode of research into our juridical history which will discover to us those controversies over "freedom of speech and of the press" which had occurred before our constitution, and which issues it was intended that our constitutions should settle forever. Furthermore, a moderately well trained mind would not stop at a mere superficial view of these past contests. It is not enough to learn that at one time the abridgment of free utterance was concerned with religion; at a second with the divine right of kings; at a third with the abolition of a censor, at a fourth with the penalizing of speech without reference to or the existence of a censor; and at a fifth that it involved the right to denounce usury, etc., etc. I say; a lawyer whose intellectual attainments are such as to make him a scientist of the law, would not content himself with the superficial view or tabulation of these controversies, which thus present so varied an aspect, and then conclude that such and only such *particular* abridgment was involved in the past issues, and only its recurrence precluded by our constitutionally guaranteed unabridgable freedom of utterance. That is the method of those afflicted with arrested intellectual development. In contrast to this, the scientifically cultivated mind will examine all these particular incidents and issues of the past abridgment of utterance, to discover the fundamental elements common to them all, though imperfectly seen and crudely expressed by the controversialists of those times. These elements, common to all these controversies, the legal scientist will generalize into principles which furnish the criteria of freedom and therein find the true meaning of our constitutional guarantee of an unabridged freedom of utterance. Although the opportunity and the duty to do this has often presented itself to our courts, seemingly no

164

judge has ever been able to see it. Even in the few cases where the courts have sustained the contention in favor of freedom of utterance, the same defective intellectual methods were used. The courts drew on their "inner consciousness," dogmatized, and made arguments showing what the Constitution ought to be, rather than analyzing what it is. In the face of this fact, may we not assert the intellectual bankruptcy of our judiciary?

I said that no court had ever pursued the historical or scientific method of inquiry as to what was meant by an unabridged freedom of utterance. They have done something much worse than merely to neglect it. In their blind unintelligent gropings for something tangible upon which to rest their emotional aversion to freedom of utterance, they adopted the pre-revolutionary declarations of English authorities, who (like many American Judges) were all passionately opposed to freedom of criticism of established opinions, and whose utterances only declared the existing practise under a system which permitted abridgment, and thus made freedom to speak only a freedom by permission, with admitted power to withhold that permission.

Under the influence of their emotional aversion to free-speech, our judges were usually unable to see the difference between the English practise of an abridgable freedom by permission, where only expediency tempers tyranny, and the American principle of an unabridgable freedom of utterance guaranteed as a matter of right and to be maintained in spite of all considerations of expediency to the contrary. I say, our courts have uniformly lacked the intellectual capacity to see this difference, and so were blindly led into following the English authorities which were uniformly opposed to freedom of utterance. By adopting their statement of what the English practise was and erroneously mistaking that mere fact of practise for a declaration of human right and of constitutional principles, our American courts have dogmatically amended our constitutional guarantees, so as to reduce liberty in this respect to just what it was in England before the time of the American Revolution. Under our constitutions, as thus judicially amended, any legislature in spite of the constitution as it originally was written, may abridge freedom of speech and press in any respect in which it and the judges who determine what is constitutional shall concur in approving, and declare to be in the interest of the public welfare.

165

These are serious charges to bring against our courts, and are not to be accepted on my mere assurance that I believe them to be true. I fear it would be no more satisfactory if I contented myself with merely citing the cases which have brought me to this conclusion, because no one would take the time and trouble to examine them. It follows that if I would convince anyone, I must reproduce the essential portion of all these judicial opinions. To do this will require much space, but that cannot be avoided. I also regret very much that like space-limits will not allow me to comment separately on each specific utterance which I shall quote, and thus aid the sluggish mind in applying the foregoing standards of judgment to the decisions actually rendered.

However, since this cannot be done, I can only request the reader to keep definitely in mind what I have said above as to the proper method of judicial interpretation, and in the light of the standards thus erected to read the following liberty-destroying judicial dogmatism, of the most pernicious and most inexcusable sort. What follows includes all the quotable and material portions of the reported judicial utterances as to the meaning of "freedom of speech and the press" which my researches have disclosed to me.

ARKANSAS.

State vs. Morrill, 16 *Ark.* 384 (40 2-3), 1855. The Arkansas Bill of Rights provides: (Sec. 7) "That printing presses shall be free to every person; and no law shall ever be made to restrain the rights thereof. The free communication of thoughts and opinions is one of the invaluable rights of man; and every citizen may freely speak, write and print on any subject, being responsible for the abuse of that liberty." The defendant was charged with criminal contempt, for the publication of an article supposed to intimate that the court had been corruptly influenced in the determination of a certain cause. The defendant invoked a statute limiting the power to punish for contempt to which the Court said: "The prohibitory clause is entitled to respect as an opinion of the legislature, but is not binding on the Courts," they possessing an "inherent" power to do their own legislating, even ex post facto, on the subject of contempt.

Upon the subject of the Constitutional right of freedom of utterance the Court said: "The last clause of the section, 'being responsible for the abuse of that liberty,' is an answer to the argument of the learned counsel. * * *

"Any citizen has the right to publish the proceedings and decisions of this court, and, if he deem it necessary for the public good, to comment upon them freely, discuss their correctness, the fitness or unfitness of the judges for their stations, and the fidelity with which they perform the important public trusts reposed in them; but he has no right to attempt, by defamatory publications, to degrade the tribunal, destroy public confidence in it, and dispose the community to disregard and set at naught its orders, judgments and decrees. Such publications are an abuse of the liberty of the press, and tend to sap the very foundation of good order and well being in society by obstructing the course of justice. If a judge is really corrupt, and unworthy of the station which he holds, the constitution has provided an ample remedy by impeachment or address where he can meet his accuser face to face, and his conduct may undergo a full investigation. The liberty of the press is one thing and licentious scandal is another. The constitution guarantees to every man the right to acquire and hold property, by all lawful means; but this furnishes no justification to a man to rob his neighbor of his lands or goods."

CALIFORNIA.

The California Constitution of 1879 provides: "Every citizen may freely speak, write, and publish his sentiments on all subjects, being responsible for the abuse of that right; and no law shall be passed to restrain or abridge the liberty of speech or of the press."

Ex parte Barry, 85 *Cal.* 603, 607-8; 25 *Pac.* 256. (1890.) Habeas Corpus proceeding on commitment for contempt in publishing an article attacking a judge for conduct in pending action.

The Court said: "This may be true in the sense that the liberty to speak and write on any subject cannot be restricted or prevented in advance, and that the only remedy is to punish subsequently, for any publication that amounts to an abuse of such liberty. That is precisely what was done in this case. * * * The liberty of the press to fairly criticise the official conduct of a judge or the decisions or proceedings of the courts, and to expose and bring to light any wrongful, corrupt or improper act of a judicial officer, is one that should

167

be carefully preserved and protected by the courts. * * *
But the publisher of a newspaper, who assumes to criticise or
censure a public officer or the proceedings of a court, must
know whereof he speaks. If he censures unjustly or charges
falsely, he must be held strictly accountable. While his right
of free speech is protected, his abuse of it must be punished.
The great trouble with the freedom of the press at the present day, so far as it affects the courts, is that it is used indiscriminately in many cases, not with the laudable purpose of
correcting abuses and exposing wrongdoing, but to gratify ill
will and passion, or pander to the passions or prejudices of
others. This tendency should be severely condemned and punished, not only for the protection of the courts and the preservation of a pure and independent judiciary, but as a means
of upholding the liberty of the press in its true sense." Writ
denied.

Ex parte Shortridge, 99 *Cal.* 526. (535). (1893.) Contempt proceeding for publishing testimony in divorce case in
violation of court order, Appellant adjudged not guilty by
Supreme Court on review.

The Court said: "Liberty of the press must not be confounded with mere license. Liberty of the press stops where
a further exercise would invade the rights of others. This
provision of the constitution does not authorize a usurpation
of the functions of the courts. Under the plea of the liberty
of the press, a newspaper has no right to assail litigants during
the progress of a trial, intimidate witnesses, dictate verdicts
or judgments, or spread before juries its opinion of the merits
of cases which are on trial. * * *

"As the article in question does not go beyond these
limitations, and as the section under which the court below
proceeded to judgment, clearly does not authorize the order
which was made, the proceedings must be annulled."

Dailey v. Superior Court of San Francisco, 112 *Cal.* 94
(99,100). (1896.) Certiorari to review order forbidding the
public performance of a play based on the facts of a pending
criminal trial. Order annulled.

The Court said: "The purpose of this provision of the
constitution was the abolishment of censorship, and for courts
to act as censors is directly violative of that purpose. [Then
the court quotes with approval Blackstone and those follow-

ing him and then concludes:] In effect the order made by the trial court was one commanding the petitioner not to commit a contempt of court; and such a practise is novel in the extreme. * * * We conclude that the order made by the trial court was an attempted restraint upon the right of free speech, as guaranteed by the Constitution of this State, and that petitioner's mouth could not be closed in advance for the purpose of preventing an utterance of his sentiments, however mischievous the prospective results of such utterance. He had the right of free speech, but at all times was responsible to the law for an abuse of that right."

COLORADO.

The Colorado Constitution(Art. II, sec. 10) provides "That no law shall be passed impairing the freedom of speech, that every person shall be free to speak, write or publish whatever he will on any subject, being responsible for all abuse of that liberty."

People v. Green, 7 Colo. 244 (250,251). (1883.) Disbarment proceedings for insulting a judge on the public street. Defendant found guilty and disbarred. Rehearing denied.

The Court said: "In this country, and in England also, the utmost liberty of speech is guaranteed by statute and enforced by the courts; the right to discuss all matters of public interest or importance is everywhere fully recognized; judicial decisions and conduct form no exceptions to the rule; the judge's official character, and his acts in cases fully determined, are subject to examination and criticism; in most of the states the office is elective, and it is proper and right that the people should be informed of the occupant's mental and moral fitness.

"True, under the guise of criticism in the public press, and otherwise, judges are often compelled to endure the sting of misrepresentation and calumny, with no other redress than an ordinary civil action; and doubtless it sometimes happens that their efficiency in office is hereby lessened, to the detriment and injury of the public service; but it is wisely considered better that these wrongs and injuries should be tolerated, than that the sacred liberty of speech, printed or spoken, should be abridged by lodging an arbitrary power to interfere therewith in the hands of the court of judge, so long as such criticism or libel is not designed to influence the mind of the judge in a cause still undetermined." * * *

169

"But we have found no case, and respondent has cited none, which extends this privilege of comment and criticism to assaults, verbal or physical, upon the judge in person."

Cooper v. People, 13 *Colo.* 337 (367); 22 *Pac. R.* 790; 6 *L. R. A.* 430 (1889.) Contempt proceeding for newspaper censure of judicial action in pending case.

The Court, after quoting Blackstone and others accepting him as an authority in Constitutional construction, affirming judgment convicting defendants, said: "We would not for a moment sanction any contraction of the freedom of the press. Universal experience has shown that such freedom is necessary to the perpetuation of our system of government in its integrity; but this freedom does not license unrestrained scandal. By a subsequent clause of the same sentence of our state constitution in which the liberty is guaranteed, the responsibility of its abuse is fixed. With us the judiciary is elective, and every citizen may fully and freely discuss the fitness or unfitness of all candidates for the positions to which they aspire; criticize freely all decisions rendered, and by legitimate argument establish their soundness or unsoundness; comment on the fidelity or infidelity with which judicial officers discharge their duties; but the right to attempt, by wanton defamation, to prejudice the right of litigants in a pending cause, degrade the tribunal, and impede, embarrass or corrupt that due administration of justice which is so essential to good government, cannot be sanctioned."

People v. Stapleton, 33 *Pac.* 167 (173), 18 *Colo.* 567 (586). (1893.) Contempt proceeding for published attack on judges.

The Court said: "The liberty of the press is one thing. The 'abuse of that liberty' is quite another. The former is guaranteed by the constitution. The latter is as clearly interdicted. If the liberty of the press is abused, the offender may be held responsible therefor. Such is the common law, such is our constitutional provision; and such offenders may be dealt with summarily for contempt, when their fabrications are calculated to impede, obstruct or embarrass the administration of justice. It has not been deemed expedient by our people that any class of persons should be privileged to attack the courts, with the view to interfere with the rights of litigants, or to embarrass the administration of justice. Hence they have never adopted any constitutional provision granting

170

such dangerous license. * * * There is far more danger to our institutions, and far more danger to the rights of the people, and especially to the rights of litigants, to be apprehended from the power of the press over the courts, than from the power of the courts over the press. * * * Thoughtful citizens now understand that the danger now threatening our institutions is that courts are not independent enough, instead of being too arbitary.

CONNECTICUT.

The Constitution provides : "Every citizen may freely speak, write and publish his sentiments on all subjects, being responsible for the abuse of that liberty. No law shall ever be passed to curtail or restrain the liberty of speech or of the press."

Atwater v. Morning News Co., 67 Conn. 504 (518). (1896.) Action for libel.

The Court said: "The administration of the law (the libel law) is concerned with two most important rights; the right of the individual to reparation for malicious injuries to his reputation, and the right of the people to liberty of speech and of the press. The two rights are not inconsistant, but interdependent. The individual has no right to demand reparation for those accidental injuries incident to organized society. Freedom of the press is the offspring of law, not of lawlessness; and its primary meaning excludes all notions of malicious injury. Indeed, any true freedom of the press becomes impossible where malicious injuries are not forbidden and punished; and the strongest guaranty of that freedom lies in an impartial administration of the law which distinguishes the performance of a public or social duty from the infliction of a malicious injury."

State v. McKee, 73 Conn. 18 (28, 29). (1900.) Appeal from conviction for selling a newspaper principally made up of criminal news, etc., under statute. Appeal sustained on technical grounds, but statute held constitutional and approved.

The Court said: "There is no constitutional right to publish every fact or statement that may be true. Even the right to publish accurate reports of judicial proceedings is limited. * * * The primary meaning of "liberty of the press" as understood at the time of our early constitutions were framed, was freedom from any censorship of the press. * * *

171

But this fundamental guaranty [the constitutional provision for free speech] goes further; it recognizes the free expression of opinion on matters of church or state as essential to the successful operation of free government; and it also recognizes the free expression of opinion on any subject as essential to a condition of civil liberty. The right to discuss public matters stands in part on the necessity of that right to the operation of a government by the people, but with this exception; the right of every citizen to freely express his sentiments on all subjects stands on the broad principle which supports the equal right of all to exercise gifts of property and faculty in any pursuit in life; in other words, upon the essential principles of civil liberty as recognized by our constitution. Every citizen has an equal right to use his mental endowments, as well as his property, in any harmless occupation or manner; but he has no right to use them so as to injure his fellow-citizens or to endanger the vital interests of society. Immunity in the mischievous use is as inconsistent with civil liberty as prohibition of the harmless use. Both arise from the equal right of all to the protection of law in the enjoyment of individual freedom of action, which is the ultimate fundamental principle. * * * The liberty protected is not the right to perpetrate acts of licentiousness, or any act inconsistent with the peace or safety of the State. Freedom of speech and press does not include the abuse of the power of tongue or pen, any more than freedom of other action includes an injurious use of one's occupation, business or property. * * *

"The general right to disseminate opinions on all subjects was probably specified mainly to emphasize the strong necessity to a free government of criticism of public men and measures. But it is specified as one of the conditions of civil liberty, and, like other conditions of a similar nature, it necessarily involves the protection of those who may suffer from the wrongful exercise of any common right. * * *

"The notion that the broad guaranty of the common right to free speech and free thought, contained in our constitution, is intended to erect a bulwark or supply a place of refuge in behalf of the violaters of laws enacted for the protection of society from the contagion of moral diseases, belittles the conception of constitutional safeguards and implies ignorance of the essentials of civil liberty."

FLORIDA.

The Constitution provides that "every citizen may freely speak and write his sentiments on all subjects, being responsible for the abuse of that right, and no law shall be passed to restrain or abridge the liberty of speech or press."

Jones v. Townsend's Administratrix, 21 *Fla.* 431 (450); 58 *Am. Rep.* 676. (1885.) Action for libel.

The Court said: "The liberty of the press means simply that no previous license to publish shall be required, but not that the publisher of a newspaper shall be any less responsible than another person for publishing otherwise the same libelous matter."

ILLINOIS.

The Constitution of Illinois (1818 and 1848) provides: "The free communication of thoughts and opinions is one of the invaluable rights of man; and every citizen may freely speak, write, and print, on any subject, being responsible for the abuse of that liberty." The constitution of 1870 is substantially the same with the first sentence omitted.

Stuart v. People, 4 *Ill.* 395 (404, 405, 406). (1842.) Action for contempt for publishing an article alleged to reflect on Court and jury, during murder trial.

The Court, reversing conviction, said: "Into this vortex of constructive contempts have been drawn, by the British Courts, many acts which have no tendency to obstruct the administration of justice, but rather to wound the feelings, or offend the personal dignity of the judge, and fines imposed, and imprisonment denounced, so frequently, and with so little question, as to have ripened, in the estimation of many, into a common law principle; and it is urged that, inasmuch as the common law is in force here, by legislative enactment, this principle is also in force. But we have said in several cases that such portions only of the common law as are applicable to our institutions, and suited to the genius of our people, can be regarded as in force. It has been modified by the prevalence of free principles, and the general improvement of society, and whilst we admire it as a system, having no blind devotion for its errors and defects, we cannot but hope that, in the progress of time, it will receive many more improvements, and be relieved from most of its blemishes. Constitutional provisions are much safer guarantees for civil liberty and per-

173

sonal rights, than those of the common law, however much they may be said to protect them.

"Our Constitution has provided that the printing presses shall be free to every person who may undertake to examine the proceedings of any and every department of the government; and he may publish the truth, if the matter published is proper for public information; and the free communication of thoughts and opinions is encouraged.

"The contempt, in this case, was by a printer of a newspaper, remarking on the conduct of an individual juror, who, whilst he was engaged in the trial of a capital case, and whilst separated from the public, and in charge of the officer of the Court, was furnishing articles for daily publication in a rival newspaper; and in admitting a communication from a correspondent, calculated to irritate the presiding judge of the court, though not reflecting upon his integrity or in any way impeaching his conduct. The paragraphs and communication published had no tendency to obstruct the administration of justice; nor were they thrust upon the notice of the Court, by any act of the plaintiff in error. * * *

"An honest, independent and intelligent court will win its way to public confidence, in spite of newspaper paragraphs, however pointed may be their wit or satire; and its dignity will suffer less by passing them by unnoticed, than by arraigning the perpetrators, trying them in a summary way; and punishing them by the judgment of the offended party.

"It does not seem to me necessary, for the protection of courts in the exercise of their legitimate powers, that this one, so liable to abuse, should also be conceded to them. It may be so frequently exercised as to destroy that normal influence which is their best possession, until, finally, the administration of justice is brought into disrepute. Respect to courts cannot be compelled; it is the voluntary tribute of the public to worth, virtue and intelligence; and whilst they are founded upon the judgment seats, so long and no longer will they retain the public confidence.

"If a judge be libelled by the public press, he and his assailant should be placed on equal grounds, and their common arbiter should be a jury of the country; and if he has received an injury, ample remuneration will be made.

"In restricting the power to punish for contempt, to the cases specified, more benefits will result than by enlarging it.

It is at best an arbitrary power, and should only be exercised on the preservative, and not on the vindictive principle. It is not a jewel of the court, to be admired and prized, but a rod rather, and most potent when rarely used."

People v. Wilson, 64 *Ill.* 195 (214, 215). (1872.) Action for contempt for publication reflecting on the action of the court in a pending matter.

The Court, finding defendants guilty, said: "Let us say here, and so plainly that our position can be misrepresented only by malice or gross stupidity, that we do not deprecate, nor should we claim the right to punish any criticism the press may choose to publish upon our decisions, opinions, or official conduct, in regard to cases that have passed from our jurisdiction, so long as our action is correctly stated, and our official integrity is not impeached. The respondents are correct in saying in their answers that they have a right to examine the proceedings of any and every department of the government.

"Far be it from us to deny that right. Such freedom of the press is indispensable to the preservation of the freedom of the people. But certainly neither these respondents nor any intelligent person connected with the press, and having a just idea of its responsibilities, as well as its powers, will claim that it may seek to control the administration of justice or influence the decision of pending causes. * * *

"Regard it in whatever light we may, we cannot but consider the article in question as *calculated* to embarrass the administration of justice, whether it has in fact done so or not, and, therefore, as falling directly within the definition of punishable contempts, announced by this court, in the case of Stuart v. The People. It is a contempt, because, in a pending case of the gravest magnitude, it reflects upon the action of the court, impeaches its integrity, and seeks to intimidate it by the threat of popular clamor."

Storey v. People, 79 *Ill.* 45 (52-53) (1875.) Contempt proceeding for publishing article reflecting on the Grand Jury. Conviction reversed.

The Court said: "This language, plain and explicit as it is, cannot be held to have no application to courts, or those by whom they are conducted. The judiciary is elective; and the jurors, although appointed, are, in general, appointed by a board whose members are elected by popular vote. There is, therefore, the same responsibility, in theory, in the judicial department, that exists in the legislative and executive departments to the people, for the diligent and faithful discharge of all duties enjoined on it and the same necessity exists for public information with regard to the conduct and character of those intrusted to discharge those duties, in order that the elective franchise shall be intelligibly exercised, as obtains in regard to the other departments of the government."

INDIANA.

The Indiana Constitution provides; "No law shall be passed restraining the free interchange of thought and opinion, or restricting the right to speak, write, or print, freely, on any subject whatever; but for the abuse of that right every person shall be held responsible.

Cheadle v. State, 110 *Ind.* 301 (312,313). (1886.) Appeal in contempt proceeding for publishing articles reflecting on the Court. Appeal sustained, judgment reversed.

The Court said: "There are cases on record from which an inference might be drawn that the statement in question constituted a contempt, as it was doubtless considered in this case; but it must be borne in mind that the force of public opinion in this country, in favor of the freedom of the press, has of late greatly restrained the courts in the exercise of their power to punish persons for making disrespectful and injurious publications. * * * No one ought to be found guilty upon a doubtful charge of indirect contempt, and especially so in a case in any manner involving the freedom of the press.

"It is true that too often, under the guise of a guaranteed freedom, the press transcends the limits of manly criticisms, and resorts to methods injurious to persons and tribunals justly entitled to moral support of all law-abiding citizens; but such digressions are not always unmixed evils, and it is only in rare instances that legal proceedings in repression of such a license can, with propriety, be resorted to.

"When such a digression becomes too flagrant to be disregarded, a prosecution for libel is usually the most appropriate and effective remedy. In such a prosecution, both parties go before a jury of the country on terms more nearly equal than they can relatively occupy in a proceeding for the punishment of an alleged contempt."

Shoemaker v. South Bend Spark Arrester Co., 135 *Ind.* 471 (478). (1893.) Action for injunction to restrain "false and malicious claims of the title," etc.

The Court, in affirming decision granting the injunction, said: "It (the case of Life Assn. v. Boogher, p. 173) is not only out of line with the holdings of this court upon that request; but it holds that the constitutional guarantee of the freedom of the press and of speech is a protection to one against equitable interference in publishing false and injurious statements. In neither of these positions can we believe it sound."

IOWA.

State v. Blair, 60 *N. W.* 486 (487) (*Iowa*). (1894.) Indictment for publicly professing to treat diseases without a license. The Iowa Constitution provides that "every person may speak, write and publish his sentiments on all subjects, being responsible for the abuse of that right. No law shall be passed to restrain or abridge the liberty of speech or of the press."

The Court said: "The statute in question is a part of a chapter regulating 'The Practice of Pharmacy and the Sale of Medicine and Poisons,' and is designed to guard against evil consequences liable to result therefrom. The prohibitive features of the act do not go to the right intended to be secured by the Constitutional provision as to speaking, writing or publishing one's sentiments, or as to abridging or restraining the liberty of the press."

KANSAS.

The Kansas Constitution (Sec. 10 of Bill of Rights) says: "The liberty of the press shall be inviolate; and all persons may freely speak, write or publish their sentiments on all subjects, being responsible for the abuse of such right."

In re Pryor, 18 *Kan.* 72. (76.) (1877.) Action for contempt for writing insulting letter to a judge, during pendency of an action.

The court found defendant guilty, but added: "It will be borne in mind that the remarks we have made apply only while the matter which gives rise to the words or acts of the attorney are pending and undetermined. Other considerations apply after the matters have finally been determined, the orders signed, or the judgment entered. For no judge and no court, high or low, is beyond the reach of public and individual criticism. After a case is disposed of, a court or judge has no power to compel the public, or any individual thereof, attorney, or otherwise, to consider his rulings correct, his conduct proper, or even his integrity free from stain, or to punish for contempt any mere criticism or animadversion thereon, no matter how severe or unjust."

In re Banks, 56 *Kan.* 242 (243, 244). (1895.) Habeas Corpus proceeding. Petitioner arrested under an act prohibiting the sale of any publication "devoted largely to the publication of scandals, lechery, assignation, intrigues between men and women, and immoral conduct of persons."

The Court said: "Without doubt a newspaper, the most prominent feature of which is items detailing the immoral conduct of individuals, spreading out to public view an unsavory mass of corruption and moral degradation, is calculated to taint the social atmosphere, and by describing in detail the means resorted to by immoral persons to gratify their propensities, tends especially to corrupt the morals of the young, and lead them into vicious paths and immoral acts. We entertain no doubt that the legislature has power to suppress this class of publications, without in any manner violating the constitutional liberties of the press."

KENTUCKY.

The constitution provides: "Printing presses shall be free to every person who undertakes to examine the proceedings of the General Assembly or any branch of government; and no law shall ever be made to restrain the right thereof. Every person may freely and fully speak, write and print on any subject, being responsible for the abuse of that liberty."

Riley v. Lee, 88 *Ky.* 603 (612, 613, 614). (1889.) Action for libel.

The Court said: "By the provisions of the United States and the state constitutions guaranteeing the 'freedom of the press,' it was simply intended to secure to the conductors of the press the same rights and immunities that are enjoyed by the public at large. The citizen has a right to speak the truth in reference to the acts of government, public officials or individuals. The press is guaranteed the same right, but no greater right. * * * *An individual may, in what he honestly believes to be in the interest of morals and good order,* and *the suppression of immorality and disorder, criticise the acts* of other individuals. So may the press. But in no case has the citizen the right to injure the rights of others, among the most sacred of which is the right to good name and fame. * * * The press must not be the vehicle of attack upon the character and reputation of a person unless the attack is known to be true. If it is not known to be true, do not publish it. The publication can seldom, if ever, do good; and the indulgence in publications of the sort not strictly true, would soon deprave the moral taste of society, and render it miserable."

LOUISIANA.

The Constitution of Louisiana provides: "No law shall ever be passed to curtail or restrain the liberty of speech or of the press; any person may speak, write, and publish his sentiments on all subjects, being responsible for the abuse of that liberty.

State v. Goodwin, 37 La. Ann. 713 (717). (1885.) Appeal from conviction for mailing threatening letter. Judgment affirmed.

The Court said: "It is a libel upon the noble privilege of free speech, guaranteed by our Constitution, to say that it embraces or protects such despicable practise."

Fitzpatrick v. Pub. Co., 48 La. Ann. 1116 (1130, 1135). (1896.) Action for libel. The Court said: "There is a marked and clear distinction to be taken between the *liberty* and the *license* of the press. * * * The freedom of speech and liberty of the press were designed to secure constitutional immunity for the expression of opinions, but that does not mean unrestrained license, nor does it confer the right upon the editor of a newspaper to print whatever he may choose, no matter how false, malicious or injurious it may be, without full responsibility for the damage he may cause."

MARYLAND.

The Constitution provides: "That the liberty of the press ought to be inviolably preserved; that every citizen of the State ought to be allowed to speak, write and publish his sentiments on all subjects, being responsible for the abuse of that privilege."

Negley v. Farrow, 60 Md. 158 (176, 177). (1882.) Action for libel.

The Court said: "It [liberty of the press] is a right which, from the introduction of the printing press down to the year 1694, did not in England belong to the subject. On the contrary, no one was allowed to publish any printed matter without the license and supervision of government, and it was against such interference on the part of the government, and in favor of the right of the citizen, that this provision, found its way into our Bill of Rights. * * * The liberty of the press guaranteed by the Constitution is a right belonging to every one, whether proprietor of a newspaper or not, to publish whatever he pleases, without the license, interference or control of the government, being responsible alone for the abuse of the privilege. * * *

"No one denies the right of the defendants to discuss and criticise boldly and fearlessly the official conduct of the plaintiff. It is a right which in every free country belongs to the citizen; and the exercise of it, within lawful and proper limits, affords some protection at least against official abuse and corruption. But there is a broad distinction between fair and legitimate discussion in regard to the conduct of a public man, and the imputation of a corrupt motive, by which that conduct may be supposed to be governed. And if any one goes out of his way to asperse the personal character of a public man, and to ascribe to him base and corrupt motives, he must do so at his peril, and must either prove the truth of what he says, or answer in damages to the party injured."

MASSACHUSETTS.

The Massachusetts Bill of Rights provides that "the liberty of the press is essential to the security of freedom in a state; it ought not therefore to be restrained in this Commonwealth."

Com. v. Blanding, 20 Mass. (3 Pick), 304 (314-314). (1825.) Action for criminal libel. The Court said: "The liberty of the press, not its licentiousness, this is the construction which a just regard to the other parts of that instrument [the Constitution] and to the wisdom of those who formed it, requires. * * * Besides, it is well understood, and received as a commentary on this provision for the liberty of the press, that it was intended to prevent all such previous restraints upon publications as had been practised by other governments, and in early times here, to still the efforts of patriots towards enlightening their fellow-subjects upon their rights and the duties of rulers. The liberty of the press was to be unrestrained, but he who used it was to be responsible for its abuse; like the right to keep fire arms, which does not protect him who uses them for annoyance or destruction."

Com. v. Kneeland, 37 Mass. (20 *Pick.*) 206 (219). (1838.) Prosecution for blasphemy.

The Court said: "The obvious intent of this provision was to prevent the enactment of license laws, or other direct restraints upon publication, leaving individuals at liberty to print, without the previous permission of any officer of government, subject to responsibility for the matter printed. * * * The intention of the article in question was, to ensure the general right of publication, at the same time leaving every citizen responsible for any offense capable of being committed by the use of language, as well when printed as when oral, or in manuscript. Any other construction of the article would be absurd and impracticable, and inconsistent with the peace and safety of the State, and with the existence of free government."

MINNESOTA.

The Constitution (Art. 1, p. 3), provides: "The liberty of the press shall forever remain inviolate, and all persons may freely speak, write and publish their sentiments on all subjects, being responsible for the abuse of such rights."

State v. Pioneer Press Co., 110 *N. W.* (Minn.) 867, (868, 869), (1907). Indictment for publishing details of an official execution contrary to statute.

The Court said: "Appellant...argues that there are no constitutional limitations upon the liberty of the press, unless the subject matter be blasphemous, obscene, seditious or scandalous in its character. This is altogether too restricted a view. The principle is the same, whether the subject matter of the publication is distinctly blasphemous, seditious or scandalous, or of such character as naturally tends to excite the public mind and thus indirectly affect the public good. If the constitutional provision has reference to restricting the publication by newspapers of unwholesome matter, or the use of the United States mails for the distribution of obscene literature * * * or the publishing of Anarchistic doctrines * * * upon the ground that it is in the interest of public morals, then for the same reason the right of restriction applies to publishing details of criminal executions. The article in question is moderate, and does not resort to any unusual language, or exhibit cartoons for the purpose of emphasizing the horrors of executing the death penalty, but if, in the opinion of the Legislature, it is detrimental to pubic morals to publish anything more than the mere fact that the execution has taken place, then, under the authorities and upon principle, the appellant was not deprived of any constitutional right in being so limited."

MISSISSIPPI.

The Constitution (Art. 1, p. 6) provides that "every citizen may freely speak, write and publish his sentiments on all subjests, being responsible for the abuse of that liberty."

Ex Parte Hickey, 12 Miss. (4 *Sm.* & *M.*) 781 (782). (1844.) Action for contempt in denouncing the act of a judge.

The Court said: "The shield which our constitution throws around the press has been held up to interpose before the power of the courts to punish for contempts. The most dearly prized offspring of our national liberty is the freedom of the press. It is so, because it can be made its most effectual protection at home, and because it can be employed as the apostle of those liberties to millions abroad. The worst enemy to freedom is ignorance. Instruct men in the knowledge of their rights, and a vindication of those rights follows as surely as light follows the rising sun. Yet the freedom of the press is abused to base and unworthy purposes. Such indeed, as sad experience teaches, is often the melancholy fate of the greatest blessings that a wise providence has bestowed upon us, or that human skill has invented. The free air we breathe is essential to our existence, but when infected with pestilential matter it becomes the most terrible weapon of death. But who would argue, because disease may float in the atmosphere, that that atmosphere should be destroyed."

MISSOURI.

The Constitution (Art II, Sec. 14) provides: "That no law shall be passed impairing the freedom of speech; that every person shall be free to say, write or publish whatever he will on any subject, being responsible for all abuse of that liberty."

Life Assn. of America v. Boogher, 3 Mo. App. 173 (180). (1876.) Action for injunction against publication of libel. The Court, holding that such injunction could not lie, said: "If it be said that the right to speak, write or print, thus se-

cured to every one, cannot be construed to mean a license to
wantonly injure another, and that by the jurisdiction claimed
it is only suspended until it can be determined judicially
whether the exercise of it in the particular case be allowable,
our answer is that we have no power to suspend that right for
a moment, or for any purpose? The sovereign power has forbidden any instrumentality of the government it has instituted
to limit or restrain this right except by the fear of the penalty,
civil or criminal, which may wait on abuse. The General Assembly can pass no law abridging the freedom of speech or of
the press; it can only punish the licentious abuse of that freedom. Courts of justice can only administer the laws of the
State, and, of course, can do nothing by way of judicial sentence which the General Assembly has no power to sanction.
The matter is too plain for detailed illustration."

Flint v. Hutchinson Smoke Burner Co., 110 *Mo.* 492 (500,
501). (1892.) Action for injunction to restrain libel of
title.

The Court said: "We live under a written constitution
which declares that the right of trial by jury shall remain inviolate; and the question of libel or no libel, slander or no
slander, is one for a jury to determine. Such was certainly
the settled law when the various constitutions of this state
were adopted; and it is all-important that the right thus
guarded should not be disturbed. It goes hand in hand with
the liberty of the press and free speech. For unbridled use of
the tongue or pen the law furnishes a remedy. In view of
these considerations, a court of equity has no power to restrain a slander or libel; and it can make no difference
whether the words are spoken of a person or his title to property."

State v. Van Wye, 136 *Mo.* 277 (234, 235). (1896.)
Indictment for disseminating a "scandalous newspaper."

The Court said: "The liberty of the press, says Lord
Mansfield, in King vs. Dean of St. Asaph, cited in 3 T. R. 431,
'consists in printing without any previous license, subject,
to the consequences of the law.' Lord Ellenborough defines it
in. Rex v. Cobbett 29 Howells State Trials, 49, in this way:
'The law of England is a law of liberty, and, consistently with
this liberty, we have not what is called an *imprimatur;* but if
a man publish a paper, he is exposed to the penal consequences,
as he is in every other act, if it is illegal.' * * * The constitu-

tional liberty of speech and the press, as we understand it, simply guarantees the right to freely utter and publish whatever the citizen may desire and to be protected in so doing, provided always that such publications are not blasphemous, obscene and scandalous in their character, so that they become an offense against the public, and by their malice and falsehood injuriously affect the character, reputation or pecuniary interests of individuals. The constitutional protection shields no one from responsibility for abuse of this right. To hold that it did would be a cruel libel upon the bill of rights itself. The laws punishing criminal libel have never been deemed an infringement of this constitutional guaranty. Equally numerous and strong are the decisions that obscene publications are without the protection of this provision of our constitution."

Marx & Haas Jeans Clothing Co. v. Watson et al., 168 *Mo.* 133 (144, 150). (1901.) Appeal from refusal of lower court to enjoin boycotting circular. Appeal dismissed.

The Court said: "Wherever within our borders speech is uttered, writing done or publication made, there stands the constitutional guaranty giving staunch assurance that each and every one of them shall be *free.* The Legislature cannot pass a law which even *impairs* the freedom of speech; and as there are no exceptions contained in the rest of the quoted section, the language there used stands as an *affirmative prescripiton* against any exception being thereto made, as effectually as if words of *negation* or *prohibition* had *expressly* and *in terms been employed.* * * * If these defendants are not permitted to tell the story of their wrongs, or, if you please, their supposed wrongs, by words of mouth or with pen or print, and to endeavor to persuade others to aid them by all peaceable means, in securing redress of such wrongs, *what becomes of free speech, and what of personal liberty?* The fact that in exercising that freedom they thereby do plaintiff an actionable injury, such fact does not go a hair towards a diminution of their right of free speech, etc., for the exercise of which, if resulting in such injury, the Constitution makes them expressly responsible. But such responsibility is utterly incompatible with authority in a court of equity to prevent such responsibility from occurring.

State ex. inf. Crow v. Shepherd, 177 *Mo.* 205 (253, 257) (1903.) Action for contempt in censuring a judgment of the Supreme Court.

The Court, adjudging defendant guilty, said: "The liberty of the press means that any one can publish anything he pleases, but he is liable for the abuse of that liberty. If he does this by scandalizing the courts of his country, he is liable to be punished for contempt. If he slanders his fellow-men, he is liable to a criminal prosecution for libel, and to respond civilly, in damages for the injury he does to the individual. In other words, the abuse of the privilege consists, principally, in not telling the truth. * * * It is the liberty of the press that is guaranteed—not the *licentiousness.* It is the right to speak the truth—not the right to bear false witness against your neighbor. Every citizen has a constitutional right to the enjoyment of his character as well as to the ownership of his property; and this right is as sacred as the liberty of the press."

MONTANA.

The Constitution provides: "No law shall be passed impairing the freedom of speech; every person shall be free to speak, write or publish whatever he will upon any subject, being responsible for all abuse of that liberty."

In re Shannon, 11 *Mont.* 67 (72). (1891.) Habeas corpus in contempt proceeding for criticism of courts. Writ granted.

The Court said: "None of these [i.e., the legal grounds for commitment for contempt], would include power to punish for the expression of sentiments through the medium of the public press or otherwise regarding the practise of the Court, or of results or abuses alleged to flow from the past administration of said Court. A power to punish for such utterance, or to silence the voice of comment upon such matters, would be the discovery of an unknown quantity in jurisprudence; and the exercise of it would be a menace to a free and spirited people.

"The constitutional right of freedom of speech * * * would be set at naught by the exercise of such a power, whenever that freedom of speech happened to be directed to the action of public courts. There is no such exception. We speak now of the discussion of matters pertaining to courts, or the practise therein, which have no tendency to affect the merits or result of particular cases pending, which class of decision is entirely distinguished from publications which are designed and put forth for the purpose and have a tendency to influence the result of particular cases."

In re Macknight, 11 *Mont.* 126 (138); 27 *Pac. R.* & 336 (339). (1891.) Contempt proceeding. In deciding that the case fell within the "constitutional sanction of the freedom of speech and press," the Court said:

"What was the purpose of this constitutional guarantee? Was it to grant freedom to ordinary speech and publication which could excite the resentment of no one? If that was the purpose, then it would be as needful to put into the Constitution a provision that people may freely walk the streets quietly and peaceably. The history of the struggle for supremacy of certain principles and ideas shows the purpose of the law, when such principles or ideas are clothed with that force and dignity, and inscribed upon our Constitution or statute. And so the history of the struggle for the establishment of the principle of freedom of speech and press shows that it was not ordinary talk and publication, which was to be disenthralled from censorship, suppression and punishment. It was in a large degree a species of talk and publication which had been found distasteful to governmental powers and agencies."

State v. Faulds, 17 *Mont.* 140 (145). (1895.) Action for contempt in publishing abuse of Court.

The Court said: "Section 10, Article 3, of the Constitution of the State provides that no law shall be passed impairing the freedom of speech; every person shall be free to speak, write or publish whatever he will on any subject, being responsible for all abuse of that liberty. While this section of the Constitution secures the largest liberty to the press, it also imposes responsibilities. It is a statute of liberty, not of 'licentious scandal.' The liberty of the press is one thing; the abuse of that liberty is quite another."

NEBRASKA.

The Constitution provides: "Every person may freely speak, write and publish on all subjects, being responsible for the abuse of the liberty."

State v. Bee Publishing Co., 60 *Neb.* 282 (296). (1900.) Contempt proceeding for publication of articles designed to affect the decision of a pending case. Defendant convicted.

The Court said: "We have, of course, no desire to restrain in the slightest degree, the freedom of the press, or to maintain the dignity of the Court by inflicting penalties on those who may assail us with defamatory publications. Our decisions and all our official actions are public property, and the press and the people have the undoubted right to comment on them and criticise and censure them as they see fit. Judicial officers, like other public servants, must answer for their official actions, before the chancery of public opinion; they must make good their claims to popular esteem by excellence and virtue, by faithful and efficient service and by righteous conduct. But while we concede to the press the right to criticise freely our decisions when made, we deny to any individual or to any class of men the right to subject us to any form of coercion with the view of affecting our judgment in a pending case."

State v. Rosewater, 60 *Neb.* 438 (439). (1900.) Contempt proceeding for publication of articles designed to affect the decision of a pending case. Defendant convicted.

The Court said: "We are told that the liberty of the press is involved, and that this proceeding is an arbitrary exercise of power, curtailing that freedom which is necessary for the conservation of public interests, and a free discussion of all questions of public concern. With the same speciousness and plausibility of reasoning, it might as well be argued that the liberty of the individual is endangered who corruptly tampers with a jury to secure an unrighteous verdict, or attempts to improperly influence the decision of a court in a case then pending before it. The issue involved is not one of the liberty of an individual or of the press, but the right of every litigant to have his case heard free from baneful external influences sought to be exerted from selfish or other improper motives. It is injecting into the case a harmful and disturbing element to the prejudice of the rights of the litigants, and inconsistent with the due and orderly administration of justice."

The Constitution provides: "Every person may freely speak, write and publish on all subjects, being responsible for the abuse of the liberty."

NEW HAMPSHIRE.

The Constitution declares: "The liberty of the press is essential to the security of freedom in a State; it ought, therefore, to be inviolably preserved."

Tenney's Case, 23 *N. H.* 162 (166). (1851.) Action for

contempt, for circulating copies of a bill in equity, containing charges against parties to the action.

The Court, finding defendant guilty, said: "Abusing parties concerned in causes before the court of chancery, and prejudicing mankind before the cause is heard, is a contempt. * * * Anything done either for the purpose of obstructing justice, or which may have that effect, may be punished as a contempt of the court before whom the proceedings are had."

Sturoc's Case, 48 N. H. 428 (432). (1869.) Action for contempt for reflecting on conduct of Court in a pending matter.

The Court, in adjudging the respondent guilty, said: "It must not be inferred that we question the right to criticize and censure the conduct of courts and parties when causes have been finally decided. The question in this case is whether publications can be permitted which have a tendency to prejudice the decisions of pending causes. The publishers of newspapers have the right, but no higher than others, to bring to public notice the conduct of courts and parties, after the decision has been made; and, provided the publications are true, and fair in spirit, there is no law, and I am sure there is no disposition, to restrain or punish the freest expression of the disapprobation that any person may entertain of what is done in or by the courts."

NEW JERSEY.

The Constitution provides: "Every person may freely speak, write and publish his sentiments on all subjects, being responsible for the abuse of that right. No law shall be passed to restrain or abridge the liberty of speech or of the press."

In re Cheeseman, 49 N. J. Law 115 (141, 142). (1886.) Appeal from contempt order for publication of articles reflecting on Court for conviction of defendant. Appeal dismissed.

The Court said: "The importance of the 'liberty of the press' is urged upon us. We do not underestimate it, but, after all, the liberty of the press is only the liberty which every man has to utter his sentiments, and can be enjoyed only in subjection to that precept both of law and of morals: *sic utere tuo, ut alienum non laedas.* In a government where order is secured, not so much by force as by the respect which citizens entertain for the law and those charged with its administration, nothing which tends to preserve that respect from forfeiture on the one hand and detraction on the other can be hostile to the commonwealth.

NEW YORK.

The New York Constitution (Art. I, Sec. 8) declares that "every citizen may freely speak, write and publish his sentiments on all subjects, being responsible for the abuse of that right; and no law shall be passed to restrain or abridge the liberty of the press."

People v. Preer, 1 *Caines* 518. (1804.) Action for contempt for comment on pending action.

The Court said: "Publications scandalizing the Court or intending unduly to influence, or overawe their deliberations, are contempts which they are authorized to punish by attachment; and, indeed, it is essential to their dignity of character, their utility and independence, that they should possess and exercise this authority."

People v. Crosswell, 3 *Johns. Cas.* (*N. Y.*), 337 (393). (1804.) Action for criminal libel, in publishing an article which accused Thomas Jefferson of hiring a pamphleteer to caluminate Washington and others.

The Court, after reviewing the constitutional provisions for free speech and a free press, said: "I am far from intending that these authorities mean, by the freedom of the press, a press wholly beyond the reach of the law; for this would be emphatically Pandora's Box, the source of every evil. * * * The founders of our governments were too wise and too just, ever to have intended, by the freedom of the press, a right to circulate falsehood as well as truth, or that the press should be a lawful vehicle of malicious defamation, or an engine for evil and designing men to cherish, for mischievous purposes, sedition, irreligion and impurity. Such an abuse of the press would be incompatible with the existence and good order of civil society. The true rule of law is that the intent and tendency of the publication is, in every instance, to be the substantial inquiry on the trial, and that the truth is admissible in evidence to explain that intent, and not in every instance to justify it. I adopt in this case, as perfectly correct, the comprehensive and accurate definition of one of the counsel at the bar, that the liberty of the press consists in the right to publish, with impunity, truth, with good motives and for justifiable ends, whether it respects government, magistracy or individuals."

Brandreth v. Lance, 8 *Paige* (*N. Y.*), 24 (26) ; 34 *Am. Dec.* 368. (1839.) Action for an injunction against the publication of a satirical biography of plaintiff, alleged to be libelous in its nature.

The Court, in sustaining a demurrer, said: "It is very evident that this Court cannot assume jurisdiction of the case presented by the complainant's bill, or any other case of the like nature, without infringing upon the liberty of the press, and attempting to exercise a power of prevention which, as the legislature has decided, cannot safely be entrusted to any tribunal, consistently with the principles of a free government."

N. Y. Juvenile Guardian Society v. Rosevelt, 7 *Daly* (*N. Y.*) 188 (191). (1877.) Motion to vacate an injunction against the publication of alleged libelous matter.

The Court, in granting the motion, on the authority of Brandreth v. Lance, 8 Paige 24, further said: "Conceding * * * that the matter thus published is defamatory and libelous, as averred, the publication cannot be restrained by a court of equity; and those injured by such publications, if they are libelous, must seek their remedy by a civil action, or by an indictment in the criminal courts; there being no authority in this court, as a court of equity, to restrain any such publication; the exercise of any such jurisdiction being repugnant to the provision of the Constitution, which declares (Art 1, p. 8) that every citizen may freely speak, write and publish his sentiments on all subjects, being responsible for the abuse of that right; and that no law shall be passed to restrain or abridge the liberty of speech or of the press."

Hart v. People, 26 *Hun* (*N. Y.*) 396 (400). (1882.) The defendants were indicted for publishing an advertisement of the Louisiana lottery. Lotteries are forbidden by the Constitution of N. Y.

The Court, in overruling a demurrer to the indictment, said: "An act of the legislature to prevent the press from discussing the legality or propriety of lotteries, or from exposing their existence as violations of law, and calling the attention of the public authorities to them, or criticising the acts or neglect of public officials in regard to enforcing the laws against them, would be violations of constitutional rights and liberties of the press. But it is a very different thing to prohibit the publication of accounts, or notices or advertisements which are designed to aid and assist in the promotion of lotteries, by informing persons desirous of engaging in such lotteries where they are to be drawn, what are the prizes therein, what are the prices of tickets or shares, and where tickets may be obtained, or otherwise aiding and assisting the unlawful act of maintaining and carrying on such violations of the statute.

"Since lotteries are regarded as public evils, in their nature, so injurious as to require express constitutional prohibition, there can hardly seem to be a doubt that laws in aid and execution of the provisions of the Constitution cannot properly be pronounced by the courts repugnant thereto and therefore void."

People v. Most, 75 *N. Y. Supp.* 591 (592, 593); 71 *App. Div.* 160. (1902.) Appeal from conviction of a misdemeanor in "seriously endangering the public peace," by the publication of an article justifying violence against rulers.

The Court, in affirming the conviction, referring to the constitutional guarantee of free speech, said: "But the provision of the constitution referred to (Art. I, Sec. 8) manifestly does not give to a citizen the right to murder, nor does it give him the right to advise the commission of that crime by others. What it does permit is liberty of action only to the extent that such liberty does not interfere with or deprive others of an equal right. In the eye of the law, each citizen has an equal right to live, to act, and to enjoy the benefits of the laws of the state under which he lives. But no one has the right to use the privileges thus conferred in such a way as to injure his fellow-citizens; and one who imagines that he has labors under a serious misconception not only of the true meaning of the constitutional provision referred to, but of his duty and obligations to his fellow-citizens and to the state itself."

People v. Most, 171 *N. Y.* 423 (431, 432); 64 *N. E.* 175 (178); 58 *L. R. A.* 309. (1902.) Appeal from affirmance of conviction for publication of alleged seditious publications. (See 75 N. Y. Supp. 591.)

The Court affirmed the conviction, and in discussing the constitutional guarantee said: "While the right to publish is thus sanctioned and secured, the abuse of that right is excepted from the protection of the Constitution; and authority to provide for and punish such abuse is left to the legislature. The punishment of those who publish articles which tend to corrupt morals, induce crime or destroy society, is essential to the security of freedom and the stability of the state. While all the agencies of government, executive, legislative and judicial, cannot abridge the freedom of the press, the legislature may control and the courts may punish the licentiousness of the press. "The liberty of the press," as Chancellor Kent declared in a celebrated case, "consists in the right to publish, with impunity, truth, with good motives, and for justifiable ends; whether it respects governments, magistracy or individuals" (People v. Crosswell, 3 Johns. Cas. 336, 393). Mr. Justice Story defined the phrase to mean "that every man shall have a right to speak, write and print his opinions upon any subject whatsoever, without any prior restraint, so always, that he does not injure any other person in his rights, person, property or reputation; and so always, that he does not thereby disturb the public peace, or attempt to subvert the government" (Story's Commentaries on the Constitution, p. 1874).

"The Constitution does not protect a publisher from the consequence of a crime committed by the act of publication. It does not shield a printed attack on private character; for the same section from which the above quotation is taken expressly sanctions criminal prosecution for libel. It does not permit the advertisement of lotteries, for the next section prohibits lotteries and the sale of lottery tickets. It does not permit the publication of blasphemous or obscene articles, as the authorities uniformly hold. It places no restraint upon the power of the legislature to punish the publication of matter which is injurious to society according to the standard of the common law. It does not deprive the state of the primary right of self preservation. It does not sanction unbridled license nor authorize the publication of articles prompting the commission of murder or overthrow of government by force. All courts and commentators contrast the liberty of the press with its licentiousness, and condemn, as not sanctioned by the constitution of any state, appeals designed to destroy the reputation of the citizen, the peace of society or the existence of the government."

Stuart v. Press Pub. Co., 82 *N. Y. Supp.* 401 (408); 83 *App. Div.* 467 (1903.) Action for libel.

The Court said: "Liberty of speech and of the press is guaranteed by the supreme law of the land, and will be zealously guarded, preserved and enforced by the courts. The provisions of the Federal and State Constitutions were designed to secure rights of the people and of the press for the public good; and they do not license the utterance of false, slanderous or libelous matter. Individuals are free to talk, and the press is at liberty to publish, and neither may be restrained by injunction; but they are answerable for the abuse of this privilege, in an action for slander or libel under the common law, except where by that law, or by statute enacted in the interest of the public policy, the publication is privileged and deemed for the general good, even though it works a private injury."

OHIO.

The Constitution (Art. I, Sec. 11) provides: "Every citizen may freely speak, write and publish his sentiments on all subjects, being responsible for the abuse of the right; and no law shall be passed to restrain or abridge the liberty of speech, or of the press."

Dopp v. Doll, 13 *Weekly Law Bull.* (*Ohio*), 335. (1885.) Action for injunction against anticipated libel.

Injunction refused as incompatible with constitutional liberty of the press. Nothing specially quotable.

Myers v. State, 21 *Weekly Law Bull.* (*Ohio*), 404. (1889.) Contempt proceeding for publishing reflections on court. Defendant found guilty. Nothing specially quotable.

In re Press-Post, 3 *Ohio N. P.* 180. (1896.) Contempt proceedings for publishing articles about case on trial. Dismissed with admonition.

The Court said: "The abuses of the freedom of the press are not as dangerous as its suppression would be. The press is a necessary, important and valuable institution in imparting information with respect to the conduct of every department of government—the judiciary as well as the legislative and executive authorities—information to which the people are entitled; but the preservation of the rights of persons who are accused of crime to a fair and impartial trial is just as essential and important in our democratic system of government."

OKLAHOMA TERRITORY.

Burke v. Ter. of Oklahoma, 2 Okla. 499 (522). (1894.) Action for contempt for article offensive to judge.

The Court said: "We decline in this case to give character to a manufactured sentiment by joining the too often repeated discussion of a perverted application of our beneficent heritage of freedom of speech and liberty of the press. During these occasions, when crime stalks abroad cloaked in the garb of liberty, and when the assassin of our highest and noblest institutions of civil government would audaciously bid the hand of justice bestow reward for punishment too long deserved, we are reminded of the historic words of Madame Roland, 'Ah, Liberty, how many crimes are committed in thy name!' and resolve that the shield of the innocent shall not be the weapon of the guilty."

OREGON.

The Constitution provides that "no law shall be passed restraining the free expression of opinion, or restricting the right to speak, write or print freely on any subject whatever; but every person shall be responsible for the abuse of the right."

Upton v. Hume, 24 Ore. 420 (432). (1893.) Action for libel.

The Court said: "The term 'freedom of the press,' which is guaranteed under the Constitution, has led some to suppose that the proprietors of newspapers have a right to publish with impunity charges for which others would be held responsible: This is a mistake; the publisher of a newspaper possesses no immunity from liability on account of a libelous publication, not belonging to any other citizen. In either case the publisher is subject to the law of the land; and, when the publication is a false and defamatory one, he must answer in damages to the injured party."

PENNSYLVANIA.

The Constitution provides: "The free communication of thoughts and opinions is one of the invaluable rights of man, and every citizen may freely speak, write and print on any subject, being responsible for the abuse of that liberty." There is much additional matter seeking specially to protect freedom for the discussion of public officials. The Pennsylvania decisions nearly all relate only to the effect of these other provisions upon actions for personal libel, and not to the general clause above quoted.

Republica v. Passmore, 3 Yeates (Pa.), 441 (442). (1802.) Action for contempt for publishing an article reflecting on a party to a pending action.

The Court said: "However libelous the publication complained of may be, we have no cognizance of it in this summary mode, unless it be a contempt of the court. But we are unanimously of opinion that in point of law it is such a contempt. * * * If the minds of the public can be prejudiced by such improper publications, before a cause is heard, justice cannot be administered."

TEXAS.

The Texas Bill of Rights provides (Sec. 8) that "every person shall be at liberty to speak, write or publish his opinions on any subject, being responsible for the abuse of that privilege; and no law shall ever be passed curtailing the liberty of speech or of the press."

Ex Parte Neill, 32 Tex. Crim. 275 (276, 277). (1889.) Appeal from denial of a writ of habeas corpus. The appellant had been arrested for selling a certain paper, contrary to the provisions of a municipal ordinance, which adjudged said paper a public nuisance, and prohibited its sale.

The Court, in pronouncing the ordinance unconstitutional and void, and discharging the relator, said: "The power to prohibit the publication of newspapers is not within the compass of legislative action in this State; and any law enacted for that purpose would clearly be in derogation of the Bill of Rights. * * *

"To prevent the abuse of this privilege as affecting the public, the legislature has prescribed penalties to be enforced at the suit of the State, leaving the matter of private injuries to be determined between the parties in civil proceedings.

"We are not informed of any authority which sustains the doctrine that a municipal corporation is invested with the power to declare the sale of newspapers a nuisance. The power to suppress one concedes the power to suppress all, whether such publications are political, secular, religious, decent or indecent, obscene or otherwise. The doctrine of the Constitution must prevail in this State, which clothes the citizen with the liberty to speak, write or publish his opinion on any and all subjects, subject alone to responsibility for the abuse of such privilege."

WASHINGTON.

The Constitution provides: "Every person may freely speak, write and publish on all subjects, being responsible for the abuse of that right."

State v. Tugwell, 19 *Wash.* 238 (253, 256). (1898.)

The Court said: The constitutional liberty of speech and the press and the guarantees against its abridgment, * * * undoubtedly primarily grew out of the censorship of articles intended for publication by public authority. Such censorship was inconsistent with free institutions and with that free discussion of all public officers and agents required for the intelligent exercise of the right of suffrage. * * * If the article is calculated to embarrass or influence a court to prevent a fair trial between suitors in court either by disturbing the independent verdict of the jury or the independent and unbiased conclusion of the court, it is contempt. * * * The right of suitors in court and persons charged with offenses to a fair trial is guaranteed by our fundamental law. * * * It is this right of impartial trial which is violated by the publication and submission of an article to the Court, while a cause is pending and yet undetermined, tending to embarrass or influence the court in its final conclusion; and the individual liberty of the citizen is gone when his personal rights are endangered or lost by such extraneous influences. It is this protection of the rights of suitors in a judicial action, which compels the courts to exercise their jurisdiction of contempt. * * * In such conclusion, it is not intended to intimate or suggest that any citizen of the state has not a legal right to comment upon, criticise and freely and without restriction from any lawful authority discuss any case determined by any of the courts of this State after the final disposition of such case; or that any restriction of fair and impartial reporting of cases pending in courts, unless forbidden by rule, is now imposed by our Laws."

WEST VIRGINIA.

The Constitution provides: "No law abridging the freedom of speech, or of the press, shall be passed; but the legislature may by suitable penalties restrain the publication or sale of obscene books, papers or pictures, and provide for the punishment of libel, and defamation of character, and for the recovery in civil actions, by the aggrieved party, of suitable damages for such libel, or defamation."

Sweeny v. Baker, 13 *W. Va.* 158 (182). (1878.) Action for libel.

The Court said: "The terms 'freedom of the press' and 'liberty of the press' have misled some to suppose that the proprietors of a newspaper had a right to publish that with impunity, for the publication of which others would have been held responsible. But the proper signification of these phrases is, if so understood, misapprehended. The 'liberty of the press' consists in a right, in the conductor of a newspaper, to print whatever he chooses without any previous license, but subject to be held responsible therefor to exactly the same extent, that any one else should be responsible for the publication."

State v. Frew, 24 *W. Va.* 416 (466, 478) : (1884.) : Contempt for proceeding for publication of an article charged with being calculated to impugn the integrity of members of the Court.

Constitutional guarantee not directly discussed.

The Court said: "In every respect of the case, the publication is clearly contempt of this Court. Can such a publication be palliated or excused? Far be it from us to take away the liberty of the press. or in the slightest degree to interfere with its rights. The good of society and of government demands that the largest liberty should be accorded the press, which is a power and an engine of great good; but the press itself will not for a moment tolerate such licentiousness as is exhibited in said editorial. The press is interested in the purity of the courts; and if it had no respect for the judges on the bench, it should respect the Court; for when the judges now on the bench shall be remembered only in the decision they have rendered, the Court will still remain; it never dies; it is the people's Court; and the press as the champion of the people's rights is interested in preserving the respect due to the Court."

Snyder, J., concurring, said: "It must be and is cheerfully conceded that public journals have the right to criticize freely the acts of all public officers—executive, legislative and judicial. It is a constitutional privilege that even the Legislature cannot abridge. But such criticism should always be just and with a view to promote the public good. Where the conduct of a public officer is wilfully corrupt, no measure of condemnation can be too severe; but when the misconduct, apparent or real, may be simply an honest error of judgment, the condemnation ought to be with-held or mingled with charity. As said by Holt in his work on Libel, chap. 9, 'It is undoubtedly within the natural compass of the liberty of the press, to discuss in a decent and temperate manner the decisions and judgments of a court of justice; to suggest even errors; and, provided it is done in the language and with the views of fair criticism, to censure what is apparently wrong; but with this limitation, that no false or dishonest motives be assigned to any party.' These views are, in my judgment, sound; and these rights should be cheerfully accorded to the press in this free and enlightened country."

WISCONSIN.

The Constitution provides; "Every person may freely speak, write and publish his sentiments on all subjects, being responsible for the abuse of that right; and no laws shall be passed to restrain or abridge the liberty of speech or of the press."

State ex rel. Attorney Gen. v. Cir. Ct. for Eau Claire Co., 97 Wis. 1 (12, 13). (1897.) Action of prohibition to check contempt proceedings for publication severely criticising the conduct on the bench of a judge, who was at the time a candidate for re-election. Peremptory writ granted.

The Court said: "Important as it is that courts should perform their grave public duties unimpeded and unprejudiced by illegitimate influences, there are other rights guaranteed to all citizens by our constitution and form of government, either expressly or impliedly, which are fully as important, and which must be guarded with an equally jealous care. These rights are the right of free speech and of free publication of the citizen's sentiments 'on all subjects' * * * also the right to freely discuss the merits and qualifications of a candidate for public office, being responsible for the abuse of such right in a proper action at law. * * * Truly, it must be a grievous and weighty necessity which will justify so arbitrary a proceeding, whereby a candidate for office becomes the accuser, judge and jury, and may within a few hours summarily punish his critic with imprisonment. The result of such a doctrine is that all unfavorable criticism of a sitting judge's past official action can be at once stopped by the judge himself, or, if not stopped, can be punished by immediate imprisonment. If there can be any more effectual way to gag the press and subvert freedom of speech, we do not know where to find it. * * * We, however, adopted no part of the common law which was inconsistent with our constitution; and it seems clear to us that so extreme a power is inconsistent with, and would materially impair, the constitutional rights of free speech and free press."

INFERIOR U. S. COURTS.

U. S. v. Hall, 26 Fed. Cas. No. 15, 282. (1871.) On demurrer to Indictment for conspiracy to intimidate and prevent free speech. Demurrer overruled.

The Court, in an elaborate argument, held that by the Fourteenth Amendment to the Constitution of the United States, the federal government assumed authority, as above the states, to safeguard the fundamental rights of the citizen, including that of free speech, and was bound to interfere, in case of State legislation hostile to these rights, or failure of the State properly to secure them.

U. S. v. Huggett, 40 Fed Rep. 636 (638, 639). (1889.) Demurrer to indictment for mailing sealed letters containing obscene matter, prior to the passage of the statute including them.

The Court, sustaining the demurrer, said: "But I am of the opinion that the adjudications which have affirmed the validity of the indictments do fall into the very latitude of construction which was condemned by the Supreme Court of the United States in the above cited cases; and that upon the somewhat gratuitous assumption that Congress intended to purge the mails of all impurity whatever * * * I say upon a gratuitous assumption, because the history of the legislation shows quite clearly, it seems to me, that, until the recent acts of Congress, that body has never come up to the elevated plane of moral action suggested by these decisions, and to be implied from putting this restriction upon the absolute freedom of that form of correspondence, but has especially refused to do that thing * * * And this reluctance to interfere with the freedom of private correspondence is readily explainable by the suggestion of Mr. Justice Field that Congress felt the difficulty of accomplishing its purpose to protect the morals of the people by a wise use of its power over the postal establishment, 'consistently with rights reserved to the people, of far greater importance than the transportation of the mail.' Ex. parte Jackson, 96 U. S. 727, 732. Free speech, and particularly free speech in private intercourse, and the aversion of our race of freemen to interfere with it, stood somewhat in the way of this legislation; at least in the popular estimation. * * *Postal officials are not supposed to examine or to appropriate to themselves the indulgence of reading that which goes into the mails in any form, but their duty is to handle and distribute it without doing that. They violate their duty when they so use any mail matter whatsoever, except for the purpose of such official inspection as may be authorized."

U. S. Harman, 45 *Fed. Rep.* 414 (415, 416). (1891.) Indictment for mailing alleged obscene publication. The Court said: "In view, however, of the fact that the defendant places so much stress along the line of his entire defense on the liberty which should be accorded to the press, it may as well be said here as elsewhere that it is a radical misconception of the scope of the constitutional protection to indulge the belief that a person may print and publish, *ad libitum,* any matter, whatever the substance or language, without accountability to law. Liberty, in all its forms and assertions in this country, is regulated by law. It is not an unbridled license. Where vituperation or licentiousness begins, the liberty of the press ends * * * While happily we have outlived the epoch of censors and licensers of the press, to whom the publisher must submit his matter in advance, responsibility yet attaches to him when he transcends the boundary line where he outrages the common sense of decency, or endangers the public safety * * * In a government of law, the law-making power must be recognized as the proper authority to define the boundary line between license and licentiousness; and it must likewise remain the province of the jury—the constitutional triers of the fact—to determine when that boundary line has been crossed."

Thomas v. Cinn, etc., Ry. Co., 62 *Fed. Rep.* 803 (822). (1894.) Contempt proceeding against labor leader for violating injunction.

The Court said: "Something has been said about the right of assembly and free speech secured by the constitution of Ohio. It would be strange, if that right could be used to sustain the carrying out of such an unlawful and criminal conspiracy as we have seen this to be. It never has been supposed to protect one from prosecution or suits for slander, or for any of the many malicious and tortious injuries which the agency of the tongue has been so often employed to inflict. If the obstruction to the operation of the road by the receiver was unlawful and malicious, it is not less a contempt because the instrument which he used to effect it was his tongue, rather than his hand."

U. S. SUPREME COURT.

Respublica v. Oswald, 1 *Dall.* (*U. S.*) 319 (325, 326). (1788.) Action for contempt for publishing comment on pending action.

The Court said: "However ingenuity may torture the expressions, there can be little doubt of the just sense of these sections (the constitutional guarantee of free speech and free press) : They give to every citizen a right of investigating the conduct of those who are entrusted with the public business; and they effectually preclude any attempt to fetter the press by the institution of license * * * The true liberty of the press is amply secured by permitting every man to publish his opinions; but it is due to the peace and dignity of society to inquire into the motives of such publications, and to distinguish between those which are meant for use and reformation, and with an eye solely to the public good, and those which are intended merely to delude and defame. To the latter description, it is impossible that any good government should afford protection and impunity.

"If then, the liberty of the press is regulated by any just principle, there can be little doubt that he who attempts to raise a prejudice against his antagonist in the minds of those that must ultimately determine the dispute beween them; who, for that purpose, represents himself as a persecuted man, and asserts that his judges are influenced by passion and prejudice —wilfully seeks to corrupt the source, and to dishonor the administration of justice."

Ex parte Jackson, 96 *U. S.* 727 (736). (1877.) Indictment for mailing lottery circular. Habeas corpus proceeding.

The Court, denying the writ, said: "In excluding articles from the mail, the object of Congress has not been to interfere with the freedom of the press or with any other rights of the people; but to refuse its facilities for the distribution of matter deemed injurious to the public morals." The Court, however, distinctly and forcibly held that Congress had no authority to prohibit the transportation of such articles in any other way than through the mails.

In Re Rapier, 143 *U. S.* 110 (134, 135). (1892.) Indictment for mailing lottery advertisement.

The Court said: "We cannot regard the right to operate a lottery as a fundamental right infringed by the legislation in question; nor are we able to see that Congress can be held, in its enactment, to have abridged the freedom of the press. The circulation of newspapers is not prohibited; but the government declines itself to become an agent in the circulation of printed matter which it regards as injurious to the people. The freedom of communication is not abridged within the intent and meaning of the constitutional provision, unless Congress is absolutely destitute of any discretion as to what shall or shall not be carried in the mails, and compelled arbitrarily to assist in the dissemination of matters condemned by its judgment, through the governmental agencies which it controls. That power may be abused furnishes no ground for a denial of its existence, if government is to be maintained at all."

Patterson v. Colo., 205 *U. S.* 454 (462). (1906.) Writ of error in contempt proceeding. Writ dismissed for lack of jurisdiction.

The Court said: "But even if we assume that freedom of speech and freedom of the press were protected from abridgment on the part not only of the United States but also of the States, still we should be far from the conclusion that the plaintiff in error would have us reach. In the first place, the main purpose of such constitutional provisions is 'to prevent all such *previous restraints* upon publications as had been practised by other governments,' and they do not prevent the subsequent punishment of such as may be deemed contrary to the public welfare."

CONCLUSION.

Having now exhibited the judicial cerebrations upon our constitutional right to unabridged freedom of speech and of the press, I proceed to restate what is claimed to be proven by the exhibit. No matter whether the result of the opinion was to uphold or to abridge the freedom of the press, I think I am warrented in making the following assertion as applicable to, and true of every opinion published upon the subject of freedom or press.

1. In no case did the court derive its standard for determining the constitutionality of the enactment under consideration by critical deductions made from the language of the constitutional phase involved. If that was too ambiguous the fact should have been stated, and the historical method of interpretation should have been pursued.

2. In no case did the court arrive at its standard for determining the constitutional meaning, by any historical study of the pre-revolutionary controversies over freedom of utterance, to discover what issues our constitutions were intended to decide, or to find the elements of unification in those past demands for such freedom, which common element of all struggles against abridgments, varied both as to subject-matter and methods of suppression, would inevitably reveal the true essence of that which those who were still in closer touch with these struggles than we can be, intended to protect us against, by the constitutional phrase in question.

3. In-so-far as any court attempted to assign reasons for its conclusions, upon either side, these justifications are never drawn from the constitutions, but are a mere statement of those considerations of expediency which might properly and perhaps effectively, be addressed to a constitutional convention, with the view to enlightening them as to what a constitution ought to contain upon this subject, but certainly not very informing as to what a constitution already in existence does in fact mean. In other words, constitutional meanings were not deduced from that instrument, but read into it, and instead of having government according to Constitutional Laws, we have government according to the arbitrary and despotic will of a judiciary, with whom a Constitutionally guaranteed unabridgable right to utter one's sentiments, means the right to utter only that which the courts deem advantageous to the public welfare.

4. From the foregoing propositions, I derive this last one. In every case wherein our constitutional guarantees for an unabridged right of utterance were involved, the alleged judicial "interpretation" expressed only the judge's emotional approval, or disapproval of the right to utter the particular sentiments then before him for judgment, and the irrelevant reasons assigned by him were deemed cogent only because they seemed to justify his prior feeling-convictions. If I am correct in this little psychologic study of the mental processes of our judges, then of course they are hardly entitled to much of that adoration usually accorded only to those possessed of very superior intellectual attainments.

It remains to be seen whether we are able to lead the way to a better method of constitutional interpretation, and make the initial attempt toward a rational generalization, such as will give us a standard of judgment for the determination of the constitutionality of every law claimed to be an abridgment of our right to utter; and thus, perhaps, ultimately we may lead the courts from mistaking their dogmatism, empirical inductions, personal emotions, moral sentimentalizing, judicial interpolations and constitutional amendment, or question-begging sophomoric declamation, for constitutional construction.

When I read the exciting grammar-school oration from the Supreme Court of Oklahoma; and when in the foregoing opinions I see it manifested again and again, that the judges of the highest courts of our land evidently do not know the difference between an analogy and a mere figure of speech, and because of that ignorance can mis-use the former as a basis of constitutional " construction "; and when I see how often "most *learned* judges" are stupid enough to think they define the limits and prescribe the criteria of constitutional liberty by the use of such meaningless epithets as "license" or "licentiousness"; and when I see "abuse" of freedom founded only upon the damaged emotions or injured vanity of judges who misconceive this mere psychologic offense—this mere constructive abuse—to be very real, without ever having even thought of the possible difference between it and an actual abuse which can only be predicated upon an ascertained, actual, real and material injury; and when I contemplate the probable fact that many readers of this paragraph will not know, even now, just what I mean by these criticisms, because I cannot take space to analyze each opinion and specifically point out its shortcomings; I say when I contemplate all these things, it makes me inexpressibly sad, because then I realize how slender a thread of intelligence sustains our liberties, and that the battle for real freedom is only just begun, because a generally accepted, intelligent conception of liberty, such as must precede its realization, for a long, long time yet will be impossible. Will the Federal Supreme Court exercise its great power to hasten the day of our liberation? Ah! there is a flattering hope, which *may* not disappoint.

The doubt which the courts have cast upon the meaning of "Freedom of Speech and of the Press" by declaring limitations upon, or exceptions to that freedom, makes it imperative that the doubt be resolved by an appeal to the historical interpretation of that constitutional phrase. Such an investigation will disclose to us whether or not our courts are warranted in blindly following, as they have done more or less directly, the declarations of Blackstone, Ellenborough, Mansfield or even Erskine, as to what is meant by freedom of the press, constitutionally guaranteed as an unabridgable right, and not a mere liberty by permission.

CHAPTER XI.

THE HISTORICAL INTERPRETATION OF "FREEDOM OF SPEECH AND OF THE PRESS."

The purpose is to re-interpret our constitutional guarantee for an unabridged freedom of speech and of the press, by the historical or scientific method, and with special reference to the specific issue raised by the judicial dogmatism thereon and my different conception of how that phrase ought to be interpreted. To clarify the issues, I restate these contradictory propositions, so the reader may have them constantly in mind during the following discussion.

My contention as to the meaning of a constitutionally guaranteed *right* to *unabridged* freedom of speech and of the press, is this: No matter upon what subject, nor how injurious to the public welfare any particular idea thereon may be deemed to be, the constitutional right is violated whenever anyone is not legally free to express any such or other sentiments, either;

First, because prevented in advance by a legally created censorship, or monopoly in the use of the press, or by other governmental power, or;

Second, because in the effort to secure publicity for any idea whatever, the equality of natural opportunity is destroyed, in that some, by subsequent legal penalties or other legal limitations, are deterred, or are impeded, in the use of the ordinary and natural methods of reaching the public, on the same legal terms, as these are permitted to any person for the presentation of any other idea, or;

Third, because the natural opportunity of all is abridged by some statutory impediment, such as taxes upon the dissemination of information placed upon all intellectual intercourse, as such, or on all of a particular class, or;

Fourth, because inequalities in State-created, or State-supported, opportunity is legalized, so that, in the effort to secure publicity for any sentiments and merely because of their nature, literary style, or supposed evil tendency, any one is discriminated against, either by law, or for any cause by any arbitrary exercise of official discretion, in the use of such State-created or State-supported facilities, or;

Fifth, because after expressing one's sentiments one is by law liable to punishment, merely for having uttered disapproved thoughts;

Provided always, that the prohibition, abridgment, discrimination, subsequent punishment, or other legal disability or disadvantage, is arbitrarily inflicted, or attaches merely because of the character, literary style, or supposed bad tendency of the offending sentiments, and their spread among sane adults, willing to read, see, or hear them, or is the result of arbitrary official discretion, and that they do not attach because of any inseparably accompanying, or other resultant penalized invasive act, constituting an actually ascertained, resultant, material injury, (as distinguished from mere speculative or constructive harm) inflicted, or by overt act attempted to be inflicted, before arrest and punishment, and in either case actually resulting from the particular utterance involved.

But, if the injury is to reputation, or loss of public esteem, and among the consequences is material injury to the libeled person, even then, truth and justifiable motive must always be recognized by law as a complete defense; and where the resultant injury consists in violence to person or property, *actually* attempted or achieved, then the *intent* to achieve such results must be of the essence of the crime, and punishment of a *mere* speaker must be only that of an accessory before the fact, if our constitutional guaranty is to be made effective. I do not discuss civil remedies.

THE JUDICIAL INTERPRETATION.

The contrary conclusion of the Courts is well summarized by a dictum, perhaps hastily uttered, of the Federal Supreme Court. These are its words: "The main purpose of such constitutional provisions is to prevent all such *previous* restraints as had been practised by other governments, and they do not prevent the subsequent punishment of such as may be deemed contrary to the public welfare"![1]

In England the licensing acts, which put a *previous* restraint upon publications, existed for only a short time, and finally expired in A. D. 1694.[2] It seems, therefore, according to the

[1]Patterson v. Colo., 205 U. S. 454, (462).
[2]Stevens' "Sources of the Constitution of the U. S.," p. 221; Patterson's "Liberty of Press and Speech," 50 and 51.

definition of our American Courts, that perfect *unabridged* liberty of speech and press obtained in England after the year 1694, because no licenser prohibited before utterance, and there prevailed a system of subsequent punishment for only such opinions as were deemed contrary to the public welfare, and for nearly a century preceding our Revolution the agitation for larger freedom of speech and of the press was a vain demand for something already enjoyed by the agitators, but not known by them to exist.

However ridiculous such judicial implications will appear to some, the official eminence of the many judges who have sanctioned that doctrine, and especially the tremendous consequence of it to our liberties, precludes levity. We will therefore proceed in all seriousness to demonstrate the error of our courts by a historical study and a scientific interpretation of the facts. Thus it will be made to appear that unabridged liberty of discussion did not obtain in England, or its American Colonies, from 1694 until the American Revolution, and that our Constitutions were designed to change the prevailing system of an abridged and *abridgable liberty of discussion by permission,* to an unabridged and *unabridgable liberty of discussion as a constitutionally guaranteed, natural right,* not to be ignored, as in England, or Russia, where the claim of such freedom was and is denied, on the plea of furthering the public welfare.

THE EARLY THEORY AS TO FREE SPEECH.

In England, "before public meetings were resorted to as an ordinary exercise of self-government, great looseness prevailed in the law, the theory apparently being that free-speech was a species of gift by the Sovereign to the people."[3] To have the power to control what others may hear or see, is of course to that extent a limitation upon their right to acquire and have opinions—thus abridging the liberty of conscience—since one cannot well acquire opinions the materials of which are withheld from him. Since the right to have a personal judgment and the right to express it existed only as a gift from kings and priests, when the issuing of pamphlets became an extended form of speech nothing was more natural than that at first "printing was treated like the making of salamoniac and apprentices were cautioned not to lay open the principles to the unfaithful "[4]

[3]Patterson's "Liberty of Press, p. 19.
[4]Patterson's "Liberty of Press," p. 43, citing, Becket v. Denison, 17 Parl. Hist., 958.

The reasons underlying such conclusions are fully appreciated only by keeping in mind the English conception of that period as to the nature of the State. The features especially to be remembered are the union of Church and State, and the King's rule of divine right, as vice-gerent for the Almighty, exercising the divinity's political omnipotence, and thus being the giver of all good, including the grant of commercial opportunity and monopoly, and being incapable of doing any wrong. It necessarily followed from such premises that the State-religion be declared the fundamental and controlling part of the laws of England, so that any statute made against "any point of the Christian religion or what they thought was the Christian religion, was void."[5]

From such considerations there grew up naturally laws against blasphemous and seditious utterances. That these found the tap-root of their justification in the union of Church and State is evident from such judicial unreason as the following: "To say that religion is a cheat, is to dissolve all those obligations whereby civil societies are preserved, and Christianity being part and parcel of the laws of England, therefore to reproach the Christian religion is to speak in subversion of the law."[6] This doctrine no longer obtains in England.[7]

Since man can impose no rightful limitations on the exercise of power by those who rule by divine right, it follows that under such a State all liberty is necessarily only liberty by permission, never liberty as an admitted natural right, and necessarily to decry religion is to inculcate treason against those whose right to rule is founded in that religion, and to attack a government conducted by divine right is in its turn irreligious and blasphemous. So, then, admitting the premises of their Church-State, the Star Chamber was quite logical when in *de famosis libellis* the court assumed "that words against the government amount to sedition; and that words against an archbishop are words against the government."[8]

Necessarily, under such a State, those who opposed the existing restrictions upon speech and press were promoting irreligion, and therefore treason against both earthly and heavenly governments. In that controversy, the demand for unabridged, or even larger freedom of heretical religious utterance, necessarily included a demand for the right to advocate even treason, and of course logically must include all the lesser

[5]Patterson's "Liberty of Press and Speech," p. 67, citing 10 St. Tr. 375.
[6]Reg. v. Taylor, Ventris, 293.
[7]See "Blasphemy and Blasphemous Libel," by Sir Fitz James Stephens, *Fortnightly Review*, Mar., 1884.
[8] Mence on Libel, p. 289.

crimes. Although in America we boast of having outgrown at least the avowed union of Church and State, we still retain that union in fact, by virtue of many repressive laws which have no other foundation than the precedents of a Church-State, and the moral sentimentalizing associated with, or anchored in, religion. In studying the English precedents we must always bear in mind the before-mentioned essential difference in our theories of government and the resultant difference between liberty merely by permission and liberty as a constitutionally guaranteed natural right.

ON CONSTITUTIONAL DESIGN.

Our constitutional guarantees upon this subject are both useless and meaningless except on the assumption that they were designed to repudiate the old theory that freedom of utterance is liberty by permission or grant, and were intended to establish intellectual liberty as a matter of constitutionally guaranteed unabridgable natural right.

If it was not the design to change the English system of *liberty by permission* to one of *liberty as a right,* then there was no reason for any constitutional provision upon the subject. If the *only* purpose was to preclude the creation of an official censor, the easiest way would have been to have had the Constitution say, "No censor shall ever be appointed," or, "No *previous* restraints shall be put upon speech or press." Thus there would be no restriction upon other modes of abridging freedom of utterance. If the intention had been that a power should remain which, by subsequent punishment, would suppress those discussions and ideas which were deemed contrary to the public welfare, then, again, there was no need for any constitutional provision upon the subject, because no other opinions than such as had been deemed contrary to the public welfare ever had been suppressed anywhere. If it is possible to assume that the purpose of amending our Federal Constitution was to preclude Congress from punishing men for publishing ideas, believed by it to be *conducive to welfare,* then we might still expect that the most appropriate language would have been used. Then our Constitution might have read thus: "Congress shall make no law abridging freedom of speech or of the press, *except* in the interest of the public welfare." But the insistence here is that such exception cannot properly be interpolated into our Constitution by judicial action.

I utterly repudiate the dogmatic paradox of our courts,

which, while claiming to construe our Constitutions, declare that the words, the legislature "shall make *no law* abridging," etc., mean that, in the alleged interest of the public welfare, it may *enact any abridging* laws it sees fit, if thereby no restraint is imposed prior to publication.

It does seem to me that these few suggestions, together with a bit of critical thought on the words themselves, as used in our Constitutions, should be all that is necessary in justification of my contention. However, the abundance of judicial dogmatism to the contrary, and the general acquiescence therein, persuade me that a more elaborate study of the historical factors is quite indispensable for most minds, even of the sort that have capacity for logical thinking upon this subject.

THE METHOD OUTLINED.

In the scientific aspect, our social and political institutions, like all other natural phenomena, are but special manifestations of the all-pervading law of evolution. With enlarged experiences, we change our conceptions of what is required by the natural law of our social relations, and accordingly we change our verbal statements of law. It follows that the laws of a State always seem to be approaching, but never attain, perfection. This seeming corresponds to the reality so long as the dominant conception of the law is nearing the truly scientific. By a scientific conception of the law, I mean one wherein the empirical generalizations have all been included in one rational generalization, which is *the law* upon the subject, because it is derived wholly from the nature of things; and, in every state of facts to which it can be applied, it conclusively determines the *how* and the *why* certain judgments must be so, and thus, the result always being derived exclusively by deductions from the ultimate rational generalization, which thus furnishes the only standard of judgment determining the decision in every particular case, that *law* must always be conformed to, irrespective of the direct estimate of the beneficence of its results in any particular instance?[9]

I venture the assertion that no one who has understandingly read the foregoing statement of the meaning of *"Law,"* and who has also read the judicial opinions as to the meaning of unabridged freedom of speech and of the press, will claim that any American court has ever attempted to declare *the law* of our Constitutions as to the freedom of utterance, because *no*

[9] See, v. 42, *Am. Law Review,* p. 360.

court has ever attempted, even in a crude way, to furnish us with any comprehensive statement of the criteria for judging the constitutionality of enactments relating to speech or press.

In England, where there is no constitutional limitation upon the power of Parliament to abridge freedom of utterance, it was said, after the passage of the Fox libel act, that "Freedom of discussion is little else than the right to write or say anything which a jury, consisting of twelve shopkeepers, think it expedient should be said or written."[10] That is freedom as a matter of expediency and by permission, the only kind of freedom of speech and press that has ever obtained in England or Russia. How useless then is our Constitution if, as the Courts quite uniformly assert, unabridged and unabridgable freedom of discussion is the right to say whatever a legislature of mediocre attainments may think it expedient to permit to be said? If our constitutional guarantees declare and determine *rights,* then these cannot be destroyed by the arbitrary decree of the legislature, even though done in the alleged interest of the public welfare. If the Constitution is a *law of right,* then its declarations are always to be obeyed, even though the legislature and court concur in the belief that in a particular case the exercise of a constitutional right is against the public welfare. Neither can such belief invest them with the authority to amend the Constitution so as to make it read, "Congress shall make no law abridging freedom of speech or of the press *except* as to those ideas which it deems contrary to the public welfare." If we are to preclude such dogmatic judicial amendments of our Constitutions, we must develop in the judicial mind, by the scientific method, a conception of constitutional law in accord with the conception of the legal scientist.

The materials for a scientific interpretation of the Constitution are antecedent historical controversies, whose issues the Constitution was intended to decide. The method must be to trace the evolution of the idea of unabridged freedom of discussion, from its inception as a mere personal protest and mere wish of the individual to be personally free from a particular interference, through unnumbered empirical inductions to the impersonal recognition of a general principle underlying all such protests and demands, and determining the rightfulness of them. To achieve this we must study the historical controversies and the primitive crude demands for a lesser abridg-

[10]Dicey, "The Law of the Constitution," p. 234.

ment of intellectual liberty, that we may discover the common elements in all these varying demands, and when we have thus discovered the elements of unification common to all these struggles for a lesser abridgment of intellectual liberty, have studied the various historical means of abridgment from which arose the controversies which were settled by our Constitutions, and have generalized the inhibition against *all* similar recurrences, we may achieve a scientific conception of what is meant by an abridgment of freedom of speech. This will be a rational generalization giving us the criteria by which to judge whether or not a particular enactment is, or is not, a breach of the constitutional right of an unabridged freedom of utterance.

THE DISPUTANTS CLASSIFIED.

I cannot resist the feeling that it is an awful reflection upon the general and the judicial "intelligence" that any argument should be deemed necessary to show the absurdity of the official "construction" of our Constitutions. Manifestly, it is urgently necessary, and it is to this end that we are to make a more precise analysis of the historical controversy which, in America, culminated in the adoption of our constitutional guarantees for *unabridged* freedom of speech and of the press. In making our analysis of the historical contentions, we must keep in mind at least three main classes of disputants.

The first and most popular class consisted of those eminently respectable and official persons who asserted, not only the existence of a proper governmental authority to abridge in every manner the intellectual liberty of the citizen, but who also defended every existing method by which the power was being exercised. This class was the only one fortified by official justifications and judicial definitions of the pre-revolutionary period.

To the second class belonged those conservative reformers who did not question the existence of a power to control legally the intellectual food-supply of the populace, but who did question some particular manner of its exercise. These usually believed in a larger liberty of speech and press, but did not demand that it be wholly *unabridged,* and usually their arguments were directed only to the inexpediency of some particular abridgment and not toward the defense of liberty as an unabridgable natural right. Among these could be found persons who demanded larger liberty for the promotion of their own heresies, but justified the punishment of other heretics; there were those who demanded liberty for the discussion of religion, but hastened to out-Herod Herod in their justification of the punishment of the psychologic crime of verbal treason. Others, like Erskine, demanded a larger liberty for the criticism of government, but hastened to give assurance of their entire orthodoxy by joining in the clamor for the punishment of religious heretics. Should we mistake any of these disputants as the defenders of *unabridged* freedom of speech and press, and adopt their definitions of liberty, as a means of constitutional construction, we should of course be led far astray and reduce our constitutional right to unabridged freedom to a limited liberty by permission.

The third class of controversialists was composed of those few who denied the existence of any rightful authority for the punishment of any mere psychologic crimes, and who therefore demanded the establishment and maintenance of *unabridged* liberty of utterance. It was the contention of these persons which was adopted into our Constitutions, and it is their statement of the meaning of "freedom of speech" which should be made the basis for constitutional construction, and not the judicial precedents of the Star Chamber, expressing the English practise from the viewpoint of the Church-State, which viewpoint was repudiated by our American States and which precedents were overruled by our American Constitutions. Unfortunately, these precedents are still often followed by our American Courts, whose judges are supposed to be the conservators, but often act as the destroyers, of our liberty, especially when unpopular and disapproved utterances are involved.

The varying conceptions of the limits of freedom of utterance, as advocated by these classes of controversialists, will now be exemplified by illustrative quotations, that we may show what was meant by an unabridged liberty of utterance, by those whose views were incorporated in our Constitutions.

LICENSING THE PRINTER.

The press was introduced into England by Henry VII. From this fact, together with the prevailing opinion that the whole matter of freedom of speech was one of permission, or gift from the Sovereign, nothing was more natural than that Edward the VI. should by patent appoint a printer, who was to print and sell all Latin, Greek, and Hebrew books, as well as all others that might be commanded, and penalties were denounced for infringing his monopoly. Subsequently, the number of licensed printers was enlarged, but for a considerable time it was limited.[11] In this form of license, the letter of the law made no discrimination against a book according to the sentiments expressed. The license seems rather to have been a business monopoly given to some court favorite, and a matter of confidence in the printer, as one having the discretion to publish nothing inimical to the grantors of his special privilege. Of course, this public printer did not publish for future reference any of the arguments against his monopoly. Could we now look back to analyze the opposition to this first form of licensing, we would seek for two possible explanations of it. According to one, freedom of the press might mean only the commercial freedom to use the press as a tool of trade, in commercial competition with the Crown-monopolists, and a modern judge, adopting that conception as a basis for constitutional construction, might uphold a law creating a censorship over only the character of the printed matter, and not directly and immediately affecting the equality of commercial opportunity in the use of the printing press as an instrument of commerce. According to this first point of view, the abolition of this monopoly was the chief, or only, end in view, and this object would not be in the least interfered with by a new form of censorship directed against particular psychologic tendencies of opinions, which would leave intellectual liberty just as much abridged as before.

The other view would be that the opposition to licensing of the printer was based principally upon the demand for a larger intellectual liberty, by equalizing the opportunity of all for using the press as an extended form of speech. In this second view, the mere abolition of the license for printers' monopoly is not an end in itself, but a mere means to the end of increasing intellectual liberty and opportunity, a viewpoint quite constantly ignored in our judicial utterances upon this subject. It is unthinkably paradoxical that the few friends of freedom of speech and of the press who existed at that time should have had no interest in the enlargement of intellectual liberty, and were interested only in the enlarged opportunity for the use of the press as a tool of trade.

Of course this view, that enlargement of intellectual op-

[11]Paterson's "Liberty of Press," p. 44.

portunity was the chief end sought, is confirmed by the related controversial literature of approximately that time. As I write this, I have open before me a volume in which are reprinted the tracts on "Liberty of Conscience" which had been published prior to 1661. These express "the first articulations of infant liberty." The arguments are in the main very crude, as arguments for liberty. They may be clearly divided into a few general classes: First, "we dissenters are right, therefore ought to be tolerated." Second, "the Bible teaches toleration, therefore we should be tolerated." Third, "it is not in the power of man to believe as he wills, but he believes as he must, and he therefore should not be punished for expressing convictions he cannot escape." This last is a good argument against the injustice of punishing "dangerous" opinions, even yet. Amid much crude thinking, there are some few very clear perceptions, excluding all mere psychological crimes from the legitimate province of government. To this end, Luther was quoted and his thought is several times restated by different authors. Luther's words are these: "The laws of civil government extend no further than over the body and goods, and that which is external: For over the Soul, [mind] God will not suffer man to rule." Such were the contentions made in behalf of liberty of speech, or, "the liberty of prophesying," as it was then often called. One would look in vain through this volume of early tracts for any suggestion that the larger liberty contended for, or an unabridged freedom of discussion, consisted only in the absence of a *prior* censorship. I do not recall even a single mention of a previous censorship as the essence of the evil, nor mere commercial opportunity to use the press as a tool of trade, as an end to be achieved. Always the demand was for, and, indeed, the arguments were all in furtherance of, a larger intellectual liberty, and sometimes demanded an unabridged liberty of utterance, by excluding all psychological offenses from the jurisdiction of the criminal law.

These early tracts, so far as they go, are a vindication of the contention, stated at the head of this essay, as that relates to the period prior to 1661. It is utterly absurd for our courts to intimate, as they do, that the real friends of unabridged intellectual opportunity were ever concerned only with the *mere time or manner* (rather than the *substance*) of the abridgment of liberty. The friends of freedom never sought the abolition of previous restraint in favor of subsequent punishment, as an end in itself, but were seeking to enlarge intellectual opportunity as against abridgment either by prior restraint or subsequent punishment.

No doubt it was in this early protest against a licensed printer that the phrase "Freedom of the Press" came into use, for here only does it have a literal signification. When the press was made free, as an instrument of trade, the shifty tyrant saw to it that no enlargement of intellectual opportunity resulted.

USURPATION BY THE "STAR CHAMBER."

Prior to 1637 there seems to have been no criminal penalties inflicted by the English secular courts, for mere psychological offenses, such as the expression of unpopular opinions. "The Common Law took cognizance of no injuries but such as affected persons or property."[12] In 1637 the Star Chamber, which never hesitated to assume the most preposterous powers, usurped the legislative function of penalizing libel, by its decree regulating the press.[13] This Judicial lawlessness, in usurping the power to punish mere psychologic crimes under *ex post facto* criteria of guilt, of course provoked criticism from those who loved liberty and knew something of its nature, and no doubt it also secured for "the watchtower of the King" the hearty approval of all tyrants, for the protection of whose reputation and prerogatives this abridgment of freedom of utterance was inaugurated. This usurped censorship and the accompanying *ex post facto* penalization of mere psychologic crimes, were among the last and most hideous of the acts of this infamous "Judicial" body, for the Star Chamber was abolished in 1640. No doubt the hostility excited by its outrageous creation and enforcement of laws against mere verbal crimes contributed much towards the downfall, but tyranny did not die with the institution that invented this special means to its end. The co-tyrants of the Star Chamber Court and their successors, prompted by the same inordinate lust for power and preferring to be relieved of the occasion for defending their official conduct, have continued, with slight modifications and very brief cessations, to this very day to act upon the precedents of the abhorred Star Chamber. Parliamentary enactment along similar lines soon took the place of Star Chamber decrees, and vagueness in the legislative defini-

[12]Mence on Libel, p. 333.

[13]Patterson on "Liberty of Press and Speech," 45; Mence, "Law of Libel," Chapt. 9, (1824); "The Freedom of Speech and Writing," pp. 47, 49, 99, (Lond., 1766).

tion of criminal libel left quite unimpaired the power for an *ex post facto* creation of the criteria of guilt. So it comes to pass that, while maintaining some of the outward seemings of law, the fundamental evils of judicial despotism still exist, even in those countries whose inhabitants are most vociferous in their stupid boast over a purely imaginary liberty. However, let it be said, that the savagery of the penalties has been a little abated, even though on the whole intellectual liberty has received no substantial enlargement. What has been gained as to some subjects has been lost as to others. Some comparison as to this would be interesting but is not within the scope of this essay.

LICENSING THE BOOK.

The licensing of one printer was succeeded by the licensing of many and later by the abolition of this system in its entirety, allowing all alike to use the printing press as an instrument of commerce, but maintaining inequalities as to its use in the distribution of ideas. Here I have reference to those various licensing acts, expiring in 1694, which succeeded to the Star Chamber decrees, and by which a censor authorized particular books to be printed, and all publications not so authorized were penalized. It was against this censorship that Milton directed his immortal essay, "Areopagitica."

Here, again, we must seek an answer to the same old question, Is it true, as our courts generally assert, that Milton and others who opposed these licensing acts were concerned only with the *manner* and not with the *substance* of this abridgment of freedom of the press? Is it true, as our courts usually imply, that the opponents of these licensing acts demanded only the abolition of the censor and *previous restraint,* and were quite willing to admit a power to punish subsequent to publication all those opinions which formerly had been denied the necessary license for getting into print? In Milton's time, one might print unpopular opinions, which the licenser had disapproved, and be punished if caught. This the Supreme Court of the United States says is an *abridgment* of freedom of the press. However, if there is no previous censorship, and although you receive the same penalty, merely for publishing the same book, because a legislature or jury deem it contrary to the public welfare, then *unabridged liberty of the press is thereby preserved,* for "the greatest judicial tribunal on earth" has said that a constitutionally guaranteed natural right to *unabridged* freedom of press calls for the cessation of "all such previous restraints as had been practised by other governments, and [but] *does not prevent the subsequent punishment of such* [publications] *as may be deemed against the public welfare."*

In other words, our courts declare that our constitutional right to unabridged freedom of utterance deals only with the manner and time of the abridgment, or the tribunal which inflicts it, and has nothing to do with unabridged intellectual opportunity to utter, to hear, and to read. Be it remembered, however, that no such distinction in favor of any *ex post facto* censorship can be deduced from the very words of our Constitutions, nor from the historical controversy culminating in their adoption, and, therefore, these exceptions to unabridged freedom are a matter of judicial creation—that is, of judicial constitutional amendment.

IN DEFENSE OF THE CENSORSHIP.

Then, as now, the advocates for the suppression of unpopular opinions refused to see that to admit the existence of the power to suppress any opinion, is, in the long run, more destructive to human well-being than the ideas against which they would have the power exercised. Then, as now, the alleged immediate public welfare was the justification of every form of censorship, and some dangerous "tendency," only speculatively ascertained and usually so in a feverishly apprehensive imagination, was always the test of guilt. "The most tyrannical and the most absolute governments speak a kind parental language to the abject wretches who groan under their crushing and humiliating weight."[14] To make this clear, it is necessary only to quote a few passages from a publication dated A. D., 1680, and written in defense of the abridgments of freedom of speech and press. Sir Robert L'Estrange in, "A Seasonable Memorial in some Historical Notes upon the Liberties of the Press and Pulpit," quotes Calvin as saying: "There are two sorts of seditious men, and against both these must the sword be drawn; for they oppose the King and God himself." He then exhibits the evolution of dangerous tendencies by these words: "First they find out corruptions in the Government, as a matter of grievance, which they expose to the people. Secondly, they petition for Redress of those Griev-

[14]Erskine in defense of Carnan.

ances, still asking more and more, till something is denied them. And then, Thirdly, they take the power into their own hands of Relieving themselves, but with Oaths and protestations that they act only for the Common Good of King and Kingdom. From the pretense of defending the Government they proceed to the Reforming of it; which reformation proves in the end to be a Final Dissolution of the order both of Church and State. * * * * Their consciences widened with their interest. * * * * First, they fell upon the King's Reputation; they invaded his authority in the next place; after that they assaulted his Person, seized his Revenue; and in the conclusion most *impiously* took away his *Sacred* Life. * * * * *The Transition is so natural from Popular Petition to a Tumult, that the one is but a Hot Fit of the other; and little more than a more earnest way of petitioning.* * * * * They Preach the People into murther, sacrilege, and Rebellion; they pursue a most gracious Prince to the scaffold; they animate the Regicides, calling that Execrable villainy an act of Public Justice, and entitling the Holy Ghost to Treason."[15]

This argument, backed by the historical fact, is unanswerable to the point that to permit freedom of criticism of Government and its officials, and to allow the presentation of petitions for the redress of grievances, is to permit that which tends to promote actual treason and rebellion. It follows that those who were demanding the opportunity to express their sentiments in criticism of official conduct were in effect demanding the right verbally to promote treason with impunity, because that was the demonstrated tendency of such utterances. That is what unabridged freedom of speech and of the press meant to its advocates, and our constitutional guarantee for an *unabridged* freedom of utterance was a final decision in favor of that view and against all mere psychologic crimes, including even verbal "treason."

THE DEFENSE OF FREEDOM, BY MILTON.

In further justification of the contention that *unabridged* freedom of utterance as a matter of right precludes the suppression of opinions having a "dangerous" tendency, either by direct prior restraint or subsequent punishment—the fear of which always operates as a prior restraint—we should contrast the foregoing argument for restricting speech with the historic argument for freedom made in Milton's "Areo-

[15]In addition to "A Seasonable Memorial," see, for similar argument, "A Discourse of Ecclesiastical Politic, wherein the Mischiefs and Inconveniences of Toleration are Represented," London, 1670.

pagitica." Here we can quote only a few paragraphs tending to show what freedom of speech meant to its friends. Not a word *can be* found to suggest *ex post facto* punishment as a substitute for previous restraint.

Milton writes: "Till then, books were ever as freely admitted into the world as any other birth; the issue of the brain was no more stifled than the issue of the womb. * * * * 'To the pure all things are pure,' not only meats and drinks, but all kinds of knowledge, whether of good or evil; the knowledge cannot defile, nor consequently the books, if the will and conscience be not defiled. For books are as meats and viands are, some of good and some of evil substance; and yet God in that unapocryphal vision said, without exception, "Rise, Peter, kill and eat," leaving the choice to man's discretion. Wholesome meats to a vitiated stomach differ little or nothing from unwholesome, and best books to a naughty mind are not unapplicable to occasions of evil. Bad meats will scarce breed good nourishment in the healthiest concoction; but herein the difference is of bad books, that they to a discreet and judicious reader serve in many respects to discover, to confute, to forewarn, and to illustrate. * * * * All opinions, yea, errors, known, read and collated, are of main service and assistance toward the speedy ascertainment of what is truest. * * * * For those actions, which enter into a man rather than issue out of him and therefore defile not, God uses not to captivate under a perpetual childhood of prescription, but trusts him with the gift of reason to be his own chooser. * * * *

"I cannot praise a fugitive and cloistered virtue, unexercised and unbreathed, that never sallies out and sees her adversary, but slinks out of the race, where that immortal garland is to be run for, not without dust and heat. Assuredly we bring not innocence into the world, we bring impurity much rather; that which purifies us is trial, and trial is by what is contrary. That virtue which is but a youngling in the contemplation of evil, and knows not the utmost that vice promises to her followers, and rejects it, is but a blank virtue, not a pure; her whiteness is but an excremental whiteness. * * * *

"Since, therefore, the knowledge and survey of vice is in this world so necessary to the constituting of human virtue, and the scanning of error to the confirmation of truth, how can we more safely, and with less danger, scout into the regions of sin and falsity, than by reading all manner of tractates, and hearing all manner of reason? * * * * Truth and understanding are not such wares as to be monopolized and traded in by tickets and statutes and standards. * * * * Give me the liberty to know, to utter, and to argue freely according to conscience, above all [other] liberties.

"Though ye take from a covetous man all his treasure, he has yet one jewel left; ye cannot bereave him of his covetousness. Banish all objects of lust, shut up all youth into the severest discipline that can be exercised in any hermitage, ye cannot make them chaste that came not hither so."

And yet Milton, though he made an unanswerable argument for a totally unabridged freedom of utterance, could not get wholly beyond all his religious prejudices, and so, although the argument made no provision for it, he found it necessary dogmatically to provide for one exception. "I mean not tolerated Popery and open superstition, which, as it extirpates all religious and civil supremacies, so itself should be extirpated." While Milton thus fell short of an unlimited intellectual toleration he yet furnished an immortal statement of reasons to guide us to an unabridged freedom of utterance, and to the invalidating of his own exception thereto.

SPINOZA.

To this same period belong the writings of Spinoza. As is to be expected, his viewpoint is different from the others of his time.

He concludes: "We have shown already that no man's mind can possibly lie wholly at the disposition of another, for no one can willingly transfer his natural right of free reason and free judgment, or be compelled to do so. For this reason the government which attempts to control minds is accounted tyrannical, and it is considered an abuse of sovereignty, and a usurpation of the rights of subjects, to seek to prescribe what shall be accepted as true, or rejected as false, or what opinions shall actuate men in their worship of God. All these questions fall within a man's *natural right,* which he cannot abdicate even with his own consent. * * * * The individual justly cedes the right of free action, though not of free reason and judgment. No one can *act* against the authorities without danger to the State, though his feelings and judgment be at variance therewith. He may even speak against them, provided that he does so from rational conviction, not from fraud, anger, or hatred, and provided that he does not attempt to introduce any change on his private authority. * * * * Thus we see how an individual may declare and teach what he believes, without injury to the authority of his rulers, or to the public peace; namely, by leaving in their hands the entire power of legislation *as it affects action;* and by doing nothing against their laws though he be compelled often to act in contradiction to what he believes, and openly feels to be best. From the fundamental notions of a State, we have discovered how a man may exercise free judgment without detriment to the supreme power; from the same premises we can no less easily determine *what opinions would be seditious. Evidently those which by their very nature nullify the compact by which the right of free action is ceded.* * * * *

"If we hold to the principle that a man's loyalty to the State should be judged, like his loyalty to God, *from his actions only*—namely from his charity towards his neighbors—we cannot doubt that the best government will allow freedom of philosophical speculation, no less than of religious belief. I confess that from such freedom inconveniences may sometimes arise, but was any question ever settled so wisely that no abuses could possibly spring therefrom? He who seeks to regulate everything by law is more likely to arouse vices than to reform them."

From these quotations it appears that Spinoza did not believe in an *unabridged* freedom of utterance. His belief in the psychologic crime of a mere verbal treason, though limited within unusually narrow range, followed logically from his erroneous conception of the sphere of government. Of this he said: "The rights of the sovereign are limited by his power." Since in his theory of government sovereign rights arise out of a cession of freedom of action by the citizen, the opinion which nullified that hypothetical compact could be called treason so long as the sovereign had the power to suppress it as such. It is quite probable, and at least consistent with his theory, that this exception may have been made by Spinoza as a condition of securing tolerance for the rest of the argument in favor of free speech.

However that may be, as Spinoza repudiated the exception to unabridged freedom of utterance reserved by Milton, so the latter annihilated the one exception made by Spinoza. The premises of each exception were specifically repudiated by the

American Declaration of Independence and American Constitutions, and hence these exceptions to unabridged liberty of utterance also must fall. However, the matter that I now wish specially to emphasize is this: The very nature of these arguments for larger freedom is such as utterly to destroy our judical assumption that the friends of unabridged freedom of utterance, who framed our Constitutional Guarantees, meant only to provide for *ex post facto* punishment as a substitute for previous restraint.

MONTESQUIEU.

Some years after the death of Milton came the birth of Montesquieu, who "commanded the future from his study more than Napoleon from his throne," and whose book on "The Spirit of the Laws" "probably has done as much to remodel the world as any product of the eighteenth century, which burned so many forests and sowed so many fields."

In the opinion of Justice O. W. Holmes, "Montesquieu had a possibly exaggerated belief in the power of legislation," which alone would not predispose him against censorship. The frequent reference to him in *The Federalist* and other discussions of the revolutionary period, as well as our Constitutions themselves, all show how the thought provoked by his book helped to shape our Institutions. This makes it all the more important to ascertain his views upon the province of the State in relation to the liberty of speech and press, because of their quite direct bearing upon the historical interpretation of our Constitution.

On the subject of religion, he emphasizes the essential difference between human and divine laws, and argues reservedly for general toleration of all religion, and concludes: "When the legislator has believed it a duty to permit the exercise of many religions it is necessary that he should enforce also a toleration among these religions themselves. * * * * *Penal laws ought to be avoided in respect to religion.*"

In the matter of verbal treason, Montesquieu seems very exact in his statements and comprehensive in his thought. Only a few lines will need quoting. He says: "Nothing renders the crime of high treason more arbitrary than declaring people guilty of it of indiscreet speeches. * * * * Words do not constitute an overt act; they remain only an idea. When considered by themselves, they have generally no determinate signification, for this depends on the tone in which they are uttered. * * * * Since there can be nothing so equivocal and ambiguous as all this, how is it possible to convert it into a crime of high treason? Wherever this law is established, there is an end not only of liberty, but even of its very shadow. * * * *

"Overt acts do not happen every day; they are exposed to the naked eye of the public, and a false charge with regard to matters of fact may be easily detected. Words carried into action assume the nature of that action. Thus a man who goes into a public market-place to incite the subject to revolt incurs the guilt of high treason, *because the words are joined to the action, and partake of its nature. It is not the words that are punished but an action in which words are employed. They do not become criminal but when they are annexed to a criminal action; everything is confounded if words are construed into capital crime, instead of considering them only as a mark of that crime.*"[16]

In this evolution to a clearer conception of the issues and the more exact statement of the claims of contending parties, we have now reached the place where unabridged intellectual liberty is defined by excluding from the category of crime every offense founded upon speech, *merely as such.*

BLACKSTONE AND HIS CRITICS.

Blackstone was the victim of most of the popular superstitions of his time, from witchcraft down. Of course he indorsed the current theory of government and consequently the current abridgments of freedom of speech and press. He had no desire or intention to vindicate man's natural right to such liberties *unabridged,* but approved and made declarations of the laws in operation, as he found them. Thus he wrote: "Everything is now as it should be with respect to the spiritual cognizance, and spirtual punishment of heresy; unless perhaps that *the crime ought to be more strictly defined,* and no persecution permitted, even in the ecclesiastical courts, till the tenets in question are by proper authority previous declared to be heretical. Under these restrictions, it seems necessary for the support of the national religion that the officers of the church should have power to censure heretics, yet not to harrass with temporal penalties, much less to exterminate or destroy them."[17]

These spiritual censures and excommunication involved

[16]Vol. I., p. 233, Aldine Edition.
[17]Vol. 4 Commentaries, p. 49.

indirect penalties, such as incapacity for "suing an action, being witnesses, making a will, receiving a legacy," etc., and these indirect consequences it would seem that Blackstone approved.

Again he writes: "The [some not unabridged] liberty of the press is indeed essential to the nature of a free state; but this consists in laying no previous restraints upon publications, and not in freedom from censure for criminal matter when published. * * * * To subject the press to the restrictive power of a licenser, as was formerly done, * * * * is to subject all freedom of sentiment to the prejudices of one man, and make him the arbitrary and infallible judge of all controverted points in learning, religion, and government. But *to punish, as the law does at present,* any dangerous or offensive writings which, when published, shall on a fair and impartial trial be adjudged of a pernicious tendency, is necessary for the preservation of peace and good order, of government and religion, the only solid foundations of civil liberty."[18]

It should be apparent from the mere reading that Blackstone was defending and describing only such *limited liberty by permission* as was then enjoyed in England, and never intended either to define or defend *unabridged* freedom of discussion, as that was contended for by his opponents, whose views, and not Blackstone's, were adopted into our Constitutions. For this reason, one may well be surprised to find the foregoing statement from Blackstone quoted by American courts as an authority on the meaning of *unabridged* freedom of utterance, which he never mentions.

One of Blackstone's critics, whose book went through more than one edition and of whom it is said,[19] "he induced the learned commentator [Blackstone] to alter some positions in the subsequent edition of his valuable work," had this to say as to the meaning of unabridged freedom of speech:

"For, though calumny and slander, when affecting our fellow men, are punishable by law; for this plain reason, because an injury is done, and a damage sustained, and a reparation therefore due to the injured party; yet, this reason cannot hold where God and the Redeemer are concerned; who can sustain no injury from low malice and scurrilous invective; nor can any reparation be made to them by temporal penalties; for these can work no conviction or repentance in the mind of the offender; and if he continue impenitent and incorrigible,

[18]Vol. 4 Blackstone's Commentaries, p. 151.
[19]Allibone's "Dictionary of Authors."

he will receive his condign punishment in the day of final retribution. Affronting Christianity, therefore, does not come under the magistrate's cognizance, in this particular view, as it implies an offense against God and Christ."[20] Here is again a clear recognition and plain statement which, like Montesquieu's, demands that actual and material injury shall be the basis of prosecution and not mere speculation about psychologic tendencies.

MANSFIELD AND KENYON.

Some of our courts, in addition to Blackstone, cite Lords Mansfield and Kenyon, as authorities on the meaning of unabridged freedom of utterance as though their views had been adopted into our Constitutions. Concerning these opinions, Sir James Fitz James Stephens (after quoting the differing definitions of Lords Mansfield and Kenyon as showing what was the official conception of freedom of the press) says: "Each definition was in a legal point of view complete and accurate, but what the public at large understood by the expression was something altogether different—namely the right of unrestricted discussion of public affairs."[21]

In other words, the judicial conception of free speech was an abridged free speech, and the popular demand was for an *unabridged* free speech. It should need no argument to prove that the latter, and not the former, was intended to be adopted into American Constitutions, and to me it is difficult to account for the contrary opinion, often expressed by our courts, which quite uniformly ignore even the existence of the pre-revolutionary contention against the English official conception as expressed by the Star Chamber, the English Parliament, Blackstone, Mansfield, or Kenyon.

BISHOP HORSLEY, REV. ROBERT HALL, AND THOMAS JEFFERSON.

The issue between "freedom of the press" in the official English sense, on the one side, and *unabridged* freedom of utterance on the other, was made clear in another English controversy following so closely upon the heels of our adoption of the first amendment as to be fairly considered an English aftermath of that agitation and of the American Revolution.

Bishop Horsley, on January 30, 1793, delivered a sermon before the House of Lords, wherein he indulged in a severe censure of that "Freedom of dispute" on matters of "such

[20]Furneaux's "Letters on Toleration," pp. 70-71, Second Edition.
[21]Vol. 2 "Crim. Law of Eng.," p. 349.

high importance as the origin of government and the authority of sovereigns," in which he laments that it has been the "folly of this country for several years past" to indulge. Of the divine right of Kings he declared: "It is a right which in no country can be denied, without the highest of all treason. The denial of it were treason against the paramount authority of God."

These premises had recently been repudiated by our Declaration of Independence, by the American Constitutions, and by the friends of unabridged freedom of utterance everywhere. One of the conspicuous critics of Bishop Horsley was the Rev. Robert Hall. In arguing against the rightfulness of punishing mere psychologic crimes, he laid down tne limits of governmental action which must be adhered to if freedom of speech is to remain an *unabridged right,* instead of mere limited liberty by permission. He said: "The law hath amply provided against *overt acts of sedition and disorder,* and to suppress mere opinions by any other method than reasoning and argument is the hight of tyranny. Freedom of thought being intimately connected with the happiness and dignity of man in every stage of his being, is of so much more importance than the preservation of any Constitution, that to infringe the former under pretense of supporting the latter, is to sacrifice the means to the end."[22]

In his discourse, this Reverend author often emphasizes the difference between ideas and overt acts and makes plain over and over that in his view actual injury should be the criteria of guilt, and not mere apprehension as to a psychologic tendency. Our constitutional definition of Treason and the guarantees of the right to carry arms, of "due process of law," and of unabridged freedom of utterance, show that it was such views as Milton argued for, and as Montesquieu and the Rev. Robert Hall expressed, and not the views of Blackstone, Mansfield, Kenyon, or Bishop Horsley, that our Constitutions sought effectually to perpetuate.

Both before and after these utterances by the Rev. Robert Hall there was most eminent American authority for the same interpretation of the meaning of a "free press." Thomas Jefferson is popularly supposed to have had much to do with framing the Declaration of Independence and shaping our American institutions. He was a dominant figure in Virginia politics for many years. Those who have familiarized them-

[22]"An Apology for Freedom of the Press," p. 18.

selves with the religious views of Jefferson,[23] will not doubt that he encouraged the passage of the Act of the State of Virginia establishing religious freedom. Although drafted with a view only to theological subjects, it contains a summary of incontrovertible reasoning in favor of the general liberty of inquiry and a clear statement as to where the jurisdiction of the state rightfully may be invoked without abridging intellectual liberty. The Virginia enactment says: "To suffer the Civil Magistrate to intrude his power into the field of Opinion, or to restrain the profession or propagation of principles on supposition of their ill tendency, is a dangerous fallacy, which at once destroys all liberty, because he, being of course judge of that tendency, will make his opinions the rule of judgment, and approve or condemn the sentiments of others only as they shall square with or differ from his own. *It is time enough for the rightful purposes of Civil Government for its officers to interfere when principles break out into overt acts against peace and good order.*" [24]

The Virginia declaration was made in 1786, several years before the adoption of the first amendment to the Federal Constitution. The Virginia enactment makes it clear that in their opinion the State has no rightful authority over opinion of any sort, and should not be suffered to interfere until ACTUAL injury has resulted. It was that conception of "freedom of the press" which America adopted, and not the English tyrants' conception, to which it was opposed, and which originated in the odious Star Chamber, found a palatable justification in Blackstone and the English Judicial decisions, and an official re-echo in American Courts, engaged in explaining away our constitutional guarantee for an *unabridged* freedom of utterance.

When the Federalist party was defeated because of its enactment of the Alien and Sedition Law, and Thomas Jefferson became President of the United States, he proceeded to pardon every man who had been convicted under this infamous statute. That the penalized utterances *tended* to sedition made no difference to him, which indicates that he too indorsed the views of Montesquieu, the Rev. Robert Hall, and the quoted enactment of the Virginia Legislature, as being the correct interpretation of the words "unabridged freedom of speech and of the press." Jefferson's own statement as to his conduct is as follows:

[23] See, "Six Historic Americans."
[24] Requoted from Wortman's, "Liberty of the Press," p. 173.

"I discharged every person under punishment or prosecution under the sedition law, because I considered and now consider that law to be a nullity, as absolute and as palpable as if Congress had ordered us to fall down and worship a golden image; and that it was as much my duty to arrest its progress in every stage as it would have been to have rescued from the fiery furnace those who should have been cast into it for refusing to worship the image. It was accordingly done in every instance, *without asking what the offenders had done,* or against whom they had offended, but whether the pains they were suffering were inflicted under the *pretended sedition law.* It was certainly possible that my motives in contributing to the relief of Callandar, and in liberating sufferers under the sedition law, might have been to protect, reward, and encourage slander; but they may also have been those which inspire odinary charities to objects of distress, meritorious or not—or, the *obligation of an oath 'to protect the Constitution,'* violated by an authorized act of Congress."[25]

This action on the part of President Jefferson was consistent with the issue upon which he was elected, and was required by his own conception of what was meant by an unabridged "Freedom of Speech and of the Press" as applied to verbal treason. His views are thus expressed in his first inaugural address: "If there be any among us who would wish to dissolve this Union or to change its republican form, let them stand undisturbed as monuments of the safety with which error of opinion may be tolerated where reason is left free to combat it."

These discussions again proclaim the historic view that *unabridged* freedom of utterance means that every man may say with impunity whatever he pleases, being held responsible and punishable only for *actual* resultant injury, that being the only abuse of such freedom which can be penalized.

TAXES ON KNOWLEDGE.

Another form of impairing natural intellectual opportunity, and therefore an abridgment of freedom of the press, was taxes upon knowledge. In America, where to a very large extent we have Government by newspapers, it seems unlikely that such taxes will ever again become a subject of controversy. However, we must briefly consider the matter as an historical

---

[25] See, 4 Jefferson's Complete Works, 556, quoted in Booth's v. Rycroft, 3 Wisconsin 183.

issue so that our final generalization as to unabridged freedom of the press may negative also this form of abridgment.

George Jacob Holyoake has briefly described the conditions against which he, and other friends of intellectual freedom before him, waged such strenuous battle. These are his words: "Yet every newspaper proprietor was formerly treated as a blasphemer and a writer of sedition, and compelled to give substantial securities against the exercise of his infamous tendencies; every paper-maker was regarded as a thief, and the officers of the Excise dogged every step of his business with hampering, exacting, and humiliating suspicion. Every reader found with an unstamped paper in his possession was liable to a fine of £20. When the writer of this published the 'War Chronicles' and 'War Fly Sheets,' the Inland Revenue Office bought six copies as soon as each number was out; thus he incurred fines of £120 before breakfast, and when the last warrant was issued against him by the Court of Exchequer he was indebted to the Crown £600,000. Besides, he had issued an average of 2,000 copies of *The Reasoner* for twelve years, incurring fines of £40,000 a week, which amounted to a considerable sum in twelve years. He who published a paper, containing news, without a stamp, was also liable to have all his presses broken up, all his stock confiscated, himself, and all persons in his house, imprisoned, as had been done again and again to others within the writer's knowledge. Neither cheap newspapers nor cheap books could exist while these perils were possible."

In his "History of the Taxes on Knowledge," Collet informs us that "The History of the Taxes upon Knowledge begins with their imposition (1711) in the reign of Queen Anne. The battle against the Press had, indeed, begun before that date." The year 1855 marked the final repeal of the last of these English stamp acts, and those requiring bonds, etc., from publishers. Those who are interested in this particular battle for larger freedom of the press are referred to Mr. Collet's interesting account.[26] In all these discussions, it is apparent that the main purpose was not to favor one system of raising revenue as against some other system, but to increase the intellectual opportunities of all, by removing *all* State-created impediments to the greatest natural freedom for the interchange of ideas.

[26]"Taxes on Knowledge, the story of their Origin and Repeal," Lond., 1899; see also Patterson on "Liberty of Press and Speech," p. 57.

THE CENSORSHIP OF MAILS.

We next consider the method of creating inequalities in intellectual opportunities, and of abridging them, by means of a State-created postal censorship, which is fast becoming an important issue in the contest for intellectual freedom in America. The American postal censorship over mail matter began in 1873, when a law was passed, without debate, making "obscene" matter unmailable. I am informed that the original draft of this bill included "blasphemy" in the unmailable list, thus again emphasizing the origin in religious intolerance, and pointing to the ultimate purpose of those who are so persistently advocating and securing extensions of our postal censorship. This censorship has already been extended, so that now even *political* literatue, which in European monarchies is spread without hindrance, has been excluded from American mails and penalized. The statutes heretofore have only provided *ex post facto* punishment for use of the mails; they did not authorize the postal authorities to prevent the transmission of prohibited matter. In several Congresses, the Postal Department asked an amendment to the laws such as would give the postmaster power to refuse transmission to forbidden matter. The amendment never was passed. Not abashed by the refusal of the Congress to confer the power, the authorities proceeded to usurp it, under the usual guise of a new "construction" of existing statutes. This usurped power, having been calmly acquiesced in by the public, soon received judicial confirmation and gradually has been extended, so that it now assumes to override the judical department by excluding from the mails publications which the courts have decided are mailable, and has excluded matter without the warrant of any statute, relying upon the absence of a remedy for the afflicted persons.

Under our modern conditions of living, with their cheap printing and postal facilities, to be denied the use of the mails for the spread of one's ideas creates a relatively greater inequality and abridgment of intellectual opportunity than ever was created by any prior form of censorship. Since private competition with our public mail service is prohibited by law, and since in these times of a cheap periodical press no one can hope ever to attain a favorable public opinion, in competition with his intellectual opponents, except by publication through the mails, therefore it follows that a postal censorship is the most effective possible abridgment of freedom of the press. Moreover, since the postal authorities now exercise a usurped censorhip over postal matter prior to publication through the mails, we have quite effectively, though unconsciously, re-establihed in some fields of thought a *"previous censorship,"* substantially like that against which Milton wrote nearly 300 years ago. If this previous censorship is upheld, in spite of our Constitutions and judicial dictums against the legal possibility of a "previous censorship," then its spread into other, and finally all, fields of thought is only a matter of time. Under present conditions, the difference between a censorship previous to printing and one after printing but previous to publication by mail, is one of no practical import, because a book that cannot get publicity by mail might as well never be printed, since without facilities for distribution by post, interstate commerce, or private competitors of the postal system, the securing of readers is practically impossible. Furthermore, a censorship after printing, and before publication by mail, is worse than one before printing, because it inflicts the needless loss of the cost of printing.

The infamous Licensing Act of England, against which Milton wrote, was passed September 20, 1649, and provided, among its pernicious abridgments of freedom of the press, that "no person whatever should presume *to send by the post, carriers, or otherwise,* or endeavor to dispense, any unlicensed book,"etc., on penalty of forfeiture, fine,and imprisonment. As if to add insult to injury, every printer was required to give a bond to *"The Keepers of the Liberties of England,"* to insure against the violation of the licensing act. It was precisely this censorship previous to publication by mail against which Milton wrote his "Areopagitica." Our courts have said that the absence of "such previous restraint as had been practised" is the one thing, at least, against which our constitutional guarantees protect us, and yet in spite of Courts and Constitutions we have for some time acquiesced in just such a usurped postal censorship previous to publication by mail. Furthermore, owing to the uncertainty of the statutory criteria of mailability, this censorship previous to publication by post is in practise an arbitrary discretion. So, then, we do not even have left the one lonely element of freedom which our courts too often have mistaken for all there is to *unabridged* freedom of the press. Even that little "all" has disappeared, and only the blank paper of our Constitutional guarantee remains. When the issue is squarely presented, will our courts confirm also the destruction of this last element of freedom of the press, and so vest Congress and our Federal bureaucracy with *all* the powers over the press which our Constitution was supposed to withhold?

An English Barrister-at-law gives us this brief account of the postal censorship in England: "The right of free speech and writing can scarcely exist in perfection without mechanical facilities for exchanging letters and printed matter between correspondents. * * * * What is desired by each and every citizen is, that he shall be entitled to send and receive all communications which he thinks material to his own interest, and that no third party shall be allowed to tamper or interfere with this operation—so that a message sent in writing or print shall be secret and inviolable from the moment it is despatched till the moment it is delivered. This has for two centuries been more or less attained. The great medium for this communication between the subjects began in 1635, on a small scale, at the suggestion of the Crown, but Parliament soon saw its importance, and in 1649 passed a resolution that the office of postmaster ought to be [at] the sole disposal of Parliament. In 1710 a statute laid down the chief rules, and one of these, continuing as it did the first sketch of a plan projected under Charles I., forbade all other persons to carry and deliver letters for hire. * * * *

"It appears to have been a century ago the common complaint of leading statesmen that their political opponents made a practise of opening their letters when they had the power. * * * *

"In 1822 complaint was made by a member of Parliament that a letter sent him by a prisoner had been opened. And, though the Government claimed the right to do so for precaution, yet many urged that it should be deemed a breach of privilege; this step, however, was not taken." Again, in 1844, instances of private letters being opened were complained of, and Parliamentary committees investigated the practise, and found sufficient confirmation of the suspicion that such a practise was not unfrequent, especially in connection with foreign refugees." Sir R. Peel said that no rule could be laid down on such a subject, and successive Secretaries of State of all

6 Parl. Deb. (2d), 282, 646.
75 Parl. Deb. (3) 1264; 76 Ibid. 212, 296.

parties had been in the habit of exercising this power at discretion."[29]

Thus, this great authority on freedom of the press informs us that, according to the English conception of it, the period of our revolution found it a matter of constant complaint that there was a post-office censorship. Those who thus complained were the friends of a larger intellectual liberty and it was their view that was adopted into our constitutional guarantee for the security of papers against unreasonable searches, and against all abridgments of freedom of utterance. These two clauses together, until judicially explained away, would seem clearly to preclude the search of unsealed as well as sealed mail-matter *for the purpose of creating inequalities of right to the public service,* according to whether the ideas transmitted are officially approved or disapproved. This is the self-evident meaning of our Constitution when viewed in the light of the issues that were agitating the public at the time of its adoption. The manifest purpose was the increase of intellectual opportunity, even though it protected such as might be inclined to sedition, and just as manifestly it was not the purpose merely to change a business policy in relation to a department of government.

To show that the advocates of unabridged freedom of the press included a mail service free from censorship as a part of their conception of freedom of speech, I will content myself with one quotation from Jeremy Bentham, as confirming the foregoing historical interpretation. After explaining that the only check to tyrannous government is "instruction, excitation, and facility of correspondence" that "the national mind be kept in a state of appropriate preparation; a state of preparation for eventual resistance," he later continues thus: "Necessary to instruction—to excitation—in a word to a state of preparation directed to this purpose is (who does not see it?) the perfectly unrestrained communication of ideas on every subject within the field of government—[which includes the · discussion of sexual physiology and psychology as a foundation for sex ethics, and the latter even from the viewpoint of the free-lover and polygamist because a democratic government must leave itself free to change even its marriage laws] the communication, by vehicles of all sorts—by signs of all sorts; signs to the ear—signs to the eye—by spoken language— by written, including printed, language—by the liberty of the

[29]Rep. of Secret Com. 1845; Patterson, "Liberty of the Press, Speech, and Public Worship," pp. 58-59.

tongue, by the liberty of the writing desk, by the liberty of the *post office*—by the liberty of the *press."* He repeats that this is necessary, "not only for instruction, but for excitation"; all "for keeping on foot every facility for eventual resistance."[20]

Bentham then pointed to the United States as a place where such liberties existed, but he could not do so now were he alive. The Declaration of Independence, the constitutional guarantees for the right of assembly, due process of law, the right to bear arms, and against searches and seizures; the declarations of the conventions of several of the States, the constitutional guarantees of unabridged freedom of speech and of the press—all proclaim the intention to protect the right of the citizen against punishment for mere psychologic crimes, to the end that he always may be prepared for eventual resistance, even of government itself.[21]

PSYCHOLOGIC TENDENCY AS CRITERION OF GUILT.

Historically considered, an inseparable part of the contention for a larger, or an unabridged, liberty of speech and of the press was the condemnation of that practise in the prosecution for libels which made the guilt of the accused depend upon "the evils which may be imaginatively and prospectively attributed to the influence of his opinions." The opposition to this uncertainty in the criteria of guilt was not limited to persons who believed in unabridged freedom of speech, but was often very forcibly urged by those who desired only a little or no enlargement of intellectual opportunity. Even Blackstone believed that the criteria of guilt for heresy and seditious utterances should be made more certain.

The protest against the uncertainty of the tests of criminality in prosecutions for seditious and blasphemous utterances was upon two distinct grounds. The first and most general of these was the historical retrospect, and was an appeal to expediency. The argument ran thus: Books once condemned for their supposed evil tendencies are now believed to have been good and useful. In making the psychologic tendency of an utterance the test of its criminality, we are again opening the door for a repetition of such error. Therefore, such criminal laws are inexpedient and should be abolished. The second reason for objecting to the tendency-test in penalized utterances was from the point of view of that larger demand for liberty which was founded upon the idea that no freeman

[20]Jeremy Bentham, "On Liberty of the Press and Public Discussion."
[21]Stevens, "Sources of the Constitution of the United States," pp. 223-224; Blackstone's Commentaries, v. 1, p. 154; Cooley, "Constitutional Law," 270.

should be deprived of his liberty except by *lawful* judgment of his peers, or by the *law* of the land. This was predicated upon the conception that every man should in justice be forewarned that his act is penalized. It could not be the law of the land if it did not impart that advance information, and could not accomplish this except an exact statement of the criteria of guilt was a part of every criminal statute. By such means the lovers of Liberty hoped to obtain *freedom under law* in contradistinction to a mere liberty by permission under lawless despotism. To such persons, it was self-evident that a speculative opinion about the psychologic tendency of an utterance upon a future, undescribed, hypothetical, reader, or hearer, when used as a criterion of guilt, could be no restraint upon the moral idiosyncracies, stupid bigotry, unreasoned hysterical apprehension, personal interest, or even the superstitious malice, of those charged with the duty of determining whether or not a verbal crime had been committed. It was seen that under such circumstances guilt must be determined by *ex post facto* standards, personal to the individuals passing judgment. This, it was argued, was government according to the lawless despotism of man, and the friends of freedom demanded as one of the conditions without which there could be no liberty of speech or press, or liberty of any sort, that the criteria of guilt be so certain that every man should know in advance, from the very letter of the law, by what standard his conduct would be adjudged criminal. It goes without saying that so long as an *ex post facto* judicial guess as to the psychologic tendency of a speech, book, or picture is the test of guilt, there can be no such thing as *liberty under the law*. Even from those to whom "free speech" meant a limited liberty by permission, there came a protest against tyranny, and the demand for the freedom of every man's opinion from that arbitrary power for the penalizing of words by standards of an *ex post facto* guess or pretense about "the evils which may be imaginatively and prospectively attributed to the influence of his opinions."

As proof of the assertion that a demand for certainty in the criteria of guilt always was a part of the agitation for more freedom of speech and press, we need but to point out that vast literature which was brought into being against constructive treason and seditious libel. Erskine's speeches are replete with the glorification and demand for such certainty.

Here it is only necessary to call attention to its existence as a part of the agitation for enlarged liberty. The discussion of the question is better treated as a subdivision of an argument to support the contention that "Due Process of Law" does not obtain unless every criminal statute prescribes the criteria of guilt with mathematical certainty.

IN CONCLUSION.

This historical review of the contentions which resulted in the adoption of our constitutional guarantees for an *unabridged* freedom of speech and of the press, is already too long for comfortable reading, and not long enough to be anything like an exhaustive treatise. I believe, however, that it adequately establishes the following propositions:

I. The contention for an *UNABRIDGED* freedom of utterance was always founded upon a demand for unrestrained intellectual opportunity, and never concerned itself primarily with preferences between different methods of abridging that freedom.

II. It opposed all past and existing restrictions upon intellectual intercourse, such as licensing printers or books, censoring the post or other means of transmission, putting taxes upon knowledge, and inflicting *ex post facto* punishments; and our Constitutions not only sought to prevent a recurrance of any of these former methods of abridging intellctual opportunity, but the antecedent discussion and the language used clearly express the determination to preclude the enforcement of any other, even theretofore untried, methods of curtailing intellectual intercourse, although again claimed to be advocated for the furtherance of the public welfare.

III. The demand for unabridged freedom of utterance always was a demand for the abolition of *all* mere psychologic crimes and all that uncertainty which attended them from the fact that the criteria of guilt were usually "the evils which may be imaginatively and prospectively attributed to the influence of one's opinions"; and the co-related demand that crime should always be predicated upon a certainty, such as an actual and material injury, or perhaps also the imminent danger of such, according to the known laws of the physical universe.

If we generalize all these contentions for a larger and an unabridged intellectual opportunity, we shall have a comprehensive statement of the historical interpretation of unabridged freedom of speech and of the press, and if the form of statement is such as to furnish us with the criteria for determining a breaching of the constitutional guarantee, we shall have a statement in substance like that at the beginning of this chapter.

If then we wish to determine whether or not any given law is violative of the free-press clause of our constitutions we must deductively apply to the law the several tests stated at the beginning of this chaper. Doing this, with reference to our ˈlaws prohibitive of sex-discussion I find them, in their separate parts, to be unconstitutional, under the second, fourth, and fifth, test of constitutionality.

One thing is certain as death: Nobody intended that our constitutions should increase the governmental authority to penalize the transmission of ideas. If it shall be held that the constitutions were not designed to enlarge intellectual opportunity, as has been hereinbefore contended, then the only alterative is the proposition that the constitutional inhibition against abridging freedom of utterance prohibits only such legislation as restricts it *beyond then existing abridgments*. In Chapter III. it has been shown that under the common-law, as it obtained in the American colonies, "obscene" literature was never penalized merely on account of its "obscenity." So then even under this anti-historical and most narrow interpretation, the statutes now under consideration are unconstitutional because they abridge freedom of utterance *beyond the existing restrictions of colonial common-law*.

CHAPTER XII.

SCIENCE *versus* JUDICIAL DICTUM.
A STATEMENT OF NOVEL CONTENTIONS AND
A PLEA FOR OPEN-MINDEDNESS.*

The occasion for this discussion arises primarily from the fact that when "obscene" literature and art were penalized, none of the statutes prescribed any test by which to determine the dividing line between that degree of obscenity which is criminal and that which is only a matter of bad taste, and non-criminal. In harmony with the pre-dominant opinion of that time, legislatures assumed, and courts decreed, that all humanity have an innate, and uniform, sense of modesty and decency, by which we may acquire a direct sense-perception of the "obscene" qualities of a book or picture. If this assumption is true, the judicial superstructure is impregnable.

If, on the other hand, that assumption is untrue, and our sense of decency, obscenity, etc., is a matter of education and experience, or is determined by each according to his personal sex-sensitiveness, or his emotional and ideational associations; determined by personal habits and moral idiosyncrasies, and is variable as these factors are variable; or if it shall develop that the only elements of unification generalized in the word "obscene" are wholly subjective to the Judge or Juror, or other person passing judgment, and not inherent in the book itself, then it might follow that all these laws are a nullity for want of a statutory definition of the crime, for while ignorance of the existence of a law can excuse no one, yet ignorance of the meaning of an undefinable criminal law must excuse everybody.

First we will exhibit the judicial dictum that the limits and test of "obscenity" are a matter of common knowledge and therefore need no statutory definition. This will be followed by the judicial statement of reasons for believing in an innate sense of the obscene and of the modest. These may be

---

* Revised from *The Alienist and Neurologist.*

contrasted with the contrary conclusions of the scientist. The issues thus formed will be followed by a statement of some of the evidences which support the contrary view of the scientists.

ARE TESTS OF "OBSCENITY" COMMON KNOWLEDGE?

Our courts have answered this question in the affirmative, but they promptly contradict that statement by framing mutually destructive tests of "obscenity" such as no dictionary-maker or other person of ordinary intelligence ever thought of. This is to be expected so long as judges, without hearing argument or considering a single factor of the scientific aspect of the problem, assume to determine the facts of natural science by mere dogmatic, judicial dictum. That is precisely what has been done.

Thus it is said: "The statute does not undertake to define 'obscene' or 'indecent.' * * * * The words are themselves descriptive. * * * * These are matters which fall within the range of ordinary intelligence."[1]

If the quoted words mean only that each person within his fund of common knowledge includes a knowledge as to what he personally deems to be "obscene," then the statement may be true, but is certainly unimportant. If, on the other hand, it is asserted that common knowledge will enable us to know under all circumstances what everyone else must deem "obscene" in all conceivable cases, and that all our judgments in such matter are alike, then the statement is untrue, and because untrue the statute is a nullity on account of the uncertainty as to what it penalizes.

Likewise the Supreme Court of the United States has implied much the same thought as the N. Y. Court when the former used these words "Everyone who uses the mails * * * * must take notice of what in this enlightened age is meant by decency, purity and chastity in social life and what must be deemed obscene, lewd and lascivious."[2]

This is true if all humans have an innate or intuitional and uniform conception of what the words in question symbolize. But such empty judicial rhetoric does not help us to a solution of the real question, which is: Have we such a uniform, innate or intuitional, immediate sensuous cognition

[1] People vs. Muller. 96 N. Y. 410.
[2] U. S. vs. Rosen, 161 U. S. 42.

of the "obscene," as to preclude the necessity for a statutory definition of that element of the crime?

Another court used these words: "There are in the language, words known as words obscene in themselves. It is not necessary in order to make a book obscene that such words should be found in it. * * * A book is said to be obscene which is offensive to decency or chastity, which is immodest, which is indelicate, impure," etc., etc.[3]

To those seeking accuracy of description for statutory crimes, the use of such mystifying epithetic tautology is not very reassuring as to the clarity of the judicial vision which could mistake it for a definition. Likewise the appeal to the consensus of opinion in "this enlightened age" has been made in support of every superstition that has ever paralyzed the human intellect. It would be more reassuring if judges had given, or would give, us a test of obscenity, in terms of the objective, sense-perceived qualities of literature, by which test alone we could unerringly and with unavoidable uniformity, draw the same, exact, unshifting line of partition between what is obscene and what is pure in literature, no matter who applies the test. Until they furnish such a test to us, their dogmatic assurance that "this enlightened age" possesses such undisclosed knowledge of standards, is not very satisfactory. Without such a test, there is no uniform law to control our conduct, nor that of our courts or juries.

The universally implied judicial assumption, that all have a uniform, innate sense of obscenity and decency, by which we all draw the same line of demarkation between the two had its origin farther back in our juridical history when such problems had a different aspect, even among scientists. By the unavoidable, yet often unfortunate, judicial habit of following precedent, courts have continued the error long after scientists have abandoned the old foundation for it.

We shall presently see that our judicial notions about the innateness of our knowledge as to standards of "obscenity" had their origin deep in the religious sentiments of the time when these laws were passed and received their first judicial interpretation. Later we will be reminded of the great change which has remoulded our religious as well as our scientific beliefs, so as to necessitate an abandonment of the premises upon which the courts built their idea of the intuitive character of our knowledge of the "obscene."

[3] U. S. vs. Bennett, Fed. Case No. 14571.

THE COURTS ON THE ORIGIN OF MODESTY.

First then we will study the foundation of the judicial dictum upon the psychologic question which is here involved. The most complete judicial vindication of the idea that our conception of modesty is innate and therefore uniform in all humanity, is found in *Ardery vs. the State,* 56 *Ind.* 329, decided in 1877. Then the court said: "Immediately after the fall of Adam, there seems to have sprung up in the mind an idea that there was such a thing as decency, and such a thing as indecency, * * * and since that time, the idea of decency and indecency have been instinctive in and, indeed, a part of, humanity. And it historically appears that the first most palpable piece of indecency in the human being was the first public exposure of his or her, as now commonly called, privates; and the first exercise of mechanical ingenuity was the manufacture of fig-leaf aprons by Adam and Eve, in which to conceal from the public gaze of each other their now but not then called privates. This example of covering their privates has been imitated by all mankind since that time, except perhaps by some of the lowest grades of savages. Modesty has ever existed as one of the most estimable and admirable of human virtues."[4]

A similar conclusion is expressed by a Federal Judge. "There is in the popular conception and heart such a thing as modesty. It was born in the Garden of Eden. After Adam and Eve ate from the fruit of the Tree of Knowledge they passed from that condition of perfectibility which some people nowadays aspire to, and, their eyes being opened, they discerned that there was both good and evil, 'and they knew that they were naked, and they sewed fig-leaves together, and made themselves aprons.' From that day to this, civilized man has carried with him a sense of shame—the feeling that there were some things on which the eye—the mind—should not look, and where men and women become so depraved by the use, or so insensate from perverted education, that they will not veil their eyes, nor hold their tongues, the government should perform the office for them in protection of the social compact and the body politic."[5]

This question-begging, by implications made from such phrases as "protection of the social compact and the body

---

[4] Ardery vs. State, 56 Ind. 329, A. D. 1877.
[5] U. S. vs. Harman, 45 Fed. Rep. 423, A. D. 1891.

politic," we must pass by, as the phrase itself belongs to an age of outgrown political speculation. So also the outrageously absurd assumption that persons may properly be denounced as moral degenerates if they have become so insensate to sensual suggestions that they can view nude humans without being ashamed, because not sexually excited nor afraid of the judgment of those who are. To many it will seem as though the sexually insensate ones are more clean-minded and decent than the judge who denounces them. However, in passing we may mention that the same opinion admits that some have "blunted sensibilities" and others acute sensitiveness, from which it follows that our sense of modesty, etc., is not always uniform, nor affords any certainty or uniformity in the enforcement of these laws.

THE CHANGES WROUGHT BY SCIENTIFIC PROGRESS.

Since 1877, when the Ardery case was decided, a great change has come to the entire intellectual world. In 1908 the public press proclaimed that a commission of scholarly Catholics, appointed by the Pope, had made a report to the effect that the books of Moses are not infallible and cannot be accepted as being in all respects literally true. Such statements are particularly weighty when we remember that the Roman Catholic Church, in such matters, is so extremely conservative as to be often stigmatized as reactionary.

In a recent Catholic cyclopedia, Benziger's *Library of Science,* the Jesuit Fathers show their accord with the main features of the doctrine of organic evolution. No Catholic, with even moderate scientific intelligence, has within two decades expressed any disagreement with the Jesuit Father, Erich Wasman of Luxemburg, when in his work, *Modern Biology and the Theory of Evolution,* he says: "The theory of evolution to which I subscribe as a scientist and a philosopher rests on the foundations of the Christian doctrine which I hold to be the only true one." Innumerable Catholic scientists have similarly expressed acceptance of the scientific doctrine of organic evolution.[6]

While, of course, there is still much controversy as to detail and incidental matter, it can be truthfully said that as between the dogmas of special creation and fixity of type, and the general features of the doctrine of organic evolution,

---

[6] For some discussion of this see: Haeckel's *"Last Words on Evolution."*

there is no longer any disagreement among educated persons.

As is to be expected, the Protestant scientists are even more outspoken than the Catholic in accepting the results of modern scientific research, and the doctrine of organic evolution is now being taught in all the theological seminaries of Europe and America. The story of creation as related in Genesis is accepted everywhere as being a myth or an allegory.

We may here content ourselves with a single quotation showing the present attitude of the great mass of educated present-day Christians toward a ready acceptance of new statements of scientific truth. Prof. James B. Pratt, of Williams College, says this: "It [religion] must forever be sloughing off an old shell and growing a new one. The shell indeed is important; but woe to the religion which identifies its life with its shell, or refuses to part with its shell when it has ceased to be a protection and has become a clamping, choking incumbrance to the growth of its inner life. * * * * If Christianity today should identify itself with the infallibility of the scriptures, or with the creation according to Genesis, or with any of the dogmas of Christology, it would condemn itself to swift decay."[7]

Creation, the fall of man, and the fig-leaf apron, according to Genesis, in their literal interpretation are no longer believed to be true by any Christian with scientific education, and thus disappears the original foundation upon which rested the judicial opinions that humans, in the Garden of Eden, acquired an innate and therefore uniform sense of the obscene, the modest, etc.

SCIENTISTS ON MODESTY AS AN INSTINCT.

The judicial dictum that modesty, as innate in man, induced the concealment of the human form, is not very important in itself. However, the discussion of the question is very material to the problem under consideration, because the evidence bearing upon that issue will illuminate the whole subject of the psychology of modesty, and especially help us to determine whether or not (within the limit of certainty essential to the validity of a criminal statute) "obscenity" is definable in terms of a book or picture, or is at all a quality residing in the thing contemplated, or, on the contrary, whether it is indefinable because resident exclusively within and depend-

---

[7] *The Psychology of Religious Belief*, 287.

ent upon the peculiar intellectual and emotional associations and predisposition of the contemplating mind.

The judicial assumption was that modesty is innate and intuitive, and therefore antedated and induced the use of clothing. Now will be quoted the contrary conclusion of scientists, that modesty instead of being the cause is an effect, a mere artificial, varying and unstable psychologic consequence, produced chiefly by the wearing of clothing.

Prof. Edward Westermarck, Ph.D., of Finland.

Westermarck (*Hist. of Marriage,* p. 211.,) after a careful review of the evidence, says: "These facts appear to prove that the feeling of shame, far from being the original cause of man's covering his body, is, on the contrary, a result of this custom; and that the covering, if not used as a protection from the climate, owes its origin, at least in many cases, to the desire of men to make themselves attractive."[8]

Prof. Ch. Letourneau, of Paris.

"In a former work[9] I have attempted to trace the genesis of a sentiment peculiar to humanity—the sentiment of modesty. It would be inexpedient here to treat the subject afresh in detail, but I will recall the conclusions arrived at by that investigation. Modesty is par excellence a human sentiment, and is totally unknown to the animals, although the procreative need inspires them with desires and passions essentially identical with what in man we call love; it is therefore certainly an artificial sentiment, and comparative ethnology proves that it must have resulted from the enforced chastity imposed on women under the most terrible penalties."[10]

Geoffrey Mortimer, of England.

"There seems to be no doubt whatever that clothing was adopted for warmth and decoration, and not from motives of decency. Drapery has always served to inflame sexual passion, and some tribes have regarded all garments as indecent. Mr. Wallace found the Brazilian Indian woman who put on a petticoat almost as ashamed of herself as civilized people would be if they took theirs off. Only prostitutes clothe themselves among the Saliras, and they dress to excite through hiding the body. * * * As Westermarck says: "It is not the

[8] Requoted from 7th Ed. of Krafft-Ebing, *Psycopathia Sexualis,* p. 15. See also: Ellis' *Studies in the Psychology of Sex* (Modesty) p. 38.
[9] *L'Evolution de la Morale.*
[10] Letourneau, *Evolution of Marriage,* 56.

feeling of shame that has provoked the covering, but the covering that has provoked the feeling of shame.' * * * Its [modesty's] origin was not in morality and a native sense of decency, though modesty is now estimated as moral and decent."[11]

Prof. Th. Ribot, of France.

"The conditions of its [modesty's] origin is little understood. H. Spencer and, after him, Sergi, maintain that it results from the habit of wearing clothes, which began with man (not with woman) from motives of ostentation and ornament. * * * Besides this special mode of expression [blushing] modesty shows itself by concentric, defensive movements, by a tendency to cover or disguise certain parts of the body. The means employed to this end are of the most various description according to race, country or period: Some hide the whole body, some the sexual parts only, or the face or bosom, some paint the body, or the face, etc. It is impossible to determine the exact part played in this diversity by circumstances, climatic conditions, and the association of ideas, compulsion, fashion, imitation, and even change."[12]

Charles Darwin.

Darwin expresses his belief "that self-attention directed to personal appearance, in relation to the opinion of others," and "not to moral conduct" is the fundamental element in shyness, modesty, shame and blushing.[13]

Prof. William I. Thomas, of University of Chicago.

"The native assumption that men were ashamed because they were naked, and clothed themselves to hide their nakedness, is not tenable in the face of the large mass of evidence that many of the natural races are naked and not ashamed of their nakedness; and a much stronger case can be made out for the contrary view, that clothing was first worn as a mode of attraction and modesty then attached to the act of removing the clothing.

"But while we find cases of modesty without clothing and of clothing without modesty, the two are usually found together, because clothing and ornament are the most effective means of drawing the attention to the person. Sometimes by

[11] *Chapters on Human Love*, by Geoffrey Mortimer, pp. 37, 38, 40, 41.
[12] Ribot, *Psychology of the Emotions*, 272.
[13] *Expression of Emotions in Man and Animals*, pp. 325-327.

concealing it and sometimes by emphasizing it. * * * * We recall the psychological standpoint that the emotions are an organic disturbance of equilibrium occurring when factors difficult of reconciliation are brought to the attention. * * * When the habits are set up and are running smoothly, the attention is withdrawn, and nakedness was a habit in the un-clothed societies, just as it may become a habit now in the artist's model. * * * When once a habit is fixed, interfer-ence with its smooth running causes an emotion. The nature of the habit broken is of no importance. If it were habitual for grande dames to go barefoot on our boulevards or to wear sleeveless dresses at high noon, the contrary would be em-barrassing."[14]

Dr. Paolo Mantegazza, of Italy.

"I acknowledge that I myself, as the years went by, changed the idea I first had of modesty, and which I treated in the *Physiology of Pleasure*. At first it seemed to me a sentiment that rises within us in childhood and youth, spon-taneous as egotism, self-respect, love; and then, again, I be-came persuaded that modesty is taught first and learned afterward; for which reason it is one of those sentiments which I term acquired or secondary. * * * * * The animals demonstrate to us some forms emanating from modesty. Many ot them conceal themselves in order to offer sacrifice to voluptuousness; numerous females sought by the male begin by fleeing, resisting, by hiding that which they desire to con-cede. And this is probably an irreflective automatic act; it is, perhaps, a form of fear, which rises before the aggressive requirements of the male; these flights, these resistances, these phantoms of modesty have the scope to excite the female as much as the male, and to prepare the soil more suitable for fecundation. . . . . Sherihat ordered the Turkish women to cover the back of the hand, but permitted them to expose the palm. The Armenian women of Southern India cover the mouth even at home, and when they go out they wrap themselves in white linen. The married live in great seclusion and for many years they cannot see their male relatives and conceal their faces even from the father-in-law and mother-in-law. These two examples, selected from a thou-sand that might be cited, suffice to persuade us that acces-sory and conventional elements are often joined to true mod-

[14]Prof. Thomas' *Sex and Society*, pp. 207 to 218.

esty which, physiologically considered, do not belong to it. We, ourselves, without leaving Europe, find that the confines of modesty are marked in many countries by the various fashions, not according to morality or the requirements of sex, but according to national mode of dress. He who exchanged these conventional elements for modesty could write the great psychological heresy, that this sentiment had its origin in the custom of covering one's self.

"*The sentiment of modesty is one of the most changeable in form and degree,* and we will write its ethical history in the volume which we will dedicate to the ethnology of love. Thus without going further than our race and time, we have women who would let themselves die rather than subject themselves to an examination with the speculum, and we have men of great intelligence and lofty passions who confess that they feel scarcely a shadow of modesty. * * *

"Modesty is one of the choicest forms of seduction and of the reticence of love; it is an extra current of the great fundamental phenomena of generation; it is a physical respect of one's self; it is one of those psychical phenomena of the highest order. * * * * * If the sentiment of modesty were not a great virtue, it would be the most faithful companion of voluptuousness, the greatest generator of exquisite joys. An ardent thirst and an inebriating bowl; what joy, but what danger of satiety."[15]

To discuss the issue thus joined will be the purpose of the immediately succeeding chapters, and these will deal unavoidably with unusual factors, mainly in the realm of sexual psychology, which are essential to a determination of the psychic essence of "obscenity." To the lawyer whose learning is limited to a memory-knowledge of judicial precedent, the new psychologic propositions to be contended for may seem a bit startling. Knowing that the disturbance of long fixed mental habits and the disruption of their association with intense moral-sentimentalism, usually produces an inhibition against the assimilation of the disturbing and disrupting argument, I feel it necessary now to devote some space to a plea for open-mindedness for the considerations supporting the following proposition:

[15]*The Physiology of Love,* pp. 91 to 97.

STATEMENT OF CONTENTIONS. *"Obscene and indecent" are never qualities of literature or art, and therefore are never a matter of sensory cognition, discoverable by unerring and uniform standards inductively derived from the nature of things, but on the contrary, these qualities reside always and exclusively in the contemplating mind, and are merely read into, or ascribed erroneously to, the book or picture. In various ways this will be proven to a demonstration. By a critical psychological analysis, it will be shown that the only unifying element generalized in the word "obscene" (that is the only thing common to every conception of obscenity and indecency) is subjective, is an affiliated emotion of disapproval, which, under varying circumstances of temperament and education, is different in different persons, and in each person at different stages of development, and is aroused peculiarly and distinctively in each individual, differently from other persons, to varying degrees of intensity by each of various stimuli, and so has become associated differently in different persons with an infinite variety of ever-changing objectives, having not even one common element in objective nature (in literature or art).*

The before stated contention will be re-inforced by an array of facts of ethnography and sexual psychology, exhibiting the great diversity in the foci of indecency and modesty; by a psychologic study of modesty showing that in actual practise judgments of modesty are usually the fear-imposed verdict of others and not rational convictions, nor deductions made from a uniform standard derived from nature, or established by statute; by a study of the uncertainty of the moral-test of "obscenity" to show it to be equally void of definite standards; by an exhibition of the varieties of official modesty and of some mutually destructive factors of the judicial legislation creating tests of "obscenity"; by authoritive confessions of their uncertainty; and by some illustrative applications of these tests to exhibit their utter absurdity.

All this is to the point that neither nature, common knowledge, science, nor the statute does or can furnish us with such a definition of the crime—such criteria of guilt— that it must unerringly fix the same unshifting line of partition between the criminally obscene and that which is innocent, when applied, no matter by whom, to every book or picture in the broad borderland of the literature of doubtful "purity." This fact will be co-ordinated with established legal maxims, as indispensable and controlling elements of constitutional construction. Although it is not absolutely essential to the correctness of my conclusions, I believe all this to be true because the only element of unification generalized in the word "obscene" is not in the quality of a book or a picture but exists solely in the contemplating mind.

STATEMENT OF ISSUE BETWEEN JUDGES AND SCIENTISTS.

The conflict between the before quoted judicial dictum and the later scientific conclusions, forms the issues now to be investigated. Before marshalling any of the evidence it is desirable to restate that issue of science and again to indicate the legal consequences toward which the conclusion should lead us.

We are to determine whether modesty is an innate attribute of all humans,—a part of human nature itself—and therefore a matter within the range of ordinary intelligence resulting in uniform judgments by a uniform intuitive standard; or whether, if those judgments are not instinctively alike, they are so variable and uncertain as to make a statutory definition essential to uniformity in the execution of the criminal statutes in question, and therefore essential to the constitutionality of the statute.

In other words, is "obscenity" a matter of sense-cognition, discoverable by unerring and uniform standards, existing in the nature of things, or does it exist wholly within the contemplating mind, so that every verdict or judgment is therefore dependent, not upon the letter of any general law, but in each person according to his personal whim, caprice, prejudice, "moral" idiosyncracies, varying personal exper-ences and different degrees of sexual hyper-astheticism or of intelligence about sexual psychology? If the latter, then the statute is clearly void for uncertainty. These issues of science we will now investigate.

I am aware how offensive some of the above claims must seem to those who may have given little or no critical thought to sexual psychology, and who therefore have not even dreamed that such a question could be raised. After this proposition was first advanced by me, in a paper before the XV Congres International de Medicine, held at Lisbon, April, 1906, some quasi-scientists have dogmatically expressed their emotional aversion to such a conclusion, but not one has had the courage to try to answer the argument. Expert psychologists, however, have expressed their agreement with my conclusions. However, the little teapot storms which my proposition raised in the minds of a very few people, credited with intelligence, again warns me that I am disrupting old convictions, resting upon established emotional associations, and that, therefore, I cannot hope for an open-mind even in the reader of more than average intelligence and that again I must take valuable space to plead for intellectual hospitality for my argument.

A PLEA FOR OPEN-MINDEDNESS.

To this end let me recall the well known anecdote of the Royal Society, to whom King Charles II proposed that they explain how it came that a vessel of water weighs no more after having a live fish put into it, though it does if the fish be dead? Various solutions of great ingenuity were proposed, discussed, objected to, and defended. After long bewilderment, it occurred to some one to try the experiment, and it was found that the fact to be explained existed only in the mind of the monarch.[16]

So now, I beg you to be patient with an argument which may prove to you that almost daily we are sending persons to a felon's cell, and are gravely discussing certain alleged "evils" which the criminal law is designed to suppress, without ever seriously inquiring if the facts which determine guilt exist anywhere except in the imagination of the judge and jury who try the accused.

It was objected to the system of Copernicus, that if the earth turned upon its axis, as he represented, a stone dropped from the summit of a tower would not fall at the foot of it but a great distance to the west, in the same manner as a stone dropped from the mast-head of a ship moving at full speed does not fall at the foot of the mast but toward the stern. To this it was answered that a stone being part of the earth obeys its laws and moves with it; whereas it is no part of a ship, of which its motion is therefore independent. The solution was admitted by some and opposed by others with great earnestness. It was not until one hundred years after the death of Copernicus that an experiment demonstrated that

---

[16] *Famous Pamphlets*, p. 255.

a stone thus dropped from the mast-head does fall at the foot of it.[17]

Could there be any harm if we made a scientific inquiry to ascertain if all the "obscenity" which we criminally punish has any existence outside of the mind and emotions of those whose unreasoned predispositions or emotional associations are offended? The laws against imaginary crimes are annulled when we destroy the superstition, if such it is, which is an indispensable assumption of the statutes.

WITCHCRAFT AND OBSCENITY, TWIN SUPERSTITIONS.

As I contemplate the difficulty of my present unpopular task, I am again and again impressed that it is not unlike that of a lawyer who should have presumed to appear before an English Judge of three centuries ago and seriously endeavored to persuade him that there were no such beings as witches. There are many things in common between the belief in the objective verity of witches and of obscenity. Both beliefs had their origin in religion, and now we are to consider if obscenity, like witchcraft, won't disappear when we cease to believe in it. I beg the reader to remember that the immediate problem is one of science and not of religion, morals or law. Let us think it over in the calm dispassion of the true scientist's quest for truth.

Fanatical as well as hospitable men and pious judges, otherwise intelligent, have affirmed the reality of both witches and obscenity and, on the assumption of their inerrancy in this, have assumed to punish their fellow-men. It is computed from historical records that 9,000,000 persons were put to death for witchcraft after 1484.[18] The opponents of witchcraft were denounced just as the disbelievers in the "obscene" are now denounced. Yet witches ceased to be when men no longer believed in them. Think it over and see if the "obscene" will not also disappear when men cease to believe in it.

In 1661 the learned Sir Matthew Hale, "a person than whom no one was more backward to condemn a witch without full evidence," used this language: "That there are such angels [as witches] it is without question." Then he made a convincing argument from Holy Writ and added: "It is also confirmed to us by daily experience of the power and energy of these evil spirits in witches and by them."[19]

A century later the learned Sir William Blackstone, since

[17] Ibid., p. 256.
[18] Gage, *"Woman, Church and State,"* pp. 217 to 247.
[19] See *Annals of Witchcraft*, by Drake, preface, page xi.

then the mentor of every English and American lawyer, joined with the witch-burners in bearing testimony to the existence of these spook-humans, just as our own courts to-day join with the obscenity-hunters to affirm that obscenity is in a book and not in the reading mind, and that therefore the publisher, and not the reader, shall go to jail for being "obscene."

Blackstone said: "To deny the possibility, nay, actual existence of witchcraft and sorcery is at once flatly to contradict the revealed word of God in various passages of both the Old and New Testament, and the thing itself is a truth to which every nation in the world hath in its turn borne testimony, either by example seemingly well tested, or by prohibitory laws which at least suppose the possibility of commerce with evil spirits."[20]

And yet when men ceased to believe in witches, they ceased to be, and so when men shall cease to believe in the "obscene" they will also cease to find that. Obscenity and witches exist only in the minds and emotions of those who believe in them, and neither dogmatic judicial dictum nor righteous vituperation can ever give to either of them any objective existence.

In the "good old days," when a few, wiser than the rest, doubted the reality of witches, the doubter, if not himself killed as being bewitched, was cowed into silence by an avalanche of vituperation such as "infidel," "atheist," or "emissary of Satan," "the enemy of God," "the anti-Christ," and some witch-finder would get on his trail to discover evidence of this heretic's compact with the devil; as is the case with obscenity, those seeking to destroy belief in witchcraft were accused of seeking to abolish morality, and as a successful scarecrow to prove this it was argued by John Wesley and others, that to give up witchcraft was in effect to give up the Bible. Let us not be frightened by such conjectural morality, but rather inquire boldly and frankly as to the objective import and reality of all that we punish as dangerous to society under the name of "obscenity."

QUESTION-BEGGING EPITHETS NOT ARGUMENT.

How this attitude toward witchcraft is duplicated in the attitude of a large portion of the public toward those who dis-

[20]Blackstone's *Commentaries*, page 59. Edition of 1850.

believe in the objectivity of "obscenity"! Whether obscenity is a sense-perceived quality of a book, or resides exclusively in the reading mind, is a question of science, and as such, a legitimate matter of debate. Try to prove its non-existence by the scientific method, and the literary scavengers, instead of answering your argument by showing the fallacy of its logic or error of fact, show their want of culture, just as did the witch-burners. They tell you that you are (quoting from Mr. Comstock) "either an ignoramus or so ethereal that there is no suitable place on earth for you," except in jail. They further hurl at you such unilluminating epithetic arguments as "immoral," "smut-dealer," "moral-cancer planter," etc., etc. Such epithets may be very satisfying to undeveloped minds, but they will not commend themselves very highly to any person wishing to enlighten his intellect upon the real question at issue. Again we say: This is a matter of science, which requires fact and argument and cannot be disposed of by question-begging villification. It is a regrettable fact that the "moral" majority is still too ignorant to know that such question-begging epithets when unsupported are not argument, and its members are too obsessed with sensual images to be open to any proof against their resultant "obscene" superstition.

Think it over and see if when you cease to believe in the existence of "obscenity," you must not also cease to find it. If that be true, then it exists only in the minds and emotions of those who believe in the superstition. Empty your mind of all ideational and emotional associations which the miscalled "pure" people have forced into your thoughts. Having done this, you may be prepared to believe that "unto the pure all things are pure; but unto them that are defiled and unbelieving is nothing pure; but even their mind and conscience is defiled."[21] Not till thus cleansed can you join in these words: "I know, and am persuaded by the Lord Jesus, that there is nothing unclean of itself, but to him that esteemeth anything to be unclean, to him it is unclean."[22]

THE JUDICIAL EPITHETIC ARGUMENT.

The courts are more refined, though not more argumentative or convincing, in their manner of denouncing dissen-

[21]Titus, 1-15.
[22]Romans 14, 14.

ters. The judicial formula is this: "When such matters are said to be only impure to the over-prudish, it but illustrates how familiarity with obscenity blunts the sensibilities, depraves good taste, and perverts the judgment."[23] Again we ask for fact and argument, not question-begging dogmatism. The statute furnishes no standard of sex sensitiveness, nor is it possible for any one to prescribe a general rule of judgment by which to determine where is the beginning of the criminal "blunted sensibilities," or the limit of "good taste," and the law-making power could not confer this legislative authority upon a judge, though in these cases all courts are unconsciously presuming to exercise it.

Furthermore, it is not clear that "blunted sensibilities" are not a good kind to be encouraged in the matter of sex. Who would be harmed if all men ceased to believe in the "obscene," and acquired such "blunted sensibilities" that they could discuss matters of sex—as we now discuss matters of liver or digestion—with an absolute freedom from all lascivious feelings? Why is not that condition preferable to the diseased sex-sensitiveness, so often publicly lauded when parading in the verbiage of "purity?" If preferable, and so-called "obscene" literature will help to bring about such "blunted sensibilities," would it not be better to encourage such publications? It requires argument and fact, rather than "virtuous" platitudes, to determine which is the more healthy-minded attitude toward these subjects. I plead for scientific research, not the brute force of blind dogmatism and cruel authority. Let us remember that "in scientific inquiry the ability to weigh evidence goes for much, but facility in declamation [and vituperation] goes for little."[24]

If, in spite of the argument by vituperation, a person refuses to submit "with humble prostration of intellect" to the demands of moral snobbery, he is cast from the temple of "good society" into jail. Then the benighted act as though by their question-begging epithets, or jail commitment, they had solved the scientific problem which is involved. Let us examine if it is not as true of obscenity, as of every witch, that it exists only in the minds of those who believe in it.

FEAR-INSPIRED AVOIDANCE OF THE ISSUE.

There is another particular in which the controversy over witchcraft resembles the controversy concerning the

[23] 45 Fed. Rep. 423.
[24] Fiske's *Cosmic Philosophy*, v. 2, p. 173.

suppression of the so-called "obscene." The earlier opponents of witchcraft always deemed it most important to anticipate and defend themselves against the influence of question-begging epithets, such as "infidel" and "atheist," etc. So we find them always explaining that this is unjust because they do not really deny the being and existence of witches, but controvert only their alleged mode of operation. Thus John Webster, in 1677, defends the whole class of anti-witch-mongers by arguments of which the following is a sample: "If I deny that a witch cannot fly in the air, nor be transformed or transubstantiated into a cat, a dog, or a hare, or that a witch maketh any visible covenant with the devil or that he sucketh on the bodies, or that the devil hath carnal copulation with them, I do not thereby deny either the being of witches, nor other properties that they may have, for which they may be so-called: No more than if I deny that a dog hath rugibility (which is only proper to a lion) doth it follow that I deny the being of a dog."[25]

Similar to this is it with the opponents of the censorship of obscenity. Every little while we have an explosive protest against the suppression of some book or work of art, but these moral heretics always hasten to explain their firm belief in "obscenity" as a quality of other books or pictures, but they protest that it does not exist where the censor or court thought. They firmly believe that "truly obscene literature" ought to be suppressed, but they assert that a great blunder has been made in suppressing the particular book in which they are unable to discover any obscenity. They hasten to approve the arbitrary power conferred by a criminal statute which fails to furnish the criteria of guilt, but complain that the arbitrary power has been abused. They like a government by the lawless will of men rather than a government by officials who are equally subjected to the law, but they prefer it should be their own lawless will and not that of another with different ideals that should govern.

As for me, I am not content to protest merely against the abuse of arbitrary power; I want that power itself destroyed. I am not content to deny the mode in which witches and obscenity are alleged to impair the morals of humanity. I demand that a searching and fearless inquiry be made as to the objective reality and essential characteristics of obscenity as well as witches. All this is said not by way of apology, but as a plea for open-mindedness for what follows.

[25] *The Displaying of Supposed Witchcraft*, p. 10.

CHAPTER XIII.

ETHNOGRAPHIC STUDY of MODESTY and OBSCENITY.

SYLLABUS of CONTENTIONS: *The ethnographic facts, a few of which are herewith presented, show that there is not a single element of objective nature which is a constituent factor of every conception of either modesty or obscenity. Thus it will be proven that the only unifying element common to all conceptions of modesty or of obscenity must be subjective —must be in the mind of the contemplating person, not in the thing contemplated. Expressed in popular English, the proposition is this: All obscenity is in the viewing mind, not in the book or picture. Since "obscene" does not generalize any fact of objective nature, it becomes impossible to define it in terms of the qualities of a book or picture, or in any terms whatever that furnish a certain or uniform standard, the application of which compels such uniformity of judgment that every one can, with unquestionable certitude, determine in advance just what must be the judgment of every court or jury as to the obscenity of any given book or picture. Later, it will be argued that because of this uncertainty the statute is unconstitutional.*

THE ETHNOGRAPHIC FACTORS.

Perhaps it is best to begin our study of modesty and nudity with a statement of conditions in ancient Greece when its civilization had reached that high place which, in some respects, we have not yet excelled. In all that follows we are always to bear in mind that we are inquiring into the innateness and uniformity of the human sense of modesty and obscenity, to see if it is possible to know from the mere reading of the statutes penalizing "obscene, indecent, filthy or disgusting" books or pictures, what conception of modesty, or what kind and degree of sex-sensitiveness, determines what is prohibited.

In Greece, "it was lawful in some cities for courtezans

to wear light, transparent garments; but at Sparta, as may be imagined, the reverse was the rule, semi-nudity being the badge of virtuous women."[26]

This is further illustrated in the fact that in their athletic games and dances the virtuous maidens appeared publicly in the nude and none were sufficiently polluted with prurient prudery to criticize. On this subject the Rev. John Potter, late Archbishop of Canterbury, has this to say: "As for the virgins appearing naked, there was nothing disgraceful in it because everything was conducted with modesty, and without one indecent word or action. Nay, it caused a simplicity of manners and an emulation of the best habit of body; their ideas, too, were naturally enlarged, while they were not excluded from their share of bravery and honour. Hence they were furnished with sentiments and language such as Gorgo, the wife of Leonidas, is said to have made use of. When a woman of another country said to her: 'You of Lacedaemon are the only women in the world that rule the men,' she answered: 'We are the only women that bring forth men.' "[27]

Among the native Mexicans, who in many respects had attained a higher civilization than their Spanish conquerors, it was found, in and before the 17th century, that the maidens went naked and only those who had parted with virginity covered the sexual parts.[28]

NUDITY AND MODESTY AMONG PRIMITIVE PEOPLE OF MORE RECENT TIMES.

Certain Mohammedan women who can easily be induced to expose their naked bodies to the male gaze are most persistent in their refusal to uncover their faces. Chinese women, who are not shocked by the exposure of the sexual parts, would have their modesty offended to quite an unbearable degree if compelled to expose their naked feet, even to one of their own sex. There are tribes who wear but little clothing, but who consider it "indecent" to eat in each other's presence, and even members of the same family turn their backs toward each other during meals. Among the Japanese, where women perform the national dance in nudity, it was found at the Jubilee Exhibition at Kyote that disgust was provoked by a painting of a naked woman, though in nature nudity was in no way offensive to them. In Lapland

[26]Sanger's *History of Prostitution*, 46.
[27]*Archaeologia Graeca*, p. 645, Glasgow, 1837.
[28]V. 3, Bayle's *Historical and Critical Dictionary*, 774. **Edition of 1734.**

woman who would prostitute themselves cheaply, will not for a large fee expose themselves before a camera. The well-bred African negress is most anxious to conceal her breasts in modesty, and exhibits shame even when discovered suckling her babe. Many civilized women are utterly indifferent to this, as one may see in the parks of any large city. So also the Arabs, who are pederasts, yet refuse to exhibit their nude bodies. In several tribes, it is as with the Naga women, who cover only their breasts. They declare that it is absurd to cover those parts of the body which every one has been able to see from their birth, but it is different with the breasts, which come later, and are therefore to be covered. Some primitive people, who unhesitatingly go about naked, still conceal themselves during copulation; others indulge openly and are not in the least affected by publicity.[29] If the tests of obscenity, decency and modesty are a "matter of common knowledge," why such varying conceptions, and where is the statutory test of "obscenity" which informs us as to which of the foregoing conceptions of modesty was incorporated into the statute?

In several countries, the consummation of the marriage by coitus in public is a part of the ceremony.[30] Among the Otaheitans, even recently, a girl is initiated into the sex-experience under the direction of a priestess as a solemn religious ceremony and in the view of a thousand. The queen gives to her and her companion, publicly, instructions as to the proper manner of its consummation. This is done with solemnity and prayer and without anything like either the leer of our stable boys or the blush of our prudes.[31]

Among some peoples modesty forbids the exposure of the male organ of generation while permitting complete female nudity, and among others the conditions are reversed. From Australia it is reported that women who did not hesitate much at exposing themselves in utter nudity, yet withdrew to a secluded place to remove their scant covering. Among some East African tribes the sentiment of modesty seems to center about the menstrual period. The Samoyed women for two months after marriage conceal their faces from their husbands and only then yield to their embraces. In some places women have been allowed to go naked until

[29] Ellis' *Modesty*, and Bebel's *Women Under Socialism*, 18, citing Bachofen.
[30] Ellis' *Modesty*, p. 17, and others.
[31] Westrop's *Primitive Symbolism*, pp. 39-40.

they were married and required to wear clothes after marriage. Among the Montana Indians, where the women readily prostitute themselves for a small consideration, they often exhibit extraordinary sensitiveness to a physician's examination. The Adamanes women "are so modest they will not renew their fig-leaf aprons in the presence of one another." In Masai it is considered as disreputable to conceal the phallus as it is to display it ostentatiously. This will to some seem a very healthy-minded attitude, which stands in great contrast to the following example of modesty.

"Native women of India have committed suicide rather than submit to examination by state surgeons under the English Government" [under a law regulating prostitution].[34]

"The Hindoos have a species of adultery, which with us would be considered mere flirtations: First, if a couple wink or smile, converse together in an unfrequented place, or bathe in the same pool; second, if a man sends sandlewood, victuals, drink or other presents to a female; the third sort seems the most serious, namely, when a man and woman sleep and dally on the same carpet, kiss and embrace, and then seek some retired place, the woman saying nothing all the while. The punishments prescribed by the shaster for adultery are too barbarous for enumeration."[35]

"It is related by Dr. Tournefort that in a Turkish harem he was allowed to see only the arm of a sick female protruded through a screen, without further opportunity for determining the nature of the malady."[36]

We are in the habit of denouncing Turkish polygamy as indecent and an argument in its favor probably could not be sent through the mails. Yet these Turks outdo us all when it comes to prudery. Where does the statute furnish the standard of judgment as between these conflicting pruderies?

VARIETIES OF CHRISTIAN MODESTY.

Here we will exhibit a variety of differing conceptions of modesty as they are found among Christian people. The purpose is always to be borne in mind, and it is to show: First, that no particular conception, standard or focus of modesty is a part of our human nature (innate in us), and second, that therefore in each individual his own notions of

---

[34]*Unmasked*, Dr. Mary Walker, p. 133.
[35]*Woman, Past and Present*, p. 338.
[36]*Woman, Past and Present*, p. 19.

modesty are determined by his educated emotional and ideational associations and the degree of his sexual hyper-æstheticism. Keeping this purpose in mind, let us review the historical evidences.

Among the early Christian Fathers we find many evidences that bundling, often in nudity, was a widespread custom, even among monks and nuns vowed to chastity. The practise always resulted in suspicion and no doubt quite frequently in something more real. Chrysostom, Jerome and Tertullian all write of it.

The Rev. Dr. Ruffner, after quoting these fathers and other evidences, summarized his conclusions as follows: "The practise of unmarried men—some of them clergymen—and consecrated virgins lying together, seems to have prevailed to a considerable extent even at this early period; but then the parties professed that there was no harm in it, seeing that there was all the while a chaste familiarity, a purely spiritual conjunction."[37]

"Some confessors, like Robert d'Arbissell (and the same has been said of Ardhelm, the English Saint, who lived before the conquest), have induced young women to lie with them in the same beds, giving them to understand that if they could prove superior to every temptation and rise from the bed as they went to it, it would be in the highest degree meritorious."[38]

Writing on the earlier period, Gibbon states this: "The primitive church was filled with a great number of persons of either sex who had devoted themselves to the profession of perpetual chastity. A few of these, among whom we may reckon the learned Origen, judged it the most prudent to disarm the tempter [by self-castration]. Some were insensible and some were invincible against the assaults of the flesh. Disdaining an ignominious flight, the virgins of the warm climate of Africa encountered the enemy in the closest engagement; they permitted priests and deacons to share their bed, and gloried amidst the flames in their unsullied purity."[39]

Washington Irving tells us of the bundling habit in New England as "a superstitious rite observed by the young people of both sexes, with which they usually terminated their

---

[37]Ruffner's *Fathers of the Desert,* 227-232-237-238; Gibbon's *History of Christianity,* p. 161, and authorities cited.
[38]*A Paraphrase on Historia Flagellatium,* p. 246.
[39]Gibbon's *History of Christianity,* p. 161.

festivities, and which was kept up with religious strictness by the more bigoted and vulgar part of the community."[40]

The practise was permitted by the Puritans and found defenders among the clergy as a custom that prevailed "among all classes, to the great honor of the country, its religion, and ladies."[41]

Tolstoi tells us that in parts of Christian Russia young people, during the years of betrothal, spend their nights together without losing their virginity. To him it illustrates the blessed possibility of spiritual communion, untainted by fleshly desire.[42]

If memory serves me, Tacitus informs us that in his time the Germans customarily went naked and that their morals were exemplary compared with those of the Romans. A recent author informs us that: "The shirt began to be worn [in Germany] in the sixteenth century. From this fact as well as from the custom of public bathing, we reach the remarkable result that for the German people the sight of complete nakedness was the daily rule up to the sixteenth century." At their public dances exposures were quite unrestricted.[43]

We find several times among Christian sects that promiscuous nudity was made a virtue and duty among them.

One such sect existed in the second century. Theodoret, Baronius Danaeus and St. Epiphaneus all mention them, as conducting their devotional exercises in complete nudity, and, according to some, those were expelled from the congregations who did not remain continent. Upon this last there is disagreement.[44]

During the earliest days of Christianity women were baptized quite nude and by men in the presence of men, their bodies being afterward anointed with oil by the priests. One of the earliest chisms in the church arose from the protest of women against this practise, and a demand that they be allowed to baptize their own sex and the opposition of priests to that demand.[45]

---

[40]*Knickerbocker Hist. of N. Y.* 4 Am. ed. p. 211; Stiles' *Bundling*, p. 49.

[41]Stiles' *Bundling*, pp. 51-58.

[42]*Die Sexuelle Frage*, 36-38.

[43]Rudeck, *Geschichte der offentliche Sittlichkeit*, p. 399.

[44]V. 1, Bayle's *Dictionary*, pp. 110-111, and citations; 1, Heckethorn's *Secret Societies of All Ages and Countries*, pp. 95-96; Gage, *Woman, Church and State*, 92; *Two Essays on the Worship of Priapus*, pp. 172-174, and authorities.

[45]Gage, *Woman, Church and State*, 215, citing Waite's *Hist. of the Christian Religion to A. D. 200*, pp. 23. 384. 385; Benson's *Christianity of Mankind*, vol. 3, 386-393, vol. 3; Analecta; *Philosophical Dictionary*; Pike's *History of Crime in England*, and citations.

Ciampini gives a large plate representing the baptism of Agilulf and Theodelinda, King and Queen of the Longobards, A. D. 591, where they both appear naked in the font, with nothing but their crowns on, and the water is poured over their heads from a pitcher.[46]

Catherine, the first wife of Peter the Great, was received into the Greek Christian Church by a similar rite. New converts to that church are plunged three times, naked, in a river or in a large tub of cold water. Whatever is the age or sex of the convert this "indecent ceremony is never dispensed with. The effrontery of a pope (priests of the Greek Church are thus called) sets at defiance all the reasons which decency and modesty never cease to use against the absurdity and impudence of this shameful ceremony."[47]

The Beghards became a distant offshoot from the Franciscan Monks in the 14th century, for the purpose of practising still greater austerities. The Beghards and another order known as the Beguines came under the influence of the Brethren and Sisters of the Free Spirit. Of those we have some very interesting accounts. Mosheim says: "And they alone were deemed perfect by these fanatics and supposed to be united to the supreme being who could behold, without any emotion, the naked bodies of the sex to which they did not belong and who, and in imitation of what was practised before the fall by our first parents, went entirely naked and conversed familiarly in this manner with males and females without feeling any tender propensities of nature. Hence it was that the Beghards (as they were nicknamed) when they came into their religious assemblies and were present at the celebration of divine worship, appeared without any veil or covering whatever."[48]

The late William Hepworth Dixon, once the distinguished editor of the *London Athenaeum*, gives us a most interesting account of these people.[49]

In the 13th century they became known as the Adamites or Picards. Under the leadership of Picard, if not before and if not in other branches, the ascetic restraint of continence was abandoned under the doctrine of perfectionism.[50]

[46]Lundy, Chapter on Baptism, *Monumental Christianity*, 389.
[47]Count Segur, in *Woman's Condition and Influence in Society*, here requoted from *Woman, Church and State*, 216.
[48]Mosheim *Eccl. Hist.* p.877, Balt. ed. 1833.
[49]*Spiritual Wives*, Chap. 14. See also Lea's *Hist. of the Inquisition*, 123-407.
[50]4, Bayle's *Historical and Critical Dictionary*, p. 628.

At Amsterdam in 1538 a dozen religious zealots, men and women belonging to the Anabaptists, went out upon the streets in nudity, and "they did not so much as leave a ribbon upon their heads to keep their hair tied."[51]

Within the past two decades we have seen a Russian Quaker sect of Canada called Doukhobors making pilgrimages in large numbers, both men and women being in entire nudity.[52]

MODESTY OF ANOTHER EXTREME.

"In the rules laid down by Augustine, he ordains that no one shall ever steadfastly fix her eyes upon another, even of the same sex, as this is a mark of immodesty."[53]

Ammon and his wife, it is reported, renounced the secular life and inhabited one common ascetic apartment in the mountains of Nitria. Uneasiness finally prompted the bride to address her husband as follows: "It is unsuitable for you who profess chastity, *to look upon a woman in so confined a dwelling.* Let us, therefore, if it is agreeable to you, perform our exercises apart." He concurred.[54]

Ligouri[55] in prescribing the requirements of modesty, which some people in "good society" still follow, while others sneer at it, says: "A religious must practise modesty in sitting . . . . she must avoid every slothful posture and must abstain from crossing her feet and putting one leg on the other."[56]

In Rome, at one period, "their sexual delicacy was indeed extreme, if the anecdote of Manlius be only moderately authentic. This patrician and senator had only inadvertently saluted his wife in the presence of his daughters, and for this indulgence he was by the censors accused of indecency. After grave deliberations on the corruptive tendency of such open osculation to the rising generation, they struck him off the list of their order."[57]

In a publication at the end of the 17th century, this statement is found: "This world too much allows nakedness in women. * * * * The faulty abuse is strengthened

[51]4, Bayle's *Historical and Critical Dictionary,* 628.
[52]Maude's *A Peculiar People,* 241.
[53]Hardy's *Eastern Monasticism,* p. 54.
[54]Day's *Monastic Institutions,* p. 5.
[55]In *True Spouse of Christ,* Chap. VIII, Sec's 1-11.
[56]Day's *Monastic Institution,* p. 266.
[57]*Woman, Past and Present,* 29. Lecky's *Hist. of European Morals,* v 2, p. 300.

through a long use, and now passed into a custom so general that it has become common almost to all women and maids of all sorts of conditions. * * * * Even at the foot of the altar and in the very tribunals of penance," they came "half-naked"! The protesting priest begs that they "at least make some difference betwixt the house of the Lord * * * * and those which are profaned by the libertinism of the age."[58]

In the portraits of that period we find ladies of quality freely exposing their entire bosom. A modified remnant of this custom is found in the evening dress of our fashionable women, by which some people are still shocked. Now, then, what is the degree of statutory sexual delicacy which limits criminality? Where between the waist and the face, does the statute draw the line beyond which nudity offends modesty? Where is the statutory test of criminality which would protect the accused against such extreme prudery, and why is there any such; is "common knowledge" upon the subject sufficiently uniform to make unnecessary a statutory definition of "obscene"?

At the close of the 18th century, we find a book written *"Chiefly on the Profligacy of our Women and its Causes."* As showing what, in the opinion of that author, "tended to deprave morals," we may extract a few sentences. He says: "For the same reason that public schools are proper for boys, they are unfit for girls. * * * Though a girl's ideas be pure as angel's on her entrance into a boarding school, she cannot remain there any time without being as knowing in the ways of pollution as any nymph in the King's palace." Further on our author says: "I cannot bear to see a woman of fashion sit down to a harpsichord at a public concert and hear her clapped by strangers on finishing her tune." The reading of fiction is denounced because "novels are full of warm descriptions run entirely on the subject of love," etc. Upon the subject of having a male physician attend upon a woman during child-birth, this author says that "the practise is repugnant to every idea of modesty, delicacy and decency. * * * * To suppose any more art necessary than what can be taught by experience, would be to arraign the goodness and wisdom of the Almighty. * * * * *Infamous as the adultress is, her crimes admit of extenuation,*

---

[58] *A Just and Reasonable Reprehension of Naked Breasts. Lond. A. D. 1678.*

and she seems pure when balanced against the pretender to modesty who sends for a doctor to be digitated. Shame on so abandoned a practise," etc., etc.[59]

Here then is a man who admits that they are "pure," and who tells us that to educate women, to allow them to play musical instruments in public, and to have a male physician attend a woman during parturition, or to argue that special skill is desirable at such times, all tend to deprave the morals of those who are open to such influences; and elsewhere he says that not one is beyond such influence.[60] On these and succeeding pages this extremely modest author strangely enough writes about the means of inducing sexual excitement that which would *now* be punished as criminally "obscene."

This same author[61] expresses opinions about the sinfulness of adultery which are logically peculiar, but in practise have the endorsement of very, very, very, many men: "When a married man commits it [adultery], he throws out no defiance to the world—for the world thinks too lightly of the offense. He makes no sacrifice of character. A man cannot sink to the level with an adultress till he has forsaken his post in battle. Courage is the male point of honor—chastity the female."

As portrayed by an epistle supposed to have been written by Clement of Rome, one of the early Christian ideals of modesty was indeed extreme. The brethren and holy sisters and maidens must not look at one another nor allow the naked hand of one to touch the uncovered hand of the other.[65] Is this conception of modesty a matter of "common knowledge" and incorporated in the statute? If not, where and what are the statutory criteria of guilt, which exclude it?

In other places these conceptions of modesty were strangely blended. "Women will scarce strip naked before their own husbands, affecting a plausible pretense of modesty," writes Clement of Alexandria, at the close of the second century, "but any others who wish may see them at home, shut up in their baths, for they are not ashamed to strip before the spectators as if exposing their persons for sale. The

---

[59]*Thoughts on the Times,* (A. D. 1779), pp. 85-94-199. To the same effect see "*Man-midwifery analyzed and the tendency of the practise exposed.*" Lond. 1764.

[60]pp. 184 and 190.

[61]p. 73.

[65]*Two Epistles Concerning Virginity,* vol. XIV, Antenicene Christian Library, p. 384.

baths are opened promiscuously to men and women. Cyprian found it necessary to upbraid even virgins vowed to chastity for continuing the custom of promiscuous bathing in the nude." For others such promiscuous bathing was the custom.[66]

"When we are told that the monks of the convent of Mount Athos accused the monks of the convent of a neighboring island with falling away from grace because they allowed hens [because being of the female sex] to be kept within the convent enclosure, we may well believe that Origines and his monks [who castrated themselves] felt that they were gradually ascending in grace when they submitted to this sacrifice."[67]

MODESTY AMONG SOME WORLDLINGS.

With only a few more illustrations as to the diversity of human notions about modesty this essay must be closed. Dr. Havelock Ellis tells us of a ballet girl who thought it immodest to bathe in the fashion customary at the sea shore and cannot make up her mind to do so, though of course, she every night appears on the stags in tights.[68] Which of these conceptions of modesty does "common knowledge" compel us to incorporate in the statute?

"A Chinaman, who lived in England some years since, acknowledged that on his first arrival he felt some difficulty in restraining himself from rudeness to women if left alone with them, and a nun that had been reared in a convent on her first escape from it imagined that every man who had opportunity would assault her virtue."[69]

With the Chinaman, accustomed to nudity, secretiveness by the use of clothing induced greater lasciviousness than nudity would evoke. The nun, through perverted education, expected lascivious designs in others when they had no existence.

Krafft-Ebing tells of a person so sex-sensitive that in the presence of ladies he thought every expression he made was an offense against decency. Thus, for example, he thought it very improper in the presence of ladies, married or unmarried, to speak of going to bed, rising, etc.[70] May the

---

[66] Ellis's *Psychology of Sex*, (Modesty), 19 and 20.
[67] *History of Circumcision*, p. 89.
[68] *Psychology of Sex*, (Modesty) p. 47.
[69] *Woman, Past and Present*, p. 212.
[70] *Psychopathia Sexualis*, 75.

statutory "obscenity" be determined and a verdict of guilt found by such persons, and if not why not?

"I have several times observed in hysterical females scruples relative to the satisfaction of natural needs, to the action of chewing, eating, micturation, defecation, which have all come to be regarded as revolting acts, which must be dissembled like crimes."[71]

The present law does not in the slightest degree protect one accused of obscenity from the whim and caprice of judges or jurors who may be thus afflicted with extraordinary sexual sensitiveness. Even the "tests of obscenity" created by judicial legislation leave the criteria of guilt just as much in doubt.

By evidences gathered from similar sources it can be demonstrated that there is not one single fact of obscenity concerning which all humanity is agreed. Even what is to us the most revolting "obscenity" is not so to all persons. Every known form of sexual perversion, from sadism, lust, murder, up and down, has been credited with the endorsement of some god and practised and sanctified by some religious society. Those who want proof of the fact need only to make themselves fairly expert in sexual psychopathy, and then study all the facts of sex-worship among the ancient Greeks and Egyptians, also the old initiations into the priesthoods of the native Mexican religions, and the sacred snake dance among the Moquis. If proof is wanted as to its expression in art, we have it in the secret Cabinet of the Museum of Herculaneum and Pompeii and other places. If doubt still remains it only becomes necessary to get the confidence of one whose sexual impulse has become completely perverted, and ask such a one about his shame when indulging only in the presence of those who are perverted like himself.

Within the available limits one can only hint at the source and character of the evidence which contradicts the judicial dictum upon the questions of science here involved. To exhaust the evidence would require a republication of volumes of ethnographical research, and most of the litera-

[71] Moral Hypochondria. Fere. *Pathology of the Emotions*, p. 389.

ture upon sexual psychology. The principal books upon the latter subject are listed for further study.[72]

Additional arguments will be offered in the succeeding chapters to demonstrate anew the subjective character of all that is generalized in the word "obscene" and the consequent unescapable uncertainty of the criteria of guilt under these obscenity statutes.

[72]*Psychopathia Sexualis* by Krafft-Ebing. *Suggestive Therapeutics in Relation to Psychopathia Sexualis*, Schenk Notzing.. *Morbid Manifestations*, by Tarnowsky. *Studies in the Psychology of Sex*, by Dr. Havelock Ellis, and especially that volume devoted to "Modesty." This literature, by exhibiting the infinite variety of foci about which center the sentiments of modesty, prove to a demonstration that we have no innate sense of modesty, nor any common standards by which to determine its opposite, nor any uniformity in the ideas which excite in us those emotions of aversion which constitute our conviction that a book or picture is obscene.

CHAPTER XIV.

PSYCHOLOGIC STUDY OF MODESTY AND OBSCENITY.

Syllabus of the Argument: Through a study of the mental processes by which we acquire the general idea symbolized by the word "obscene", (or its opposite) and of those by which we usually form a judgment as to the modesty or obscenity in a particular case, it will be redemonstrated that the word "obscene" does not stand for any sense-perceived quality of literature or art but is distinguished only by the likeness or unlikeness of particular emotions associated with an infinite variety of mental images. Therefore, obscenity is only a quality or contribution of the viewing mind—a subjective state—which, by synchronous suggestion or prior experience, is linked, in the contemplating mind, with the particular matter presented by the contemplated book or picture or with the special conditions under which these are being viewed. When this association, thus formed, asserts itself in consciousness the subjective "obscene" attachment is erroneously ascribed to and read into the objective factor of its conceptual associate. All this is only a technical way of telling how the "obscenity" of the viewing mind is referred to the book or picture before it.

As supporting these claims we see the fact that "obscenity" never has been, nor can be, described in terms of any universally applicable test, consisting of the sense-perceived qualities of a book or picture, but ever and always it must be described as subjective, that is, in terms of the author's suspected motive, or in terms of dreaded emotions imagined to exist in the mind of some superstitious reader.

With some knowledge of the psychologic processes involved in acquiring a general conception, it is easy to see how courts, as well as the more ignorant populace, quite naturally fell into the error of supposing that the "obscene" was a quality of literature, and not—as in fact it is—only a contribution of the reading mind. By critical analysis, we can exhibit separately the constituent elements of other conceptions, as well as of our general idea of the "obscene." By a comparison, we shall discover that their common element of unification may be either subjective or objective. Furthermore, it will appear that in the general idea, symbolized by the word "obscene," there is only a subjective element of unification, which is common to all obscenity, and that herein it differs from most general terms. In the failure to recognize this fundamental unlikeness between different kinds of general ideas, we shall discover the source of the popular error, that "obscenity" is a definite and definable, objective quality of literature and art.

THE PSYCHOLOGIC ARGUMENT.

A general idea (conception) is technically defined as "the cognition of a universal, as distinguished from the particulars which it unifies." Let us fix the meaning of this more clearly and firmly in our minds by an illustration.

A particular triangle may be right-angled, equilateral or irregular, and in the varieties of these kinds of triangles, there are an infinite number of shapes, varying according to the infinite differences in the length of their boundary lines, meeting in an infinite number of different angles.

What is the operation when we classify all this infinite variety of figures under the single generalization "triangle"? Simply this: In antithesis to those qualities in which triangles may be unlike, we contrast the qualities which are common to all triangles, and as to which all must be alike.

These elements of identity, common to an infinite variety of triangles, constitute the very essence and conclusive tests by which we determine whether or not a given figure is to be classified as a triangle. Some of these essential, constituent, unifying elements of every triangle are now matters of common knowledge, while others become known only as we develop in the science of mathematics. A few of these essentials may be re-stated. A plain triangle must enclose a space with three straight lines; the sum of the interior angles formed by the meeting of these lines always equals two right angles; as one side of a plain triangle is to another, so is the sine of the angle opposite to the former to the sine of the angle opposite to the latter.

These, and half a dozen other mathematical properties belong to every particular triangle; and these characteristics, always alike in all triangles, are abstracted from all the infinite different shapes in which particular triangles appear; and these essential and constant qualities, thus abstracted, are generalized as one universal conception, which we symbolize by the word "triangle."

Here it is important to bear in mind that these universal, constituent, unifying elements, common to all triangles, are neither contributions nor creations of the human mind. They are the relations of the separate parts of every triangle to its other parts, and to the whole, and these uniform relations inhere in the very nature of things, and are of the very essence of the thing we call a "triangle."

As the force of gravity existed before humans had any knowledge of the law or its operation, so the unifying elements of all triangles exist in the nature of things, prior to and independent of our knowledge of them. It is because these unifying elements, which we thus generalize under the word "triangle," are facts of objective nature, existing wholly outside of ourselves, and independent of us, or of our knowledge of their existence, that the word "triangle" is accurately definable.

We will now analyze that other general term, "obscene," reducing it to its constituent, unchanging elements, and we shall see that, in the nature of things, it must remain incapable of accurate, uniform definition, because, unlike the case of a triangle, the universal element in all that is "obscene" has no existence in the nature of things objective. It will then appear that, for the want of observing this difference between these two classes of general terms, judges and the mob alike erroneously assumed that the "obscene," like the "triangle," must have an existence outside their own emotions, and, consequently, they were compelled to indulge in that mystifying verbiage which the courts miscall "tests of obscenity."

COMMONPLACE FACTORS OF THE PSYCHOLOGIC ARGUMENT.

First of all, we must discover what is the universal constituent, unifying element common to all obscenity. Let us begin with a little introspection, and the phenomena of our everyday life. We readily discover that what we deemed "indecent" at the age of sixteen, was not so considered at the age of five, and probably is viewed in still another aspect at the age of forty.

We look about us, and learn that an adolescent maid has her modesty shocked by that which will make no unpleasant impression upon her after maternity, and by that which would never shock a healthy physician. We know, also, that many scenes are shocking to us if viewed in company, and not in the least offensive when privately viewed; and that, among different persons, there is no uniformity in the added conditions which change such scenes to shocking ones.

We see the plain countyman shocked by the decollete gown of our well-bred society woman; and she, in turn, would be shocked into insensibility if, especially in the presence of strange men, she were to view some pastoral scenes which make no shocking impressions upon her rustic critic. The peasant woman is most shocked by the "indecency" of the society woman's bare neck and shoulders, and the society woman is shocked most by the peasant woman's exhibition of bare feet and ankles, at least if they are brought into the city woman's parlor. We see that women, when ailment suggests its propriety, quite readily undergo an unlimited examination by a male· physician, while with the sexes reversed much greater difficulty would be experienced in securing submission. This not because men are *more* modest than women, but because other social conditions and education have made them *differently* modest.

It would seem to follow that the universal qualities which we collect under the general term "obscene," as its constituent elements are not inherent in the nature and relations of things viewed, as is the case with the triangle. Taking this as our cue, we may follow the lead into the realm of history, ethnology, sexual psychology and jurisprudence. By illustrative facts, drawn from each of these sources, it will be shown to a demonstration that the word "obscene" has not one single universal, constituent element in objective nature.

Not even the sexual element is common to all modesty, shame or indecency. A study of ethnology and psychology shows that emotions of disgust, and the concept of indecency or obscenity, are often associated with phenomena having no natural connection with sex, and often in many people are not at all aroused by any phase of healthy sexual manifestation; and in still others are aroused by some sensual associations and not by others; and these, again, vary with the individual according to his age, education and the degree of his sexual hyperaestheticism.

HYPERÆSTHETICISM AND EDUCATION.

Everywhere we find those who are abnormally sex-sensitive and who, on that account, have sensual thoughts and feelings aroused by innumerable images, which would not thus affect the more healthy. These diseased ones soon develop very many unusual associations with, and stimulants for, their sex-thought. If they do not consider this a lamentable condition, they are apt to become boastful of their sensualism. If, on the other hand, they esteem lascivious thoughts and images as a mark of depravity, they seek to conceal their own shame by denouncing all those things which stimulate sensuality in themselves, and they naturally and erroneously believe that it must have the same effect upon all others. It is essential to their purpose of self-protection that they make others believe that the foulness is in the offending book or picture, and not in their own thought. As a consequence, comes that persistence of reiteration, from which has developed the "obscene" superstition, and a rejection—even by Christians—of those scientific truths in the Bible, to the effect that "unto the pure all things are pure," etc. We need to get back to these, and reassert the old truth, that in literal fact all genuine prudery is prurient.

The influence of education in shaping our notions of modesty is quite as apparent as is that of sexual hyperaesthesia. We see it, not only in the different effects produced upon different minds by the same stimulants, but also by the different effects produced upon the same person by different objects bearing precisely the same relation to the individual. When an object, even unrelated to sex, has acquired a sexual association in our minds, its sight will suggest the affiliated idea, and will fail to produce a like sensual thought in the minds of those not obsessed by the same association.

Thus, books on sexual psychology tell us of men who are so "pure" that they have their modesty shocked by seeing a woman's shoe displayed in a shop window; others have their modesty offended by hearing married people speak of retiring for the night; some have their modesty shocked by seeing in the store windows a dummy wearing a corset; some are shocked by seeing underwear, or hearing it spoken of otherwise than as "unmentionables;" still others cannot bear the mention of "legs," and even speak of the "limbs" of a piano. A book published in England informs me of some who speak of the "bosom" of a chicken because of the immodesty of saying "breast." Surely, we have all met those who are afflicted in some of these ways.

Since the statutes do not define "obscene," no one accused under them has the least protection against a judge or jury afflicted with such diseased sex-sensitiveness, or against more healthy ones who, for want of information about sexual psychology, blindly accept the vehement dictates of the sexually hyperaesthetic as standards of purity. But whether a judge or a juror belongs to either of these classes, or rejects their dictum as to what is pure in literature, in any and every event, he is not enforcing the letter of a general law, but enacting and enforcing a particular *ex post facto law* then enacted by him solely for the particular defendant on trial. What that law shall be in any case depends on the experiences, education and the degree of sex-sensitiveness of the court, and not upon any statutory specification of what is criminal.

Among more normal persons, we see the same difference as to what is offensive to their modesty, depending altogether upon whether or not they are accustomed to the particular thing. That which, through frequent repetition, has become commonplace no longer shocks us, but that which, though it has precisely the same relation to us or to the sensual, is still unusual, or is seen in an unusual setting, does shock us.

Some who are passive if you speak of a cow, are yet shocked if you call a bull by name. In the human species, you may properly use the terms "men" and "women," as differentiating between the sexes, but if you call a female dog by name, you give offense to many. So, likewise, you may speak of a mare to those who would take flight if you called the male horse by name. With like unreason, you may speak of an ox or a capon to everybody, of a gelding to very many, but of a eunuch only to comparatively few, without giving offense. No one thinks that nudity is immodest, either in nature or in art, except the nudity of the human animal; and a few are not opposed to human nudity in art, but find it immodest in nature.

The Agricultural Department of the United States distributes information on the best methods for breeding domestic animals, and sends those to jail who advocate the higher stirpiculture, for the sake of a better humanity, if they are equally specific in the manner of treating the subject or advocate the adoption of the same method for improving humanity.

THE ONLY UNIFYING ELEMENT IS SUBJECTIVE.

It thus appears that the only unifying element generalized in the word "obscene," (that is, the only thing common to every conception of obscenity and indecency), is subjective, is an affiliated emotion of disapproval. This emotion under varying circumstances of temperament and education in different persons, and in the same person in different stages of development, is aroused by entirely different stimuli, and by fear of the judgment of others, and so has become associated with an infinite variety of ever-changing objectives, with not even one common characteristic in objective nature; that is, in literature or art.

Since few men have identical experiences, and fewer still evolve to an agreement in their conceptional and emotional associations, it must follow that practically none have the same standards for judging the "obscene," even when their conclusions agree. The word "obscene," like such words as delicate, ugly, lovable, hateful, etc., is an abstraction not based upon a reasoned, nor sense-perceived, likeness between objectives, but the selection or classification under it is made, on the basis of similarity in the emotions aroused, by an infinite variety of images; and every classification thus made, in turn, depends in each person upon his fears, his hopes, his prior experience, suggestions, education, and the degree of neuro-sexual or psycho-sexual health. Because it is a matter wholly of emotions, it has come to be that "men think they know because they feel, and are firmly convinced because strongly agitated."

This, then, is a demonstration that obscenity exists only in the minds and emotions of those who believe in it, and is not a quality of a book or picture. Since, then, the general conception "obscene" is devoid of every objective element of unification; and since the subjective element, the associated emotion, is indefinable from its very nature, and inconstant as to the character of the stimulus capable of arousing it, and variable and immeasurable as to its relative degrees of intensity, it follows that the "obscene" is incapable of accurate definition or a general test adequate to secure uniformity of result, in its application by every person, to each book of doubtful "purity."

Being so essentially and inextricably involved with human emotions that no man can frame such a definition of the word "obscene," either in terms of the qualities of a book, or such that, *by it alone,* any judgment whatever is possible, much less is it possible that by any such alleged "test" every other man must reach the same conclusion about the obscenity of every conceivable book. Therefore, the so-called judicial "tests" of obscenity are not standards of judgment, but, on the contrary, by every such "test" the rule of decision is itself uncertain, and in terms invokes the varying experiences of the testors within the foggy realm of problematical speculation about psychic tendencies, without the help of which the "test" itself is meaningless and useless. It follows that to each person the "test," of criminality, which should be a general standard of judgment, unavoidably becomes a personal and particular standard, differing in all persons according to those varying experiences which they read into the judicial "test." It is this which makes uncertain, and, therefore, all the more objectionable, all the present laws against obscenity. Later it will be shown that this uncertainty in the criteria of guilt renders these laws unconstitutional.

As the final proofs are being read there comes from the press the sixth volume of Dr. Havelock Ellis' elaborate "Studies in the Psychology of Sex," the earlier volumes of which I have often quoted herein. At page 54 I find this gratifying indorsement of the main contention of this chapter. He says: "Anything which sexually excites a prurient mind is, it is true, 'obscene' *to that mind,* for, as Mr. Theodore Schroeder remarks, obscenity is 'the contribution of the reading mind'."

P. S.—The rest of the Psychologic Study of Modesty, which should be a part of this chapter, will be found at pages 315 to 325. This misplacement is one of the defects arising from the literary mechanics, by which I tried hastily to make a book by the use of a paste pot and some magazine articles, where I should have rewritten the whole.—T. S.

CHAPTER XV.

UNCERTAINTY OF THE "MORAL" TEST OF OBSCENITY.*

Our Courts, in their blind non-logical gropings for some practical criteria of guilt under these vague statutes against "obscenity," have often amended the statutes so as to make the criminality of admitted facts depend, not upon the literal application of the letter of the statute, but upon the jury's opinion, according to its personal standards, as to whether or not the matter is such as might tend to deprave the morals of some hypothetical person who might be open to such immoral influences. Assuming now for the sake of argument that this judicial legislation is entirely proper as a matter of legitimate statutory construction, then the question arises whether this makes the statutory criteria of guilt so certain in meaning as is necessary to constitute this statute "due process of law." If courts can be said to have answered a question which they have not even considered, because the answer is a necessary inference from their acts, then the courts have answered this question in the affirmative. Is this answer by implication correct?

The inquiry now to be pursued is as to whether or not there exists an agreement as to the criteria of the ethical right in general, and of sex ethics in particular, such as enables the "moral" test of obscenity to satisfy the constitutional requirement as to the necessary certainty of the criteria of guilt in a penal statute. The method will be to study the various schools of ethics, and to exhibit what the various leaders of thought have to say upon the subject.

RELIGION AND SCIENCE DISTINGUISHED.

The most conspicuous line of cleavage between differing schools of morals, is that which separates religious morality from ethical science. The matter of differentiating the ethics of science from religious morality, is but a sub-division of the larger problem of the distinctions between religion and science

*Revised from the *Truth Seeker.*

in general. In *The Arena*[1] (Jan. 1, 1908), I discussed this latter question, rather too briefly, but summarized my conclusions as to the difference between science and religion in the following language:

"In religion the source of authority for its beliefs and activities is subjective experiences, believed not to be dependent for their existence upon material objective stimuli. To describe these subjective processes for the acquisition of religious knowledge such phrases are used as *an act of faith, an assurance of the heart, the inward miracle of grace,* and *the inward monitions of the spirit.*

"Science, on the contrary, deals only in objectives, and in our relation with them finds its only source of knowledge. Even when psychic phenomena are being studied the scientist must consider them objectively.

"From this difference in the sources of religious and scientific knowledge, comes an unavoidable difference of method to be pursued for the acquisition of their respective truths. The religionist resorts to faith, to prayer, to spiritual exercises, to silent communion with unseeable powers, superhuman intelligences, or extra-physical personages, as a means of securing those subjective experiences by which he knows because he feels, and is firmly convinced because strongly agitated. The scientist on the contrary can sum up his method in an application of the processes of synthesis and analysis to our human experience with our material environments.

"From these differences of source and method comes also a difference of aim. The scientist is concerned with the laws of nature, under which are included not merely things and their forces, but men and their ways, to the end that human happiness here and now may be increased by a more perfect adjustment to the conditions of our present material well-being. On the other hand, religion is primarily concerned with the laws of our 'spiritual,' (that is, our alleged superphysical) nature, to the end that man's happiness, primarily in some other existence, may be increased through the individual's adjustment to the conditions of 'spiritual' growth and 'spiritual' well-being.

[1]January, 1908. The Religious and Secular Distinguished.

"The scientist, or secularist, never subordinates the human happiness of this existence to that of any other. The religionist on the other hand, whenever a conflict arises between the joys of this life and those of some other kind of existence, always must sacrifice the present for the advancement of that other, super-physical, existence."

What is thus true of the difference between religion and science in general, is equally true of the difference in the particular, between religious and scientific ethics. That the general sources of religious authority, method for discovering religious truth, and the ends to be achieved by it, are all true of religious ethics in particular, is quite generally understood. The antipathy between religious and secular morality is not so generally known. Indeed, very few, even among those who have left the churches, seem to know anything definite about secular morality, and blindly continue to follow the moral dogmatism and sentimentalism of their abandoned religion. Religious morality either directly, or indirectly through the meditation of holy writ or a holy priest or priesthood, rests upon the authority of some *a priori* sanctity, whose inerrancy is certified to by some subjective experience, sometimes personal, at others adopted through imitation. The morality of science is always based upon experienced consequences of conduct, and between these differing moral standards there is, and always will be, an irrepressible conflict, arising from their different source of authority, of method, and of end to be achieved. This I will now try to make more plain.

THEOLOGICAL MORALS.

Prebendary Wace says: "Morality *cannot* for practical purposes be left to rest on scientific experiences. * * * * * It is essential in practice, to the welfare of individuals and of society alike, that the chief false routes of moral life should be barred by plain and authoritative prohibitions."[2] He also informs us that: "The eternal relations of the *heart* to a perfect being, towards whom every emotion of love and gratitude can be indulged to the highest degree," is a higher purpose and motive for morals than can be supplied by natural law.

Prof. Sedgwick considers *the moral ought* as an "ultimate and unanalyzable fact."[3]

---

[2] Ethics and Religion by Prebendary Wace. In *Journal of the Victoria Institute*, 1901, vol. 33.
[3] *Mind*, Oct., 1889.

Mortensen says: "Truly if the Light of religion be extinguished no reason is perceptible for leading a moral life in all these finite and temporal relations."[4]

"Blind obedience to extraneous law does not approve itself to us as really moral. * * * * The question concerning the ground of our moral obligations finds an adequate solution only in God,"[5] says the Rev. Otto Pfleiderer.

In religious ethics the appeal is to "the reality which transcends that which now is and that which now is known, "[6] is the opinion of the Rev. George Wm. Knox.

Notwithstanding the persistence of the clerical falsehoods to the contrary, Thomas Paine was a theist, and although his religious emotions no longer prompted him to adopt the Bible, or the priest, as embodying the divine will, he nevertheless did not place his morality upon a scientific basis. His words are: "The practice of moral truth, or in other words a practical imitation of the moral goodness of God, is no other than our acting towards each other as he acts benignly toward us."

Such theistic morality, though strictly religious in an unsectarian sense, yet is the associate of a conspicuous deviation from the habit of applying the religious method to all the factors of life. Thus is marked the beginning of a transition from the all-religious to the complete secularization of our thinking.

THE TRANSITION TOWARDS SECULAR MORALITY.

With that religionist whose mind is *wholly* "uncorrupted" by the scientific method, his religion, its methods and aims, will determine his ethical ideals. As a man gets away from the religious habit of mind, he gradually acquires moral and other ideals whose authority will dominate and determine his religious convictions. This is the transitional stage of some advanced theologians and the ethical culturists. When these dominating ethical ideals have become wholly scientific, then the secularization of morals is complete. The following illustrates the second stage of secularizing influence in an advanced theologian. "Religion must ever anew measure its inherited ideas and customs against the standard of the ethical

[4]Christian Ethics, p. 16.
[5]Rev. Otto Pfleiderer in *Am. Journal of Theology*, April, 1899, vol. 3, p. 239.
[6]"Religion and Ethics by Rev. Geo. Wm. Knox of Union Theol. Sem. in *International Journal of Ethics*, v. 12, p. 315.

ideals, [otherwise acquired?] and in so far as they do not harmonize with that, it must strive for their purification and progressive development. * * * * * It may be justly demanded that its teachings shall not conflict with what has been established as theoretical or practical truth, and especially that it shall not lag behind our ethical ideals."[7]   But how are we to judge of differing standards, which is the one that is lagging behind and which running ahead?   This author seems to demand that even the religious authority in matters of ethics may properly be subordinated to the standards of science.

In this progression toward the secularization of our morals, the ethical culture movement represents the "last ditch" of religion, in resisting the secular advance.   Here the religious method, and its subjective source of authority, are still in full operation as to morals, but the theology and the use of the religious method in every other branch of human thinking may have been abolished.   In the following quotation we see a non-theological religious morality in full force, with the ecstatic joy and hysterical enthusiasm of the revival convert but slightly impaired.   One can readily imagine the exhorter's impassioned tones accompanying this statement from the Ethical Culturist.

"There is," he says, "no reason why men, become conscious of their responsibilities and of the great issues at stake, [in ethical conduct,] should not be touched with reverence and awe as they think of these things, should not become hushed and subdued.   Morality would then become a religion to men, in the fundamental and indeed universally recognized sense of the term.   Morality as I conceive it, morality as I have tried—and yet too well know I am unable, to picture it— Morality as conscious willing glad subordination to the universal law of life, morality as lifting one to comradeship with suns and stars, because it is faithful as they, Morality *loving the law of life more than life,* Morality ready to die rather than to be untrue—that Morality may be the very ideal which one may seek all one's life to follow, *that may be the supreme passion to a man, down on his knees he may bow before it,* as he may before Jesus, or before Buddha, or any other son of man, who has exemplified the ideal, or made it any brighter

[7]Rev. Otto Pfleiderer in *Am. Journal of Theology,* April, 1899, vol. 225-249.

before his eyes. Aye, then it is plain the sense in which Religion and Morality may become one."[8]

It is apparent that the ethical culturist has that same unreasoned, passionate devotion to his moral law which the Brahmin manifests for the law of Manu, the Persian for the laws of Zoroaster, the Mohammedan for his Koran, the Protestant Christian for his Bible, the Catholic for his "permanent oracle of the divine will" at Rome, and the Mormon for the utterances of his "Prophet, Seer, and Revelator," who is the Utah Pope; and each endorsing something which some other denounced as immoral. It is also apparent that the same subjective source of authority exists in all cases though it attaches itself to varying standards. Take these words of Mr. Mangasarian, when he was still connected with the Ethical Culture movement, as conclusive proof. "Ethical Culture is the religion of the spirit. * * * * * Ethics is the heart of religion. * * * * * *It is impossible to learn from the physical world the lesson of morality.* * * * * Whenever we protest against wrong *it is from within* that we draw our inspiration. * * * * * Ethical Culture is a spiritual religion."[9]

RELIGION WITHOUT MORALS.

Not by this method, alone, but also by historical investigation, can it be shown that we can have, not only religious morals without theology, but also that we may have religion without a moral code. Here again eminent authorities also sustain our contention. We may begin by calling the Rev. Dr. Batchelor to the witness stand. He says: "Religion does not begin in ethics. It did not grow out of ethics. It was before ethics in origin and has during a great part of human history wrought in life independently of, and not infrequently in distinct opposition to, the ethical sentiment. Let all sense of ethical obligation be destroyed, or reduce it again to the level of the pre-historic standard, and still religion would none the less be a power in human life not to be disregarded."[10]

Next we quote Professor Everett, of Brown University. He says:[11] "That religion may be non-ethical, finds numerous illustrations in the history of the world's religions. Indeed,

[8]Rev. W. Salter in Morality and Religions, p. 33.
[9]The Religion of Ethical Culture, by Mangasarian, Philadelphia.
[10]Religion its own Evidence, p. 19.
[11]*International Journal of Ethics,* v. 10, p. 479.

at a certain stage, many primitive religions appear to have been non-ethical. That of Rome continued for centuries, remaining to the last almost exclusively formal and ritualistic. The statement that ethics may be non-religious, finds abundant support in modern life, as in the case of the positivists."

To this we may add the testimony of the Rev. Geo. Wm. Knox, of Union Theological Seminary.[12] He says: "Religion is to be distinguished from ethics. Even when somewhat developed, it may have no ethical code. It is said that Shinto has as its teaching only this: Fear God and obey the Emperor! But in its earlier books there is not even this teaching, nothing which implies either as an ethical maxim. The later writers explain this unusual feature by saying that the Japanese, being holy by nature, need no moral code; which was invented by immoral folk like the Hindoos and the Chinese."

Aristotle and Bacon separated the sphere of religion and ethics by assigning to the former those matters relating to an after-life, and to the sphere of the latter those actions which relate only to the present life. Of course many others would insist that according to their conception of the after life, *all* conduct here is related to it, affects it. Probably most of our present day orthodox Christians hold with Thomas Aquinas that God is the direct source of all the theological virtues, and the indirect source of all earthly virtues. While thus agreeing as to the source of authority with all believers in theistical religions, there is the widest range of belief as to what the Deity really considers virtue. See the varying attitudes toward sex problems entertained by Catholics, Shakers, Methodists, Bible Communists, Mohammedans and Mormons, all being Christian sectarists.

In practically all Christian ethics the foundation tenet is that God requires obedience to his law, not because it is good, but because it is his law. As to its goodness, finite humans have neither capacity nor right to sit in judgment, except to approve and obey. His moral law is good, not in itself, but only as the expression of the Divine will. God might have willed to the contrary and then his will would still have been good.

ETHICS OF SCIENCE.

When we contrast this with any scientific conception of

[12]*International Journal of Ethics*, v. 12, p. 305.

ethics the irrepressible conflict at once manifests itself. Here responsibility rests upon the individual, not merely as to choosing which God, or whose interpretation or conception of God's will, it is to which he will yield blind and unquestioning obedience, but also for the choice of conduct according to its social utility. Conduct now is moral or not according to its consequences, determined by its being a violation, or not, of the natural law of our social organism. But the good and ill of consequences are relative, so morality becomes a relative matter instead of an absolute thing. Responsibility now cannot be shifted on to God, for having imposed an inscrutable injurious "duty," and each person must decide for himself what is to be his own moral code, and himself must take the consequences of judging wrong and violating nature's moral law. For the breaching of nature's inexorable laws there is no forgiveness, nor vicarious atonement. In natural law all *must* take the natural consequences of their conduct. No priest can save us. We must readjust, get in harmony with the law—or perish. No wonder then that Cotton Mather denounced ethics as "a vile form of paganism."[13]

THE NON-RELIGIOUS, NON-THEOLOGIC MORALITY OF SCIENCE.

To make the irresistible conflict between religious and scientific morals still more evident it becomes desirable to quote some of the standard writers upon ethics, to show what is their source of ethical authority and what are their varying criteria of the moral life.

As to the source of ethical authority, "Clifford says that the 'Maxims of ethics are hypothetical maxims, derived from experience and based on the assumption of the uniformity of nature.' "[14]

Another offers this: "Morality springs from those human relationships in which the individual finds himself compelled to live and act. It has its roots in the needs physical and mental which other human beings can satisfy and in the sympathies which answer to those needs." Science "seeks to find the sanction of morality in the natural and inevitable results of the conduct itself and to establish morality on a rational basis by exhibiting the inescapable consequences of right and wrong action, of good and evil character, as in

[13]See Hall's Adolesence, v. 2, pp. 287-288.
[14]Religion and Ethics, by Rev. Geo. Wm. Knox, of Union Theol. Sem. in *International Journal of Ethics*, v. 12, p. 305

themselves sufficient grounds for the choice of the one and the avoidance of the other. As a science it does not even inquire if there is a supreme being."[15]

While all scientific students of ethics agree that nature is the ultimate source of authority in ethics, yet when it comes to formulating a general statement of what is required of us by the natural law of our interhuman relations there is, at least seemingly, a wide range of difference in the statement. This is quite inevitable in the present undeveloped state of our attainments in the social sciences. We are as yet too near the beginnings of our investigation into these subjects to have arrived at any comprehensive and ultimate rational generalizations.

Let me now portray the criteria of moral guilt according to various students of ethical science. I will begin with John Stuart Mill whose ethical views are still very popular with the masses, but have lost much of their authority with the more modern scientists.

He says: "According to the greatest-happiness principle as above explained, the ultimate end, with reference to and for the sake of which all other things are desirable (whether we are considering our own good or that of other people) is an existence exempt as far as possible from pain, and as rich as possible in enjoyment, both in point of quantity and quality; the test of quality and the rule for measuring it against quantity, being the preference felt by those who in their opportunities of experience, to which must be added their habits of self-consciousness and self-observation, are best furnished with the means of comparison. This being according to the utilitarian opinion the end of human action, is necessarily also the standard of morality."[16]

Another statement of such views is the following: "James Mackaye, in 'The Economy of Happiness,' states that a right act is an act of maximum utility, that act, among those at any moment possible, whose presumption of happiness is a maximum, and that 'a wrong act is any alternative of a right act.' The test therefore to be applied to an act is, does it produce happiness? If so it is a moral act."[17]

As a criterion of conduct these statements are still vague.

[15]Prof. Everett of Brown University in vol. 10, p. 479, *International Journal of Ethics*.

[16]P. 28 of Mill's Utilitarianism.

[17]Arthur Smith in *The Arena*, August, 1907, p. 160.

Whose conception of the good and the useful has nature pre-scribed as a measure of moral values? Is it right for a majority, deliberately and for its own pleasure, or good, or both, to do injustice and inflict pain on a helpless minority? Most people seem to think so, if we may accept the great popularity of the dogma: "The greatest good to the greatest number," without limiting this test to such conduct as necessarily in-volves social consequences as its direct result. The few, with a more refined sense of justice, as it seems to me, decline to give their assent to a doctrine which permits the greatest number to do any wrong, no matter how outrageous, if only in their own opinion the greatest number (to wit, them-selves) deems it even momentarily to be advantageous to them-selves, in its overweighing goodness.

Out of such speculations come conflicting ethical theories, according to whether the emphasis is put upon the individual good, the majority's good or the racial good. Others with a broader vision and a more refined sense of justice, as it seems to me, repudiate such notions of morality. "The highest morality demands, therefore, careful judgment. The factors to be considered are the complicated relations of men in the society of which the judge and the actor himself is a mem-ber; morality may thus be identified with justice in the highest sense of the word."[18]

"Every action is right which in itself, or in the maxim on which it proceeds is such that it can co-exist along with the freedom of the will of each and all in action, according to a universal law. If then my action or my condition generally can co-exist with the freedom of every other, according to a universal law, any one does me a wrong who hinders me in the performance of this action, or in the maintainance of this condition. For such a hindrance or obstruction cannot co-exist with freedom according to universal law."

The last quotation, from Emanuel Kant's Philosophy of Law, is but the rule of natural justice applied to the problem of personal liberty, and justifies all conduct which, according to Herbert Spencer's formula, is not an invasion of another's greatest liberty, is consistent with an equality of liberty.

Even if the seeming differences thus far exhibited can be reconciled, still others confront us. These, as it seems to me,

---

[18]Williams' Evolutional Ethics, 445.

result mostly from a partial view of the individual's relations to his fellowman and the rest of the universe, and from this defective view comes an undue emphasis upon some one aspect or some one phase of the ethical problem. Thus the Egoist finds the chief factor of moral obligation to be in the personal good of each actor for himself. From the evolutional view-point we have racial advantage emphasized most. Pres. G. Stanley Hall states it thus: "The basis of the new biological ethics of today and of the future is that everything is right that makes for the welfare of the yet unborn, and all is wrong that injures them, and to do so is the unpardonable sin—the only one that nature knows."

It may be a matter of interesting speculation to inquire if these two seemingly divergent views are really in conflict. The question then would be whether an individual can injure himself without injury to his progeny and whether future generations can possibly be injured except by first injuring some one of the present generation? To ask these questions already suggests the possibility that all these seemingly vary-ing standards can be harmonized by reference to some broad generalization of nature's moral law. Some such general statements have already been attempted and will now be quoted to emphasize further the inevitable and irreconcilable conflict between the morality of religion and the results of ethical science. Charles Lee says: "Vice represents an incomplete response to the guidance of the law of life. * * * * Like every other arbitrary standard, that of morality must be regarded as the interpretation of the law of life for the guidance of the individual man. * * * * Perfect freedom is only to be found in absolute obedience to nature's law. All human laws are but interpretations thereof, and according to the degree of their imperfections the individual response to the guidance of na-ture is fettered, and social sickness becomes more or less acute."[19]

But "the law of life" is still a vague phrase, and the law itself but partially understood. However, it points clearly the direction of our search for the ethical sanction. De Fleury tries to be more specific when he says:

"The new morality is hygienic, science raising itself to the dignity of a practical philosophy; it is therapeutics dealing

[19]Cosmic Ethics, pp. 143-152-203.

with the temporary weakness, or more serious paralysis of our will, the great regulator of the human machine; disorder in love, disorder in work, insensate anger or vain sadness; these are the sins of enfeebled will. If the hygiene which we desire succeeds in teaching men to live worthily, and to work well then it in truth is a sound morality, for except loving and working, what is there of serious import here below? (p. 356) * * * * I believe firmly that our vices develop themselves only in unhealthy soil; that the way to cure the mind is to treat the brain; that henceforth the moralist is inseparable from the doctor. (p. 361) * * * * * If we look at love from the point of physiology or of Naturalist philosophy, platonic love will surely appear to us the most harmful as it is the most immoral."[20]

But this again is perhaps a partial view. Many without being unhealthy, develop vices through mere ignorance, imitation or misinformation, and when they come, diseases, personal and social, are often a consequence and not a cause. This is more especially true in the realm of sexual ethics than anywhere else, because here moral sentimentalism and the theology of sex are constantly and successfully forcing their misinformation and anti-natural ideals upon a long suffering public, with the result that our insane asylums and sanitariums for the treatment of nervous diseases are full to overflowing. A wiser view will some day abolish the dogmatic sex-morality of religion, and substitute a truly scientific ethics in its stead, which will not only be prophylactic and therapeutic, from the individual viewpoint, but will also discover to perfection and also live up to nature's rule of justice which is always moral, as among all humans. Thus only will we attain our highest degree of perfection and our most elevated conception and realization of human joys.

To me it seems as though Herbert Spencer has given us the most rational view of the criteria of right conduct and indicates most clearly what is the object of ethical science. As to the first he says: "Conduciveness to happiness is the ultimate test of perfection in man's nature." Further on he says: "Before we can fully understand the ethical aspects of chastity, we must study its biological and sociological sanctions. *Conduciveness to welfare, individual or social or both, being the*

[20]De Fleury in Medicine and Mind, p. 300.

ultimate criterion of evolutionary ethics, the demand for chastity has to be sought in its effects under given conditions. * * *
We saw, too, that in some cases, especially in Thibet, polyandry appears more conducive to social welfare than any other relation of the sexes. It receives approval from travelers, and even a Moravian missionary defends it; the missionary holding that 'superabundant population, in an unfertile country, must be a great calamity, and produce "eternal warfare or eternal want." ' "[21]

Likewise a convention of Christian missionaries, for the moment subordinating the absolute moral creed of their religion to practical ends, once resolved that Mohammedan polygamy was not a barrier to acceptance of the convert to the orthodox fold.

But, I must return to Spencer. It seems to me that when we have achieved a truly scientific ethics, we will probably have unified all the scientists' seemingly conflicting criteria of right conduct. The work before us is outlined by him in these words: "The view for which I contend is, that Morality properly so-called—the science of right conduct—has for its object to determine *how* and *why* certain modes of conduct are detrimental, and certain other modes beneficial. These good and bad results cannot be accidental, but must be necessary consequences of the constitution of things; and I conceive it to be the business of Moral Science to deduce, from the laws of life and the conditions of existence, what kind of actions necessarily tend to produce happiness, and what kinds to produce unhappiness. Having done this, its deductions are to be recognized as laws of conduct; and are to be conformed to irrespective of a direct estimation of happiness or misery."[23]

As the stars do not create the laws which they obey, so men cannot create the moral laws, which compel obedience, or the acceptance of disaster. The law of individual life is rather a physical than an ethical law, because an enlightened self-interest will preclude self-infliction from becoming a social menace. The ethical problem begins only when others are directly affected without their consent, and the ethical law, which is only the law of life in the social organism, necessarily inheres in the nature of things, and it is the purpose

---

[21]Spencer's Principles of Ethics, v. 1, pp. 448-449. Italics are mine.—T. S.
[23]Principles of Ethics, vol. 1, p. 57.

of ethical science to discover, amid infinite complexities, what is the natural law of life in interdependent human existence. Just as fast as we acquire a clear comprehension of what that law is, either in part or in whole, we are by imperative self-interest irresistably impelled to live in accordance with it, and avoid the penalties of its violation. Like gravity, nature's moral law is unavoidable, and for its violation there is no forgiveness nor vicarious atonement, and knowledge of the law of its operation only facilitates such an adjustment as enables us to live in harmony with its condition of well-being—that is to avoid its pain and to insure its blessings.

It is believed that I have now demonstrated that "morality" is not a fixed and certain thing, about which all are agreed; but on the contrary that the criteria of the ethical right, even in their broadest outline, are tremendously in conflict. Of course this conflict acquires indefinitely greater variety when these varying standards are applied to concrete problems, in which event even the same verbal standards of judgment take on various hues, according to each individual's own peculiar experiences. It is also believed that I have demonstrated that there is an irreconcilable conflict between the morality of all religions and ethical science, which conflict arises out of an inevitable difference in their respective sources of authority, their different methods for the ascertainment of moral truths, and their difference in the end to be achieved by living the ethical life.

From this conflict between the numerous varieties of ethical standards, and the conflict between these and the religious conceptions of the right life, emerge some practical results which our legislators and judges should, but do not, bear in mind. Which of the foregoing varying standards of morals does the statute, or the judicial legislation, direct jurors to apply in determining whether or not a particular book is "obscene?" Where is the legislative authority for the selection if one is made?

But careless thinkers may be tempted to say that it makes little difference by what standard of ethics the judgment is determined, since we all reach pretty much the same conclusion as to what is the moral right in matters of sex. There are two answers to this specious argument. First: From the viewpoint of the judge it makes all the difference between a constitutional and unconstitutional statute, whether a man of ordinary intelligence is, or is not, able from a mere reading of the law to know in advance of a verdict *by what criteria of guilt* the verdict will be determined. The second answer is, that it is not a fact that we all reach the same conclusion as to what is the ethical right in relation to sex problems. The variety in statutes by which we regulate marriage, divorce and other phases of sexual activities, sufficiently evidences this.

This difference may be further illustrated by quotations from modern ethicians who have entertained opinions or made arguments bearing upon sex-ethics which are of a character such as have not yet received general approval.

REV. JOHN NORRIS.

"For if pleasure as such were against the good of the community, then every particular pleasure would be so, because every particular pleasure partakes of the common nature of pleasure, which would then be enough to render it evil. * * * Now concerning particular pleasure I propose these two general canons, which I think will hold in all instances whatsoever: First that that pleasure which has no trouble or pain annexed may, nay indeed cannot but be embraced; as on the contrary, the pain which has no pleasure annexed is to be avoided. If unusual pleasure were evil in itself, or as such, it would be so in all its instances. This is an undeniable consequence. But now that it is not so in all its instances, is plain from the divine institution of marriage and therefore it is not evil in itself. For it must not be thought (as some seem to fancy) that marriage makes that good which was in itself evil. For if once evil in itself it must eternally and universally be so, and consequently even in marriage itself, that as to sensual pleasure being the same with fornication or adultery. But sensual pleasure is not evil in marriage, therefore not in itself or as such. This is demonstration. * * * * We will state the question * * * and it shall be whether the pleasure of the sixth sense have any moral turpitude in it. Wherein I will venture to pronounce that it has not as such. But to be captivated to that pleasure, so as to make us less capable of that which is better, or to break the laws of what is just and decorous, this is the turpitude that is contracted therein. * * * If there be no moral turpitude in the simple conception of venerial pleasure, then all abstracted acts of it, such as voluntary pollution, lascivious embraces, etc., must be accounted lawful, which are yet condemned by all moral and divine writers. The reason for the consequence is, because there seems to be nothing in such abstract act besides the simple perception of the pleasure of the sixth sense. For, as for excess, captivation of spirit, too sensitive applications and the like, these are merely accidental, and equally incident to the same acts in all other circumstances."[24]

JOHN STUART MILL.

"Baron Wilhelm von Humboldt, in an excellent essay, [Sphere and Duties of Government] from which I have already quoted, states it as his conviction that engagements which involve personal relations or services should never be legally binding beyond a limited duration of time; and that the most important of these engagements, marriage, having the peculiarity that its objects are frustrated unless the feelings of both of the parties are in harmony with it, should require nothing more than the declared will of either party to dissolve. * * * * * Even if, as von Humboldt maintains, the circumstances of the marriage ought to make no difference in the legal freedom of the parties to release themselves from the engagement (and I also hold that they ought not to make much difference), they necessarily make a great difference in the moral freedom. A person is bound to take all three circumstances into account, before resolving on a step which may affect such important interests of others, [that is, the other spouse, or their children, no one else.] * * * Fornication, for example, must be tolerated."[25]

REPORT OF PROF. FELIX ADLER AND COMMITTEE OF FIFTEEN.

"The proposition is to exclude prostitution from the category of crime" [and treat it only as a sin.][26]

PROF. CH. LETOURNEAU.

"It is therefore probable that a future more or less distant will inaugurate the regime of monogamic unions, freely contracted, and, at need, freely dissolved by simple mutual consent, as is already the case with divorces in various European countries—at Geneva, in Belgium, in Roumania, etc., and with separation in Italy. In these divorces of the future, the com-

---

[24]The Theory and Regulation of Love, pp. 92-99-171-173-179.
[25]On Liberty, pp. 165-172, 174, Burt Edition.
[26]The Social Evil, p. 177.

294

munity will intervene only in order to safeguard that which is of vital interest to it—the fate and education of the children."[27]

HERBERT SPENCER.

"As monogamy is likely to be raised in character by a public sentiment requiring that the legal bond shall not be entered into unless it represents the natural bond; so perhaps it may be that the maintenance of the legal bond will come to be held improper if the natural bond ceases. * * * *

"Whereas at present the union by law is thought the more important and the union by affection the less important, there will come a time when union by affection will be held of primary moment, and the union by law as of secondary moment."[28]

WORDSWORTH DONISTHORPE, M. P.

"If permanent unions are the natural outcome of civilized instincts, they will come without the assistance of the sexual tinker. If they are not, then we are fighting against nature as the Titans warred on the gods, in vain. The system is artificial and rotten and must fall. For my part, I do not believe that even the approximation to monogamy observable to-day among civilized races could have been imposed upon them from without. Even the terrors of religion could not have prevailed against the impulses of love, any more than the terrors of the deep prevailed against the voices of the siren. Throughout all the ages Religion has conformed to the prevailing sexual customs. The gods of Olympus sided with the abductors of Briseis; the god of the Hebrews rewarded the virtue of Solomon with hundreds of wives and concubines; the god of the Koran offers eternal promiscuity to the faithful, and the god of the dark ages only followed the rule binding the gods generally, by enjoining monogamy on all who would be saved. No; the tendency comes from within. I believe in monogamy, not because it is good for the race, not because it is good for the husband, not because it is good for the children, but because an uncoerced monogamy, the result of a state of evolution not yet attained, will be best for each and all."[29]

C. STANISLAND WAKE.

"Some explanation is perhaps due why sexual morality

[27]Evolution of Marriage, p. 358.
[28]Principles of Sociology, v. 1, part 2, p. 765 Appleton's Edition.
[29]Law in a Free State, p. 211.

has not been more fully considered in the following pages. Its phenomena are frequently referred to when describing the character of particular peoples, but the subject embraces so wide a range that it was found impossible to do it justice in the present work. Moreover, as most of those phenomena are wanting in an element, injury to others, which is essential to the idea of immorality they are better fitted for independent inquiry."[30]

DR. HAVELOCK ELLIS.

"The State regulation of marriage has undoubtedly played a large and important part in the evolution of society. At the present time the advantages of this artificial control no longer appear so obvious (even when the evidence of law courts is put aside) ; they will vanish altogether when women have attained complete economic independence. * * *

"Sexual relationships, so long as they do not result in the production of children, are matters in which the community has, as a community, little or no concern, but as soon as a sexual relationship results in the pregnancy of the woman the community is at once interested. It is at this point clearly the duty of the state to register the relationship."[31]

EDWARD CARPENTER.

"Thus the family institution in its present form, and as far as that form may be said to be artificial, will doubtless pass away. * * * While to-day this sight [of offspring] reconciles husband and wife to the legal chains which perforce hold them together, in a free society, we may hope, it will more often be the sign and seal of a love which neither requires or allows any kind of mechanical bond."[32]

ELSIE CLEWS PARSONS, PH.D.

"We have, therefore, given late marriage and the passing of prostitution, two alternatives, the requiring of absolute chastity of both sexes until marriage or the toleration of freedom of sexual intercourse on the part of the unmarried of both sexes before marriage, i. e., before the birth of offspring. In this event condemnation of sex license would have a different emphasis from that at present. Sexual intercourse would not be of itself disparaged or condemned, it would be disapproved

[30]Evolution of Morality, v. 1, p. VI.
[31]Revised reprint from *Westminster Review*, Oct., 1888.
[32]Loves Coming of Age, pp. 147-148.

of only if indulged in at the expense of health or of emotional or intellectual activities in oneself or in others. As a matter of fact, truly monogamous relations seem to be those most conducive to emotional or intellectual development and to health, so that, quite apart from the question of prostitution, promiscuity is not desirable or even tolerable. It would, therefore, seem well from this point of view to encourage early *trial* marriage, the relation to be entered into with a view to permanency, but with the privilege of breaking it if proved unsuccessful, and in the *absence of offspring* without suffering any great degree of public condemnation."[33]

GEOFFREY MORTIMER.

"Strictly speaking, a marriage is felicitious when, through a fortunate chain of circumstances, there is complete mental and physical adaptation of two fervid lovers to each other's tastes, opinions, sympathies and passional desires. * * * * Thousands of persons gifted with insight and social prescience, and endowed with a zeal for the welfare of humanity, are convinced by study, observation, and mature reflection that the single lifelong union of the sexes is not adapted in the highest sense to the individual and collective needs and desires of our age, and that such associations will be even less fitted to survive in the society of the near future. * * * * Every marriage is a trial, an experiment which may fail or succeed. * * * * Marriage must be free. Lovers when they join hands must agree to live together so long as the natural tie of affection holds them with its silken strands. Any other pledge, civil or religious, mocks at morality, derides the promptings of a healthy conscience and scoffs at reason."[34]

PROF. WESTERMARCK.

"When both the husband and wife desire to separate, it seems to many enlightened minds that the State has no right to prevent them from dissolving the marriage contract, provided that the children are properly cared for; and that for the children also it is better to have the supervision of one parent only, than of two who cannot agree [p. 398] * * * It is obvious that the extreme horror of fornication which is expressed in the Christian doctrine is in the main a result of the same ascetic principle which declared celibacy superior

[33]The Family, p. 348.
[34]Chapters on Human Love, pp. 221-234-236.

to marriage, and tolerated marriage only because it could not be suppressed. [p. 439.] * * * When a man and a woman, tied to each other by a deep and genuine affection, decide to live together as husband and wife, though not joined in legal wedlock, the censure which public opinion passes upon their conduct seems to an unprejudiced mind justifiable, at most, only in so far as it may be considered to have been their duty to comply with the laws of their country and to submit to a rule of some social importance.

"Sexual intercourse between unmarried persons of opposite sex is thus regarded as wrong from different points of view under different conditions, social or psychical, and all of these conditions are not in any considerable degree combined at any special stage of civilization." [p. 440.][85]

DR. DE FLEUREY.

"If we look at love from the point of view of physiology or of natural philosophy, platonic love will surely appear to us the most harmful as it is the most immoral."[86]

As I am reading proof there comes to me a journal edited by John Trevor, the author of "My Quest for God" and Pastor of the Labor Church, Manchester, England. From his words I quote the following few paragraphs:

"I know a young man of unusual ability in his profession who has been giving his energies devotedly to his work, while his brain was being wasted by the results of the suppression of passion. The consequence is that he has had to be sent to a lunatic asylum. Even should he recover, his whole life is blighted. He has been robbed of his manhood, of his personality, of that love without which life is not life.

"The doctrine of the essential antagonism of the Spirit and the Flesh is a fiction of Traditional Religion which Natural Religion must destroy. It is only in harmonious blending of the two that the fullness of Manhood and Womanhood is realized. The passion of love suppressed like a disease has developed a mass of festering sores.

"One of the most amazing facts in the history of Humanity is this of Man's abject submission to unnatural restraints in the name of some Revelation from God. When incapable of submission, he has called his revolt a Sin—a

[85]The Origin and Development of the Moral Ideas, vol. 2, at pages noted.
[86]Medicine and Mind, p. 856, et seq.

still more groveling submission.. For many hundreds of years Man has tried to submit to an unnatural standard of virtue, not having the virtue of revolt.

"Natural Religion, to grow up naturally, demands a Natural Life. The right to live naturally Traditional Religion denies, and the State enforces the denial.

"When a plant you cherish is about to flower, you are more careful than ever that its conditions shall be such as Nature requires. When youth is about to flower, the conditions imposed are as unfavorable as can well be imagined.

"To return to the symbol of the acorn—as the fall of the acorn from the oak is the birth of a soul into the world. Puberty is the swelling of the acorn under the genial influences of Spring. Then the soul of youth has need of Knowledge and Culture and Freedom for Self-expression. These the world refuses. This is the Tragedy of Youth. The world sears with a hot iron the acorn that begins to swell. The man never recovers wholly from the injury done to the youth. I have no doubt the same is true of the woman also.

"To make man submit to this irremediable injury, and to provide him with palliatives of its consequences, is one of the principal functions of the churches. Much of the social work of the churches to-day is inspired by the necessity of keeping young people from thinking of sexual matters. It is called keeping them off the streets.

"The churches are the wreckers of youth, and live largely on the results of their wreckage. The Right of Youth to Self-expression through love is the great principle over which the coming fight must be waged between Tradition and Life.

"The Redemption of Love from the curse of Tradition in the name of Natural Religion is the work to which I must devote the rest of my life."[37]

PREDESTINATION AND IMMORALITY.

This then brings me back to the starting point of the conflict between religious morals and ethical science which, in one of his essays, Thoreau sums up in these words: "To regret religion is the first step towards moral excellence." Macaulay in his essay on "Civil disabilities of the Jews," uses this language: "The doctrine of predestination, in the opinion of many people, *tends* to make those who hold it utterly immoral. And certainly it would seem that a man who believes

[37] *The One Life.* No. 1, pp. 19-20.

his eternal destiny to be already irrevocably fixed *is likely to indulge in passions without restraint* and to neglect his religious duties."—Italics are mine, T. S.

In his youth the illustrious Milton was inoculated with the doctrine of predestination, and it may be possible that it was this which first determined his conclusions concerning divorce and polygamy, as to which Macaulay remarks that he does not think "any reader acquainted with the history of his life ought to be much startled in the matter." All this suggests again the very practical question whether the doctrine of predestination, and Milton's views about divorce and polygamy and the numerous opinions of secular scholars herein quoted, are criminally obscene because a court and jury believe the "tendency" of these doctrines "is to deprave and corrupt the morals of those whose minds are open to such influence and into whose hands a publication of this sort may fall."[38]

Judges, with Comstockian or ascetic minds or some peculiar religious bent, may answer "yes" and can point to a considerable quantity of loose judicial utterance to support them. An eminent English law-writer has answered in the negative. He says: "I have found no authority for the proposition that the publication of a work, immoral in the wider sense of the word, is an offense. A man might with perfect decency of expression, and in complete good faith, maintain doctrines as to marriage, the relation of the sexes, the obligation of truthfulness, the nature and limit of the right of property, which would be regarded as immoral by most people, and yet (I think) commit no crime. Obscenity and immorality in this wide sense are entirely distinct from each other. *The language used in some of the cases might throw doubt on this,* but I do not think that any instance can be given of the punishment of a decent and *bona fide* expression of opinions commonly regarded as immoral."[39] Italics are mine, T. S.

Who is right? Sir James Stephens or the loose language used in some cases? Even if we follow Stephens, what are the criteria of "decent expression of opinion?" Where does the legislative enactment determine the question? How can

---

[38]U. S. *vs.* Debout, 28 Fed. R. 523.

[39]Sir James Stephen's "Digest of the Criminal Law," page 97. If one were to consider critically the matter of finding the dividing line between "immorality in the broader sense" and other kinds of immorality, he might conclude with Dr. A. W. Herzog that "Morals are imaginary." See *Harper's Weekly* June 12—1909. For other unorthodox views of sexual morality, see " Blasting the Rock of Ages," by Harold Bolce, in *The Cosmopolitan Magazine* for May, 1909.

a man from reading the statute or even the judicial legislation under it inform himself by which standard of "decent expression," or of "morals," his production will be judged "obscene?" It must now be self-evident that every conviction under "obscenity" statutes is according to an *ex post facto* standard of judgment, dictated by caprice, not by any legislatively created criteria of guilt.

CONCERNING " MORAL POISON."

Suppose a person to be indicted for selling a deadly poison in violation of law. It is proven or admitted that the defendant sold some of the alleged poison to many persons, who ate heartily thereof. No witness is introduced to prove that a chemical analysis has been made and that such proves the substance in question to be a deadly poison. No one testifies that any of those who have eaten of it were injured thereby.

Suppose then that in spite of these facts the court should submit to the jury the question of guilt, and instruct them that they may look at the alleged poison, and smell of it, and that if they do not like its appearance, or smell, they are authorized to believe it to be poisonous, and must find the defendant "guilty." It requires no argument for anyone to see the outrageousness and utter lawlessness of such a proceeding.

In all cases of "obscenity" juries are instructed to determine guilt according to their conviction as to the existence of "moral poison" which, in all its varied forms of statement, is a mere figure of speech, or a doubtful speculation without definite tests, and so guilt is determined by just such uncertain, whimsical "standards" as we have probably agreed, just hereinbefore, to be outrageous. Why then don't judges see the outrageousness of it and discharge all such defendants? In the case of actual poison we all know of the existence of conclusive and certain tests and the very fact of that knowledge makes us see the necessity for insisting upon their application in every such trial. In the case of "obscenity" we know of no such certain standard for determining the existence of "moral poison" and so have not that knowledge to remind us of the necessity for having and applying such certain standards of judgment, and popular "ethical" sentimentalizing and the fear of the judgment of "moral" snobs precludes the efficacy of those other reminders which, *at least to lawyers,* should suggest the indispensable necessity of mathematically-certain criteria of guilt.

CHAPTER XVI.

VARIETIES OF OFFICIAL MODESTY.[73]

Here we will concern ourselves only with the further demonstration of the uncertainty of these laws by evidences taken from our variety of judicial and official manifestations of modesty. Later we will make some unofficial applications of the judicial tests of obscenity to demonstrate their utter absurdity.

The early prosecutions for obscenity of literature and art occurred when the influence of puritanism was stronger than at present, and a court said: "I am for paying some respect to the chastity of our records."[74]

And so the rule came to be that indictments need not reproduce the alleged obscenity, and that rule is still in force. If "records" can be literally "chaste," then they can also be deprived of that chastity by rape. If, on the other hand, chastity is not a real quality of records, then we have the spectacle of a judicial tribunal solemnly and deliberately creating rules of pleading upon the foundation of a mere figure of speech, misconceived as an analogy. The English courts have taken the latter view, and upon having their attention called to the American precedents, they pronounced our judicial reason for them too "fanciful and imaginary."[75]

The courts of olden times seem to have given but a limited sanction to judicial prudery or to the official moral snobbery over "chastity of records." I infer this from the following extract taken from "An Explanation Concerning Obscenities," written by the learned Pierre Bayle in the seventeenth century. He says:

"When a nation [are] agreed in calling some words immodest . . . all the members of the society are obliged to respect it. The courts of justice afford us a remarkable instance of it, for lawyers are not allowed to repeat such words when

<hr>

[73]Republished from *The Am. Journal of Eugenics*, Dec., 1907, and *The Albany Law Journal*, Aug., 1908.

[74]*Com. vs. Sharpless, 2 Serg. N Rawle*, 91-113 (Penn. 1815). *Com. vs. Tarbox*, 1 *Cush. (Mass.)* 66. *Com. vs. Holmes*, 17 *Mass.* 336.

[75]*Bradlaugh vs. Queen*, 3 *Q. B.* 607-620. See also *Peop. vs. Daniley*, 68 *Hun*, 579, and, *State vs. Hanson* 23 *Tex.* 234.

they plead for punishment of those who have used them in reviling their neighbors. They will have public modesty respected in the hearing of a cause; but when they judge by report, they not only permit the reporter to mention the very words of the offender, though never so obscene, but also command him to do it. This I have from a counselor in the Parliament of Paris, who told me within these few years, that, having used a circumlocution the first time he reported such a cause, the president gave him to understand that there was no occasion to have a regard to chaste ears, but to judge of the nature of the offence, and that therefore he was obliged to speak the very word it consisted in. I fancy the Inquisition uses the same method."[76]

We have not to go far back in our own juridical history to find a very different judicial conception of modesty from that which is now dominant, and one wherein "nakedness was so little feared that adulterous women were led naked through the streets."[77]

In England, for several centuries, before and during the eighteenth century, and probably later, in order to forestall spurious heirship, the ecclesiastical courts compelled widows, claiming to be pregnant by their deceased husbands, to submit to a physical examination by the sheriff, in the presence of twelve knights and as many women. Later, it became the practise also judicially to prescribe the place of her abode during pregnancy, and to require that parturition take place in the presence of five women appointed by the next of kin. Other women, to a fixed limit, might be present; but all must first submit to a physical examination as to their own pregnancy, before being admitted to the chamber of parturition.[78]

The above-described mode of judicially determining material sexual facts, and the "judicial congress," which will be presently discussed, are both the outgrowth of a very ancient custom of judicially and ecclesiastically determining the virginity of women by physical examination. Even in the last decade of the nineteenth century a Morman chief of police in Salt Lake City, Utah, (but without statutory authority) compelled some young girls, arrested on a suspicion of being "streetwalkers"—which, however, proved unfounded—to submit,

---

[76]V. 5, *Historical and Critical Dictionary*, 848. Edit. of 1787.

[77]Remy de Gourmont, *Le Livre des Masques*, p. 184, requoted from Ellis, *Studies in Psychology of Sex: Modesty*, p. 21.

[78]Nelson's *Rights of the Clergy*, pp. 78-80. (A. D. 1709.)

at the police station, to an examination as to their virginity. A decade later a "gentile" judge of the Juvenile Court in the same city ordered a like examination under like circumstances, and again without finding any evidence of lost virginity. If it were not for our legislatively enforced ignorance of sexual matters it would have been known that examinations of the hymen furnish no evidence as to chastity."[79]

Out of such practises among the early Christians evolved the "judicial congress," by which a wife might demand of a husband charged with impotency in an action for marriage dissolution, or the husband might offer to give ocular demonstration of his capacity for copulation, by its consummation in the very presence of the court.

"Pope Gregory the Great, who was raised to the pontificate in 590, appears to have been the first to confer upon bishops the right of deciding this description of questions. . . The great antiquity of this custom is proved by the seventeenth article of the Capitulars of Pepin, in the year 752, which bears a direct allusion to it; inasmuch as that article established as a principle that the impotency of a husband should be considered as a lawful cause for divorce, and that the proof of such impotency should be given, and the fact verified, at the foot of the cross. . . That the 'Congress' originated with the church, who considered it as an efficacious means for deciding questions of impotency, is still further proved by the President Boutrier and by other writers, who assert that the ecclesiastical judges of other times were alone empowered (to the exclusion of all secular ones) to take cognizance of cases of impotency. It is well attested that during the sixteenth and seventeenth centuries all the courts of law in France held the opinion that a marriage be annulled on the demand of a wife who claimed the Congress."[80]

The erudite Pierre Bayle has preserved for us some of the arguments by which was justified this practise of judicial decrees ordering a sexual intercourse in the presence of the court, as a means of determining an issue of potency. He quotes as follows:

"The congress is the usual and most certain proof that can be used in a case of impotency; witness Lucian in his *Eunuchus. 'Nec inimicum videri debet probationis genus*

---

[79]Maj. R. W. Shufeldt, M.D., in *Pacific Medical Journal* for January, 1906.
[80]Davenport, *On the Powers of Reproduction*, p. 52.

quod solum est,' says Quintilian in his seventh declamation; at least the bishops' courts in France have admitted it, and the court has authorized it by several decrees, particularly that of the 20th of January, 1597, made against one who, being accused of wanting testicles, would not submit to it. . . .

"Certainly the best precaution that can be used is to come to an actual trial; especially when we are induced to it by a desire of peace, which will better excuse a lawful copulation, though done openly, than all clandestine doings can justify an unlawful divorce. Otherwise it would be an absurd thing to admit, for the proof of adultery, the evidence of one who should say that he has seen, and likewise that, in order to avoid the supposition of a child, the civil law should permit the inspection of a woman; and yet that, to justify the validity of a marriage (which is a thing much more important), one should be unwilling to see, *impactum Thyrsum horto in cupidinis.* . . .

"It is to no purpose to say that his wife, pretending to modesty when it is too late, and upon an occasion when it is not necessary, objects that she would be ashamed to have her secret parts inspected, and to go to the congress; for she must be forced to it, since she has brought things to such a pass.

"I add, that in such cases the inspection is usual, so that it cannot be said that there is any injustice in requiring that which is practiced by the common law: for we learn from St. Cyprian in his epistles, and from St. Augustine and St. Ambrose, that in cases relating to the defloration of virgins inspection has always been practiced; nay, we are told by Clemens Alexandrinus (*7 Strom.*), and by Suidas *in verbo* Jesus, that the Virgin Mary submitted to it, the sanhedrim of the high priests having ordered that she should be inspected, to discover whether she remained a virgin, and whether our Lord, whom they had a mind to adopt into their own order, should be matriculated in their registers as the son of Joseph, or as the son of the living God and of a virgin-mother. Chaffanæus recites the story at length in the fourth part of his *Catalogus gloriæ mundi, distinct.* 6."[81]

The date of origin of this "judicial commerce" appears to be in doubt. In the district of the Parliament of Paris it was abolished February, 1677, and the judicial custom then

---

[81]4, Bayle's *Historical and Critical Dictionary*, 805. Edition 1787.

reverted to the physical examination of the sexual parts; but elsewhere the trial by judicial commerce continued to be the accredited method of determining impotence. From the standpoint of our present modesty, the physical examination, not in the presence of the court, did not much improve the situation, for we are informed that "the men have, in some trials, inspected the women, and the women have been admitted to inspect the men." At present, the former would not be deemed so intolerable if the men were physicians, but to have women physicians thus examine men would seen to us much more intolerable. This distinction, let it be remembered, has no logical foundation, but rests only in our difference of educated emotions as associated with the differences of sex.[82]

CONFLICT AS TO THE NUDE IN ART.

Very many people to this day entertain the same view about the immorality of all nudity in art as that which was expressed by St. Chrysostom in these words: "A naked image and statue is the devil's chair."[83]

The contrary view is thus expressed: "Nakedness is always chaster in its effects than partial clothing. A study of pictures or statuary will alone serve to demonstrate this. As a well-known artist, Du Maurier, has remarked (in *Trilby*), it is 'a fact well known to all painters and sculptors who have used the nude model (except a few shady pretenders, whose purity, not being of the right sort, has gone rank from too much watching) that nothing is so chaste as nudity. Venus herself, as she drops her garments and steps on the model-throne, leaves behind her on the floor every weapon in her armory by which she can pierce to the grosser passions of men.' Burton, in the *Anatomy of Melancholy* (Part III, Sec. ii, subsec. iii), deals at length with the 'allurements of love,' and concludes that the 'greatest provocations of lust are from our apparel.' "[84]

The Rev. Frederick George Lee, in an expostulation with the Royal Academy of Art, at considerable length endorses the position of St. Chrysostom, above quoted; but the academy continues to hold to the contrary view. Dr. Lee in part says:

---

[82]4, Bayle's *Historical and Critical Dictionary* 803 to 807. Edition of 1737. Davenport, *On the Powers of Reproduction*, pp. 47 to 60.

[83]*A Just and Reasonable Reprehension against Naked Breasts*, 28.

[84]Ellis, *Psychology of Sex: Modesty*, 39, and *Erotic Symbolism*, p. 15. See also *Fables of the Female Sex*, p. 62. (1766.)

"Permit me, in the remarks being made, to start with the axiom that nothing should be represented by the artist's brush for exhibition in public which may not be rightly and properly looked upon by the people in general (p. 7). . . . They [pictures of the nude] offend against Christian morals, directly pervert good taste, and distinctly maim modesty (p. 10)."

Further on he tells us of a London prostitute who thought to make some honest shillings by becoming a nude model to the life-class of an art school. After much hesitancy, she disrobed, and from behind a temporary curtain stepped upon the model's stage.

"On doing so, and finding herself suddenly under the glare of gaslight, naked, before forty or fifty students, the poor frightened creature threw up her arms, and with a shriek fell fainting on the floor. On recovering, she, uttering fearful language, dashed the money on the ground, huddled on her garmets, and rushed from the place in a storm of passion."[85]

Here, then, we have a clear portrayal of two distinct and conflicting conceptions of modesty: St Chrysostom, the Rev. Dr. Lee, and the unfortunate woman representing the one, and Du Maurier, the professional model, and the sexual psychologist representing the other.

Our obscenity statutes give us no information as to whether the legislature intended to endorse the prostitute's conception of modesty, or that of the clean-minded, unblushing, and unashamed professional models who daily exhibit themselves in nudity before the life-classes of every art school in the civilized world. While the statute gives us no clew as to which conception of modesty is adopted, the judicial legislation upon the subject seems to favor the latter.[86]

RABELAIS AND BOCCACCIO.

In England a publisher, to escape criminal punishment, has consented to destroy his stock of Rabelais and Boccaccio.[87] In Indiana a village bookseller was induced to plead guilty and pay a fine of $5 for sending through the mail an obscene book, to wit, *Decameron* of Boccaccio. On the strength of this a postoffice inspector affirms "this book has been declared

[85]Lee, *Immodesty in Art,* 13.
[86]*People vs. Mueller,* 96 *N. Y.* 408, 48 *Am. Rep.* 635. *U. S. vs. Smith,* 45 *Fed. Rep.* 477.
[87]See Buchanan's *On Descending Into Hell,* p. 89.

non-mailable."[88] The United States District court of Utah also had before it an unexpurgated edition of Boccaccio on an indictment of its obscenity. Accompanying the book were some loose laid-in pictures, which the court instructed the jury were "obscene, lewd, and lascivious under the statute, and constituted the very kind of literature that the law was aimed against." No instruction was given to the jury concerning the unexpurgated edition of *Decameron,* nor was the question of its obscenity even submitted to the jury. The judge evidently did not consider it obscene.[89]

In the state courts of New York, a brief to the contrary having been submitted by Mr. Comstock, it was decided that Rabelais and Boccaccio were not obscene.[90]

After the foregoing decision, the United States district Court of the Western District of the Southern District of Ohio fined one Stiefel $5 for sending *Decameron* by express from Cincinnati to Crawfordsville, Ind.[91]

Which of these conflicting views is correct, and where does the statute fix the standard for deciding whether Boccaccio is "obscene" or not?

BRIEFER MISCELLANY.

In a former chapter, I called attention to the case of Mrs. Carrie Nation, wherein a U. S. Commissioner had discharged her, deciding that her magazine was not "obscene", and the postal authorities continued to exclude it from the mail because it was "obscene."

At this writing the case of the Art Students League Catalogue is yet fresh in our memory. The Post Master General had declared it mailable. Postal Inspector Comstock, disagreeing, made arrests under the N. Y. statute against "obscenity." A great protest went up over the country. The accused were induced to plead guilty and received a suspended sentence.

Hereinbefore I wrote of Dr. Parke's arrest, and that he had been bound over to await the action of the grand jury, and that the Federal grand jury had determined that his book "Human Sexuality" was not "obscene." He was indicted and is awaiting trial. What kind of whim will determine his guilt?

[88]See Frankenstein's *A Victim of Comstockism,* pp. 16-17.
[89]See Record in *U. S. vs. Shepard,* in U. S. Circuit Court of Appeals, 154, 155.
[90]*Matter of Worthington Co., 30 N. Y. Sup.* 361, *62d St. Rep.* 115, *24 L. R. A.* 110.

In one of the larger cities of Massachusetts an influential business man was arrested for dispensing "obscene" literature and pleaded guilty. His prominence and popularity was such that all newspapers considerately suppressed mention of the fact, and I am making only a vague mention of it so as not to do him any unnecessary injury. The same book which got him into trouble has had a New York market for over a quarter of a century, and one of the chief beneficiaries of its sale has been a frequent contributor to the N. Y. Society for the Suppression of Vice. Mr. Comstock never thought the book "obscene," and like Mr. Colgate (elsewhere referred to), the N. Y. vendors escape prosecution.

These contradictions between postal officials, grand juries, and trial juries and between federal and state authorities under statutes of identical wording, could be multiplied greatly. While deeming that undesirable, I cannot refrain from calling attention to the case of People vs Eastman, (188 N. Y. 478) when we find a divided court, each side dogmatizing against the other and each ignoring the statute, leaving the non-legal motive for the dogmas quite rarely exposed.

IS THE BIBLE CRIMINALLY "OBSCENE"?

Under the laws against "obscene" literature, one of the first American prosecutions of note was that of the distinguished eccentric, George Francis Train, in 1872. He was arrested for circulating obscenity, which, it turned out, consisted of quotations from the Bible. Train and his attorneys sought to have him released upon the ground that the matter was not "obscene," and demanded a decision on that issue. The prosecutor, in his perplexity, and in spite of the protest of the defendant, insisted that Train was insane. If the matter was not "obscene," his mental condition was immaterial, because there was no crime. The court refused to discharge the prisoner as one not having circulated obscenity, but directed the jury, against their own judgment, to find him not guilty, on the ground of insanity; thus by necessary implication deciding the Bible to be criminally obscene. Upon a hearing on a writ of habeas corpus, Train was adjudged sane and discharged. Thus an expressed decision on the obscenity of the Bible was evaded, though the unavoidable inference was for its criminality.[92]

[92]For partial statement see *Medico-Legal Journal*, December,1906, p. 490; also Train's published autobiography, *My Life in Many States*, p. 328.

In his autobiography, Train informs us that a Cleveland paper was seized and destroyed for republishing the same Bible quotations which had caused his own arrest. Here, then, was a direct adjudication that parts of the Bible are criminally indecent, and therefore unmailable.[93]

In 1895 John B. Wise, of Clay Center, Kansas, was arrested for sending "obscene" matter through the mail, which consisted wholly of a quotation from the Bible. In the United States court, after a contest, he was found guilty and fined. Just keep in mind a moment these court precedents where portions of the Bible have been judicially condemned as criminally "obscene," while I connect it with another rule of law. The courts have often decided that a book to be obscene need not be obscene throughout the whole of it, but if the book is obscene in any part it is an obscene book within the meaning of the statute.[94]

You see at once that under the present laws, and relying wholly on precedents already established, juries of irreligious men could wholly suppress the circulation of the Bible, and in some states the laws would authorize its seizure and destruction. We also have the decision of a federal court seemingly of the opinion that the Bible is "obscene," but that, notwithstanding this fact, a successful prosecution thereon is ridiculously impossible. The decision reads thus:

"As a result [according to the contention of the defendant's counsel] not only medical works, but the writings of such authors as Swift, Pope, Fielding, Shakespeare, and many others, even the *Bible* itself, would be denied the privileges of the United States mails. *Undoubtedly there are parts* of the writings of said authors, and others equally noted, which *are open to the charge of obscenity and lewdness,* but any one objecting to such works being carried through the mails would be laughed at for his prudery."[95] Italics are mine. T. S.

But if "undoubtedly there are parts" of the Bible "which are open to the charge of obscenity and lewdness," as the judge seems to admit, and as John Wise and another found out to their sorrow, what consolation is it to the convicted man that his persecutors are laughed at for their prudery,

[93](Here, I think, Train must be referring to the conviction of John A. Lant, publisher of the Toledo *Sun.*)
[94]*U. S. vs. Bennett, Blatchford,* 388, Fed. Case, 14571.
[95]*U. S. vs. Harman,* 38 *Fed. Rep.* 828.

while he pays a fine, or goes to prison for conduct which he could not know to be a crime until after conviction?

On the contrary side we have the opinion of an assistant attorney-general that the Bible is not "obscene" in any of its parts, but he carefully points out that the law is so uncertain that courts might take a different view. Under date of Dec. 4, 1891, James N. Tyner in his official capacity as assistant attorney-general of the United States, wrote to E. Q. Morton, Esq., of Daphne, Ala., as follows:

"The law is made up of two clauses: One concerns the mailability of obscene, lewd, lascivious, or indecent publications, and this is determinable by the postmaster-general. The other branch of the law provides punishment for violating its provisions, and this is enforceable by the courts. I cannot therefore properly pass upon the "liability" in any case, even if it were submitted in proper form and detail, for that would be an attempted usurpation of the power of the judicial branch of the government; I can, however, state to you as I now do, that I do not regard the *Holy Bible as a whole, or any part of it published separately,* as being unmailable within the meaning of the laws." Italics are mine. T. S.

Voltaire informs us, on the authority of St. Jerome, that the synagogue did not permit the reading of Ezekiel till after the thirteenth year of age; but that was for fear their youth should make a bad use of the too lively description in the sixteenth and twenty-third chapters, of the whoredoms of Aholah and Aholibah."[95a]

Now we demand to know whether the Bible is "obscene" in any of its parts, and where is the statutory test which determines the quesion?

THE TAYLOR AND LAWTON CASES.

In Minnesota, Miss Rebecca Taylor, having a zeal for reform, encountered the interests of C. B. Gilbert, superintendent of the St. Paul Schools. As a part of her work of purifying the schools she thought it necessary to publish in a paper edited by her (*Truth,* May 8th, 1897) parts of certain affidavits which were part of a judicial record, reflecting upon Mr. Gilbert. This was at a time when he was negotiating for a position as superintendent of the Newark, N. J. public schools, the intention being to circulate these papers in Newark. Gilbert's friends, hearing of the enterprise, persuaded the

[95a]Treatise on Toleration, p. 170, Edition of London, 1764.

postal authorities of St. Paul to refuse to transmit the paper because of the "obscenity" of these affidavits. Miss Taylor had the matter presented to the authorities at Washington. The Assistant Attorney General for the Post-Office Department rendered a lengthy written opinion to the effect that the matter was not "obscene" and the paper therefore mailable. The Assistant Post Master General accordingly instructed the St. Paul post-master to transmit the paper. Thereafter A. W. Lawton, editor of *The White Bear Breeze,* republished from *Truth* the larger part of the same affidavits.

Notwithstanding the opinion of the Washington postal authorities, the United States Attorney at St. Paul secured the indictment of both editors for sending these "obscene" affidavits through the mail. They had a separate trial. In neither case was there any question about the publication or mailing, and the only question for the jury was, "Is this matter obscene?" The Taylor jury answered "no" and Miss Taylor was acquitted. The Lawton jury answered "yes" and Lawton was found guilty and punished.

Again it is self-evident that these contradictory verdicts were not derived from applying any statutory criteria of guilt, but from the total absence of such criteria, and a mere difference of whim on the part of the two juries. The opinion of the Attorney General's office was offered in evidence, and excluded as immaterial. As between these juries and the U. S. Attorney General, who was right? Where and how does the statute decide? How can any man know even now if it is a crime to send this matter through the mail? If the Federal Statutes, *as interpreted and applied by the Attorney General of the United States,* do not safeguard against prosecution, *even in the Federal Courts,* then how can we have such a thing as "law" or "due process of law"? How can this law be "the sanctuary of the innocent"?

"CUPID'S YOKES."

Another book, the history of which strikingly illustrates the outrageous uncertainty of the laws against "obscene literature," is one entitled *Cupid's Yokes; or, The Binding Forces of Conjugal Love. An Essay to Consider Some Moral and Physiological Phases of Love and Marriage, Wherein is Asserted the Natural Right and Necessity of Sexual Self-Government,* by E. H. Heywood. The author was a rather

312

conspicuous co-laborer of such abolitionists as Parker and Garrison. He was also the author of considerable controversial literature upon other subjects. He was convicted June 25, 1878, for sending his pamphlet, *Cupid's Yokes,* through the mails, and sentenced to two years at hard labor. Attorney-General Devens did not consider it "obscene." He wrote, under date of Jan. 13, 1879:

"I do not confound it with those obscene publications, the effect and object of which is to excite the imagination and inflame the passions."[96]

President Hayes in December, 1878, pardoned Mr. Heywood, —no doubt because to him the pamphlet did not seem obscene.

Before this, D. M. Bennett had been arrested, under the New York state statute, for selling *Cupid's Yokes,* and the prosecution had been dropped. Just before the pardon of Heywood, Bennett was again arrested, this time for sending *Cupid's Yokes* through the mails. He was convicted,[97] and President Hayes again signed a pardon—which, however, was not issued, because of some representations that Bennett had also been guilty of adultery.[98]

In April, 1878, Mrs. Abbie Dyke Lee was tried under the Massachusetts state statute against selling "obscene" literature, which consisted of *Cupid's Yokes.* The Jury disagreed, the case was thereupon dismissed, and the book continued, without molestation, to circulate in Massachusetts. In 1882, Heywood was again arrested for sending *Cupid's Yokes* through the mails. Judge Nelson, after hearing the pamphlet read, said: "The court is robust enough to stand anything in that book," and refused to admit the government's plea that it was too "obscene" to spread upon the records, later instructing the jury to acquit on the first two counts of the indictment, those relating to *Cupid's Yokes* and the *Word Extra.*

Here, then, we have two convictions, one jury disagreement and consequent dismissal, one instruction to acquit because the book was not "obscene," and one pardon upon the same ground, and one abandonment of prosecution. There was never any dispute about the contents or meaning of the book. The uncertainty is therefore wholly in the law. After five arrests—resulting in one abandonment of prosecution, two

[96]See *Liberty and Purity,* p. 62.
[97]See *U. S. vs. Bennett,* Fed. Case No. 14571.
[98]See *Liberty and Purity,* p. 63.

discharges as not guilty, two convictions—the opinions of the attorney general of the United States and of the United States circuit court, and the judicial "constructions" of the statutes against "obscene" literature as applied to this particular book, no man on earth can tell, even now, whether it is a crime to send *Cupid's Yokes* through the mail. If any one claims to know whether the law condemns this book, I ask him to point to a statutory test which is decisive.

Even if in every case *Cupid's Yokes* had been declared not to be "obscene," still this would be no protection to the next vendor of the book, because the next jury might reach a different conclusion as to what the law prohibited. Indeed, the courts might, as courts have done, instruct the jury to disregard a precedent of acquittal by another court deciding that the same matter was not "obscene." This I understand to be the effect of all tests of obscenity, and also of the following charge from Judge Butler, Eastern District of Pennsylvania, as unofficially published by Mr. Comstock from the official stenographer's report. The judge charged: "It is wholly unimportant what may have occurred elsewhere in the consideration of this question, if it ever has been considered; you have nothing to do with it at this time."[100]

Prof. Andrew D. White tells us that: "At a time when eminent prelates of the Older Church were eulogizing debauched princes like Louis XV and using the unspeakably obscene casuistry of the Jesuit Sanchez in the education of the priesthood as to relations of men and women, the modesty of the church authorities was so shocked by Linnaeus' proof of a sexual system in plants, that for many years his writings were prohibited in the Papal States and in various parts of Europe where clerical authority was strong enough to resist the new scientific current."[101]

Now, one may with impunity discuss the sexuality of plants, but a publication of the writing of Sanchez and others like him has landed good men in jail, though it was done for the best of motives.[102]

The foregoing record illustrates and demonstrates the baneful uncertainty and conflicting results coming from an exercise of arbitrary judicial power in determining innocence under a penal statute which fails to furnish criteria of guilt.

[100]*U. S. vs. Sherman*: See *Morals, Not Art or Literature*, p. 33.
[101]*Hist. of the Warfare of Science and Theology*, v. 1, p. 60.
[102]Queen vs. Hicklin L. R. 3 Q. B. 369,—U. S. vs. Price, 165 U. S. 311.

Tests of obscenity were never deduced from the statutes, but read into them. The decisions express only *ex post facto* legislative judgments as to what was believed ought to be the result as applied to the facts of each given case. The uncertain statutes furnish the pretext, and the judicial legislation creating equally uncertain "tests" of obscenity furnishes the unconstitutional means by which the emotionally demanded result is attained and "justified." These miscalled "tests" are the mere empty verbalisms by which judges attempt to objectivize their emotional pre-disposition, and they are considered cogent only because responding to the prior feeling-conviction which called them into being. The "tests of obscenity" are seldom the real reason for the decision, but are a misleading consequence of it. Our emotions, and the public demand that something be done, produce that unconscious shamming, to consumate which meretricious and factious "tests of obscenity" are judicially and unconstitutionally created and interpolated into the statute.

A PSYCHOLOGIC STUDY OF MODESTY. [108]

What then is the nature of modesty which is now seen to manifest itself in such illimitable and ever changing variety? What is the relation of that essential nature of modesty to the practical problem of determining the existence of "obscenity" in literature and art by the test of shocking modesty? What is the moral value of a shock to modesty, as a means of determining the existence of "obscenity"? These matters will now be discussed. After this will come a demonstration of the uncertainty of the "moral" test of obscenity, and this in turn will be followed by a discussion of the legal consequences which must flow from this wholly indeterminable nature of the "obscene" and the consequent total absence, either in the statute or the unconstitutional judicial legislation under it, of anything like uniform criteria of guilt.

The Rev. Dr. Stoddard has told us that "All visible signs are common to converted and unconverted men, and a relation of experience among the rest." To this the Rev. Jonathan Edwards adds: "No external manifestations and outward appearances whatsoever that are visible to the world are infallible evidence of grace."

[108]Republished from *The Medical Council*, Jan., 1909.

What is thus true of religion is equally true of modesty. No external manifestation or outward behavior, nor the habitual presence of clothing or its absence, nor the verbal relation of experience, nor crimson blushes are unmistakable criteria of a commendable (that is, healthy minded) modesty, and all are consistent with the highest degree of nasty mindedness. The true modesty of healthy mindedness is but a mental attitude, which in the presence of healthy nature always maintains an imperturbable poise, akin to the inward grace of the religionist, and which can not be infallibly inferred from appearances or conduct. Like health in any other particular, it eludes exact definition, because it fades so gradually into its opposite of disease that none can tell precisely where one ends and the other begins.

We can not assume that all have the desirable healthy modesty who claim it or who can blush. We may, however, analyze the symptoms and trace them to their source, and so we can, at least in an abstract way, determine the criteria of the modesty of a healthy-minded, physically perfect man.

The first form of spurious modesty I shall designate as the modesty of unconscious and uncoerced sympathetic imitation. This, perhaps, is oftenest found in the (simulated) modesty of children, and not infrequently in adults. If you should ask them why they denounce certain acts as immodest they could give no reply except that "they say" it is so. In this form there is no emotional aversion nor any fear of the judgment of others. It is the simplest form of imitation, unconsciously enacted and because not so fixedly habitual as to be involved with the emotional life, therefore it does not yet induce objective moral valuations and is not really esteemed a virtue. Here there may be a most perfect healthiness of mind, which, however, for the want of a definite appreciation of the factors and evidence of its health, and a consequent ignorance and absence of all consciousness of definite standards of healthy mindedness in relation to sex or modesty, is non-assertive and may be led to imitate the verbally expressed sex-overvaluation of the most unhealthy sensualists, of either repression or indulgence.

When this modesty of an unconscious, ignorant, sympathetic imitation becomes habitual and evolves to self-consciousness, and acquires associated emotions, with all the other factors unchanged, it becomes the conscious modesty of imitation through cowardice. This, perhaps, is the most general and popular kind of modesty among adults, and is about the only kind of modesty that has received scientific study, and has often been generalized as being all that there is of modesty.

An idea related to sex, the harboring of which would invoke adverse criticism, may and usually does produce an emotional fear, which is readily transfused into an emotional approval of an opposing idea, and this emotional approval is quite apt to have its intensity determined by the degree of fear-emotion, which it really is, and the degree of the individual's sexual hyperaestheticism.

Let us now quote the statements of intelligent observers as to this form of modesty, which is a mere imitation through fear. In the seventeenth century I find the scholarly Peter Bayle making this observation as to modesty: "An honest woman will justly be offended if any one tells her an obscene story; but she will not blame an historian for relating it, provided he abstain from filthy words. An historian speaks to the public, and not to such and such a woman in particular, and therefore what he says is not offensive, as it would be if it was said in a conversation or in a letter. In these two last cases *he would have no very favorable notion of the modesty of those to whom he speaks or writes, and that it is that gives offense.*"[104].

In this analysis it is clear that such modesty consists only in a fear of the judgment of those who know that she suffers in her presence the telling of that which those others esteem "obscene." The "obscenity" disappears—that is, the offense is non-existent—when the fear of that judgment is non-existent, either ideally or actually.

When some dominant character, through fear of him or her, has forced generally upon any community some particular standard of "modesty," we have the condition described by Dr. Havelock Ellis in these words: "Modesty thus comes to have the force of tradition, a vague but massive force, bearing with special power on those who can not reason."[105]

It seems to me that the following quotation is pregnant with the same suggestion that a healthy natural woman is not ashamed to discuss sex or see sex in the presence of men, un-

[104]*Historical and Critical Dict.,* Vol. V, page 133, Edition of Lond., A. D. 1738.

[105]*Studies in the Psychology of Sex,* page 43.

less first reminded that she is a woman and that therefore she must fear adverse judgment unless she acts differently than she would do if unafraid or if she were a man.

"I have conversed, as man with man, with medical men on anatomical subjects and compared the proportions of the human body with artists, yet such modesty did I meet with that I was never reminded by word or look of my sex, of the absurd rules which make modesty a pharisaical cloak of weakness. And I am persuaded that in the pursuit of knowledge women would never be insulted by sensible men and rarely by men of any description if they did not by mock modesty remind them that they were women; actuated by the same spirit as the Portuguese ladies, who would think their charms insulted if, when left alone with a man, he did not at least attempt to be grossly familiar with their persons. Men are not always men in the company of women; nor would women always remember that they are women if they were allowed to acquire more understanding."[106]

The same thought that fear of the judgments of others is the essence of modesty comes from another woman. Madame Celine Renooz, in a recent "elaborate study of the psychological differences between men and women," says: "Modesty *is masculine shame attributed to women* for two reasons: First, because man believes that woman is subject to the same laws as himself; second, because the course of human evolution has reversed the psychology of the sexes, attributing to women the psychological results of masculine sexuality. This is the origin of the conventional lies which by a sort of social suggestion *have intimidated women.* They have in appearance at least *accepted the rule of shame imposed on them* by men, but only custom inspires modesty for which they are praised. It is really an outrage to their sex."[107]

In support of her views the authoress points out that the decolette constantly reappears in feminine clothing, never in that of the male; that missionaries experience great difficulty in persuading uncivilized women to cover themselves; that while women accept with facility an examination by male doctors, men cannot force themselves to accept examination by a woman doctor, etc., etc.[108]

Professor James of Harvard is more specific in his state-

[106]Woolstonecraft, *"Vindication of the Rights of Women,"* page 132.

[107]*Psychologie Comparre de Homme et de la Femme,* pages 85-87, requoted from Ellis's *Psychology of Sex* (Modesty), page 4.

[108]Ellis's *Psychology of Sex* (Modesty), page 5.

ment when he informs us that modesty is "The application in the second instance to ourselves of judgments primarily passed upon our mates."[109]

Ribot concurs in these words: "I look upon it [modesty] as a binary compound capable of being resolved into two primary emotions—self-feeling and fear. The emotional state which lies at the root of modesty, shame and other similar manifestations arises from the application in the second instance to ourselves of a judgment primarily passed upon others. * * * Modesty can not be considered an instinct in the strict sense of the word, *i. e.*, as an excitomotor phenomenon. Under the influence of custom, public opinion, civilization it passes through its evolution till it reaches the New England pitch of sensitiveness and range, making us say stomach instead of belly, limb instead of leg [even limbs of a piano], retire instead of go to bed, and forbidding us to call a female dog by name."[110]

In practically every discussion of modesty the same conclusion is implied, even when not expressed. I will quote a few illustrative statements: "But here we come round to the altruistic and moral emotions, for *shame is present only where the individual has a desire to please and is pained at the disapproval of others.*"[111]

Darwin expresses his belief "that self-attention directed to personal appearance *in relation to the opinion of others,*" and *"not moral conduct,"* is the fundamental element in shyness, modesty, shame and blushing.[112]

Professor Thomas, of the Chicago University, expresses himself thus: "Now, taking them as we find them, we know that such emotions as modesty and shame are associated with actions which injure and *shock others and show us off in a bad light.* * * * When once a habit is fixed interference with its smooth running causes an emotion. The nature of the habit broken is of no importance. *If it were habitual for grandes dames to go barefoot on our boulevards, or to wear sleeveless dresses at high noon, the contrary would be embarrassing. . . .*

"Our understanding of the nature of modesty is here further assisted by the consideration that *the same stimulus*

---

[109]*Principles of Psychology,* Vol. II, page 435.
[110]*Psychology of the Emotions,* pages 273-275.
[111]Williams's *Evolutionary Ethics,* 439.
[112]*Expressions of Emotion in Man and Animals,* pages 325-327.

does not produce the same reaction under all circumstances, but, on the contrary, may result in totally contrary effects. . . . Similarly, modesty has a two-fold meaning in sexual life. *In appearance it is an avoidance of sexual attention, and in many moments it is avoidance in fact.* But we have seen in the case of the bird that the avoidance is at the pairing season only a part of the process of working up the organism to the nervous pitch necessary for pairing." [No doubt it is this same thought as applied to man, which, in about 1751, induced Helvetius to say: "Modesty is only the invention of a refined voluptuousness."]

"Modesty with reference to personal habits has become so ingrained and habitual, and to do anything freely is so foreign to woman, that even freedom of thought is almost in the nature of immodesty in her."[113]

Dr. Havelock Ellis, probably the world's most famous specialist in sexual psychology, has this to say: "That modesty —like all the closely allied emotions—*is based on fear,* one of the most primitive of the emotions, seems to be fairly evident."[114]

"IMMODESTY" NO PROVOCATIVE.

Among uneducated people, the test of shock to modesty is esteemed of importance because, being founded on their feelings, they confound the moral valuation of circulating a disagreeable idea, with the moral sentimentalism associated with the accused presentation. This makes it desirable to make a little inquiry into the relation of modesty and sensualism. The more precise question of standards of morals will be left for a later discussion. Here it will suffice to show that thoughtful men dispute the mob's opinion that nudity is usually provocative of lust.

The poets, more than most other people, meditate upon love and the associated subjects. It is not surprising, therefore, to find that some of these should have hit upon the same thought. Here is a sample:

"The maid, who modestly conceals
Her beauties, while she hides, reveals.
Give but a glimpse, and fancy draws
Whate'er the Grecian Venus was.
From Eve's first-fig-leaf to brocade,

113Fables for the Female Sex (3rd Edition, 1766) pp. 66-65.
114*Studies in the Psychology of Sex* (Modesty), pp. 1-27.

All dress was meant for fancy's aid,
Which evermore delighted dwells
On what the bashful nymph conceals.
Whenever Celia struts in man's attire,
She shows too much to raise desire;
But from hoop's bewitching round,
Her very shoe has power to wound.
The roving eye, the bosom bare,
The forward laugh, the wanton air,
May catch the fop, for gudgeons strike
At the bare hook, and bait, alike;
While salmon play regardless by,
Till art, like nature, forms the fly.
     *   *   *   *   *   *   *
To wiser heads attention lend,
And learn this lesson from a friend.
She who with modesty retires,
Adds fuel to her lover's fires,
While such incautious jilts as you,
  By folly your own schemes undo."[115]

Burton (*Anatomy of Melancholy*, Part III, Sec. 2, Sub. 3, is quoted by Ellis, *Modesty*, page 39) as writing that "The greatest provocations to lust are our clothing." Burton further says: "Some are of the opinion that to see a women naked is able of itself to alter his affection, and it is worthy of consideration, saith Montaigne, the Frenchman, in his essays, that the skillfullest master of amorous dalliance appoints for a remedy of venerous passions a full survey of the body; which the poet insinuates:

The love stood still that ran in full careire,
  When once it saw those parts should not appear."[116]

If, as all the scientists seem agreed, modesty is but "the application in the second instance to ourselves of judgments primarily passed upon others," then we have ready explanation why, though there are no definite criteria of guilt, the verdict is quite uniformly "guilty." The defendant is denounced by the prosecuting attorney, and the widely advertised morality of "vice-societies." This avalanche of righteous vituperation is often reinforced by an impassioned stump speech from a popularity-seeking judge, who abuses the op-

[115]Fables for the Female Sex (3rd Edition, 1766), pp. 66-65.
[116]Burton's *Anatomy of Melancholy*, Vol. II, page 371.

portunity given him to instruct the jury. Thus the jury is informed how contemptible they will be in the eyes of these exemplars of "virtue" should they disagree with them as to the "obscenity" of the book under investigation. Neither the statute nor his own knowledge of the psychology of modesty, furnish him with any criteria of obscenity; the juror, therefore, is wholly without the instruments by which to fortify himself against the terrible charges that are already laid at his door should he find the accused publication to be unobscene. Thus from the sheer absence of any other standard of judgment he renders a verdict of guilty, solely to insure the esteem of the prosecutors. This is the inevitable result of the absence of statutory criteria of guilt, and of submitting to the jury's modesty the question of what shall constitute the essence of guilt.

That there is no such uniform and necessary connection between "immodesty" and sexual "immorality" as is popularly supposed and judicially assumed, is further testified to by other scholars.

Dr. R. W. Felkin remarks concerning Central Africa, that he nowhere met with more indecency than in Ugabda, where the death penalty is inflicted on an adult found naked in the streets. To this we may add the testimony of H. Crawford Angus, who has spent many years in Azimba land, Central Africa. He writes: "It has been my experience that the more naked the people, and the more, to us, obscene and shameless their manners and customs, the more moral and strict they are in the matter of sexual intercourse."[117]

Among the Druses, where incest is practised, divorce is easy and the elect, or spiritualists, have most licentious and sacred debaucheries, the women yet wear veils and their faces are unseen except by immediate relatives.[118]

"There is a great truth underlying the fact which the Governor of Uganda has just proclaimed, namely, that the more clothes the Bakedi women wear the less moral they are. Among all the unclothed Nilotic tribes, he says, a notable degree of morality exists; whereas those who have always been addicted to wearing apparel are of notoriously lax habits. It is the same everywhere."[119]

[117]Burton's *Anatomy of Melancholy*, Vol. II, page 371.
[118]"*Woman*," by Talmey, pages 10, 11.
[119]*Pall Mall Gazette*, now requoted from *Truth Seeker*, May 8, 1909.

These testimonies demonstrate quite conclusively that there is no necessary connection between "immodesty" and sexual orthodoxy, and that with those in whom a healthy-minded naturalness has not been tainted by a prurient prudery, the absence of clothing does not usually operate as a provocative to lust, and thus we see that the passions are best stimulated by concealment and mystery.

It follows quite logically from what has preceded that those who have become dominated by the idea that the sex impulse is a deplorable passion, and therefore a condition to be ashamed of, will manifest shame proportionate to the intensity of their own sex-sensitiveness, that they so intensely desire to conceal. This sexual hyperestheticism is more than the foundation of modesty and the determinant of the quality and quantity of its resultant shame. This same sensitiveness to suggestion is also the foundation of psycho-sexual impotency. Thus it comes that excessive lewdness very often induces excessive modesty and shame, and these in turn, by the very fact of their abnormal intensity and the resultant abnormally intense fear, produce a psychic inhibition against the natural physiological consequences of an otherwise appropriate objective sex-stimulus.

When this modesty, of diseased nerves, and a consequent abnormal lasciviousness, have produced psychic immunity to a normal sex-stimulation, their victims often are credited, by themselves and by others, with being unusually "virtuous." This erroneous conclusion involves two false assumptions. The first of these is the implication that incapacity for normal and healthy activity of any bodily organ can by any possibility be credited with moral value; the other false assumption is that mere psychic impotence as to normal sex-functioning implies general indifference to sex, for nothing can be farther from the facts as they are known to sexual psychologists. Practically all sex-perverts are hyperesthetic, and probably a majority of them are indifferent to or impotent as regards normal indulgence. The prude who, through fear, has become psychically unresponsive to what otherwise would be an effective sex-stimulus, has not been deprived of even the least quantity of the subjective conditions of excessive lasciviousness, either psychological or physiological. Since a psychic inhibition against some particular manifestation of the sex-impulse does not at all imply any decrease in the imperativeness of the impulse itself, it would seem to follow that wherever excessive modesty imposes a continuing inhibition against normal sexuality it is almost certain to promote and be the accompaniment of the perversion of the sex impulse. All writers upon sexual psychopathy have given us abundant examples to show the concurrence of excessive modesty and perverted sexuality.

I think we may consider it an established fact that the most prevalent kind of modesty is but a manifestation of conscious cowardice, quailing in fear of the anticipated adverse judgment of those whose favorable opinion is most valued. Also that in its more acute manifestations modesty and shame will be intense just to the degree that the sexual hyperestheticism (lewdness) is excessive. So it comes to this, that all genuine modesty and prudery are founded on excessive sensuality, and all mere seeming modesty and prudery are the unreasoned and fear-induced imitation of the former.

Furthermore, if this theory is correct we should expect that the most vehement denial of it must come from the very persons who feel that by our analysis we have uncovered the very thing in themselves which they are most anxious to conceal. As further evidence of the correctness of our theory it will, no doubt, appear that those who are most vehement in their protestations against it, because their weakness has been discovered, will not base their denials upon any psychologic study of modesty objectively considered. In other words, their denial will rest wholly upon subjective authority—that is, upon their personal and emotional desire that others shall not believe the theory true, at least as to themselves.

"They [prudes] do not recognize that normal, well-ordered amativeness is a physiological and moral virtue, while manifestations of spurious spirituality are often induced by some perversion. Indifference to amatory pleasures is frequently professed by those who resort to artificial stimulants. Prudery only betrays impurity. Prudery is the affectation of innocence, and consequently implies guilt. To the really innocent and pure all things are pure. Only the immoral or those most occupied with amatory delights feign to look with contempt upon the generative organs and to despise their wonderful functions.

"Yet the prudery and obscenity of such as these have succeeded in distorting our judgment on questions of sex in such a way that any desire for scientific instruction in these subjects has become inextricably confused with ideas of prurience or impropriety. Matters pertaining to the generative functions and to the sexes, which were formerly discussed with perfect familiarity and directness, with no thought of impropriety and immodesty, as every reader of the Bible or other ancient classics well knows, are now excluded even from treatises on physiology or gynecology. But for the anatomists and alienists nothing would be known about the physiology of normal love. The zealots wish to persuade us that the population of the earth increases by the stork method. These victims of a diseased imagination and perverted moral sense have succeeded in creating a false modesty which hinders free discussion."[120]

Thus far we have considered perverted sexuality only as an associate and as a consequence or cause of prurient prudery. We have not yet arrived at the origin of prudery and modesty when racially considered. By the way, it is worthy of remark that prudery and modesty are not in the least distinguishable except that as an epithet prudery is applied to those particular manifestations of modesty which come only from others and which we do not happen to like.

The question still remains, How came the first prude into existence? What manner of man first inspired that unnatural shame for healthy--minded sensualism by making others afraid of his criticism, should they admit by word and act their own healthy naturalness? Here I cannot take up this question, except to hint my conclusion that, phylogenetically, human modesty, as we now understand it, had its principal sources in sexual hyperestheticism and a perverted sex-impulse, and its secondary source in clothing, religious customs, etc. But that must be left for another discussion.

The foregoing considerations, it is believed, demonstrate that modesty is but the fear-imposed judgment of others, and in itself is devoid of moral value and from its very nature is incapable of furnishing anything like a uniform or certain criterion of "obscenity" such as is essential to the validity of the statute in question.

[120]"*Woman*," by Talmey, pages 10, 11.

325

CHAPTER XVII.

VARIETIES OF CRITERIA OF GUILT.

Our study of psychology, ethnography, and juridical history, in relation to modesty, has revealed the fact that the statutory words "obscene and indecent," etc., do not in and of themselves furnish either uniform, or any, criteria of guilt, such as should enable every man of ordinary understanding, under all circumstances, to know with certainty whether or not his proposed conduct is penalized, and without which certainty in the criteria of guilt no penal statute can be "due process of law."

It remains to inquire how far the unconstitutional judicial legislation in the creation of criteria of guilt has supplied the necessary certainty in the tests of obscenity. That this is not accomplished is the opinion of hundreds who have been convicted for a mere difference of opinion with the censors, as it seemed to them, and some of these have left valuable and intelligent protests. But these are not alone.

At the National Liberal League's convention held in Philadelphia July 1st to 4th, 1876, the following resolution was adopted:

"Resolved, That this League, while it recognizes the great importance and the absolute necessity of guarding by proper legislation against obscene and indecent publications, whatever sect, party, order, or class such publications claim to favor, disapproves and protests against all laws which, by reason of indefiniteness or ambiguity, shall permit the prosecution and punishment of honest and conscientious men for presenting to the public what they deem essential to the public welfare, when the views thus presented do not violate in thought or language the acknowledged rules of decency; and that we demand that all laws against obscenity and indecency shall be so clear and explicit that none but actual offenders against principles of purity shall be liable to suffer therefrom."[1]

[1]Comstock's Frauds Exposed. page 446.

The annual meeting of the National Purity Federation, Oct. 11, 1906, unanimously adopted a resolution praying for relief from the evils of this uncertainty. From the preamble of this resolution I quote the following: "In view, however, of the fact that Purity workers are constantly placed in jeopardy because of the uncertainty of the judicial test of obscenity and because these laws have in some instances been made the means of injustice and cruel wrong; and in view of the fact also that the indefinite character of the law renders it impossible for anyone to know whether he is acting within the law, or is violating the law, and because the law has been made a menace and a hindrance to many earnest workers whose efficient help is most seriously needed," etc.[2] Similar resolutions, complaining of the uncertainty of the law and offering definite suggestions for amendment, were adopted by the joint session of the medical and surgical sections of the State Medical Society of Illinois.[3]

The foregoing statements are entitled to great weight because in each case they come from persons who expressly approve the general purposes of the laws in question, and their complaints are in the nature of an admission against interest.

Lawyers have also noted the difficulty of knowing what is penalized. Thus Edward Livingston, one of the greatest lawyers of his time,[4] while revising the penal code of Louisiana, when he came to that class of offenses against "morals," wrote to a distinguished colleague, thus: "There is another evil of no less magnitude, arising from the difficulty of defining the offense. Use the general expression of the English Law, and a fanatic judge with a like-minded jury will bring every harmless levity under the lash of the law. Sculpture and painting will be banished for their nudities, poetry for the warmth of its descriptions, and music, if it excites any forbidden passion, will hardly escape."[5]

A noted English law-writer makes this comment: "It is impossible to define what is an immoral or obscene publication. To say that it necessarily tends to corrupt or deprave the morals of readers supplies no definite test."[6]

2*The Light*, Nov., 1906.
3*Medical Record*, Oct. 12th, 1907, p. 599-600.
4See *Columbia Law Review*, p. 32, Jan., 1902.
5Life of Edward Livingston, by Chas. Haven Hunt, p. 289.
6Paterson, Liberty of Press and Speech, etc., p. 70.

There is also judicial admission of the uncertainty and consequent arbitrariness of the statute. Thus it is said, "the law is arbitrary."[7] In a concurring opinion in the leading English case this language is used: "Therefore it appears to me very much *a question of degree,* and if the matter were left to a jury, it would *depend very much on the opinion, which the jury might form of that degree* in such a publication as this."[8a] One American court speaks of "the elasticity of the language used by Congress, necessarily [?] so general in its description of the offense."[9] Another court admits that, "Whether act or language is obscene depends upon circumstances,"[10] which circumstances, however, are not defined in the statute. Again it is declared: "The views that different persons might entertain of the tendency and effect of such publications *are so various* that these questions ought to be submitted to a jury,"[11] and so, instead of being a matter of statute law, every case in effect "is one which addresses itself largely to your [the jurors'] good judgment, common sense, and knowledge of human nature and the weakness of human nature."[12] The same thought comes from another court: "Now what are obscene, lascivious, lewd, indecent publications is largely *a question of your own conscience and your opinion,*"[13] and not a matter of statutory definition. "The question whether the contents of the publication in question come within the prohibition of the statute is one upon which *there might be a difference of opinion,*"[14] because the statute has not defined the crime. Again: "The question of obscenity in any particular article *must depend largely on the place, manner, and object* of its publication,"[15] but how, and why, these control is nowhere defined with any precision. "It is wholly unimportant what may have occurred elsewhere in the consideration of this question,"[16] because there is no common standard of judgment binding upon all Federal Courts. Another court declared: "Obscenity is determined by the common sense and *feelings* of mankind and not by the skill of the learned,"[17] nor by the statutes or even the judge-made tests.

---

[7] U. S. *vs.* Harman, 45 Fed. Rep. 421.
[8] Queen *vs.* Hicklin, L. R. 3, Q. B. 378.
  a In this, as in most other quotations, the italics are mine.—T. S.
[9] U. S. *vs.* Davis, 38 Fed. Rep. 327.
[10] U. S. *vs.* Smith, 45 Fed. Rep. 477.
[11] U. S. *vs.* Clarke, 33 Fed. Rep. 502.
[12] U. S. *vs.* Clarke, 38 Fed. Rep. 734.
[13] Instruction approved in Dunlop *vs.* U. S. 165 U. S. 500.
[14] In re Coleman, 131 Fed. Rep. 152.
[15] U. S. *vs.* Harman, 38 Fed. Rep. 829.
[16] U. S. *vs.* Sherman, unofficially reported by Mr. Comstock in "Morals, not Art or Literature," p. 33.
[17] Commonwealth *vs.* Landis, 8 Phila. 453.

Even the judicial legislation has not improved matters. The words "obscene, indecent," etc., "can not be said to have acquired any technical significance."[18] The same comes from another court: "It would therefore appear that the term 'public indecency' has no fixed legal meaning, is vague and indefinite."[19] And so after all the judicial legislation in aid of the statute, "The word [obscene] can not be said to be a technical term of the law, *and is not susceptible of exact definition in its juridical uses.*"[20]

However, it may be suggested that all this admitted uncertainty is due to uncertainty of evidence and not to the uncertainty of the law. It has been shown that the statutory words do not furnish any definite criteria of guilt, and that often the practical operation of the statute is to produce contradictory results when applied by different courts to the same subject-matter. It remains to show by a comparison of the judicial legislation creating criteria of guilt, that these are so conflicting as to leave undiminished the uncertainty as to what are the standards of judgment. It is quite apparent that the tests of obscenity are determined by the necessities of each case, and adjusted to accomplish the judicial desire, predetermined by considerations other than those expressed in the statute and derived from mere moral sentimentalism and feeling-convictions. Even when taken separately, the judicial tests of obscenity are as uncertain as the statute, upon which they engraft unconstitutional amendments on the pretense of interpretation. Taken collectively, they leave us in a worse muddle than could have been imagined from a mere reading of the statute.

FACT OR LAW?

"Whether obscene or not is *a question of law* and not of fact; that question is for the court to determine and not for the jury."[21]

The pictures "should be exhibited to the jury for them to determine as *a matter of fact* in the exercise of their good sense and judgment whether or not they were obscene or indecent."[22]

[18]U. S. *vs.* Harman, 45 Fed. Rep. 417.
[19]McJunkins *vs.* State, 10 Ind. 145. See also Redd *vs.* State (Ga.) 67 So. East. Rep. 709.
[20]Timmons *vs.* U. S. 85 Fed. Rep. 205, C. C. A.
[21]McNair *vs.* People, 89, 111, 441; U. S. *vs.* Bennett, Fed. Case, 14571, p. 1099; in U. S. *vs.* Shepard, 160 Fed. Rep. 584 (Utah) Trial 9 court directed verdict of guilty, see record in C. C. A. Also in U. S. *vs.* Heywood, trial court directed a verdict of guilty.
[22]People *vs.* Muller, 32 Hun. 211.

"The Judge may rightfully express his opinion respecting the evidence and it may sometimes be his duty to do so, yet *not* so as to withdraw it from the consideration and decision of the jury."[23]

"Ordinarily it is a question for the determination of a jury. But it is within the province of the court to construe the objectionable document so far as necessary to decide whether a verdict establishing its obscenity would be set aside as against evidence and reason."[24]

"The ultimate solution of that *rests with the jury* to the same extent that in civil prosecutions for libel and in criminal prosecutions since the declaratory act of the 32 Geo. III, c. 60."[25]

"Rather is the test what is *the judgment of the aggregate sense of the community* reached by it."[26] "It is a question for the jury to pass upon under proper instructions."[27]

IS THE STATUTE TAUTOLOGICAL?

"Obviously the words 'obscene' and 'of an indecent character' are treated in this opinion [165 U. S. 311] as *convertible* expressions, equivalent in meaning."[28]

"The word 'lascivious' is very nearly *synonymous* with the word 'lewd'; so nearly so that I will not undertake to draw a distinction between the two words."[29]

"The words 'obscene', 'lewd', and 'lascivious' as employed in the statute *are not used interchangeably*."[30]

MAY COMPARISONS BE MADE?

"You [jurors] are not sent here to try other books *nor to compare this book with other books,* and you heard the court rule out all other books."[31]

"So far as your experience goes, the effect that Shakespeare's writings, or any other author's writings, have had in the world, notwithstanding certain passages that they contain, you have the right to resort to that experience in determining what will be the probable effect of the publication

[23]Commonwealth *vs.* Landis, 8, Phila. 453.
[24]U. S. *vs.* Smith, 45 Fed. Rep. 418.
[25]U. S. *vs.* Clarke, 38 Fed. Rep. 50; U. S. *vs.* Harman, 45 Fed. Rep. 418.
[26]U. S. *vs.* Harman, 45 Fed. Rep. 417.
[27]U. S. *vs.* Moore, 129, F. R. 160.
[28]Timmons *vs.* U. S. 85 Fed. Rep. 205. (C. C. A.)
[29]U. S. *vs.* Clarke, 38 Fed. Rep. 733.
[30]U. S. *vs.* Smith, 45 Fed. Rep. 477; U. S. *vs.* Bennett, Fed. Case No. 14571,—16 Blatch. 338; U. S. *vs.* Britton, 17 Fed. Rep. 733; U. S. *vs.* Males, 51 Fed. Rep. 42.
[31]U. S. *vs.* Bennett, Fed. Case 14571, p. 1105.

involved in this case, *provided you think such comparison,* or reference to such experience, will be of service and will aid you in reaching a correct conclusion."[32]

DOES THE DEPOSIT COMPLETE THE OFFENSE?

"The act of depositing [obscene matter in the mails] must be held to constitute the entire offense."[33]

"The statute does not make criminal the mere depositing in a post-office of obscene matter, even though it be 'knowingly' deposited."[34]

CONTRADICTION AS TO "KNOWINGLY" IN INDICTMENT.

"It [the indictment] is defective because it does not allege that the defendant knew that the writings, papers, etc., which she is charged with having deposited in the mail, for mailing and delivery, were of an obscene, lewd, and lascivious character."[35]

"The indictment alleges that the defendant knowingly deposited this non-mailable picture * * * * Believing that the defendant was fully informed of the matter charged against him, notwithstanding the cases cited to me of Com. *vs.* Boynton, 12 Cush. 499; U. S. *vs.* Slenker, 32 Fed. Rep. 691, I am constrained to hold that this indictment is sufficient."[36]

EVIDENCE ALIUNDE.

"If the terms employed do not in and of themselves reasonably *convey the suggestion* of obscenity, lewdness, or lasciviousness, they cannot be eked out by evidence aliunde."[37]

Yet in the case of U. S. *vs.* Bennett *et al,* of the N. Y. Herald, such evidence was the sole reliance of the prosecution; Advertisements leading to immoral resorts were basis of the charge. I believe the same was true in the case of U. S. *vs.* Dunlop.

AS TO OBSCENITY ON SUSPICION.

Indictment on letter from a married man to an unmarried woman inviting her to visit a neighboring city with him clandestinely, the purpose of the visit not being disclosed in the letter, and it was free from immoral language. "The court

---

[32] U. S. *vs.* Clarke, 38 Fed. Rep. 735.

[33] U. S. *vs.* Commerford, 25 Fed. Rep. 903.

[34] U. S. *vs.* Brazeau, 78 Fed. Rep. 465.

[35] U. S. *vs.* Slenker, 32 Fed. Rep. 695; in U. S. *vs.* Macfadden, 165 Fed. Rep. 51 (N. J.). First indictment was dismissed on this ground; Com. *vs.* Boynton, 12 Cush. 499.

[36] U. S. *vs.* Clark, 37 Fed Rep. 107-108; Shephard *vs.* U. S., 160 Fed. Rep. 584.

[37] U. S. *vs.* Moore, 129 Fed. Rep. 160.

cannot see how any other construction can be put upon them than that they are within the meaning of the statute. * * * * It is difficult to conceive what can be more shocking to the modesty of a chaste and pure-minded woman than the proposition contained in these letters."[38]

In a similar case, a "letter free from the immoral language inhibited by the statute, written apparently for the purpose of seduction or assignation," produced the following opinion: "For a letter to be obnoxious to this statute *its language must be obscene,* lewd, or lascivious and it must be of indecent character. The statute does not declare that the letter must be written for an obscene or indecent purpose, but that the letter itself, in its language, shall be of indecent character. When a law denounces a letter containing obscene language, and does not denounce a letter decent in terms but written for an indecent purpose, an indictment founded only upon the obscene purpose cannot be maintained."[39]

"The language, 'go to bed with me,' is itself neither obscene nor vulgar, and has never before been so held. * * * * Taken in connection with the surrounding circumstances in this case, the conclusion is very natural that the defendant intended this as a proposition to violate chastity. * * * * As there is nothing obscene or vulgar in the language itself, though it makes a proposition that ought, in my opinion, to be criminal, I do not feel at liberty to embrace it by construction."[40]

WHOSE OPINION, THE JUROR'S, THE PUBLIC'S, OR THE PURIST'S?

"Sitting, as the court does in this case, in the stead of the jury, it may not apply to the facts its own method of analysis or process of reasoning as a judge, but should try to reflect in the findings the common experience, observation, and judgment of the jury of average intelligence."[41]

Here, then, was a judge with much more intelligence than an average jury, who, by applying his "own method of analysis and reasoning," might conclude that a book was not "obscene," but, believing that a jury of lesser intelligence would conclude otherwise, he decided it would be his duty to find the defendant guilty. The test of obscenity was the

---

[38]U. S. *vs.* Martin, 50 Fed. Rep. 921.
[39]U. S. *vs.* Lamkin, 73 Fed. Rep. 463.
[40]Dillard, *vs.* State, 41 Ga. 279. See concurring opinion. See also, Edwards *vs.* State, 85 S. W. Rep. 797. (Tex.)
[41]U. S. *vs.* Harman, 45 Fed. Rep. 418.

"judgment of the jury of average intelligence" and the jury's "*own opinion.*"[42]

"A book to be obscene must appear so *to the mind of the pure not to the impure merely.*"[43]

IMMORAL INFLUENCE ON ADDRESSEE DECISIVE.

"The inquiry as to the tendency of the letter must be narrowed to the liability to corrupt the addressee."[44]

"Even an obscene book, or one that in view of the subject matter would ordinarily be classed as such, may be sent through the mails or be published to certain persons for certain purposes. For example, a treatise on venereal diseases might be sent through the mail or delivered to a student or practitioner of medicine, and perhaps to other persons for certain purposes."[45]

"I cannot doubt that proper and necessary communication between physicians and patients touching any disease may be properly deposited in the mail. The statute is not to receive a strained construction."[46]

"IMMORAL" INFLUENCE ON ADDRESSEE IMMATERIAL.

"Without regard to the character of person to whom they are directed."[47]

"Have sexual intercourse with me" is held obscene even though "addressed to a prostitute."[48] Even her morals are guarded against impure suggestion by this tender and maternal statute.

"IMMORAL" INFLUENCE ON ORDINARY READER DECISIVE.

"It must be calculated with the ordinary reader to deprave him."[49]

"Tendency to vitiate the *public taste* and to debauch the public morals."[50]

"IMMORAL" INFLUENCE ON THE MOST LEWD IS DECISIVE.

"The matter must be regarded as obscene if it should have a tendency to suggest impure and libidinous thoughts *in the*

[42]Dunlap *vs.* U. S. 165, U. S. 488.
[43]Com. *vs.* Abbie Dyke Lee. Unofficially reported in Heywood's Defense, p. 29.
[44]U. S. *vs.* Wroblensky, 118 Fed. Rep. 496; U. S. *vs.* Moore, 129 Fed. Rep. 163; Edwards *vs.* State, 85 So. W. Rep. 797.
[45]U. S. *vs.* Clarke, 38 Fed. Rep. 502.
[46]U. S. *vs.* Smith, 45 Fed. Rep. 478.
[47]U. S. *vs.* Cheeseman, 19 Fed. Rep. 498.
[48]Kelly *vs.* State, 55 So. E. Rep. 482.
[49]Ruling approved in Dunlap *vs.* U. S. 165 U. S. 488.
[50]Montross *vs.* State, 72 Ga. 266.

minds of those open to the influence of such thought. * * * *
Whether the tendency of the matter charged as obscenity is
to deprave and corrupt *those whose minds are open to such
immoral influence,* and into whose hands a publication of this
sort *may* fall."[51]

FITNESS FOR "MORAL" INSTRUCTION TO CHILDREN IS DECISIVE.

"Such as should go into their [the jury's] families and
be handed to their [the jurors'] sons and daughters, and
placed in boarding schools for the beneficial information of
the young and others, then it was [the jury's] duty to acquit
the defendant."[52]

"UNBECOMING" LITERATURE.

The mere quality of being "unbecoming" is criterion of
"obscenity."[53]

On the contrary, it is held that "unbecoming or even
profane" language is not within the inhibition of the statute.[54]

CONFLICTS AS TO "TASTE" AND "SHOCK" AS TESTS.

The general notion is that protection to "morality" was
the only thing sought. But, according to some, the esthetic
sense was also to be protected. However, here as everywhere
else there is conflict of authority.

"Offensive to delicacy" is held sufficient."[55]

"*Shocks* the ordinary and common sense of men as an
indecency."[56]

"Tendency to vitiate the public *taste*" is a material element
according to another court.[57]

"If it is such as to *offend the sense of delicacy.*"[58]

"An obscene writing was defined as one offensive to
decency, *indelicate,* impure, and an indecent one, as one *unbecoming,* immodest, unfit to be seen."[59]

"That which *shocks* the ordinary and common sense of
men as an indecency is the test," AND YET!!

"The court must * * * * not allow a hypercritical judgment to take advantage of the elasticity of the language used

[51]U. S. *vs.* Bennett, Fed. Case, 14571, p. 1104; U. S. *vs.* Debout, 28 Fed.
Rep. 523; U. S. *vs.* Slenker, 32 Fed. Rep. 693.

[52]Com. *vs.* Landis, 8 Phila. R. 454; U. S. *vs.* Heywood, Off. Sten. Rep.
Morals, not Art or Lit. 22; U. S. *vs.* Silas Hicks, Off. Sten. Rep. Morals, not Art
or Literature; U. S. *vs.* Cheeseman, 19 Fed. Rep. 498.

[53]U. S. *vs.* Williams, 3 Fed. Rep. 485.

[54]U. S. *vs.* Smith, 11 Fed. Rep. 664.

[55]U. S. *vs.* Britton, 17 Fed. Rep. 733.

[56]U. S. *vs.* Davis, 38 Fed. Rep. 328.

[57]Montross *vs.* State, 72 Ga. 266.

[58]U. S. *vs.* Sherman, (from official Stenog. notes, see Comstock's Morals,
not Art or Literature, p. 33.)

[59]U. S. *vs.* Williams, 3 Fed. Rep. 485.

by Congress, * * * * by bringing within the act words and thoughts that are only rude, impolite, or *not in good taste,* according to the standard of decency prescribed by the purists in language and thought."[60]

ARE WORDS OBSCENE PER SE?

"There are in the language words known as words obscene in themselves."[61]

"There is *not a single word* in the language, however coarse, low, or vulgar, that may not be and is not often used to convey proper and decent ideas, and it is a mawkish and realy an indelicate and immodest sensitiveness that blushes at a word which may be used obscenely, but which the occasion and the context show not to be so used."[62]

MUST THE LANGUAGE BE "OBSCENE"?

"Inasmuch as every letter is written, and is a composition of words, it necessarily follows that for a letter to be obnoxious to this statute *its language must be obscene, lewd, or lascivious,* and it must be of an indecent character."[63]

"The language or communication may be free from the condemnation of the statute in one instance while it would clearly fall within it when addressed to other persons."[64] But who are these authorized obscenists?

"It is of no consequence that the language employed may be pure."[65]

"The poison of the asp may lie beneath the honeyed tongue just as a beautiful flower may contain a deadly odor. *It is the effect of the language* employed * * * * which is struck at by the statute."[66]

WHEREIN MUST THE OBSCENITY BE?

Here then it is held that the words sent through the mail must be obscene. Other cases say that the words need not be obscene; it is enough, though expressed in choicest words, if the idea is obscene. Again it is said that neither the words nor the idea actually expressed need be obscene; it being enough if these convey only to the most prurient

[60]U. S. *vs.* Davis, 38 Fed. Rep. 327; U. S. *vs.* Smith, 11 Fed. Rep. 664; U. S. *vs.* Wightman, 29 Fed. Rep. 636.

[61]U. S. *vs.* Bennett, Fed. Case, 14571, p. 1102; U. S. *vs.* Harman, 38 Fed. Rep. 829.

[62]Dillard *vs.* State, 41, Ga. 280.

[63]U. S. *vs.* Lamkin, 73 Fed. Rep. 463; Dillard *vs.* State, 41 Ga. 279.

[64]U. S. *vs.* Wroblensky, 118 Fed. Rep. 496.

[65]U. S. *vs.* Smith, 45 Fed. Rep. 478; U. S. *vs.* Males, 51 Fed. Rep. 421; U. S. *vs.* Hanover, 17 Fed. Rep. 444.

[66]U. S. *vs.* Moore, 129 Fed. Rep. 160.

imagination a mere *suggestion of obscenity*. And again it is decided that it can not be that every suggestion of lascivious ideas is prohibited. ·

"It *can not be that every writing or publication which in any way suggests a thought of the relation of the sexes is obscene, lewd, and lascivious*. That would place upon the court a vast burden of separating the little matter that is mailable from the grand mass and majority of literature which would be non-mailable."[67]

INTENT IS MATERIAL.

"I have but little patience with those self-constituted guardians and censors of the public morals who are always on the alert to find something to be shocked at, who explore the wide domain of art, science, and literature to find something immodest, and who attribute impurity where none is intended. * * * * The question of obscenity in any particular article must depend largely on the place, manner, and *object of its publication*."[68]

"The question of the violation of the statute rests upon the import and *presumed motive*."[69]

"Words get their point and meaning almost entirely from the time, place, circumstances *and intent* with which they are used. * * * * *The intention of the defendant* who used the language and the purpose for which he used it * * * * *constitutes the offense*."[70]

"We think it would also be a proper test of obscenity in a painting or statue *whether the motive* of the painting or statue, so to speak, as indicated by it, is pure or impure."[71]

INTENT IS IMMATERIAL.

"A mistaken view of the defendant as to the character and tendency of the book, if it was in itself obscene and unfit for publication, would not excuse his violation of the law."[72]

"The statute does *not* declare that the letter must be written *for an indecent or obscene purpose*."[73]

"The criminal character of the publication is not affected

[67] U. S. *vs.* Larkin & Adams (Wash. March 11, 1902) from Official Stenog. Rep.

[68] U. S. *vs.* Harman, 38 Fed. Rep. 828-9.

[69] U. S. *vs.* Wroblensky, 118 Fed. Rep. 496; Smith & Crocker, *vs.* State, 24 Tex. Cr. App. 1.

[70] Dillard *vs.* State, 41 Ga. 280-281. The second sentence is from a concurring opinion.

[71] People *vs.* Muller, 96 N. Y. 410.

[72] Com. *vs.* Landis, 8 Phila. 455.

[73] U. S. *vs.* Lamkin, 73 Fed. Rep. 463.

or qualified by there being some *ulterior object* in view *of a different and honest character.*"[74]

"I have stated *the object with which the book is written is not material, nor is the motive which leads the defendant to mail the book material. * * * * His motive may have been ever so pure; if the book he mailed is obscene, he is guilty.*"[75]

"Where the writings * * * * are of an obscene, lewd, or lascivious character, the fact that they were sent in *the real or supposed interest of science,* philosophy, or morality, is immaterial." (syllabus)[76]

UNCERTAINTY AS TO MEDICAL BOOKS.

"I am *not prepared to say* and it is not necessary now to decide whether these medical books could be sent through the mails without violating the statute."[77]

"Nor does the truth or falsity of the publication make any part of the offense."[78]

If, as many cases hold, truth and good motives are immaterial, and the character of the person to whom the matter is sent is also immaterial, then a book which would be obscene if handed to an adolescent or pubescent child must also be so if mailed to a physician. However, sometimes the judicial dictum repudiates this logical consequence.

"I *have no doubt* that under the statute, under which this indictment is found, standard medical works * * * * may be sent through the mails *to persons* who buy or call for them for the purpose of seeking information."[79]

However, according to another authority they may *not* be offered to *all* with a view to stimulating the desire for information.

"Even scientific and medical publications containing illustrations exhibiting the human form, if wantonly exposed in the open markets, with a wanton and wicked desire to create a demand for them and not to promote the good of society by placing them in proper hands for useful purposes, would, if tending to excite lewd desires, be held to be obscene

---

[74]Regina *vs.* Hicklin, L. R. 3, Q. B. 360; Steele *vs.* Brannan, L. R. 7, C. P. 261.

[75]U. S. *vs.* Bennett, Fed. Rep., Case 14571, p. 1102; U. S. *vs.* Clarke, 38 Fed. Rep. 502; U. S. *vs.* Debout, 28 Fed. Rep. 524.

[76]Charge quoted in U. S. *vs.* Slenker, 32 Fed. Rep. 691; State *vs.* Brown, 27 Vt. 619.

[77]U. S. *vs.* Cheeseman, 19 Fed. Rep. 498.

[78]U. S. *vs.* Debout, 28 Fed. Rep. 525; Com. *vs.* Landis, 8 Phila. 453; U. S. *vs.* Bennett, Fed. Case 14571.

[79]U. S. *vs.* Clarke, 38 Fed. Rep. 733; U. S. *vs.* Smith, 45 Fed. Rep. 478.

libels." * * * * That it is 'true and scientifically correct' is immaterial."[80]

"The object no doubt is to display the nature of a particular disease and the effect of a particular medicine, but it is not commendable, even to medical men, to display such representations in public."[81]

Mr. Comstock tells of one Sherman who was three times arrested for circulating a book on hernia. The first two trials resulted in acquittal, because the jury did not consider it obscene. On the third trial the court instructed the jury that they must consider the verdict of other juries as immaterial, and then invented some new test of obscenity which resulted in conviction.[82]

JUDICIAL TESTS OF "OBSCENITY" APPLIED.

Nowhere else is the judicial "intelligence" so utterly devoid of real enlightenment as when dealing with these problems of abnormal psychology and sex-psychology. Were it not so pathetic, we could find great humor in the judicial hysteria over "obscene" literature. Unconscious of the fact that the obscenity is the contribution of the reading mind,[84] our "most learned judges" when trying to objectivize the judicial moral-sentimentalism, by judicial legislation creating tests of obscenity, make standards which are not only very contradictory but also very ludicrous when examined from the view-point of the scientist. It seems as though judges think of themselves as possessed of a capacity for acquiring a knowledge of science by some mysterious occult means, which make it unnecessary for them to investigate before expressing a judicial determination involving scientific problems.

Probably the most frequently used "tests" of obscenity, etc., are the following: "Where the tendency of the matter is to deprave and corrupt the morals of those whose minds are open to such influences and into whose hands a publication of this sort may fall * * * * the statute uses the word 'lewd,' which means having a tendency to excite lustful thoughts."[85] I intend to apply the foregoing "tests of ob-

[80]Com. vs. Landis, 8 Phila. 453; U. S. vs. Burton, 142 Fed. Rep. 58; U. S. vs. Cheeseman, 19 Fed. Rep. 498.

[81]Reg. vs. Grey, 4 Foster and Finlanson, 79.

[82]U. S. vs. Sherman, Morals, not Literature or Art, p. 33.

[84]Ellis' Studies in the Psychology of Sex, Vol. VI. p. 54; Varieties of Official Modesty, Albany Law Journal, Aug. 1908; Legal Obscenity and Sexual Psychology, Alienist and Neurologist, Aug. 1908; What is Criminally Obscene, Albany Law Journal, July 1906.

[85]U. S. vs. Bennett, Fed. Case, No. 14571, Vol. 24, p. 1102.

scenity" to a few related facts, well known to the psychiatrist, in order that their connection, and the crass judicial ignorance concerning the import of these "tests," may become more generally known.

Krafft-Ebing, in quoting the confession of a masochist, gives this as the language of the afflicted one: "That one man could possess, sell, or whip another caused me intense excitement; and in reading 'Uncle Tom's Cabin' (which I read about the beginning of puberty), I had erections. Particularly exciting to me was the thought of a man's being hitched up before a wagon in which another man sat with a whip, driving and whipping him."[86]

Here then is a case where conviction would have been dependent, not upon the jurors' mere *a priori* speculation, but upon the admitted fact that the "tendency" of "Uncle Tom's Cabin," according to the judicial ignorance, is to "deprave and corrupt the morals of those whose minds are open to such influences" and that it has a *demonstrated* "tendency to excite lustful thoughts." Thus, by the generally accepted judicial tests of obscenity, our "most learned" judges condemn "Uncle Tom's Cabin" as being an "obscene" and a "lewd" book, and it is a crime to sell it, or to send it by mail or express, if the "law" (?) is uniformly enforced.

One need but know the facts of sexual fetichism and apply the judicial "test" of obscenity, to an apron, feathers—any item of female attire, such as the shoe, furs, handkerchiefs, gloves, silks, velvets, or even a woman's hand, or hair, or perfumes, and thus demonstrate that in themselves each of these is an object of "public indecency" and "obscenity" because "to those whose minds are open to such influences," to wit, certain sexual fetichists, it has a *demonstrated* "tendency to excite lustful thoughts."

Dr. Havelock Ellis recently wrote this: "The case has lately been reported of a young schoolmaster who always felt tempted to commit a criminal assault by the sight of a boy in knickerbockers; that for him was an 'obscene' sight—must we, therefore, conclude that all boys in knickerbockers should be forcibly suppressed as 'obscene'?[86a] Most assuredly! If the judicial tests of obscenity and lewdness are to be applied, it becomes a public indecency, in many States criminally punishable, to permit a boy in knickerbockers to be seen in public,

[86]Psychopathia Sexualis, Chaddock translation, p. 105.
[86a]Free Press Anthology, p. 224.

and a picture of such a boy would be an "obscene and indecent, a lewd and lascivious" print, within the meaning of the postal law, because it has a *demonstrated* "tendency to deprave and corrupt the morals of those whose minds are open to such influences"; because in such persons the picture of a boy in knickerbockers has a *demonstrated* "tendency to excite lustful thoughts."

The literature of sadism also furnishes illustrations of the crass ignorance involved in our judicial "tests of obscenity." "There is a case of a boy who experienced sexual feeling by viewing the picture of a battle scene,"[87] hence such pictures are "obscene and indecent, lewd and lascivious," and, therefore, criminal if sent by mail. Again our author writes: "A surgeon confessed to the writer that while reading in a surgical work a description of the puncture of a festered wound, he found himself, to his astonishment, in a state of sexual excitement." Therefore, according to the judicial "test of obscenity," a book on surgery is non-mailable because "obscene and indecent," etc., it being now a *demonstrated* fact that such books have "a tendency to excite lustful thoughts," and, therefore, by the official "logic," a tendency "to deprave and corrupt the morals of those whose minds are open to such influences and into whose hands a publication of this sort may fall," to wit, certain sadists.

Maj. R. W. Shufeldt, a distinguished scientist and a retired army-surgeon, while denouncing the absurdity of suppressing the literature of human topographical anatomy, said: "My studies have brought me much evidence in this matter. It is only the sadist who quivers with sexual excitement as he or she stands and views the whips and a few other implements in the windows of a harness-store, and not the normal being; it is only the hopeless sexual pervert who is driven to libididinous gratification after viewing the piston copulating with the cylinder on the side of a locomotive, and not the healthy minded engineer in the cab. * * * * One case came to my knowledge of a man who was so delicately balanced sexually that he could not view in the window of a fish store a lot of hard-shelled clams that the association of the name, and the outline of the posterior aspect of the bivalve, did not suggest to his mind the external sexual parts of woman and greatly excite him as a consequence. All this constitutes no valid reason,

87Arthur MacDonald in *Medico-Legal Journal*, for March, 1907.

however, for our prohibiting a whip display in a trademan's window, do [ing] away with the locomotive, or suppress [ing] the public sale of clams."[88]

Here then we have it demonstrated according to the most generally accepted judicial criteria of "obscenity" that "Uncle Tom's Cabin," a book on surgery, a hard-shelled clam, a horse-whip, a lady's shoe, glove, handkerhcief, and, in fact, everything on earth is legally "obscene, indecent, lewd, or lascivious," because to *some* minds lewdness has been or may be suggested by it.

There was a time when the Federal Supreme Court still subordinated the will of its judges to constitutional law. Then it was said: "It would certainly be dangerous if the legislature could set a net large enough to catch all possible offenders, and leave it to the courts to step inside and say who could be rightfully detained and who shall be set at large."[89] Will it adhere to that doctrine when moral sentimentalism is involved? In many fields of jurisprudence we are the helpless victims of the arbitrary will of a lawless judiciary. This lawless judiciary in the matter of obscenity has legislated into existence "criteria of guilt" so contradictory as to be meaningless, so inclusive as to make everyone a criminal, and, when applied to all conceivable cases, so fantastic in their result as to make our courts a laughing stock of the alienist. And these courts, which unconstitutionally enact such contradictory and extremely absurd criteria of obscenity, tell us: "These are matters which fall within the range of ordinary intelligence";[90] and, "Everyone who uses the mails * * * * must take notice of what in this enlightened age is meant by decency, purity, and chastity in social life and what must be deemed 'obscene,' lewd, and lascivious."[91] BAH!!!

But, our judges are not solely to blame for being so densely ignorant as not even to suspect the fact. The blame lies farther back with our moralists for revenue, who, with the stupid sentimentalists, have so nearly suppressed all literature not in harmony with the theology of sex that the average physician is quite as ignorant as our "most learned judges."

Dr. Wm. J. Robinson edits several journals for his profes-

---

[88]*Pacific Medical Journal*, March, 1909, p. 152.
[89]U. S. *vs.* Reese 92 U. S. 219-221.
[90]People *vs.* Muller, 96, N. Y. 410.
[91]U. S. *vs.* Rosen 161 U. S. 42, See also, Redd *vs.* State, 176 Fed. Rep. 944.

sional brethren, and makes something of a specialty of venereal subjects. Yet he, who is accounted among the leaders in his profession, wrote this: "And so [as in the case of beauty and ugliness] it is in regard to obscenity; the thing in itself is not obscene; in the midst of the desert or at the bottom of the sea, it is not obscene. But if it induces some people, *however small a number,* to commit indecent, unhealthy things, then the thing is indecent, and no amount of sophistry can do away with the fact."[92]

No! the judges are not the only ones whose minds are "uncorrupted by learning" on sexual psychology, and they are not to be blamed for their ignorance, only for their unwillingness to be enlightened. But what shall we say of the moralists for revenue and the quack-moralists in the medical profession?

CONCLUSION.

It has been demonstrated that, whether viewed as a problem of abstract psychology, of sexual psychology, abnormal psychology, ethnography, juridicial history, or considered in the light of the mutual distructiveness of the judicially created criteria of guilt, or their all inclusiveness and the grotesqueness resulting from their general application, in every aspect we find *absolute demonstration* of the correctness of the occasional judicial admission that the statutes under consideration do not prescribe the criteria of guilt by which judge or jury determines that the law has been violated.

It will next be exhaustively shown that such certainty in the criteria of guilt is essential to the validity of a penal statute. The conclusion contended for is well stated in a recent case where it is said: "A crime can be created only by a public act, and the language of the act must be sufficient to *completely declare and define* the crime and affix the punishment. * * * * The discretion of fixing what facts import criminality is exclusively that of the lawmaker as distinguished from the executive,"[93] or court. It follows from the coordination of these propositions that all of these laws are nullities, because "Where the law is uncertain there is no law," and, consequently, no "due process of law."

[92] *Altruria,* 1907, p. 2. Italics are mine.—T. S.
[93] U. S. *vs.* Louisville and N. Ry. Co. 176 Fed. Rep. 944.

CHAPTER XVIII.

"DUE PROCESS OF LAW" IN RELATION TO STATUTORY UNCERTAINTY AND CONSTRUCTIVE OFFENSES.

PART I.

The Scientific Aspect of "Law." [1]

In all the annals of the past, one of the most conspicuous features in the struggle for liberty has been the fight against constructive crimes, which includes that against punishment for imaginary or psychologic injuries. The condition of England, before the days of the revolution, is thus described by Edward Livingston, Secretary of State under President Jackson, and reputed to be "the greatest lawyer of his time," in his official report to the Louisiana Legislature.

"The statute gave the texts, and the tribunals wrote the commentary in letters of blood, and extended its penalties by the creation of constructive offenses. The vague and sometimes unintelligible language employed in the penal statutes gave a *seeming* color of necessity to this assumption of power, and the English nation have submitted to the legislation of its courts, and seen their fellow-subjects hanged for constructive treason, and roasted alive for constructive felonies, quartered for constructive heresies, with a patience that would be astonishing, even if their written law had sanctioned the butchery."

It appears, historically, that those baneful constructive crimes developed from several specific causes. A union of church and state resulted in punishing the mere constructive injury of heretical speech; the witchcraft superstition resulted in punishing the mere constructive cause of material injuries; the abridgment of the freedom of speech and of the press also punished psychologic crimes based upon mere constructive injuries; these, with the evils of judicial legislation in defining the criteria of guilt, were all of the sources for those evils

[1] By special permission revised and republished from the *American Law Review*, for June, 1908.

which are so often denounced under the name of constructive offenses. Our ancestors saw the evils and their practical concrete origins, but apparently did not concern themselves with the generalization of the ultimate tests by which to determine the essence of all constructive offenses. Notwithstanding this, they very effectively barred the door against any recurrence of such evils, if we will but construe our constitution in the light of a truly scientific conception of *the law,* such as will be formulated hereinafter.

To obviate the recurrence to punishment of mere psychologic or constructive injuries, our forefathers prohibited the union of church and state, and the abridgment of freedom of speech and of the press. To the same end, and to preclude judicial legislation and its arbitrary tyrannies, they separated the functions of the legislative and judicial branches of our government, and then, as including all these and more besides, they made the more general and comprehensive guarantee that no man should be deprived of life, liberty or property without due process of *law.*

In spite of all these safeguards, and innumerable judicial denunciations of the punishment of constructive offenses, it seems to me that all about me I discover such penalties being inflicted, without its inducing much of a protest. In seeking for an explanation, I have been led to the conclusion that it is to be found in the fact that in reducing the lawyer's calling from a profession to a business, we have put so high a premium upon his commercial acumen that we have reduced the lawyer from a scientist of the law to a business executive. The result is that not one lawyer in ten thousand has a truly scientific conception of *the law,* or of its essential nature. As best I can I intend to point out the nature of "law" as I believe the few intelligent lawyers view it, and then I will endeavor to deduce therefrom criteria for determining what are constructive offenses, especially in their relation to *"due process of law."*

THE LAW AS A SCIENCE.

It is often said, let us hope not always in sarcasm, that the law is a science. I wonder if those who speak these words really know what they signify. I shall undertake, I fear in an inadequate way, to state what such words mean to me. Men have a scientific conception of the law only when they see legal truth as a formulated expression of the natural law of our social organism. To conceive this as a "law" we must understand it, not as a mere acquaintance with, or memory-knowledge of, the verbally uttered decision in this case or that, or under these or other special states of fact, but we must understand these special legal truths in all their necessary relations to one another, as constituent elements in the induction leading to the most comprehensive generalization; and again, all must be seen according to their own necessary logical classifications as mere special examples of the broadest rational generalization of legal truth, to which all concrete instances must be referred, and from which all specific decisions must be made, by the process of deduction. It is not enough that we discover some more or less crude analogies between these facts and those, and thus by an empirical induction make the decision in that case fit this; on the contrary, the law has not reached the dignity of a science until we see the relation of all its special cases to those general principles which are decisive of all causes belonging to the same general class. Let me make a quotation by way of illustration. "During its early stages, planetary astronomy consisted of nothing more than accumulated observations respecting the positions and motions of the sun and planets; from which accumulated observations it came by and by to be empirically predicted, with an approach to truth, that certain of the heavenly bodies would have certain positions at certain times. But the modern science of planetary astronomy consists of deductions from the law of gravitation—deductions showing *why* the celestial bodies necessarily occupy certain places at certain times."

To have accumulated a knowledge of the kind of judgments entered in a large number of cases is not to know "law" —nor to be a scientist of the law. To make empirical inductions from such accumulated knowledge may enable us to decide cases with an approach to truth and justice, but the result is not "law" in the only sense in which a scientist of the law can use that word. The lawyer, whose intellectual attainments are such as to make him a scientist of the law, must have adopted the scientific method for the ascertainment of legal truth. The scientific method requires that his empirical generalizations shall have been included in a rational generalization, which is the formulated statement of *the law,* because it determines conclusively from the nature of things *how* and *why* certain judgments must be so and thus, the result always being derived by deductions from the ultimate rational generalizations, by which process *the law* thus determines the decision in every particular case, which *law* must always be conformed to, irrespective of a direct estimate of the beneficence of its result in any particular instance. It is this, and this alone, which, in my judgment, makes the law a science, and though I should be convinced that not many lawyers are legal scientists, still I would not despair. If our conception of the law falls short of being a scientific one, it can be only because the judges and legislators whose duty it is to formulate verbal statements of the law have not attained the intellectual stature of scientists.

If *"the law"* is a system of rational generalizations to which all specific controversies must be referred, and by deductions from whose uniform standards all controversies must be conclusively decided, then it follows that if no such certain and uniform controlling standard is prescribed by the legislative enactment, and where, because of that fact (especially in criminal cases), courts are left free to pronounce their judgments (of guilt or innocence) by empirical inductions based upon their differing personal experience, then, under such circumstances I say, courts do not declare, and are not governed by *"the law,"* but themselves are unconsciously seeking by their judicial legislation to create law, and enforce their own arbitrary edicts; they are not enforcing or maintaining natural law according to the formulated precepts of it, made by the proper authority, but instead they become the executioners of their own lawless wills. All this is but another way of vindicating the maxim, "where the law is uncertain there is no law." From the foregoing speculations it already appears that *the law* is something outside of and independent of the judicial mind. Let us now make further inquiry as to the nature of *law,* from the scientific viewpoint.

ON THE NATURE OF THE LAW.

If we would know what is to be understood by a constructive breach of the law we must first achieve a very definite conception of the nature of *law.* After that we can better discern all the conditions which might constitute its constructive breach, as distinguished from its actual infraction.

Just as the laws of mathematics are not created by the mathematicians, nor the physical laws by the physicists, who discover or make formal statements of them, as also the laws of our thinking are not products of thinking, so the laws— *the real laws*—of a state are never products of judicial cerebration. All *laws* are pre-suppositions which alone make our thinking about them, and statement of them, possible. The province of the court is to discover, declare and enforce, the prior existing *law,* and never to construct or create law. To declare *the law* means only to formulate a verbal statement of it as it exists, prior to and apart from the judicial formula, and outside of the judicial mind. Thus the civil-state *law,* in its proper and technical sense, is but natural justice, as we find it in the very nature of our inter-human relations, and in the formulated statements of it and such other artificial legislatively created rules of conduct as the law-making power properly may enact, but enact *only* in furtherance of the security and realization of natural justice among sentient beings. These considerations it seems to me are the reasons underlying the following language from the Supreme Court of the United States: "In the ordinary use of language it will hardly be contended that the decisions of courts constitute law. They are, at most, only evidence of what the laws are; and are not of themselves laws."[2]

ON THE REQUIREMENT OF NATURAL JUSTICE.

The laws of natural justice are in the nature of things and exist wholly independent of our knowledge of them, and would still exist though every verbally expressed statement of them should be destroyed. It follows that judicial opinions and statutes should do no more than merely to declare our highest conception of the most refined sense of natural justice to which humanity has now attained, and to provide for its practical realization. If it does either less or more than this, it is a misconception of *the law,* and its enforcement should be declared beyond the power of any court. To declare otherwise would be to assert that our state machinery may be used deliberately and consciously to accomplish a wrong—to violate natural justice, or, what for practical purposes amounts to the same thing, our best human conception of it.

[2]Swift v. Tyson, 16 Peters 18.

In accordance with the foregoing conception of law as existing in the nature of things, or as being a human regulation conducing to the practical maintenance of natural justice, it follows that juridical systems must always conform to right reason, because the essence of right reason consists in the very fact of a conformity of our thinking with the natural order of things outside our minds. More technically expressed, we say legal truth, which is but a subordinate department of truth as a whole, is "the exact correspondence between the subjective order of our [the judge's] conception and the objective order of the relation among things."[3] If then a true conception of law in civil matters is one which is an exact correspondence with natural justice, as this exists in and is derived from the very nature of things, and as a mere part of the natural law of our social organism, then our formulated statements of *the law* must always conform to right reason, because such conformity is the very essence of a true conception of *the law*. Thus understood it is hardly possible to disagree with Blackstone and those authorities following him, who say: "Statutes which violate *the plain and obvious principles of common right* and common reason are null and void."[4]

Upon the supremacy of natural law, as the original of all our formulated statements of law, Montesquieu wrote this: "How iniquitous the law which, to preserve a purity of morals, overturns nature, the origin and the source of all morality."[5]

Later Blackstone expressed himself about the supremacy of natural law in these words: "No human laws are of any validity if contrary to the law of nature; and such of them as are valid derive all their force and all their authority from this original."[6]

Statutes have been held unconstitutional merely because "manifestly contrary to the first principles of civil liberty and natural justice."[7]

"Reason and the nature of things, which will impose laws even upon the Diety."[8]

[3]Fiske's, Cosmic Philosophy.
[4]Bennett v. Bogge, Fed. Case, No. 1319; Morrison v. Barksdale, 1 Harp. (So. Car.), 101; Taylor v. Porter, 4 Hill 140. (N. Y., 1843)
[5]"The Spirit of the Laws," Aldine edition, vol. 2, p. 556.
[6]Blackstone's Commentaries.
[7]Holden v. James, 11 Mass. 405; Durkee v. City of Janesville, 28 Wisc., 465 and cases; Calder v. Bull, 3 Dallas, 387-388. (U. S.)
[8]Fletcher v. Peck, 6 Cranch, 143, see dissenting opinion; Wilkinson v. Leland, 2 Peters, 1-658; Terrett v. Taylor, 9 Crauch, 50-52.

I am well aware that many courts, without having weighed the foregoing considerations as to the nature of *law,* have held otherwise, but such courts repudiate and contradict the expressly declared purpose of our Constitution and so discredit themselves.

There is little excuse for the existence of government except as affording a method for the authoritative formulation of our best conception of natural rules of justice and promoting their realization in practise. Although the preambles of our Federal, and perhaps most of our State constitutions, proclaim their purpose "to establish justice * * * * * and secure the blessing of liberty," and though to the end of establishing justice "due process of law" was made mandatory, yet judges, guiltless of the scientific conception of *the law,* have not hesitated to contradict the constitutionally avowed purpose of government, and of "due process of law," by declaring that these words do "not mean merciful *nor even just laws.*"[9]

Judges capable of saying that a state may violate the *obvious* demands of natural justice (as distinguished from an enforcement of laws deciding disputed problems of justice), discredit the state, and invite for themselves contempt. To uphold many such laws as constitutional would justify and might necessitate a revolution by violence, as a means of restoring liberty and justice.

If, in a criminal case, a court should undertake to enforce upon any person a judgment which was not in the furtherance of natural justice as that must be viewed in our secular states, dealing only with material factors, and which did not conform to general, uniform and certain rules of conduct, having an exact, verbally formulated existence outside the mere arbitrary will of the court, and well known, or easily accessible to all, prior to the acts constituting the offense then before the court—I say, if a court should undertake to enforce anything different from such a law, it would not be enforcing *the law* at all, and to submit to it would be submission to a government by the arbitrary and despotic will of a judiciary, unrestrained by subjection to *the law,* and not in any sense would this be a government by courts *according to law* Criminal punishment under such circumstances would be punishment for constructive crimes.

[9]Eames v. Savage, 77 Me. 212.

If the state, in violation of the foregoing injunctions, should be permitted to penalize an act which is not an essential element in doing actual violence to natural justice in relation to material factors, the statute could not be one enacted in the furtherance of the governmental purposes to establish justice and secure the blessings of liberty, and therefore such a law could not be within the legitimate province of such a government as we profess to maintain. Furthermore such a statute, penalizing an act which is not an essential element in violating such natural justice in relation to material things, must in itself be the creation of an injustice—that is, it must in itself and from its very nature authorize an invasion of liberty, unwarranted by any necessity for defending natural justice or maintaining equality of liberty, and therefore the enforcement of such a statute would be the deprivation of liberty without due process of *law,* as we now understand *law* in the light of our foregoing study of its nature. I conclude that every such statute as I have last hereinabove described is an attempt to punish for a constructive offense—is a violation of our constitutional guarantee of "Due Process of Law." With so much by way of preliminary discussion, we may proceed to some preliminary classification of constructive offenses under several heads, indicative of the different sources from which comes the tendency toward the construction of offenses and the wrongful infliction of penalties based upon the creation.

MATERIAL INJURY ESSENTIAL TO CRIME.

It follows from the fact that human justice and a secular State can deal only with material factors, that an offense to be real, and not merely constructive, must be conditioned upon a demonstrable and ascertained material injury, or an imminent danger of such, the existence of which danger must be determined by the known laws of the physical universe. Our Constitution, both in its guarantee of freedom of speech and press, and in its guarantee of due process of *law* (as we now understand *the law,* according to the foregoing analysis) precludes the construction of mere psychologic crimes. The offenses which are based only upon ideas, expressed or otherwise, such as constructive treason, witchcraft and heresy, either religious or ethical, and all kindred psychologic, or other constructive injuries, are prohibited, because the very nature of *the law,* whose supremacy and processes our Constitution guarantees, is such that American legislators cannot be permitted to predicate crime upon mere psychologic factors. Manifestly this does not preclude punishment when these psychologic factors have ceased to be *merely* such, by having resulted in actual material injury as distinguished from constructive and speculative injury; for example, it does not preclude punishment in cases of personal libel, or where the uttered opinion has resulted in crime, under such circumstances as to make one an accessory before the fact, or such as proves a conspiracy to secure its commission. Under such circumstances, no man is punished for a mere speech *as such,* nor for its psychologic effect merely as a psychologic effect, but he is punished for his practical contribution toward the actually realized ascertained material injury, the speech being only the evidence of his complicity in the achievement of the resultant invasion and material damage.

I have spent so much space in efforts to clarify the vision as to this phase of constructive crimes because it seeems to me to be very little understood and very often disregarded. In its practical application, no doubt, the tests which I have prescribed will occasionally run counter to certain moral sentimentalizing which, however, we can afford to dispense with, and which our legislators and courts will refuse to regard seriously when we get an enlightened view of liberty. For this class of constructive crimes the responsibility rests primarily with the legislative department. For the others, now to be discussed, the courts are chiefly to blame.

JUDICIAL LEGISLATION UNDER PRETENSE OF INTERPRETATION.

The next class of constructive offenses is a little better understood. Here the act under investigation is one which, under the former tests, may properly be penalized, but is not within the plain letter of the prohibitive statute: First, because the statutory tests of criminality, though certain in meaning and covering acts of the same general character, do not include the conduct under investigation; or, second, because the language of the statute is ambiguous and the act under investigation is not clearly within every possible meaning of the words descriptive of the crime; or third, because the statute is uncertain in that it prescribes no certain and decisive tests of criminality, thus making it necessary, if the statute is to be enforced at all, judicially to interpolate such tests. These are the three classes of judicial legislation which are prohibited in criminal cases by the guarantee of "Due Process of Law."

THE JUDICIAL ENLARGEMENT OF THE STATUTE.

In the first of these instances a judicial enlargement of the field plainly marked out by the statute is so universally recognized as improper, because judicial legislation and therefore within the domain of prohibited constructive offenses, as to need no argumentative support. Indeed, all our judicial rules for the strict construction of criminal statutes are founded upon the necessity of prohibiting judges from creating law.

AMBIGUOUS STATUTES JUDICIALLY AMENDED.

The second case, that of ambiguous penal statutes, oftener seduces judges into an abuse of their power by a misapplication of rules of construction. Where the words descriptive of a crime are ambiguous (open to several interpretations, some or all of which are very certain and definite as to the criteria of guilt), it is erroneously assumed by many courts that it is an exercise of the judicial function of statutory interpretation to select that one among the possible meanings of the statute which is to be enforced. I do not conceive it so. The judicially selected meaning may not be the one which the legislature intended to enact. Certainly it has not received the specific sanction of the legislative branch of the government any more than every other possible interpretation, and the only conduct which can with certainty be known to be within the legislative prohibition (that is within *the law*) are those acts which are clearly within *every possible meaning* of the statute. If this rule has not been always observed in the matter of ambiguous statutes it is because judges have not seen clearly the true relation between such ambiguity and *the law*.

UNCERTAIN STATUTES AND JUDICIAL LEGISLATION.

In the third case, where definitive description of the crime is wholly wanting (as distinguished from ambiguity in the definition), because there is an absence of any certain, clear, universal, and decisive tests of criminality, we have a case for the application of the old maxim: "Where the law is uncertain there is no law." In such case, if the court should supply the tests of criminality so indispensable to the enforcement of every such statute, those tests would not have the sanction of the legislative branch of the government, and therefore could not be *the law,* in any criminal case. Supplying these criteria of guilt is therefore clearly a matter of judicial legislation, by means of statutory interpolation, as distinguished from interpretation, and punishment thereunder is punishment for a constructive offense, and not "due process of law."

If, then, we do as we ought and look to the very nature of our social organism to derive therefrom our conception of law, as that word is used in our state constitutions, and the fifth amendment of our federal constitution, then, because the very essence of "law" is natural justice, and because the establishment of that justice is expressly declared to be the purpose of our constitutions, it follows that "law" must always stand as the destroyer of every vestige of arbitrary power, which is always open to be capriciously exercised or unequally applied, and therefore opens the gates to the worst forms of legalized injustice. In the scientific aspect, the "law" is a general rule of civil conduct (not religious, nor merely self-regarding, nor relating to matters of opinion or of speech so long as the material effect of these terminate with the individual) which rule of *civil conduct* must exist in the nature of things or be duly enacted, in the furtherance of natural justice, by the duly constituted law-making power, and the enactment and its publication must precede the conduct to which it is to be applied; which rule of conduct to be "law" must not do violence to natural justice, and therefore every statute penal in character, or one creating artificial rights, if it is to be "law," from the inherent necessity of its formal statement (not by accidental uniformity in the judicial interpolation or construction) must be general and equal, fixed and certain, as to all persons who in the very nature of things bear the same relationship to one another and to the state; and such statute cannot from its inherent necessity be general and equal in its application to all similarly situated, unless it be also so plain and exact in its description of the right created or the conduct prohibited, and in its criteria of guilt, that every man of average intelligence, from a mere reading of the statute may know with mathematical certainty, in every conceivable state of fact, *why* and *how* his legislatively created

right attaches or lapses, and whether or not his proposed conduct is permitted or penalized; furthermore, a penal statute can predicate an offense and its punishment only upon an actually ascertained material injury, or the imminent danger of such, ascertained according to the known laws of our physical universe, which material injury must be imminent to, or actually realized by, some sentient being, not giving a voluntary, undeceived consent, or one who from immaturity or infirmity is incapacitated for giving that consent. If a statute does not conform to all these requirements, then I believe it cannot be *the law,* and all penalties inflicted under such other statutes are the deprivation of life or property for mere constructive offenses, and cannot constitute "due process of law." We pass now from these general considerations to the more specific consideration of uncertainty in criminal statutes.

CHAPTER XIX.

"DUE PROCESS OF LAW" IN RELATION TO STATUTORY UNCERTAINTY AND CONSTRUCTIVE OFFENSES.

PART II.

General Considerations Concerning Uncertainty and Due Process of Law.[10]

That a deprivation of liberty or property may be due process of law, two things must occur. First, there must be a valid "law," within the meaning of that word in the constitutional phrase "due process of law," and secondly the process prescribed by that law must be accurately pursued. Here I am directly concerned only with one phase of the question: What is essential as to the content of a legislative enactment to make it a criminal "law" within the meaning of the Constitution? Judicial opinions have often commented upon uniformity and universality of application, to all who in the nature of things are similarly situated, as an essential to the very existence of a law. Here it is proposed to discuss only the effect of uncertainty in a criminal statute, as related to the non-existence of "law", because under such uncertain statutes courts must indulge in constitutionally prohibited judicial legislation; and because statutory uncertainty excludes the requirement of unavoidable uniformity of application to all who are naturally similarly situated. In other words, it is proposed to resurrect the ancient maxim, *"Ubi jus incertum ibi jus nullum"* (where the law is uncertain there is no law) and to make it a rule for the interpretation of the "due process of law" clause of our constitutions.

In order that my conclusions may not be discredited by the use of false analogies, I deem it wise to begin with a short analytical statement which will differentiate the problem which I propose to discuss from kindred problems arising from uncertainties of other than criminal statutes, and the probable

[10]Revised from *The Central Law Journal*, Jan. 3, 1908.

different effect which uncertainty may produce in different classes of legislation. Even though the preliminary discussion may be superficial, it seems needful since I have nowhere found any general discussion of the subject.

UNCERTAIN STATUTES CLASSIFIED.

It is conceivable that some civil enactment of a legislature would merely be an effort verbally to declare, and legally to establish and maintain, some rule of natural justice, which is inherent in the nature of things and of the social organism. Uncertainty in such a statute, resulting from an unfortunate choice of words, could do no serious injustice even though the court, either by legitimate construction or judicial legislation, should make it certain, if in doing so nature's rule of justice was not violated, nor artificial penalties inflicted. It is probable that uncertainty in such a statute would not necessarily effectuate its annulment. At any rate, I exclude that class of cases from my discussion. A second class of statutes which might be objected to because of uncertainty, are those which create artificial civil remedies for the maintenance of natural justice. Here again ambiguity and uncertainty can be judicially eliminated in accordance with the legislative intent, if that is reasonably ascertainable from the act itself, and no injury result to innocent parties, because the postulate was that the maintenance of natural justice was the only end to be achieved by the use of this new artificial remedy. For the same reason such laws may also be retroactive.[11]

The third class of uncertain statutes consist of such as declare a rule of justice not derived from nature as such, but finding its foundation in some artificial condition of legislative creation. The limitation of the liability or rights of corporate stockholders might be an illustration. When in such legislation the effect is to curtail the responsibility which naturally should flow from one's act, great exactness in expressing the legislative intent to that effect would be required, since every intendment must be indulged in favor of the natural consequences of one's act operating under natural conditions. But I'm not going to discuss this either. I have mentioned these classes only to point out superficially their probable difference from the next class, so that, in the mind of the reader, my

[11]Chamberlain v. City of Evansville, 77 Ind. 551; Davis v. Ballard, 1 Marshall (Ky.), 579.

argument may not be subjected to unmerited discredit, because of the thoughtless use of false analogies.

The fourth class of legislation, of which uncertainty may be an attribute, includes all those laws which are intended to create and enforce artificial rights or which are punitive in their character. The creation of artificial rights such as arise from the establishment of a public postal system, patent rights, and copyrights, are all laws of this character wherein the statute must describe with the accuracy required for a penal statute upon what conditions the right may vest or be destroyed, else again we are governed by the arbitrary will of men, and not according to *the law*.

The relationship of "due process of law" to an uncertainty in the statutory specification of that which is made punishable by it, is the special matter here to be discussed.

Every State in the union has from one to several score of penal statutes in which no words of exact meaning serve to define with any certainty what it is that is prohibited. In the last thirty years, under only one class of these uncertain statutes, about 5,000 convictions have been secured, and it is fair to assume that under all others, including an infinite variety of vague municipal police regulations, there have been some 20,000 more citizens deprived of liberty and property, and yet seemingly no one has ever doubted that a conviction under such statutes constitutes "due process of law." This makes me wonder if I am dreaming or if the whole rank and file of the bar and judiciary have forgotten the original meaning and purpose of "the law of the land." I do not even except the Supreme Court of the United States, because it, like all the appellate courts of all the states, has repeatedly enforced such laws without a doubt ever crossing its mental horizon, originating either with the court or the attorneys appearing there to argue in such cases.

The most conspicuous and most generally approved examples of these many and outrageously uncertain laws, are those which in various ways penalize "indecent, obscene, filthy or disgusting" literature and art. Those who need to have a concrete example in mind, while the discussion proceeds, may be thinking of those laws as a sample of many others which must be annulled if my contention is correct.

UNCERTAIN AND AMBIGUOUS STATUTES DISTINGUISHED.

First of all we must bear in mind the distinction between an ambiguous statute and an uncertain one. An ambiguous statute I conceive to be one which is expressed in words some of which have several different meanings, all, or some of which meanings, would leave the statutory signification so certain as not to require any additional words to make its meaning plain and uniform beyond doubt, to every man of average intelligence. When that is the case the problem is one of construction, in the method of which due regard is to be had, first for the liberty of citizens and second for the legislative intention, which, however, must be gathered exclusively from the words of the act itself. The rules for statutory construction will always protect the accused, so he shall not be punished if there be any reasonable doubt as to whether his act necessarily comes within the very letter of all of the possible meanings of the statutory prohibition. If it does not come within every possible interpretation of the legislative language, the accused must have the benefit of the doubt under the rule of strict construction. In a statute which is only ambiguous, we can thus avoid all possibility of raising the constitutional question which I am proposing to discuss. If in criminal cases such rules for a strict construction do not safeguard the liberties of citizens, they are convicted under judicial legislation, and not by "due process of law."

By an uncertain statute, as contradistinguished from an ambiguous one, I mean a statute which is uncertain because incomplete in its description of the artificial rights created by it, or the act which it proposes to punish. Thus an uncertain statute is one which, when applied to undisputed facts of past or present existence, is incapable of any literal enforcement, or incapable of enforcement with absolute certainty and uniformity of result, except by the judicial addition of words, or tests, which may or may not have been intended by the legislature, but which are not unavoidable implications from the statutory language alone. It will be contended that such an uncertainty in a statute, creating an artificial right or punishment, makes the enactment unconstitutional because in its practical operation and enforcement it unavoidably involves *ex post facto* judicial legislation in defining the crime, and therefore is not "due process of law," and is an arbitrary government of men and not of *law*.[12]

UNCERTAINTY OF EVIDENCE AND OF LAW DISTINGUISHED.

These generalizations can hardly provoke much antagonism. It therefore seems to me that the difficulty lies chiefly in a clouded vision concerning their application to concrete facts. We shall presently see how in some instances it is not at first clear whether the uncertainty is inherent in the statute or arises from doubt as to the probative value of the evidence adduced under it. We must first take notice of that kind of uncertainty which arises because the statute attempts to make guilt depend, not solely upon facts of present or past existence, but also requires a decision upon an essential element of the crime concerning speculative and problematical tendencies towards future results, of such a character as are undeterminable with accuracy and uniformity by the known laws of the physical universe. Again we must observe the difference between a doubtful sufficiency of evidence to establish a fact of past or present existence, and which beyond all question is of a demonstrable character, and that other case of doubtful sufficiency of evidence to establish a fact, not of past or present material actuality, and one which from its very nature is incapable of certain demonstration, under the known laws of the physical universe, but is by the statute required to be proven as an element of the crime. In the former case the uncertainty of guilt or innocence is not chargeable to uncertainty of the statute. In the latter case it is wholly due to such uncertainty, because a conclusion as to the present existence of an unrealized, non-physical or psychologic tendency, is but an unsupported belief as to the doubtful possibility of a future doubtful event. Where such an uncertainty inheres in the statute itself, and is of the essence of the crime it attempts to define (as is the case with our obscenity statutes and the judicial legislation creating tests of obscenity), then in the very nature of things guilt must always be determined by surmise, speculation, caprice, emotional association, ethical sentimentalizing, moral idiosyncrasies or mere whim on the part of judges or jurors. Punishment for such a "crime," or under such a statute is the arbitrary deprivation of property,

[12]As to the requirement of certainty in laws creative of artificial civil rights, see: Blanchard v. Sprague, Fed. Case No. 1517, and cases; also, Bittle v. Stuart, 34 Ark. 229-232; Ferrett v. Atwill, 1 Blatchford, 157.

or liberty, or both, according to the arbitrary dictates of men not vested with legislative authority, and therefore is not according to "due process of law."

UNCERTAINTY CONCERNING THE "OBSCENE."

In the obscenity statutes there is no question of construing involved verbiage, but solely one of defining the word "obscene." Let us first clearly understand what we mean by a "definition." If the word "water" had been used in a statute, every average man would at once translate that word into the same general mental picture. Every such reader would probably define the word "water" as standing for a certain transparent, odorless fluid, of the identical kind with which he, and every one else, has had abundant experience. There never would arise in any man's mind any doubt as to what concrete concept the general word "water" symbolized, even though it might become a matter of inquiry whether a particular substance was water or peroxide of hydrogen. That doubt is not as to the meaning of the word, but one concerning the past or present existence of the corresponding objective fact; one of classifying the matter as water. When such an issue has arisen we do not resort to a definition of the word, for the purpose of making certain what concept the word "water" was intended to convey; instead, we call in experts to apply the chemical tests by which the objective material, "water," is differentiated from peroxide of hydrogen.

To determine the classification of a particular substance we apply mathematically exact and always uniform tests, not created by statute and not a part of a judicial definition of any word used in the statute. If such exact tests exist in the nature of things there will be no occasion for legislatures or courts to prescribe them. If they do not exist in the nature of things perhaps the legislature has the right and power to create its own artificial tests or definitions, but in a criminal statute they must be of equal certainty with the ascertained laws of the physical universe. If neither science nor the statute furnishes us with a definite test by which to determine the existence of those things expressed by statutory words and which are essential to a definition of a crime, then the law is void for uncertainty and the lack of statutory tests of criminality cannot be supplied by the courts since that would be judicial penal legislation, and *ex post facto* at that.

If such tests were not a matter of exact science, but merely a matter of speculation, or necessary judicial creation in the attempt to enforce such an uncertain law, then they would be unconstitutional judicial legislation and not definition nor statutory interpretation. Furthermore, if such tests were not of mathematical certainty, then the law would be a nullity because "where the law is uncertain, there is no law." Let us now keep in mind the word "water" (in contrast with the word "obscene"), and the character of those differentiating tests, not of statutory origin, nor necessarily implied in the statutory words, but by which we, as a matter of physical science, distinguish the substances of that for which the words stand.

With the foregoing distinction in mind, I affirm that no human can define the word "obscene" so that every reader, even with the help of the test, or definition, must receive therefrom the same concrete mental picture. The reason obviously is, that unlike the word "water," the word "obscene" stands for no particular concrete objective quality, but always and ever stands for an abstraction, in which is generalized only subjective states, associated with an infinite variety of objectives, and therefore in the concrete it will always have a different significance for every individual, according to what he has personally abstracted, from his peculiar and personal experience, and classified according to his own associated emotions of disapproval, and included within his personal generalization, "obscene." Each individual therefore reaches a judgment about obscenity according to his own ever-varying experiences, and the peculiarly personal emotional associations (of approval or disapproval) which are evolved from these, as well as the degrees of his sexual hyperaestheticism.

From this indisputable fact, it follows that the word "obscene" is indefinable as a matter of science and the criminal statute, of which that word is an indispensable element, is void, because "where the law is uncertain there is no law," and no "due process of law."

We must make still clearer, if possible, the difference between the uncertainty of the "obscene" and other remotely similar uncertainties. Some will ask, Is not the uncertainty of the existence of a special intent, which sometimes is made an essential element of a crime, just as uncertain as the unrealized psychologic tendencies of a book, which are the judicial test of its obscenity? I answer "No!" The existence of that intent as to past acts is in its nature a demonstrable fact. The accused, if he would tell the truth, could settle it beyond a doubt. Here the uncertainty is one of evidence not of statutory tests of crime. An unrealized psychologic potential tendency of a book upon its hypothetical future reader has only a speculative future existence, not determinable with exactness by any known law of the physical universe, and therefore is not a demonstrable fact, but one that we only guess at, and as to which neither the accused, nor any one else, can furnish certain information, nor have any certain advance knowledge as to just exactly what will induce the court or jury to judge it to be criminal. The criminal intent of a man charged with crime is a fact which in point of time antedates the indictment and verdict, and has such prior existence objectively to the mind of the juror or trial court. Not so with obscenity. The test by which juries are instructed to determine the existence of "obscenity" depends upon their speculation about the psychologic tendency of a particular book upon a future hypothetical reader, which tendency has not yet become actualized at the time of indictment or trial, and which psychologic tendency is not known to us to be controlled by any exact known law having the immutability of the physical laws of our material universe. It follows that, unlike specific intent, which is a demonstrable fact of past existence and objective to the mind of the court, the unrealized psychologic tendency by which a particular book is judged "obscene" has no demonstrable existence except as a belief about a doubtful future possibility, and exists exclusively as a mere belief in the mind of the trial judge or jury, and without any known proven or provable present, corresponding objective. Such an uncertainty is one of law and not of evidence, because it arises out of the fact that the statute (or the judicial legislation under it as to the tests of obscenity) predicates guilt upon a conclusion about an undemonstrable factor of speculative future existence.

No legislature has the power to penalize travel in an automobile at a "dangerous speed," and leave to the trial court or jury to say in each case whether the speed is dangerous or not. What is a "dangerous" speed is a legitimate subject for the exercise of legislative discretion, and is determinable only by the legislature, and its authority cannot be delegated to the varying judgments of varying juries. So likewise what is to be deemed of dangerous moral tendency is a matter exclusively of legislative discretion, and must be determined and definitely fixed by decisive definition of the law-enacting power, and the formulation of tests cannot be delegated to the varying judgments of varying courts or juries. Since the "obscenity" of a book is not by the statute defined to consist in any of its sense-perceived qualities and since therefore the legislature has not completed nor expressed its legislative discretion to decide what is deemed to be of "dangerous tendencies," and since that legislative function cannot be delegated to the jury or judge to be exercised *ex post facto* or otherwise, it follows that there is no law upon the subject and no due process of law in any such prosecution.

ON THE CERTAINTY ESSENTIAL TO THE VALIDITY OF A CRIMINAL STATUTE AGAINST OBSCENITY.

To constitute a valid criminal law the statute under consideration must so precisely define the distinguishing characteristics of the prohibited degree of "obscenity" that guilt may be accurately and without doubt ascertained by taking the statutory description of the penalized qualities and solely by these determine their existence in the physical attributes inherent in the printed page. Judicial tests of "obscenity" cannot be read into the statutory words. Nor can official or judicial speculations (of a character not calculated to discover such definitely penalized physical qualities in the book), be permitted so long as they deal only with a mere unrealized psychologic potentiality for influencing in the future some mere hypothetical person. Such speculative psychologic tendencies are never found with certainty in any book, but are read into it, with all the uncertainty of the *a priori* method, as an excuse for a verdict of guilty. Even if the legislative body attempted to authorize such a procedure it would be a nullity under the maxim, "Where the law is uncertain there is no law." Therefore, such procedure cannot be "due process of law." An unrealized psychologic tendency cannot be made the differential test of criminality, even though we should admit that such a tendency may properly appeal to the legislative discretion and may properly result in penal laws wherein the statutes and not the courts specifiy the tests, definite and certain, by which to determine what it is that is deemed to possess the criminal degree of such dangerous tendency.

GENERAL STATEMENT AS TO THE REQUIRED CERTAINTY OF CRIMINAL STATUTES.

We now come to the contention that a criminal statute cannot constitute "due process of law," unless it is general, uniform, fixed and certain. These qualities are more or less related, since if a law is not fixed and certain it can seldom be general and uniform in its application. Now we are specially interested to get a more condensed summary as to what is meant by the requirement of fixity and certainty, in a statute.

Our claim is that a criminal statute, to constitute "due process of law," must define the crime in terms so plain, and simple, as to be within the comprehension of the ordinary citizen, and so exact in meaning as to leave in him no reasonable doubt as to what is prohibited. Those qualities of generality, uniformity, and certainty, must arise as an unavoidable necessity out of the very letter of the definition framed by the law-enacting power, and not come as an incidental result, from an accidental uniformity in the exercise, by courts, of an unconstitutionally delegated legislative discretion. If a statute defining a crime is not self-explanatory, but needs interpretation or the interpolation of words or tests to insure certainty of meaning, or because its ambiguity permits of more than one judicial interpretation, then it is not *"the law of the land,"* because no such selected interpretation of the courts has ever received the necessary sanction of the three separate branches of legislative power, whose members alone are authorized and sworn to define crimes and ordain their punishment. Laws defining crimes are required to be made by the law-making branch of government because of the necessity for limiting and destroying arbitrariness and judicial discretion in such matters. That is what we mean when we say ours is a government by law and not by men. It follows that it is not enough that uniformity and certainty shall come as the product of judicial discretion, since "law" is necessary for the very purpose of destroying such discretion in determining what is punishable.

CHAPTER XX.

"DUE PROCESS OF LAW" IN RELATION TO STATUTORY UNCERTAINTY AND CONSTRUCTIVE OFFENSES.

PART III.

Historical Interpretation of "Law" in Relation to Statutory Certainty.[13]

As I view history, the evolution of organized government toward liberty, especially in its relation to laws which are penal in character, is clearly divided into three general stages of tendency. The first of these manifests itself in the effort to restrain autocratic sovereigns and their minions in the arbitrariness of their power to punish, by subjecting their wills and penalties to the authority of prior known rules or laws. The second step in this evolution toward liberty is to curtail the authority of the lawmaking power as to the manner of its exercise, so that it may not, even under the forms of law, violate that natural justice which requires uniformity of the law in its application to all those who in the nature of things are similarly situated, which uniformity, of course, is impossible unless the law is certain in the definition of what is prohibited. The third tendency is marked by the curtailment of the legislative power as to the subject matter of its control, so as to conserve a larger human liberty by excluding certain conduct —and progressively an increasing quantum thereof—from all possible governmental regulation, even by general, uniform and certain laws. This should later limit legislation to the prohibition of only such conduct as in the nature of things necessarily involves an invasion of the liberty of another, to his material and ascertainable injury. I have no doubt it was such a government, of limited power to regulate human affairs, that the framers of American constitutions intended to establish.

The stage before the evolution above indicated we gener-

[13]Revised from *The Albany Law Journal*, April, 1908.

ally term a lawless government of men, in contradistinction to a government by men according to law, and such a government of men is always despotic and arbitrary, although it may at times be a relative benevolent despotism. The first advance means a government by men according to prior established rules, which rules may be as invasive and unjust as the legislative power sees fit to make them. This condition is aptly described as tyranny by the laws, of which we find many examples all around us. The second progressive stage is that wherein men strive to limit the exercise of the law-making power so that it may not, even under the forms of law, do violence to that natural justice which demands definiteness and uniformity affecting those who are similarly accused.

The third stage wherein the legislative power is limited to the suppression of acts which are necessarily, directly, and immediately, invasive, is aptly termed liberty under the law. Our present stage of evolution, so far as the leaders of thought are concerned, is probably to be located near the beginnings of this stage, and in the course of a few thousands of years we may attain to something approximating real liberty under the law; and in another million years we may attain to the Anarchist ideal, which is liberty without law, made possible because no one has the inclination to invade his neighbor, and all are agreed as to what constitutes an invasion. The great mass of Americans, and humans generally, are now in that stage of their development which compels a love of tyranny under the forms of law—a tyranny tempered only by the discretion of the ignorant, such as know nothing of liberty in the sense of an acknowledged claim of right to remain exempt from authority.

The transition from despotism to government by law in its earlier stages is marked by the misleading seemings of law, which, however, are devoid of all its essence. This is illustrated in many of the miscalled laws of the Russian Tsar, and also in the Chinese code, which latter prescribes a punishment for all those who shall be found guilty of "improper conduct," without supplying any further criterion or test of guilt. Manifestly under such authority the magistrates are justified in punishing anything which whim, caprice, or malice might prompt them to adjudge "improper." Accordingly, we have a state of affairs wherein under the misleading appearances of law everything is condemned, and the arbitrary will of the officers of the State again creates the penalty instead of merely enforcing *"the law"* as they find it. Thus, while observing the outward forms and seemings of law, the people are still governed by the mere despotic wills of officials.

Upon the questions as to what are all the essentials of *law,* and what are the limits of liberty, we still have, in the main, very crude thinking and perhaps still more crude efforts toward generalizations. So far as my investigations have informed me, no court has had the confident clarity of vision to even attempt the formulation of a comprehensive general statement as to the limits of liberty and governmental control. This of course means that our judges are still in that early stage of their intellectual development wherein this branch of the law has not become a science. However, it is a most deplorable state of mind which too often impels courts to confess to the permanent intellectual bankruptcy of the judiciary by asserting that such definitive generalizations are impossible.

The present purpose is to inquire into the historical verdict as to the reasons which make *law* a necessity and especially the verdict of all lovers of liberty as to the degree of certainty required to make a penal statute THE LAW, and its enforcement "due process of law." The method will be to exhibit the facts and the authoritative declarations concerning this question as these appear in our juridical history. This fragmentary material often includes very crude statements of imperfectly conceived principles, as well as mere empirical generalizations, but out of it we will later erect a rational generalization, and this will be done so far as is necessary to determine the degree of certainty required in *the law,* as the same is formulated in penal statutes.

I confess that it seems to me as though men claiming to be learned in the law should be presumed to know all that follows, and yet it is self-evident that they do not. I say self-evident, because the fact is notorious that among the many uncertain criminal statutes those only which are directed against "obscene, indecent, filthy or disgusting" literature and art, which words are as vague as a London fog, have resulted in over 5000 persons being deprived of life, liberty, or property, and yet it seems *hardly* to have occurred to any one connected with these cases to question the constitutionality of those laws because of their uncertainty. Such facts, and numerous equally vague statutes and municipal ordinances which are continually being enforced, without having their constitutionality questioned, demonstrate that the intelligence of the profession in general has not yet risen to the point where there is any need to apologize for attempting to enlighten its members concerning the constitutional requirement of certainty in penal statutes.

EARLY WRITERS ON THE NECESSITY OF LAW.

John Adams, in "A Defense of the Constitution and Government of the United States," defends at some length the proposition that even under laws to which all are equally subject the Majority may oppress the minority. In this connection he speculates about the meaning and limits of liberty, in the course of which discussion he quotes from numerous old authors about the necessity of a government according to *law* to prevent the tyranny of arbitrary punishments by the magistrate. I will now reproduce some of Mr. Adams' quotations and speculations, asking the reader as he scans these quotations concerning the necessity for having princes and judges govern according to *law,* always to bear in mind the essential nature of *the law,* in contradistinction to arbitrary edicts.

"It is weakness rather than wickedness which renders men unfit to be trusted with unlimited power. * * * Junius says: 'Laws are intended, not to trust to what men will do, but to guard against what they may do.' Aristotle says that 'A government where the Laws alone should prevail, would be the kingdom of God.' This indeed shows that this great philosopher had much admiration for such a government. Aristotle says, too, in another place, 'Order is law, and it is more proper that *law* should govern, than any one of the citizens; upon the same principal, if it is advantageous to place the supreme power in some particular persons, they should be appointed to be only guardians, and the servants of the laws.' These two are very just sentiments, but not a formal definition of liberty. Livy, too, speaks of happy, prosperous, and glorious times, when *'Imperia legum potentiora fuerant quan hominum.'* But he nowhere says that liberty consists in being subject only to the *legum imperio.* Sidney says, 'No sedition was hurtful to Rome, 'until through their prosperity some men gained a power above the laws.' In another place he tells us too, from Livy, that some, whose ambition and avarice were impatient of restraint, complained that *'leges rem surdam esse, inexorabilem, salubriorem inopi quam potenti.'* And in another that no government was thought to be well constituted 'unless the laws prevailed against the commands of men.' But he has nowhere defined liberty to be subjection to the laws only. Harrington says, 'Government *de jure*, or according to ancient prudence, is an art, whereby a civil society of men is instituted and preserved upon the foundation of common interest, or, to follow Aristotle, and Livy, it is an empire of laws and not of men.' And government, to define it according to modern prudence, or *de facto*, is an art, by which some man, or some few men, subject a city or a nation, and rule it according to his or their private interest, which, because the laws in such cases are made according to the interest of a man, or a few families, may be said to be the empire of man, and not of laws. Sidney says, 'Liberty consists solely in an independency on [of] the will of another, and, by a slave, we understand a man who can neither dispose of his person or goods, but enjoys all at the will of his master.' And again, 'As liberty consists only in being subject to no man's will and nothing denotes a slave but a dependence upon the will of another; if there be no other law in a kingdom but the will of a prince [or of the judiciary] there is no such thing as liberty!' "[14]

It appears sufficiently evident from these past contentions for liberty that the necessity for statutes in criminal cases arises out of the necessity for strengthening the weakness and curbing the passions of judges, who, according to all experiences and while remaining human, cannot be safely trusted with arbitrary power to determine what shall be punishable. Since such are the reasons uniformly assigned by the older philosophers for their insistence upon subjecting the will of judges to *law*, it follows that criminal statutes fall short of satisfying the demand for *law*, if by their uncertainty they compel, or permit, judges to exercise a discretion in framing tests of criminality such as are not specifically written into the very words of the penal code.

Let us now briefly trace these same influences in the origin of Magna Charta and the English conception of "the law of

[14]"A Defense of the Constitution," etc., letter XXVI in Vol. 1.

OBSCENE LITERATURE AND CONSTITUTIONAL LAW.

the land." This of course is re-stated, without being altered, in our American constitutional guarantee of "due process of law." A little farther on we consider the later unfoldment of the judicial interpretation of "law."

MAGNA CHARTA AND "THE LAW OF THE LAND."

The ancient prohibition against an infliction of penalties "without due process of law," or, what usually amounts to the same thing, those inflicted under "ex post facto laws," or for mere constructive injuries or crime, was the most essential and fundamental guarantee of an Englishman's liberty.

King John, we are told, filled his coffers by confiscation and cruel extortions. He invited dignitaries to London, then declared them prisoners until they should pay large fines. These penalties were not inflicted for offenses against any general or prior known laws, such that with certainty could have informed the citizens in advance that their conduct was illegal, or warn them of the penalty thereof. "Liberty of all kinds was vendible in the reign of John" precisely because there was no law, in the sense of general rules with undoubted certainty of meaning, to define the limits of liberty or furnish a refuge of defense for the citizen in the exercise of his liberty, or to curtail the arbitrary power of a tyrant King, or his judiciary.

To prevent this lawlessness of official power as exemplified in the arbitrary infliction of penalties, the barons by force exacted the Magna Charta. In that document, as confirmed by Henry the III and Edward I, we find it stated that "No free-man shall be taken or imprisoned or disseized of his freehold or liberties, * * * but by lawful judgment of his peers or by the law of the land."[15] If read in the light of the historical facts which brought this into being, it is manifest that the primal purpose of all this was that no man might be deprived of his property or liberty or be tricked into criminality by any unknown or uncertain rules, such as would not warn him in advance, and with unerring certainty, that his conduct was prohibited.

The Magna Charta required only that criminal statutes should be certain and general. It did not yet by its strict letter prevent their being made so after the fact charged as crime, if the King and Parliament saw fit then to prescribe a punish-

[15]Chap. 29 Magna Charta.

ment. This furnished the opportunity for shifty tyrants to evade the spirit of Magna Charta, and they did it. In the 25th Edward III, a law provided thus: "It is accorded, that if any case, *supposed* treason, which is not above specified, doeth happen before any justices, the justices shall tarry without any going to judgment of the treason, till the cause be showed and declared before the King and his Parliament whether it ought to be judged treason or other felony."[16] Thus tyrants kept the letter of the "due process of law" provision of Magna Charta, and yet accomplished quite effectively the repudiation of its spirit and of the very essence of *law*, and thus they again successfully destroyed liberty. From such circumstances grew the demand which resulted in a charter-prohibition against *ex post facto* laws.

However, the tyrants are always fertile in the evasion of charters and constitutions, such as are intended to limit their arbitrary power and correspondingly to protect the citizen against official invasion. So next we find men imprisoned under the authority of a special royal commission, which implied a process similar to our present occasional executive legislation. There were not wanting Judges who, impelled by a lust for power or even more base motives, were ready to affirm the validity of such evasions of the English Charters of Liberty, by the judicial engraftment of exceptions, called "martial law." And so it became necessary to make English liberties more safe, by perfecting the Writ of Habeas Corpus, and securing the re-affirmance of the former safeguards of liberty. In all of the English charters of liberty, and their various re-affirmations, one principle is always discernable in the use of such words as "due process of law," and the "law of the land." It was not the purpose to change the person of the despot, or to transfer despotic power from an autocrat to the judiciary; neither was it intended merely to influence those vested with despotic power to change the mode of exercising their discretion under it. On the contrary, the plain purpose was to destroy the discretion itself, so as, at the trial of an accused, to preclude every possibility of an arbitrary judicial determination as to what should be the criminal statutes as applied to his acts. All along the history of these stormy times, it is made plain that the charter phrases, for the protection of liberty, were designed to mean that no

[16]English Liberties 64.

man should be deprived of liberty or property except by a prior, duly enacted, publicly promulgated law, which to be *"law"* must be general in terms, equal in its application to all who in the nature of things are similarly situated, and to accomplish this it must be so certain as to its meaning that no man of ordinary intelligence could be misled by it. The manifest intention was to safeguard liberty, against every arbitrary determination of guilt, in a manner that could not be realized if an enactment should lack any of these qualities, and in consequence we must say that a conviction under such statute would not be according to *the law,* and therefore would not be within Magna Charta or our own constitutionally guaranteed "due process of law." If a statute defines a crime in uncertain terms, a judge who, under the pretext of construing it, should attempt to supply the absent but necessary certainty of meaning, through judicially created tests of criminality, then, as to the person on trial, such a judge would be enacting an *ex post facto law.* If such judicial legislation should thereafter be uniform in all subsequent cases, the uniformity would still be a matter of accidental uniformity in the exercise of arbitrary judicial legislation, and not a compulsory uniformity imposed by definite and certain legislative enactment. Even under uniformity of judicial legislation there would still be the absence of that unavoidable uniformity which should result from subjecting the judicial will to the certainty of a statute and which compulsory conformity is an indispensable requirement of "law," and of "due process of law." Now let as inquire how far this interpretation of the historical events harmonizes with the views of the early writers, interpreting the charter phrases which were incorporated into our constitution. Here let it be remembered that our constitutional guarantee of "due process of law" was adopted after most of the following construction had been placed upon the word "law," and probably because of these constructions.

THE EARLY LAW WRITERS ON THE MEANING OF "LAW."

"Every law may be said to consist of several parts: One declaratory, whereby the right to be observed, and the wrong to be eschewed, are *clearly defined* and laid down."[17]

Although there is much in Montesquieu's "Spirit of the

---

[17]Blackstone in his Introduction, Book 1, p. 55.

Laws" that we have outgrown, yet he was the precursor of most that is good in modern political institutions, and, as it appears by the frequent references to him in The Federalist, his book did much to shape our own constitution. It is nearly two centuries since he wrote:

"Under moderate governments, the law is prudent in all its parts, and *perfectly well known,* so that even the pettiest magistrates are capable of following it. But in a despotic state, where the prince's will is the law; though the prince were wise, yet how could the magistrate follow a will he does not know? He must certainly follow his own.[18] In despotic governments there are no laws, the judge himself is his own rule."[19]

The following words, also from Montesquieu, show what the contest for certainty of the law meant with special reference to intellectual crimes, and, with a very few verbal changes, will be seen to bear with unusual force against the validity of our present obscenity laws. He said: "Nothing renders the crime of high treason [and we may add obscenity] more arbitrary than declaring people guilty of it for indiscreet speeches. Speech is so subject to interpretation; there is so great a difference between indiscretion and malice; and frequently little is there of the latter in the freedom of expression, that the law can hardly subject people to a capital punishment for words *unless it expressly declares what words they are.* Words do not constitute an overt act; they remain only in idea. When considered by themselves, they have generally no determinate signification, for this depends on the tone in which they are uttered. It often happens that in repeating the same words they have not the same meaning; this depends on their connection with other things, and sometimes more is signified by silence then by any expression whatever. *Since there can be nothing so equivocal and ambiguous as all this, how is it possible to convert it into a crime of high treason? Wherever this law is established, there is an end not only of liberty, but ever of its very shadow."[20]* Italics are mine, usually, in all these quotations, T. S.

Beccaria, who profited by studying Montesquieu, also elab-

[18]Aldine Edition, Vol. 38, p. 79.
[19]Vol. 1 Aldine Edition, p. 19.
[20]The Spirit of the Law, v. 1, p. 232, Aldine Edition.

orates this theme of the necessity of certainty of law as a condition of liberty. In part he wrote as follows:

"Judges, in criminal cases, have no right to interpret the penal laws, because they are not legislators. They have not received the laws from our ancestors as a domestic tradition, or as the will of a testator, which his heirs, and executors, are to obey; but they receive them from a society actually existing, or from the sovereign, its representative. * * * There is nothing more dangerous than the common axiom: The spirit of the laws is to be considered. To adopt it is to give way to the torrent of opinions. This may seem a paradox to vulgar minds, which are more strongly affected by the smallest disorder before their eyes, than by the most pernicious, though remote, consequence produced by one false principle adopted by a nation. *When the rule of right which ought to direct the actions of the philosophers, as well as the ignorant, is a matter of controversy, not of fact, the people are slaves to the magistrate. If the power of interpreting laws be an evil, obscurity in them must be another, as the former is the consequence of the latter.* This evil will be still greater if the laws be written in a language unknown to the people; who, being ignorant of the consequences of their own actions, *become necessarily dependent on a few, who are interpreters of the laws, which instead of being public, and general, are thus rendered private and particular.* If this magistrate should act in an arbitrary manner, and not in conformity to the code of laws, which ought to be in the hands of every member of the community, he opens a door to tyranny, which always surrounds the confines of political liberty. *I do not know of any exception to this general axiom, that every member of society should know when he is criminal, and when innocent.* If censors, and, in general, arbitrary magistrates, be necessary in any government, it proceeds from some fault in the constitution. *The uncertainty of crimes hath sacrificed more victims to secret tyranny than have ever suffered by public and solemn cruelty.*

"No Magistrate then (as he is one of the society) can, with justice, inflict on any other member of the same society *punishment that is not ordained by law. Judges in criminal cases have no right to interpret the penal laws, because they are not legislators.* Who then is their lawful interpreter? The sovereign that is the representative of society, *and not the judge, whose office is only to examine if a man have or have not committed an action contrary to the law.*"[21]

An American commentator writing before the Revolution defines "The law of the land" to mean, By the common law or by the statute law, by the due course and process of law. He quotes Lord Coke as thus interpreting the clause in question, "the law is the surest sanctuary that a man can take, and the strongest fortress to protect the weakest of all. * * * No man is deceived while the law is his buckler. * * * The law is called right because it discovereth that which is crooked or wrong; for as right signifieth law, so crooked or wrong signifieth injuries; injury is against right. A right line is both declaratory of itself and the oblique. *Hereby the crooked chord of that which is called discretion appeareth to be unlawful,* unless you take it as it ought to be, *discreti est discerne per legem, quid sit justum*—discretion is to discern by the law what is just."[22]

"It is the function of a judge not to make but to declare the law according to the golden metewand of the law, and not by the crooked cord of discretion." Coke.

It must be apparent from this conception of "law" that under "due process of law" as used in the English charters and defined before the days of our constitution, and with such interpretation incorporated into these constitutions, no man can be deprived of property or liberty for acts made criminal, by any exercise of power, which seeks to invest either judges or juries, either directly or indirectly, with a discretion to determine whether or not any undisputed act shall be penalized; but, on the contrary, the very essence of *"law"* in "due process of law," in criminal cases at least, is that *all such discretion shall be destroyed by the very explicitness of the law itself,* and that all juridical discretion shall be limited to discovering the facts and discerning solely from the letter of the law whether these ascertained facts constitute a crime. Only thus can statutes curb the tyranny of arbitrary judicial power. Here is another authoritative statement as to the requirement of the law, which again is a prerevolutionary authority, in the light of which our constitutional phrase must have been adopted.

[21]An Essay on Crimes and their Punishment. (Edition of 1775) pp. 12-41.
[22]English Liberties, by Henry Carr and William Nelson, pp. 21 to 27. Providence, R. I., 1774.) 2 Coke's Institutes, marginal page 56.

"It is further essential to political freedom *that the laws be clearly obvious to common understanding,* and fully notified to the people. * * * When the people first learn the law by fatal experience, they feel as if the judge was in effect legislator, and as if life and liberty were subjected to arbitrary control. * * * *The same will be the consequences where the law is imperfectly and indefinitely expressed.* The style thereof should be clear, and as concise as is consistent with clearness; general terms also should be particularly avoided, as liable to become the instruments of oppression. Under the Act 14 Geo. 11 c. 6, stealing sheep *'or other cattle'* was made felony without benefit of clergy; but those general words 'or other cattle' being considered as too vague to create a capital offense, the act was properly holden to extend only to sheep."[23]

That judicial interpretation of "Law" just quoted was adopted into our constitutional guarantee of "Due Process of law," and, measured by that standard, all uncertain criminal statutes must be annulled because not *"Law"* and not constituting "due process of law."

In the debates of the English Parliament frequent references can be found in which certainty of the law is advocated. (See 4 Parliamentary History, pp. 115-117-118 for illustrations). In 1792 (Stat. 32 Geo. 111, c. 60) was passed the act which in cases of criminal libel made the jury the judge of both law and fact. Before this (in 1784) an English court denounced uncertainty of the law of libels or its administration in no uncertain terms. Here is the language officially reported.

"Miserable is the condition of individuals, dangerous is the condition of the state, if there is *no certain law,* (or which is the same thing) no certain adminstration of law, to protect individuals or to guard the state. * * * Under such an administration of the law *no man could tell, no counsel could advise, whether a paper were or were not punishable. I am glad that I am not bound to subscribe to such an absurity, such a solecism in politics."*[25]

If the English courts have not so uniformly ignored uncertain statutes as might be desired, the explanation may perhaps be found in the fact that Magna Charta is a limitation upon only the sovereign, and not upon Parliament, in the sense

[23]Lord Auckland's Principles of Penal Law. pp. 312-314 (1771).
[25]King v. Dean of St. Asaph, 3 Terms Rep. 431. (1784)

in which our American constitutions operate to limit legislative power. If therefore English courts, because of uncertainty, are to annul an enactment of Parliament, the justification therefore can be found only in the very nature of their institutions, without any fundamental written authority making such natural law a limitation upon legislative power.

Erskine, although he did not believe in an unabridged freedom of speech, did believe in more such liberty than was current in his time, and he did believe in "Law" in the true sense. I think it worth while in this connection to quote a few paragraphs from his speech in defense of Lord George Gordon, as illustrating his view of the point now under discussion. He said:

"In nothing [else] is the wisdom and justice of our laws so strongly and eminently manifested, as in the rigid, accurate, cautious, explicit, unequivocal definition of what shall constitute this offense. * * *

"If treason, where the government itself is directly offended, were left to the judgment of its ministers, without any boundaries—nay, without the most broad, distinct and inviolable boundaries marked out by law—there could be no public freedom—and the condition of an Englishman would be no better than a slave's at the foot of a Sultan; since there is little difference whether a man dies by the stroke of a sabre, without the forms of a trial, or by the most pompous ceremonies of justice, if the crime could be made at pleasure by the state to fit the fact that was to be tried. * * *

"A long list of new treasons, accumulated in the wretched reign of Richard the Second, from which (to use the language of the act that repealed them) 'No man knew what to do or say for doubt of the pains of death,' were swept away in the first year of Henry the Fourth, his successor; and many more, which had again sprung up in the following distracted arbitrary reigns. * * *

"This wise restriction [against arbitrary judicial determination of what shall be treason] has been the subject of much just eulogium by all the most celebrated writers on the criminal law of England. Lord Coke says, 'The Parliament that made it was on that account called Benedictum or Blessed'; and the learned and virtuous Judge Hale, a bitter enemy and opposer of constructive treasons, speaks of this sacred institution with that enthusiasm which it cannot but inspire in the breast of every lover of the just privileges of mankind."

Again in his argument insisting on the definiteness of the law, he contends that it shall "be extended by no new or occasional constructions—to be strained by no fancied analogies—to be measured by no rules of political expediency—to be judged by no theory—to be determined by the wisdom of no individual, however wise—but to be expounded by the simple genuine LETTER of the law."[26]

Although Erskine lauded the certainty of the statute, and no doubt thought it at least certain enough to preclude the conviction of his client, Lord Gordon, we still find an abundance of complaint, after his time. Here is a sample taken from a protest of the Peers in 1819. "The offense of publishing a libel is, more than any other that is known to our law, undefined and uncertain. Publications which at one time may be considered innocent and even laudible may at another, according to circumstances and the different view of public accusers, of judges and of juries, be thought to be deserving of punishment, and thus the author or publisher of any writing dictated by the purest intentions on a matter of public interest, without any example to warn, any definition to instruct, or any authority to guide him, may expose himself to a long imprisonment and a heavy fine."[27]

THE MAXIM REQUIRING CERTAINTY.

From such solicitude for that liberty which ever depends upon the certainty of meaning in the criminal statute came the ancient maxim: *Ubi jus incertum, ibi jus nullum*—"Where the law is uncertain, there is no law."[28]

Here it is important that we examine a little further into the importance of maxims in general and this last one quoted in particular: "All great judges and writers have been led by maxims. * * * Where the maxims lead and illumine the great ends of jurisprudence have been advanced; constitutions and their implications have been respected. Judges who understand, respect and cite maxims, save great principles from clouds of doubt and miserable equivocation. * * * Nothing more greatly obstructs usurpation, abuse of power, and arbitrariness in its edicts than do maxims. * * * All

[26]Erskine's Speeches, Vol. 1, pp. 72 to 78. Edition of 1810.
[27]41 Parl. Deb. 747.
[28]Black's Law Dictionary, p. 1196; Bouvier's Law Dictionary, Rawl's Revision v. 2, p. 381.

of the admittedly authentic maxims are expressions of mercy, reason and moderation, and are often highly Christain in spirit and suggestion. Lovers of liberty consecrate the maxims, oppressors desecrate them. * * * Maxims are the condensed good sense of all nations. They are the essence of wisdom in all ages. Whenever the law is the perfection of reason, they are not excluded but they must necessarily be included. Jurisprudence can lay claim to no other element so lustrous, so illuminating and attractive, as its great fundamental maxims."[29]

Upon the subject of the particular maxim with which we are now concerned, namely "where the law is uncertain, there is no law," Mr. Hughes, among other things, has this to say, all of which is applicable to our present judicially enacted tests of the "obscene, indecent, filthy and disgusting" literature and art.

"Where the rule is alternating, as antipathy or affection, caprice or whim dictates, there is no law. And so it is where for one the foundation for a judgment must be one kind of matter, and for another, a different. Where for one there must be allegations and proofs and for another anything, even palpably sham and false statements."

Concerning jurisprudence, he says: "Its value depends on a fixed and uniform rule of action. * * * If water at one time would extinguish fire and at another would spread a conflagration; if on one day it would bring life and the next death, its value would be destroyed. * * * And so it is in language, when words have no fixed meaning. * * * Those who rule in disregard of obligation and reason, may be likened to the sailor who bores a hole in the ship upon which the safety of all depends."[30]

POST-REVOLUTIONARY DISCUSSION ON REQUIREMENTS OF THE LAW

Alexander Hamilton in discussing this subject, among other things wrote: "I agree [with Montesquieu] that there is no liberty if the power of judging be not separated from the legislative and executive powers. [p. 484.] *To avoid an arbitrary discretion in the courts, it is indispensable that they should be bound down by strict rules and precedents, which serve to define and point out their duty in every particular case that*

---

[29]Hughes on Procedure v. 2, pp. 1003-1007; see also, Coke on Littleton, 11, a, (marginal).

[30]Hughes on Procedure, v. 2, p. 1237.

comes before them; * * * The creation of crimes after the commission of the fact, or, in other words, the subjecting of men to punishment for things which, when they were done, were breaches of no law [or could not have been ascertained to be such because of the uncertainty of the statute]; and the practice of arbitrary imprisonment have been in all ages the favorite and most formidable instruments of tyranny. [p. 490.] The courts must declare the sense of the law; and if they should be disposed to exercise will instead of judgment, the consequence would equally be the substitution of their pleasure to [for] that of the legislative body." [p. 487.][30a]

"It is law which has hitherto been regarded in countries calling themselves civilized, as the standard by which to measure all offenses and irregularities that fall under public animadversion. * * * It [the law] has been recommended as 'affording information to the different members of the community respecting the principles which will be adopted in deciding upon their actions. It has been represented as the highest degree of inequity to try men by *ex post facto* law, or indeed in any other manner than by the letter of a law, formally made and sufficiently promulgated.' "[31]

Prof. Thomas Cooper quotes with approval the following words of Richard Carlile (about A. D., 1820), which have as direct and certain applications to the uncertain meaning of "obscene" as to the uncertainty about the meaning of "blasphemy" or "Christianity." Carlile wrote: "No one can understand what is meant by blasphemous publications, or by Christianity; and what no one can understand, no law can justly take cognizance of, or support."[32]

Before this Blackstone had made a similar protest against the heresy statutes, although he approved of most of the superstitions of his time, including witchcraft and the prosecutions for heresies and blasphemy, yet he had too good a legal mind not to see the evils of uncertainty as to the criteria of guilt, even in laws the object of which he approved. He says:

"What doctrines shall therefore be adjudged heresy was left by our constitution to the determination of the ecclesiastical judge who had herein a most arbitrary latitude al-

[30a]The Federalist, at pages indicated.
[31]2, Godwin's Political Justice, p. 289. (A. D., 1796.)
[32]Laws of Libel and Liberty of the Press, p. 157.

lowed him. * * * What ought to have alleviated the punishment, the uncertainty of the crime, seems to have enhanced it
in those days of blind zeal and pious cruelty."

Commenting on the statute I. Eliz. c. 1 repealing forme
statutes against heresy, he says: "Thus was heresy reduced
to a greater certainty than before, though it might not have
been the worse to have defined it in terms still more precise
and particular; as a man continued still liable to be burnt for
what perhaps he did not understand to be heresy till the ecclesiastical judge so interpreted the words of the canonical Scripture. * * * Everything is now as it should be with respect to
the spiritual cognizance, and spiritual punishment of heresy,
unless perhaps that crime ought to be more strictly defined,
and *no prosecution permitted even in the ecclesiastical courts
till the tenets in question are by proper authority previously
declared to be heretical.*"[32a]

In 1884 Sir Fitz-James Stephens, of the court of King's
Bench, seems almost to agree with Carlile. In the course of
an argument for the repeal of all statutes against blasphemy,
which he refers to as "an admitted blemish in the existing
law," and as "essentially and fundamentally bad," he points
out the irreconcilable conflict in the various judicial tests of
guilt in blasphemy prosecutions, and reducing the uncertainty
of some of these to an absurdity, he describes them "as destitute of that manly simplicity which ought to be the characteristics of the law. There is no reason why the law should
be so indistinct."[33]

Unfortunately in England there is no constitutional limitation upon the power of Parliament such as would preclude
the enactment of uncertain laws. What Sir Fitz-James Stephens contends for as a matter of wisdom to be acted upon by
the Parliament, in America is a constitutionally guaranteed
right, and no American judge, conscious of uncertainty in a
penal statute, can enforce it without violating his oath of office.

Edward Livingston, a U. S. Senator, Secretary of State
under Pres. Jackson, and Minister to France, reputed to be
one of the greatest American lawyers of his time, in 1822
wrote these words: "This dreadful list of Judicial cruelties
was increased by legislation of the judges, who declared acts
which were not criminal under the letter of the law to be

[32a] Blackstone, Book IV., pp. 45 to 49.
[33] See, "Blasphemy and Blasphemous Libel," 41 *Fortnightly Review,* 289-314,
March, 1884.

punishable by reason of its spirit. The statute gave the text and the tribunals wrote the commentary in letters of blood, and extended its penalties by the creation of constructive offenses. *The vague, and sometimes unintelligible, language* employed in the penal statutes gave a color of necessity to this assumption of power, and the English nation have submitted to the legislation of its courts, and seen their fellow subjects hanged for constructive felonies, quartered for constructive treason, and roasted alive for constructive heresies, with a patience that would be astonishing even if their written laws had sanctioned the butchery. *The first constructive extension of a penal statute beyond its letter is an ex post facto law, as regards the offense to which it is applied, and is an illegal assumption of legislative power, so far as it establishes a rule for further decisions.* In our republic, where the different departments of government are constitutionally forbidden to interfere with each other's functions, the exercise of this power would be particularly dangerous. * * * It may be proper to observe that the fear of *these consequences is not ideal, and that the decisions of all tribunals under the common law justify the belief that without some legislative restraint our courts would not be more scrupulous than those of other countries in sanctioning this dangerous abuse.* [p. 17-18.] It is better that acts of an evil tendency should for a time be done with impunity than that courts should assume legislative powers, which assumption is itself an act more injurious than any it may purport to repress. There are therefore no constructive offenses. [p. 118.] *Penal laws should be written in plain language, clearly and unequivocally expressed, that they may neither be misunderstood or perverted.* * * * The accused in all cases should be entitled to a public trial, conducted by known rules," etc. [p. 113.][34]

At the time when Livingston wrote, Puritan prudery had scarcely made a beginning toward its legalization. Under the common law of England before the revolution "obscenity" in literature had been punished only when it was incidental to treasonable or blasphemous utterances. Some American judges, with that peculiar intellectual capacity which enables them without research to determine historical facts of the past on the mere testimony of their inner consciousness, have often asserted the contrary, but the fact remains that prior to the

[34]"Report made to the General Assembly of the State of Louisiana on the plan of a Penal Code," by Edward Livingston, at pages as indicated in the text.

Revolution there is no recorded case of punishment for an obscene libel wherein the obscenity of the publication, merely as such obscenity and dissociated from treason and blasphemy, was ever punished.[35]

Thus far we have examined the statements of those persons without whose warfare against tyranny we would to-day enjoy less liberty than is permitted us. We have everywhere found that the necessity for law arises from the fact of everyday experience that frail human beings cannot lose their weakness by receiving judicial office, and that, because of this, we must submit to the penalties which may be determined by whim, caprice, prejudice, moral idiosyncrasies and sentimentalism, or even malice, unless the judge's will is always held in subjection to the same law which is designed to warn all others and defines the conduct to be punished. We have also seen that it was the desire to achieve this result which prompted the demand for the English Charters of liberty, and we know the terrible havoc which has resulted from the neglect of this requirement that the criminal law should be certain. Furthermore we have seen how the judge who insisted on the charter-rights, refused to enforce, except as to sheep, a statute penalizing the theft of sheep "or other cattle" because the word "cattle" was too vague, holding that since it required judicial legislation to make it certain it could not be "the law of the land." It was after that construction of "law," and with it, that we adopted our constitutions guaranteeing "due process of law."

I therefore conclude that the historical interpretation of the word "law" is in accord with its significance as derived from a study of its essential nature, and that among other qualities which must inhere in every penal statute, in the absence of which it cannot be *the law,* nor constitute "due process of law," is that of certainty in the description of the conduct penalized. In other words, according to the historical interpretation of "law," "No penal law can be sustained unless its mandates are so clearly expressed that any ordinary person can determine in advance what he may or may not do under it," and by that test all statutes against "obscene, indecent, filthy or disgusting" literature and art, and a large number of other statutes similarly vague, fail to constitute "due process of law." Next we will pass to a study of the modern decisions as affecting the problem under discussion.

[35]"Obscene Literature under the Common Law." *Albany Law Journal,* **May, 1907;** or published in Chapter III.

CHAPTER XXI.

"DUE PROCESS OF LAW" IN RELATION TO STATUTORY UNCERTAINTY AND CONSTRUCTIVE OFFENSES.

PART IV.

Certainty Required By Modern Authorities.

The modern authorities are quite as definite as the older ones in insisting upon absolute certainty in the definition of that which is penalized, and we will now proceed to a mere compilation of authoritative utterances bearing upon the requirement of statutory certainty. Most of these quotations are from cases construing punitive statutes. In others, however, we find the principle definitely applied to the end of declaring uncertain statutes to be unconstitutional. First will be collected some of the authorities which show that the historical interpretation of "law," which requires certainty in the meaning of penal statutes before they can constitute "law," was perpetuated by our constitutional guarantees of "due process of law." After that will be quoted some judicial opinions which specifically declare that the destruction of all arbitrariness of courts, by the certainty of meaning in the statutory statement of the criteria of guilt, is a prerequisite without which penal statutes do not furnish "due process of law."

For the benefit of the lazy and the very busy man, I violate my ideals of what a legal argument ought to be and pursue the method of merely compiling quotations from judicial opinions, which are deemed more or less material to the contention which I am making. If I merely cited the opinions instead of quoting them, I fear not many of them would be read.

THE HISTORICAL AND SCIENTIFIC INTERPRETATION OF "LAW" IS
PERPETUATED BY OUR CONSTITUTIONS.

In reading the following quotations it is necessary always to bear in mind that the "settled maxims"—"the principles which were before the constitutions"—"the ancient rights and liberties of the subject," from the time of *Magna Charta* down, always included the protection of those accused of crime by insistance upon the maxim *"Ubi jus incertum, ibi jus nullum"* (where the law is uncertain there is no law).

"Due process of law" means "an exercise of the powers of government *as the settled maxims of the law permit* and sanction, under such safeguards as these maxims prescribe for the class of cases to which the one in question belongs."[36]

"Even in judicial proceedings we do not ascertain from the constitution what is lawful process but we must test their action by *principles which were before the constitution* and the benefit of which we assume that the constitution was intended to perpetuate."[37]

"These phrases [of the Constitution] did not mean merciful nor even just laws but they did mean equal and general laws, *fixed and certain.* * * * The English colonies in America were familiar with the conflict between customary law and arbitrary prerogative and claimed the protection of these charters. When they came to form independent governments, they sought *to guard against arbitrary* and unequal governmental action by inserting the same phrase in their constitutions. * * * It does not follow that every statute is 'the law of the land,' nor that every process authorized by a legislature is 'due process of law.' "[38]

"No man shall be arrested, imprisoned or exiled or deprived of his life, liberty or estate, but by the judgment of his peers, or the law of the land, is so manifestly conformable to the words of *Magna Charta,* that we are not to consider it as a newly invented phrase, first used by the makers of our constitution, but we are to look at it as the adoption of one of the greatest securities of private right, handed down to us among the liberties and privileges which our ancestors enjoyed at the time of their emigration, and claimed to hold and retain as their birthright. These terms, in this connection, cannot, we think, be used in their most bold and literal senses to mean the law of the land at the time of the trial, because the laws may be shaped and altered by the legislature from time to time; and such a provision, intended to prohibit the making of any law

[36] State v. Board of Med. Exams. 34 Minn. 387-389, Meyer's Vested Rights, p. 196.
[37] Weimer v. Bunbury, 30 Mich., 301 (213)   State v. Doherty, 60 Me., 504.
[38] Eames v. Savage, 77 Me., 212 (220, 221), 1885; Meyer's Vested Rights, p. 192.

impairing *the ancient rights and liberties of the subject,* would under such a construction be wholly nugatory and void. The legislature might simply change the law by statute, and thus remove the landmark and barrier intended to be set up by this provision in the bill of rights. It must therefore have intended the ancient established law and course of legal proceedings, by an adherence to which our ancestors in England, before the settlement of this country, and the emigrants themselves and their descendants, had found safety for their personal rights."[39]

This would include the requirement of certainty in tests of guilt, as laid down by Coke, Blackstone and others, as quoted in the "Historic Interpretation of 'Law,'" and the maxim, "where the law is uncertain there is no law."

"By 'due process of law' is meant such general and legal forms and course of proceeding as were known either at common law or were generally recognized at the time of the adoption of the provision."[40]

"The words, 'due process of law,' were undoubtedly intended to convey the same meaning as the words, 'by the law of the land' in *Magna Charta.* Lord Coke in his commentary on these words (2 Inst., 50) says they mean due process of law. It is manifest that it was not left to the legislative power to enact any process which might be devised. The article is a restraint on the legislative as well as the executive and judicial powers of the government, and cannot be so construed as to leave Congress free to make any process 'due process of law,' by its mere will. We must look to those settled usages and modes of proceeding existing in the common and statute law of England, before the emigration of our ancestors, and which are shown not to have been unsuited to their civil and political conditions by having been acted on by them after the settlement of this country."[41]

These authorities sufficiently show that the Federal and State constitutions guaranteeing "Due Process of Law," adopted the conception of "Law" which requires from the law-making power an absolute certainty in the statement of its criteria of guilt before a penal statute is *the law* of the land. This still further vindicates the historical interpretation of

[39] Jones v. Robbins, 8 Gray (74 Mass.), 329 (342, 343); Meyer's Vested Rights, 195.
[40] Gibson v. Mason, 5 Nev., 283 (302); McCarrol v. Weeks, 5 Hayw. (Tenn.), 246.
[41] Murry v. Hoboken, etc., 18 How., 272 (276), (U. S., 1855); Davidson v. New Orleans, 96 U. S., 97 (1877).

"law" as hereinbefore made, and aids us to resurrect and re-vivify the ancient maxim, "Where the law is uncertain there is no law." It is hoped that thus may be destroyed all those tyrannous laws whose meanings no one knows until after trial, and as to which no lawyer can advise, because they are born of a stupid moral sentimentalism, fathered by those whose dense ignorance of the meaning of law and liberty is evidenced in the fact that mere question-begging vituperative epithets, so often expressing only diseased emotions, supplant the necessary statutory definitions of that which is prohibited. Next we shall examine the judicial utterances in so far as they may bear upon the required certainty in statute law.

CERTAINTY IN CIVIL AND POLITICAL STATUTES.

These disquisitions were primarily designed to discuss the requirement of certainty in penal statutes. In the foregoing essays it seemed necessary to the clarification of our thinking to point out how and why certainty is equally a requisite of those statutes which seek to do something else than merely to declare and enforce natural justice. As confirming that part of my speculations which asserts that "law" presupposes the abolition of all arbitrary power such as unavoidably results from the enforcement of uncertain statutes, as well as to em-phasize the importance of the maxim, "Where the law is un-certain there is no law," a few opinions in civil cases will be quoted, in which the principle of the maxim is applied to non-penal statutes.

"It is impossible for a man to regulate his conduct by a rule that has no existence; it therefore follows of necessity that laws can influence the conduct of men only after they are made."[42]

"An act may be passed and published by legislatures na-tional, state and territorial, with all the usual formalities and appendages, and yet be pronounced no law when put to the judicial test. * * * Strip this act of its outside appendages, leave it solitary and alone, is it possible for any human being to tell by what authority the seat of Government of Washing-ton Territory was to be removed from Olympia to Vancou-ver?"[43] (On the implied negative the legislative act was annulled.)

[42]Davis v. Ballard, 1 Marshall (Ky.), 577.
[43]Seat of Government Case, 1 Wash. Ter. Rep., 123.

"The word equity in the oath administered to the special jury is synonymous with *law, and does not mean some undefined and undefinable notion which the jury may entertain of the justice of the case,* but a system of jurisprudence governed by established rules and bound down by fixed precedents. The special jury is sworn to try the cause according to equity and the opinion they entertain of the evidence, and not their opinion of equity, as well as the evidence."[44]

"Every duty becomes such because the law makes it so. It is fixed and certain. *Unless fixed and certain it cannot be a duty,*" said in civil action for damages from negligence.[45]

"Unless then the description [in an act of Congress] *is so clear and accurate* as to refer to a particular patent [or unerringly describe the characteristics which make the book 'obscene'] so *as to be incapable of being applied to any other, the mistake is fatal."*[46]

"We cannot make the language for the law-making power, when the means of construing the language used, in any other than its literal and grammatical sense, is not furnished by the act itself or unmistakably indicated by the circumstances. * * * It [the legislative act] is *void* because it cannot be ascertained from its terms, with any reasonable certainty, what territory is assigned to Dallas County."[47]

These decisions sufficiently demonstrate that as to those civil and political statutes which create or enforce artificial rights, it is unavoidable that we apply the old maxim, "Where the law is uncertain there is no law," or else submit to the arbitrary tyranny of judicial legislation.

THE TEXT-BOOK WRITERS ON CERTAINTY IN PENAL STATUTES.

"The penal law is intended to regulate the conduct of people of all grades of intelligence within the scope of responsibility. It is therefore essential to its justice and humanity that it be expressed in language which they can easily comprehend, *that it be held obligatory only in the sense in which all can understand it,* and this consideration presses with increasing weight according to the severity of the penalty. Hence every provision affecting any element of a criminal offense involving

[44]Thornton v. Lane, 11 Ga., 461-538.
[45]Evansville St. Ry. Co. v. Meadows, 15 Ind. App. Ct., 159.
[46]Blanchard v. Sprague, Fed. Case 1517, v. 3, p. 647, and cases.
[47]Bittle v. Stuart, 34 Ark., 229-232; see also, Ferrett v. Attwill, 1 Blatchford, 157; Henry v. Evans, 97 Mo., 47.

life or liberty is subject to the strictest interpretation. * * *
It is the legislature, not the court, which is to define a crime
and ordain its punishment."[48]

Under "Due Process of Law," Ordronaux says: "Every
enactment is not necessarily 'the law of the land.' * * *
The phrase means * * * judgment rendered under and
according to *a general system of law* which the community has
esablished for the protection of the civil rights of all its members."[49]

I have made no investigation of English decisions, but
chanced to run upon the following expression, which I have
thought best to preserve by inserting it here, though it will
add a little to the disorderly character of the compilation of
this chapter.

"It would be extremely wrong that a man should, by a
long train of conclusions, be reasoned into a penalty when the
express words of the act of Parliament do not authorize it."[50]

THE STATE COURTS.

"All must have the equal protection of the law and its in-
strumentalities. The same rule must exist for all in the same
circumstances,"[51] which cannot be the same if the criterion of
guilt is uncertain, as it must be where left for judicial creation.

"Words cannot be imported into a statute for the purpose
of construing it."[52]

"The office of interpretation is to bring sense out of the
words, not to bring a sense into them."[53]

All the judicial "tests of obscenity" violate these rules of
construction. All such tests are in fact interpolated by unauthorized and unconstitutional judicial legislation, and vary
according to the exigencies of each case and the moral idiosyncracies of each judge.

"By the 'Law of the Land' is meant, *not the arbitrary
edict of any body of men,* not an act of assembly, though it
may have all the outward form of law, but due process of
law."[54]

[48]Southerland, Statutory Construction, 1st Ed., pp. 438-9.
[49]Ordronaux's Constitutional Legislation (1891), p. 255.
[50]Rex v. Bond, 1 B. and Ald. at page 392.
[51]Chic., St. L. & R. v. Moss, 60 Miss., 641, (647); Pearson v. Portland, 69
Me., 278.
[52]State v. Payne, 29 Pac. Rep., 787.
[53]McClusky v. Cromwell, 11 N. Y. (1 Kern), 593, (602).
[54]Palairet's Appeal, 67 Penn. St., 479, (485); Meyer's Vested Rights, 196.

"The rights of every individual must stand or fall by the same rule of law that governs every other member of the community under similar circumstances, and every partial or private law which directly proposes to destroy or affect individual rights, or does the same thing *by affording remedies leading to similar consequences,* is void."[55]

"Under the requirement of due process of law, the law must provide some just form or mode in which the duty of the citizen shall be determined before he can be visited with a penalty for non-performance of an alleged duty"[56]; which is not done if criteria of guilt are left uncertain, and consequently to be supplied by the court.

"Due process of law is a general expression and is equivalent to the 'law of the land.' It permits the deprivation of life, liberty or property according to law, not otherwise. *It shields such right from arbitrary power.* Due process of law, in a [criminal] case like this, *requires a law describing the offense.* The definition of the offense, and the authority for every step of the trial, must be found in the law of the land. Nothing essential can emanate from arbitrary power."[57]

"These uncertainties [arising from a statute] as to whether a man would be subject to fine or imprisonment, are not the qualities of law, but rather the qualities of anarchy. * * * That laws shall exist which are not plainly in exact words prescribed, so that an individual may know them, which are not passed by the deliberation of the three legislative departments, each member in each branch sworn to exercise his best judgment for the people upon his own responsibility, is directly opposed to every principle of the American or any [other] good government."[58]

The judicially prescribed and ever varying "tests of obscenity" never had the indorsement of any branch of any legislature.

"The clause 'law of the land' was defined in our earlier cases to mean 'a general and public law, equally binding upon every member of the community,' but by our later cases it is

[55]Wally's Heirs v. Kennedy, 2 Yerg., 554, (555); Bank of the State v. Cooper, 2 Yerg., 599.

[56]Philadelphia v. Scott, 81 Penn. St., 80, (90); Craig v. Kline, 65 Penn. St., 899.

[57]State v. Bates, 14 Utah, 293, (300).

[58]Thornton v. Ter. of Wash., 3 Wash. Ter. Rep., 488, (494).

defined to mean a law 'which embraces all persons who are or may come into like situation and circumstances.' "[59]

If the criteria of guilt are left for judicial creation *the law* does not uniformly embrace all persons who may come into like situation.

"It is obvious there can be no certain remedy in the laws where the legislature [or courts in criminal cases] may prescribe one rule for one suitor or a class of suitors in the courts, and another for all others under like circumstances, or may discriminate between parties to the same suit."[60]

The city council of Hagerstown, Md., had been authorized to pass ordinances "to prevent nuisances and to regulate and control offensive trades" and passed an ordinance prohibiting the herding and keeping of domestic animals "without permit therefore first had and obtained from the mayor and council," but no general rules were prescribed which would control the granting of such permits. The defendant was arrested for violating the ordinance. The ordinance was attacked among other reasons for this, that "it places unreasonable, arbitrary, and oppressive power in the hand of the mayor and council."

The court said: "In re Christensen (C. C.) 43 Fed. 243, it is said: 'The fact that it *permits* arbitrary discriminations and abuses in its execution, depending upon no conditions or qualifications whatever other than the unregulated arbitrary will of certain designated persons, is the touch-stone by which its validity is to be tested.' In Cicero Lumber Co. v. Cicero, 176 Ill. 9, 51 N. E. 758, 42 L. R. A. 705, 68 Am. St. Rep. 155, in a well considered case, says: 'The ordinance in so far as it invests the Board of Trustees with the discretion here indicated is unreasonable. It prohibits that which is in itself and as a general thing lawful and leaves the power of permitting or forbidding the use of traffic teams upon the boulevards to an unregulated official discretion when the whole matter should be regulated by permanent local provisions operating generally and impartially. * * * The ordinance in no way regulates or controls the discretion thereby vested in the Board. It prescribes no conditions upon which the special permission of the Board is to be granted. Thus the Board is clothed with the

---

[59]Stratton Claim v. Morris Claim, 89 Tenn. 521, cases; Harbison v. Knoxville Iron Co., 103 Tenn., 434.
[60]Durkee v. Janesville, 28 Wisc., 464, (471).

right to grant the privilege to some and to deny it to others. Ordinances which thus invest a city council or board of trustees with a discretion which is purely arbitrary and *which may be exercised in the interest of a favorite few*, are unreasonable and invalid. The ordinance should have established a rule by which its impartial enforcement could be secured.' "[61]

"We hold the ordinance here in question to be invalid and contrary to law."[62]

"It has been wisely and aptly said that this is a *government of laws and not of men;* that there is *no arbitrary power* located in any individual or body of individuals; but that all in authority are guided and limited by those provisions which the people have, through the organic law, declared shall be the measure and scope of all control exercised over them."[63]

FEDERAL COURTS.

"A court is not however permitted to arrive at this [Legislative] intention by mere conjecture, but it is to collect it from the object which the Legislature had in view and the expressions used, which should be competent and proper to apprise the community at large of the rule which it is intended to prescribe for their government. For although ignorance of the existence of a law be no excuse for its violation, yet if this ignorance be the consequence of an ambiguous or obscure phraseology, some indulgence is due to it. *It should be a principle of every criminal code, and certainly belongs to ours, that no person be adjudged guilty of an offense unless it be created and promulgated in terms which leave no reasonable doubt of their meaning.* * * * A court has no option where any considerable ambiguity arises on a penal statute, but is bound to decide in favor of the party accused. 'It is more consonant with the principles of Liberty,' says an eminent English judge, 'that a court should acquit when the Legislature intended to punish, than that it should punish when it was the intent to discharge with impunity.' If no sense can be discovered in them [the words used in the statute] as they are here introduced, the court had better pass them by as unintelligible and useless than to put on them, at great uncertainty, a very harsh

[61] Citing Mayor v. Radecke, 49 Md. 250, 33 Am. Rep. 239; Bostock v. Sams, 95 Md. 400, 52 Atl. 655, 59 L. R. A. 282, 93 A. S. R. 394; Cov. Stockyards v. Keith, 139 U. S. 128, 11 Sup. Ct. 461, 35 L. Ed. 73; Crowley v. Christensen, 137 U. S. 89, 11 Sup. Ct. 13, 34 L. Ed. 620.
[62] Mayor, et al. v. B. & O. R. Co., 68 Atl. Rep. 490.

signification and one which the Legislature may never have designed."[64]

Here we may adapt to new uses the words of Chief Justice Best, in Fletcher v. Lord, Sondes, 3 Bing., 580. He says: "If this rule is violated, the fate of the accused person is decided by the arbitrary discretion of judges and not by the express authority of the laws." Also: "The courts have no power to create offenses but if by a latitudinarian construction they construe cases not provided for to be within legislative enactment, it is manifest that the safety and liberty of the citizen are put in peril, and that the legislative domain has been invaded. * * * *The doctrine is fundamental in English and American law that there can be no constructive offenses; that before a man can be punished, his case must be plainly and unmistakably within the statute;* that if there be any fair doubt whether the statute embraces it, that doubt is to be resolved in favor of the accused. These principles admit of no dispute, and often have been declared by the highest courts, and by no tribunal more clearly than the supreme court of the United States."[65]

"Such an interpretation is not to be adopted, to give effect to particular words, *which will require* on the part of the court *the introduction of new provisions and auxiliary clauses, which the statute neither points out nor even hints at,* and yet which are indispensable to make such interpretation serviceable or practicable."[66]

The rule of this last decision is violated by every one of the judicial "tests of obscenity."

"Penal statutes cannot be extended beyond the OBVIOUS meaning of their terms on any plea of failure of justice."[67]

"Statutes creating crimes will not be extended by judicial interpretation to cases not plainly and unmistakably within their terms. If this rule is lost sight of the courts may hold an act to be a crime when the Legislature never so intended. * * * The sense of indignation against such vocation or conduct should not permit a violation by the courts of established rules of law, or an unlawful exercise of jurisdiction."[68]

"The words 'by law' in section 967 [U. S. Stat.] are em-

---

[64] Enterprize, Fed. Case No. 4499, Vol. 8, pp. 734-5.
[65] U. S. v. Clayton, Fed. Cas. No. 14814, Vol. 25, p. 460.
[66] U. S. v. Bassett, v. 24, Fed. Cases p. 1034, No. 14589.
[67] U. S. v. Garretson, 42 Fed. R., 25.
[68] U. S. v. Whittier, Fed. Case No. 16688.

phatic and refer in my judgment to a *fixed rule* in respect to time and manner, *and not to a discretionary power* vested by statute in a state court."[69]

Uncertainty arising from absence of specific standards of judgment necessarily involves the exercise of discretionary power in determining what shall be the essence of guilt.

"A citizen desiring to obey the laws would search the acts of Congress in vain to find that grazing sheep upon a forest reserve without the permit of the Secretary of Agriculture, is a criminal offense. It has been suggested that the acts under which the indictment is drawn give notice that the Secretary may make rules and regulations, and the search would not be complete and the inquiry concluded until it be ascertained whether he has made such rules and regulations, the violation of which it is expressly declared shall be a criminal offense. But here we are led back to a delegation of legislative power. The rules prescribed by the heads of the departments are not necessarily promulgated. While they may be procured, they are not as easily available as are statutes of the United States; nor does our system contemplate an examination of those rules for the ascertainment of that which may or may not be a crime, for *the right to prohibit a given thing under penalty, belongs to Congress alone. * * * It cannot authorize any other branch of the government [not even the courts] to define that which is purely legislative, and that is purely legislative which defines rights, permits things to be done, or prohibits the doing thereof.*"[70]

"In order to constitute a crime, the act must be one *which the party is able to know in advance whether it is criminal or not. The criminality of an act cannot depend upon whether a jury may think it reasonable or unreasonable.* There must be some definiteness and certainty."[71]

How can any man know in advance from a mere reading of the statute by what "test of obscenity" the judge or jury may determine the guilt or innocence of his conduct in circulating a book or picture? Of course he can't know and therefore such laws cannot constitute "Due Process of Law."

"No penal law can be sustained unless its mandates are so clearly expressed that *any ordinary person can determine in*

[69]Meyers v. Tyson, Fed. Case 9995-13 Blatch, 242.
[70]U. S. v. Mathews, 146 Fed. Rep. 308; U. S. v. Eaton, 144 U. S., 687.
[71]Tozer v. U. S., 52 Fed. Rep., 919.

advance what he may and what he may not do under it. [citing authorities] Lieb. Herm. 156. In this the author quotes the Chinese Penal Code which reads as follows: 'Whoever is guilty of improper conduct and of such as is contrary to the spirit of the laws, though not a breach of any specific part of it, shall be punished at least forty blows, and when the impropriety is of a serious nature, with eighty blows' There is very little difference between such a statute and one which would make it a criminal offense to chage more than a reasonable rate.'"[71a]

"But to punish a man for the non-performance of a duty, it is not sufficient that the law impliedly requires him to do the act. *The statute must be clear and explicit in its terms, in defining that duty, in order that he may know what he is called upon to do, and what it is his duty to avoid.*"[72]

CERTAINTY REQUIRED BY THE U. S. SUPREME COURT.

The Supreme Court of the United States whenever called upon to express an opinion upon the subject has been uniformly insistent upon the requirement of certainty in the statutory definition of crimes.

"There can be no constructive offenses."[73]

"It is axiomatic that statutes creating and defining crimes cannot be extended by intendment, and that no act, however wrongful, can be punished under such a statute unless clearly within its terms."[74]

Chief Justice Marshall said this:

"The rule that penal laws are to be construed strictly, is perhaps not much less old than construction itself. It is founded on the tenderness of the law for the rights of the individuals; and on the plain principle that the power of punishment is vested in the legislative, not in the judicial department. *It is the legislature, not the court, which is to define a crime,* and ordain its punishment. . . . To determine that a case is within the intention of a statute its language must authorize us to say so. It would be dangerous, indeed, to carry the principle that a case which is within the mischief of a statute, is within its provisions so far as to punish a crime not enumerated in the statute, because it is of equal atrocity, or of kindred character, with those which are enu-

[71a]Chic. etc. Ry. Co. v. Dey 35 Fed. Rep. 866-867.
[72]U. S. v. Dwyer, 56 Fed. Rep. 468.
[73]U. S. v. Lacher, 134 U. S. 628.
[74]Todd v. U. S., 158 U. S. 282.

merated. If this principle has ever been recognized in expounding criminal law, it has been in cases of considerable irritation which it would be unsafe to consider as precedents forming a general rule for other cases.[75]

Before this the Supreme Court had said: "The effect of the provision [requiring Due Process of Law] is to secure the individual from the *arbitrary* exercise of the powers of government."[76]

"If the language is clear it is conclusive. There can be no construction where there is nothing to construe. The words must not be narrowed to the exclusion of what the legislature intended to embrace, *and they must be such as to leave no reasonable doubt upon the subject."*[77]

"Laws which prohibit the doing of things, and provide a punishment for their violation, should have no double meaning. A citizen should not unnecessarily be placed where, by an honest error in the construction of a penal statute, he may be subjected to a prosecution for a false oath, and an inspector of elections should not be put in jeopardy because he, with equal honesty, entertains an.opposite opinion. . . . *If the legislature undertakes to define by statute a new offense and provide for its punishment, it should express its will in language that need not deceive the common mind. Every man should be able to know with certainty when he is committing a crime. . . . It would certainly be dangerous if the legislature could set a net large enough to catch all possible offenders and leave it to the court to step inside and say who could be rightfully detained, and who should be set at large. This would to some extent substitute the Judicial for the legislative department of the government."*[78]

"When we consider the nature and theory of our government, the principles upon which they are supposed to rest, and review the history of their development, we are constrained to conclude that *they do not mean to leave room for the play and action of purely arbitrary power"*[79]*;* such as must result if the statute leaves the test of criminality uncertain.

"No language is more worthy of frequent and thoughtful

[75]U. S. v. Wiltberger, 5 Wheat. 95; see also Ferrett v. Atwill, 1 Blatchford 157.

[76]Bank of Columbia v. Oakley, 4 Wheat. 235 (244), Meyer's Vested Rights 196.

[77]U. S. v. Hartwell, 73 U. S. (6 Wall) 396.

[78]U. S. v. Reese 92 U. S. 219-221.

[79]Yick Wo, v. Hopkins, 118 U. S. 356-359.

consideration than these [foregoing] words of Mr. Justice Mathews."[80]

"The words 'due process of law' come to us from England, and their requirements were there designed to secure the subject against the arbitrary action of the crown and place him under the protection of the law. . . . In this country the requirements are intended to have a similar effect against legislative power, that is, *to secure the citizen against any arbitrary deprivation of his rights whether relating to his life, his liberty or his property. . . . The great purpose of the requirements is to exclude everything that is arbitrary and capricious in legislation affecting the rights of the citizens.*"[81]

"*Laws which create crime ought to be so explicit that all men subject to their penalties may know what acts it is their duty to avoid.* U. S. v. Sharp, Pet. C. C. 118, Fed. Case No. 16264."[82]

"In the administration of the criminal justice no rule can be applied to one class which is not applicable to all other classes"[83]; which is not insured if the tests of criminality are of judicial creation.

"*It is all important that a criminal statute should define clearly the offense which it purports to punish,* and that when so defined it should be within the limits of the power of the legislative body enacting it."[84]

LOUISVILLE & N. RY. CO. V. COMMONWEALTH.

Perhaps the lengthiest statement concerning the requirement of certainty in a criminal statute is made by the Court of Appeals of Kentucky, in declaring unconstitutional a statute penalizing transportation companies for charging more than a just and reasonable rate of toll for the transportation of passengers and of freight. In that case the court among other things said this:

"That this statute leaves uncertain what shall be deemed a 'just and reasonable rate of toll or compensation,' cannot be denied; and that different juries might reach different conclusions, on the same testimony, as to whether or not an offense

[80]Gulf C. & S. Fe. Ry. v. Ellis, 165 U. S. 159.

[81]Dent v. West Virginia, 129 U. S. 114; s. c. Meyer's Vested Rights, 195; Millett v. People, 117 Ill. 294. (1886).

[82]U. S. v. Brewer, 189 U. S. 288, 11 Sup. Ct. Rep. 538; U. S. v. New Bedford Bridge Co., Fed. Case No. 15867.

[83]Gibson v. Mississippi, 162 U. S. 591.

[84]James v. Bowman, 190 U. S. 127.

has been committed, must also be conceded. The criminality of the carrier's act, therefore, depends on the jury's view of the reasonableness of the rate charged, and this latter depends on many uncertain and complicated elements. That the corporation has fixed a rate which it considers will bring it only a fair return for its investment does not alter the nature of the act. Under this statute it is still a crime, though it cannot be known to be such until after an investigation by a jury, and then only in that particular case, as another jury may take a different view, and, holding the rate reasonable, find the same act not to constitute an offense. There is no standard whatever fixed by the statute, or attempted to be fixed, by which the carrier may regulate its conduct. And it seems clear to us to be utterly repugnant to our system of laws to punish a person for an act, the criminality of which depends, not on any standard erected by the law, which may be known in advance, but on one erected by a jury; and especially so, as that standard must be as variable and uncertain as the views of different juries may suggest, and as to which nothing can be known until after the commission of the crime.

"If the infliction of the penalties prescribed by the statute would not be the taking of property without due process of law, and in violation of both state and federal constitutions, we are not able to comprehend the force of our organic laws. In Louisville & N. R. Co. v. Railroad Commission of Tennessee, 16 Am. & Eng. r. Cas. 15, a statute very similar to the one under consideration was thus disposed of by the learned judge (Baxter) : 'Penalties cannot be thus inflicted at the discretion of a jury. Before the property of a citizen, natural or corporate, can be thus confiscated, the crime for which the penalty is inflicted must be defined by the law-making power. The legislature cannot delegate this power to a jury. If it can declare it a criminal act for a railroad corporation to take more than a 'fair and just return' on its investments, it must, in order to the validity of the law, define with reasonable certainty what would constitute such 'fair and just return.' The act under review does not do this, but leaves it to the jury to supply the omission. No railroad company can possibly anticipate what view a jury may take of the matter, and hence cannot know, in advance of a verdict, whether its charges are lawful or unlawful. One jury may convict for a charge made on a basis of 4 per cent., while another might acquit an accused who had demanded and received at the rate of 6 per cent., rendering the statute, in its practical working, as unequal and unjust in its operation as it is indefinite in its terms.' The Supreme Court of the United States, in Railroad Commission Cases 116 U. S. 336, 6 Sup. Ct. 334, 348, 388, 391, 1191, refers to this Tennessee case, and substantially approves it by distinguishing the case then before the court from the Tennessee case. This case is also used to support the text in 8 Am. & Eng. Enc. Law, p. 935, where it is said: 'Although a statute has been held to be unconstitutional which left it to the jury to determine whether or not a charge was excessive and unreasonable, in order to ascertain whether a penalty is recoverable, yet where the action is merely for recovery of the illegal excess over reasonable rates, this is a question which is a proper one for a jury.' Mr. Justice Brewer, in the case of Railway Co. v. Dey, 35 Fed. 866, had under consideration the provision of a statute similar to the one we have before us, and, while the statute was upheld, it was only because there was a schedule of rates provided in the act which rendered the test of reasonableness definite and certain. The learned judge there said: 'Now the contention of complainants is that the substance of these provisions is that, if a railroad company charges an unreasonable rate, it shall be deemed a criminal, and punished by fine, and that such a statute is too indefinite and uncertain, no man being able to tell in advance what in fact is, or what any jury will find to be, a reasonable charge. If this were the construction to be placed upon this act as a whole, it would certainly be obnoxious to complainant's criticisms, for no penal law can be sustained unless its mandates are so clearly expressed that any ordinary person can determine in advance what he may and what he may not do under it. In Dwar. St. 652, it is laid down that it is impossible to dissent from the doctrine of Lord Coke that 'acts of Parliament ought to be plainly and clearly, and not cunningly and darkly, penned, especially in legal matters.' See also U. S. v. Sharp, Pet., C. C. 122. Fed. Cas. 16, 264; The Enterprise, 1 Paine, 34, Fed. Cas. No. 4, 499; Bish. St. Crimes 41 ; Lieb. Herm. 156. And the learned judge concludes there is very little difference between a provision of the Chinese Code, which prescribed a penalty against any one who should be guilty of 'improper conduct,' and a statute which makes it a criminal offense to charge more than a reasonable rate. The same learned judge discussing the kindred subject of unreasonable difference in rates in Tozar v. U. S. 52 Fed. 917, said: 'But, in order to constitute a crime, the act must be one which the party is able to know in advance whether it is criminal or not. The criminality of an act cannot depend upon whether a jury may think it reasonable or unreasonable. There must be some definiteness and certainty. When we look on the other side of the question, we find the contention of the State supported by neither reason or authority. No case can be found, we believe, where such indefinite legislation has been upheld by any court when a crime is sought to be imputed to the accused. In the case from 77 Ill. the court said: 'That section, by itself, makes the offense to consist in taking more than a fair and reasonable rate of toll and compensation, without reference to any standard of what is fair and reasonable. In such case it may be seen different persons have different opinions as to what is a fair and reasonable rate. Courts and juries, too, would differ, and at one time or place a defendant might be convicted and fined in a large amount for the same act which in another place or at another time, would be held to be no breach of the law, and what might be thought a fair and reasonable rate on one road might be thought otherwise upon another road. There would be no certainty of being able to comply with the law. A railroad corporation, with the purpose of conforming to the law, might fix its rates at what it believed to be reasonable, and yet be subjected to the heavy penalties here prescribed. The statute furnishes evidence that it did not intend to leave the railroad in this state of uncertainty and danger, and exposed to such seeming injustice. The eighth section provides how reasonable rates shall be ascertained, what they shall be, and that the railroad and warehouse commissioners for each of the railroad corporations in the State a schedule of reasonable maximum rates thus furnishing a uniform rule for the guidance of the railroad companies. These authorities and the argument abundantly supporting them are sufficient.

"Other objections to the judgment below need not be discussed, as the one noted is fatal, and the statute cannot be enforced as a penal statute."[85]

In the aggregate the foregoing authorities prove and dem–

[85]Louisville & N. R. Co. v. Commonwealth, 35 S. W. Rep. 129-131.

onstrate that though often neglected, the ancient maxim *"Ubi jus incertum, ibi jus nullum"* (Where the law is uncertain, there is no law), is still a fundamental part of our jurisprudence, and that in consequence all uncertain penal statutes are unconstitutional because not constituting "due process of law."

Since the foregoing essays were first published by me, several cases have been decided or come to my notice which are more or less related to the principle for which contention is herein made. These cases are cited in the footnote.[86]

[86]Mc Junkins vs. State, 10 Ind. 145 (A. D. 1858).

CHAPTER XXII.

"DUE PROCESS OF LAW" IN RELATION TO STATUTORY UNCERTAINTY AND CONSTRUCTIVE OFFENSES.

*PART V.—The Synthesis and the Application.**

In the foregoing chapters, I justified with considerable elaboration the proposition that in the United States no man can be punished for mere constructive offenses.

I have gone further and have attempted to formulate a statement of the nature of law as viewed in the scientific aspect, in contradistinction to that arbitrary power which punishes constructive offenses, and I have undertaken to make a comprehensive discussion as to what is a constructive offense in relation to "due process of law." Here I shall undertake only to summarize those conclusions, already justified in various ways, and apply them to our laws against "obscene" literature and art.

CONSTRUCTIVE CRIMES CLASSIFIED.

Constructive offenses naturally divide into two general classes. In the first of these the more direct responsibility for the prohibited construction rests with the courts, and arises from the judicial engraftments made upon legislative enactments, while the second class includes those where the more direct responsibility for the evil primarily rests with the legislature for having attempted to construct a wrong, by penalizing conduct not in itself injurious nor of injurious tendencies according to any known laws of the physical universe. These two general classes of constructive crime readily lend themselves to a further subdivision according to the various conditions which conduce to such baneful punishments for mere constructive wrongs. These different sources of such error will now be pointed out with a little more system and elaboration, and it is believed that the following statements are justified by, and generalize all, that is included in the dis-

*Revised from *The Central Law Journal,* Dec. 18th,1908.

cussion and the authorities cited in the several chapters on "due process of law."

JUDICIAL LEGISLATION UNDER PRETENSE OF INTERPRETATION.

The first class of constructive offenses is best understood. Here the act under investigation is one which under any of the tests prescribed hereafter, may properly be penalized, but it is not within the plain letter of the prohibitive statute because the statutory tests of criminality, though certain in meaning and covering acts of the same general character, manifestly do not specifically include the conduct under investigation. In such a case the judicial enlargement of the field plainly marked out by the statute is so universally recognized as improper, because judicial legislation, and therefore within the domain of the prohibited constructive offenses, as to need no argumentative support. Indeed, all judicial rules for the strict construction of criminal statutes are founded upon the necessity of precluding judges from creating law.

If the act penalized by the statute under consideration is assumed to be one which may be penalized, and the contention herein made, namely, that none of the judicial tests of "obscenity" has that certainty required by the Constitution, is held good, then the last declared principle has no application. On the other hand, if the judicial tests of "obscenity" do have the certainty required, then this principle still does annul the law, because these "tests" of guilt are clearly of judicial creation, extending the statute beyond what the words of the legislative enactment necessarily imply.

AMBIGUOUS STATUTES.

The second class of constructive offenses is less perfectly understood. Here the act under investigation is again one which, under any of the tests prescribed hereafter, may properly be penalized, but the statutory language is ambiguous in its specification of the criteria of guilt. Such statutes often seduce judges into an abuse of their power by a misapplication of rules of construction. Where the words descriptive of the crime are ambiguous (open to several interpretations, some or all of which meanings, taken separately, are very certain in their application to all specific facts), it is erroneously assumed by many courts that it is an exercise of the judicial function of statutory interpretation to select that one among all the possible meanings of the statute which is to be enforced. I do not conceive it so. The judicially selected interpretation may not be the one which the legislature intended to enact. Certainly it has not received the specific sanction of the legislative branch of the Government, any more than every other possible interpretation, and the only conduct which can with certainty be known to be within the legislative prohibition (that is, within *the law*) consists of those acts which are clearly within every possible meaning of the statute. If this rule has not been always observed in the matter of ambiguous statutes it is because judges have not seen clearly the true relation between such ambiguity and *the law*, as a scientist must view it, nor the distinction between judicial legislation and judicial interpretation. Very many of the prosecutions under the laws in question have resulted merely from a difference of opinion between the prosecutor and some sex-reformer as to which of the speculative meanings of "obscene" was to be enforced. It is an outrage that these defendants were never given the benefit of the doubt.

UNCERTAIN STATUTES.

The third class of these prohibited constructive offenses consists of those where definite description of the crime is wholly wanting (uncertainty as distinguished from mere ambiguity), because there is total absence of any certain, clear, universal and decisive tests of criminality. Then we have a case for the application of the old maxim: "Where the law is uncertain there is no law." In such a case, if the Court should supply the tests of criminality so indispensable to the enforcement of every statute, those tests would not have the sanction of the legislative branch of the Government, and therefore could not be *the law*, in any criminal case. Supplying these tests, or criteria of guilt, is therefore clearly a matter of judicial legislation, by means of statutory interpolation, as distinguished from interpretation, and punishment thereunder is punishment for a constructive offense, and not due process of law.

If in a criminal case a Court should undertake to enforce upon any person a judgment which did not conform to general, uniform and certain rules of conduct having an exact, verbally formulated existence, which were wholly created by the legislative department, and therefore existing outside the mere will of the Court, and well known or easily accessible to all prior to the inception of the cause of action then before the Court—I say, if a Court should undertake to enforce anything different from such a law, it would not be enforcing *the law* at all, and to submit to such penalties would be submission to a government by the arbitrary and despotic will of the judiciary, and not in any sense would this be a government according to *law,* and this must always be the case where the statutory criteria of guilt are uncertain. Criminal punishment under such circumstances would be punishment for constructive crimes, and not due process of law.

This is perhaps the most appropriate place to quote a few opinions in which this principle has been applied to statutes, similar at least in the nature of the uncertainty of their criteria of guilt, sometimes resulting merely in the discharge of the defendant, and at others in the more specific annulment of the statute.

INSTRUCTIVE PRECEDENTS.

The highest court of the State of Indiana has left us two instructive opinions. The court is construing a statute against "notorious lewdness or public indecency." No question of the constitutionality of the statute was before the court, yet after reviewing English authorities, the court continues its reflections thus: "It would therefore appear that *the term 'public indecency' has no fixed legal meaning—is vague and indefinite, and cannot in itself imply a definite offense.* And hence, the courts, by a kind of judicial legislation, in England and the United States, have usually limited the operation of the term to public displays of the naked person, the publication, sale or exhibition of obscene books and prints, or the exhibition of a monster—acts which have a direct bearing on public morals, and affect the body of society. Thus it will be perceived that so far as there is a legal meaning attached to the term, it is different from and more limited than the commonly accepted meaning given by Webster to the word indecency. A statute relative to a misdemeanor of the grade and character of this, and prescribing so severe a penalty as the deprivation of liberty by imprisonment, *ought to be clearly worded, so as to leave no doubt or ambiguity about its meaning,* before it should be construed to include a large and undefined class of offenses against morality. * * * This statute, under such circumstances, should be in itself explicit, and should not depend for vitality upon another act defining the meaning of words. * * If the statute is given the broad construction contended for by the prosecution, who is to determine what phrases amount to an offense under it? Is the public sentiment of each locality to be reflected through the jury?"[87] Conviction reversed because act not within the statute, that being all that was before the court.

The next case was an appeal from a conviction under a statute against heavy hauling on turnpike roads. The statute was held void for uncertainty, and the court said: "The language of a criminal statute cannot be extended beyond its reasonable meaning, and, whenever the court entertains a reasonable doubt as to the meaning, the doubt must be resolved in favor of the accused. The court must expound what it finds written, and cannot import additional meaning without sufficient indication thereof in the words of the statute, with such aids thereto as the established rules of law authorize. * * * Where the terms of the statute are so uncertain as to their meaning that the court cannot discern with reasonable certainty what is intended, it will pronounce the enactment void. * * * There must be some certain standard by which to determine whether an act is a crime or not."[88]

In another place I find a quotation to the point, but the original source of which I do not know with certainty. From the connection in which it is published, I infer that it is quoted from an unofficial report of the remarks of the late Judge Lowell, of Boston, while imposing a nominal fine upon one Jones, who had pleaded guilty to distributing *Clark's Marriage Guide* through the mails. This is of course unofficial, but its logic is incontrovertible.

"Crime should be so clearly defined that there can be no mistaking it; murder, homicide, arson, larceny, burglary, forgery, are so defined that they cannot be misunderstood. If obscenity is a crime punishable by fine and imprisonment, it ought to be so clearly described that we may know in what it consists, and that accused persons may not be at the mercy of a man or a number of men who construe what is obscene, indecent or immoral by their own special opinion or notion of morality or immorality. What is obscene to one man may be

---

[87]Cook vs. State, 59 N. E. (Ind.) 489-490 (1901)
[88]Requoted from Heywood's Defense, p. 29.

pure as mountain snow to another. One man should not and cannot decide for other men."[89]

In another case a similarly vague statute made it a misdemeanor to "commit any act injurious to the public health, or public morals, or the perversion or obstruction of public justice or the due administration of the law." The court said: "We cannot conceive how a crime can, on any sound principle, be defined in so vague a fashion. Criminality depends, under it, upon the moral idiosyncrasies of the individuals who compose the court or jury. The standard of crime would be ever varying, and the courts would constantly be appealed to as the instruments of moral reform, changing with all fluctuations of moral sentiment. The law is simply null. The Constitution, which forbids *ex post facto* laws, could not tolerate a law which would make an act a crime, or not, according to the moral sentiment which might happen to prevail with the judge or jury after the act had been committed."[90]

One United States Court, although not asked to do so, has all but declared the postal laws against "obscene" literature to be unconstitutional—as the necessary result of their uncertainty.

"We have been taught to believe that it was the greatest injustice toward the common people of old Rome when the laws they were commanded to obey, under Caligula, were written in small characters, and hung upon high pillars, thus more effectually to insnare the people. How much advantage may we justly claim over the old Romans, if our criminal laws are so obscurely written that one cannot tell when he is violating them? If the rule contended for here is to be applied to the defendant, he will be put upon trial for an act which he could not by perusing the law have ascertained was an offense. My own sense of justice revolts at the idea. I cannot give it my sanction. * * * The indictment is quashed, and the defendant is discharged."[91]

LEGISLATIVE PENALIZING OF MERE CONSTRUCTIVE INJURIES.

Fourth: It follows from the fact that human justice and a secular state can deal only with material factors, that an offense to be real and not merely constructive must be condi-

---

[89]Ex parte Andrew Jackson, 45 Ark. 164.
[90]U. S. v. Commerford, 25 Fed. Rep. 904. West Dist. of Tex.
[91]*See Pub. Weekly*, p. 1218, dated April 21, 1906.

tioned upon a demonstrable and ascertained material injury, or upon the imminent danger of such, the existence of which danger is determined by the known laws of the physical universe. Our Constitution, both in its guarantee of freedom of speech and press, and in its guarantee of due process of law (as we must understand *the law,* according to the scientific viewpoint), precludes the construction of mere psychologic crimes. The offenses which are based only upon ideas expressed or otherwise, such as constructive treason, witchcraft, and heresy, either religious or ethical, and all kindred psychologic or other constructive crimes, are prohibited, because the very nature of *the law* whose supremacy and processes our Constitution guarantees is such that American legislators cannot be permitted to predicate crime upon mere psychologic factors. Manifestly this does not preclude punishment when these psychologic factors have ceased to be merely such, by having resulted in actual material injury as distinguished from constructive and speculative injury. For example, it does not preclude punishment in cases of personal libel, which has resulted in material injury, or where the uttered opinion has resulted in actual crime, under such circumstances as to make one an accessory before the fact, or as to prove a conspiracy to secure its commission.

Furthermore, if the State should be permitted to penalize an act which is not an essential element in doing violence to that natural justice which can deal only with material and physical factors, such a statute could not be one enacted in the furtherance of the governmental purpose to establish justice (material justice), and therefore such a law could not be within the legitimate province of such a government as we profess to maintain. Furthermore, such a statute, penalizing an act which is not an essential element in violating natural justice, must in itself be the creation of an injustice—that is, it must in itself, and from its very nature, authorize an invasion of liberty, unwarranted by any necessity for defending natural justice, or maintaing the greatest liberty consistent with equality of liberty, and therefore the enforcement of such a statute would be the deprivation of liberty without due process of *law,* as we must understand "law" if we view it in the scientific sense. I conclude that every such statute as I have last hereinabove described is also an attempt to punish for a constructive offense—is a violation of our constitutional guarantee of due process of law.

DIFFICULTY IN THE APPLICATION.

It hardly seems possible that there can be much conflict of opinion about the foregoing generalities. The differences of opinion I apprehend will arise chiefly when we come to make deductions therefrom for application to some particular statute, and the result comes in conflict with our moral sentimentalism. Under such circumstances we are all predisposed to error, because our emotions will necessarily blur our intellectual insight as to the difference between certainty in the very words of the statute, and a strong feeling-certitude within us that the legislature must have meant to prohibit exactly what *we feel* that it ought to have prohibited. Thus moved by our feelings, just to the extent that they are intense, we shall be certain to read our feeling-convictions into the statutes, which, often by reason of their very uncertainty, readily lend themselves to this dangerous and almost inevitable evil of judicial penal-legislation. If this evil can be avoided it will be only because our intellectual development is of that superior order which dominates the feelings, without ever being overcome by them, and which at the same time enables us to possess an illuminated view of the point of contact and division between judicial (so called) statutory construction and a judicial usurpation of the legislative function, under the guise of statutory interpretation. These considerations seem to make it desirable that the foregoing principles be more elaborately restated with some special attention to the factors which necessarily imply unconstitutional uncertainty and form the tests by which statutes will be adjudged to be uncertain, and consequently a nullity. Thus we shall still further clarify our intellect and fortify ourselves against the dangerous, liberty-destroying tendency to punish for constructive offenses.

PENALIZING ABSTRACTIONS AND EMOTIONS.

If the legislative verbiage in a criminal enactment is so involved as to make its significance doubtful, or if the offense is bunglingly described by words which symbolize and generalize only a subjective (emotional) state, associated in the minds of different persons with a variety of mere, peculiarly personal, abstractions incapable of an accurate, concrete definition that is uniformly applicable to every conceivable case, and decisive beyond all speculative doubt, then, in either event, that enactment must be declared a nullity, because "where the law is uncertain there is no law." If courts were allowed to decide which of possible or conflicting descriptions is to be made effective and which annulled, or were allowed to create the criteria of guilt, when the legislature has failed to do so, this would be judicial legislation. The legislature having furnished no exact material for definition, the courts can declare only that to be the law which its judges, in the exercise of legislative discretion, believe ought to be the law. Instead of deriving that legislative intent exclusively by deductions made from the legislative language, the judges of necessity read their own personal desires into the statutes and dogmatically declare these to have been the legislative intent.

The judicial power over criminal statutes must be limited to a mere re-declaration, or restatement of that which, to every intelligent person, is already definitely and clearly manifest from the actual words of the enactment, and from these alone. If it requires more than this to make the statute enforcible, or applicable to a particular case, then the statute is a nullity under the maxim, "Where the law is uncertain, there is no law." To do less than this, for every word used in the enactment, or to do more by importing and engrafting into a criminal statute facts and phrases not actually placed there by the legislative body, is again a judicial usurpation of the power to enact criminal legislation.

It follows that if those words which alone are actually employed in the statute do not unavoidably import such an exact definition that every man of average intelligence, *by the use of the statutory definition alone,* can determine with mathematical certainty whether a particular act is a crime (or a particular book is obscene), then the legislative body has failed to create a criminal "law" and the court, being without legislative power, has nothing to execute, but must declare the pretended statute a nullity, because, "Where the law is uncertain, there is no law."

STATUTORY WORDS MUST SYMBOLIZE DEFINITE AND UNIFORM CONCEPTS.

Not quite identical with the foregoing proposition is this truism: The power of courts is limited to deductions made from the legislative words; that is, the general concept symbolized by the statutory words may be made concrete to determine if the specific act is necessarily included in the legislative general conception, as that is exclusively revealed in the legislative language. In other words, the court cannot create such a concept where the legislative word-symbols do not stand for definite concepts. That again would be judicial legislation, not interpretation, because, "where the law is uncertain there is no law," and a law which requires this to make it effective is void.

If courts can be credited with any power to construe penal statutes, the occasion and subject-matter of construction must be found solely in the ambiguity of the word-symbols used in the criminal statutes and not in the translation of the interpolated ideas of the judge. The latter is an act of judicial legislation, under the guise of interpreting the indefinable nature of that which the legislative words in fact do symbolize. Any other rule would authorize arbitrary *ex post facto* judicial legislation and punishment, and where the legislative word-symbols do not stand for definite concepts the enactment is a nullity because "where the law is uncertain there is no law."

To clarify our minds let this be restated in another way. When the word-symbols descriptive of the crime do not stand for definite or concrete concepts, nor any sense-perceived, objective quality or activity of matter, of present or past existence, but represents to each individual only a subjective relation between his own purely personal experiences, or the abstractions made from them, and his purely personal emotions of approval or disapproval, then the words used to describe this subjective condition must, because of its abstractions and emotional element, ever making it personal and individual, always elude accuracy of definition, and the law is void "because where the law is uncertain there is no law."

Whenever we neglect the requirement that every crime must be predicated upon some actual sense-perceivable and proven material injury, or the imminent danger of such, determined to be imminent by the known laws of the physical universe, and therefore accurately definable and so defined in the statute—I say, whenever we abandon these requirements, we are condemning men on mere metaphysical speculations about unrealized psychologic tendencies, or according to the personal ethical sentimentalizing, whim, caprice, malice, etc., etc., on the part of those charged with the execution of the law, and thus the judge arrogates to himself the rôle of legislator; and under such enactments convictions are never secured according to the uniform express authority of any statute, and all such convictions inflict punishment for mere constructive injuries and are an unconstitutional deprivation of liberty and property because not "due process of law." This error, I repeat, is one easily made if we are but careless about the proper different attitudes of mind which should characterize our outlook upon penal statutes and those of a civil nature which declare and enforce only natural justice; or if our vision is clouded as to the difference between deductions made from the statutory phrases and our feeling-convictions read into statutes, made hospitable thereto because uncertain, and therefore containing little or no limitation upon the reading-in process.

Under our system (especially that of the Federal Criminal law), where legislative power is definitely placed, accurately limited, and incapable of transference to a jury, star-chamber, or any other department of government, and where in addition *ex post facto* laws are prohibited, it is manifest that the maxim against uncertainty in statute: must be treated as an inseparable, inalienable and inherent part of that liberty of the citizens which is guaranteed by every American constitution. Without certainty before the fact, as to what is the law in relation to it, there can be no such thing as "due process of law" in any conviction. If the criminal statute is uncertain, then courts and juries become legislators after the fact, if any enforcement of the statute is had.

It follows that if any American legislative body should create a crime without defining it, such enactment would be a nullity. Should an attempt be made to penalize the commission of "screw-loos-ibus," without defining the word, such a law would be unenforcible and void. It is intolerable that courts should resort to current history and therefrom deduce meanings to be read into a penal statute whose words are devoid of all definiteness of meaning. By such a process the court might conclude that a legislature by "screw-loos-ibus" intended to penalize certain unpopular practices of "Christian" Scientists or Spiritualists. If courts may thus speculate inductively from current history, personal emotions and prejudices, and read the result into penal statutes by dogmatically asserting that this or that was the legislative intent, then we have re-established judicial despotism. In the absence of a generally known and *accurately definable* meaning for the word, an enforcement of the law against "screw-loos-ibus" would necessarily involve the exercise of legislative power, by the court or jury charged with its execution, and this enactment, by an unauthorized delegation of legislative power, must be specially made at each trial to cover only the acts then under investigation and must always be *ex post facto*. For each of these reasons a law which in its practical administration necessarily involves such objections must be judicially annulled.

If a criminal law is so vague as to need interpretation, then it should be declared a nullity for uncertainty. Any other course necessarily involves on the part of the interpreting judge that as among all possible meanings he exercise his own legislative discretion and read the result into the legislative intent and phraseology. If the words to be interpreted symbolize emotions as their only element of unification, and therefore are incapable of accurate general definition, or if the materials for a judgment as to the applicability of the law to every conceivable case, are varying in different persons, then to allow judges or juries to interpret or apply such a doubtful statute is to admit their authority to enforce *ex post facto* criteria of guilt; which are not public nor general, but of private origin in the court, and particular for each defendant.

The foregoing speculations suggest all that has occurred to me by way of specifying in general terms the principal sources of that outrageous remnant of absolutism which so often results, even in our time and country, in the damnable practise of punishing men for mere constructive offenses. The motive for these wrongs is usually a stupid moral sentimentalism and self-righteousness, and very often has its roots in religious superstitions of the past. The remedy can be found only in securing judges whose intellectual development is such as to make them true scientists of the law, and who with clear intellectual insight shall combine that moral courage which will make them dare to resist the "moral" rant of a politically potent but intellectually bankrupt professional reformer. I am sure there are such judges and that with persistance and diligence they can be found.

413

THE STANDARD OF CERTAINTY.

The standard of certainty and constitutionality is that a criminal statute to constitute "due process of law" must define the crime in terms so plain, and simple, as to be within the comprehension of the ordinary citizen, and so exact in meaning as to leave in him no reasonable doubt as to what is prohibited. Those qualities of generality, uniformity, and certainty must arise by an unavoidable necessity out of the very letter of the definition framed by the law-enacting power, and not come as an incidental result, from an accidental uniformity in the exercise, by courts, of an unconstitutionally delegated legislative discretion. If a statute defining a crime is not self-explanatory, but needs interpretation, or the interpolation of words or tests to insure certainty of meaning in the criteria of guilt, then it is not *the law* of the land, because no such judicial test of criminality has ever received the necessary sanction of the three separate branches of legislative power, whose members alone are authorized and sworn to define crimes and ordain their punishment. Laws defining crimes are required to be made by the law-making branch of government because of the necessity for limiting and destroying arbitrariness and judicial discretion in such matters. That is what we mean when we say ours is a government by *laws* and not by men. It follows that it is not enough that uniformity and certainty shall come as the product of judicial discretion, since "law" is necessary for the very purpose of destroying such discretion in determining what is punishable.

In chapters 13 to 17 inclusive it has been exhaustively shown that, whether studied from the viewpoint of abstract psychology, sexual psychology, abnormal psychology, ethnography, juridical history, ethics or moral sentimentalism, or, considered in the light of the mutual destructiveness of the judicially created criteria of guilt, or their all-inclusiveness and the grotesqueness resulting from their general application, in every aspect we find absolute demonstration that the statutes against "obscene" literature and art prescribe NO criteria of guilt.

In chapters 18 to 22 inclusive it has been demonstrated that the maxim, "where the law is uncertain there is no law," is an essential ingredient of our constitutional guarantee of "due process of law," and that therefore all penal statutes are unconstitutional if they do not prescribe the criteria of guilt with such precision that every man of ordinary understanding may know with absolute certainty whether or not his proposed conduct is a violation of law.

Co-ordinating these foregoing propositions, we are lead by irresistible logic to the conclusion that all statutes herein under investigation are void for the uncertainty, yes, the total absence, of criteria of guilt. *But, in the determination of these issues,* WHEN THE CONFLICT COMES BETWEEN LOGIC AND LAW ON THE ONE SIDE AND MORAL SENTIMENTALISM ON THE OTHER, WHICH WILL CONTROL?

CHAPTER XXIII.

EX POST FACTO CRITERIA OF GUILT ARE UNCONSTITUTIONAL.

Statement of Contention: *All statutes against "obscene,"* *"indecent," and "disgusting" literature and art are violative* *of section 9, article 1, of the Federal Constitution, which* *provides that* "No * * * * EX POST FACTO LAW SHALL BE PASSED," *or are violative of similar limitations in State Constitutions.*

From every conceivable viewpoint it has now been demonstrated that neither these statutory vituperative epithets against "obscene, indecent, lewd, lascivious, or filthy" literature or art, nor the unconstitutional, contradictory, and absurd judicial legislation under them, afford any certainty in the criteria of guilt, and are incapable of exact or literal application, or of producing uniformity of result. From this it follows that every conviction under these mis-called "laws" is according to *ex post facto* standards of judgment, created by the court or jury, during the trial of the accused, and enacted only for the one case of the defendant then being prosecuted. In other words, every conviction under these "laws" has been demonstrated to be according to *ex post facto* criteria of guilt. The Congress and State Legislatures, being inhibited against the passage of *ex post facto* laws, the right, thus preserved against legislative infringement, cannot be destroyed by the trick of authorizing courts to enact the prohibited *ex post facto* criteria of guilt. Neither does it make any difference whether the prohibited legislative power is directly and expressly delegated to the courts in plain terms, or is indirectly and impliedly delegated, by leaving uncertain the statutory definition of the crime, and thus, by silent implication, conferring upon courts or juries the seeming duty and consequent implied authority, *ex post facto,* to enact the necessary tests of criminality. It must be a self-evident truism that no American legislative body can delegate to courts any legislative power to define crime, and that, even if such general authority could be delegated, it could not include a power to enact *ex post facto* criteria of crime. Such *ex post facto* judicial legislation violates every modern conception of "law" and cannot constitute "due process of law." What the legislative department is prohibited from doing directly it cannot do indirectly, by a clouded attempt to confer upon the judicial department constitutionally-prohibited legislative discretion, nor authorize the latter to enact laws of such a character as even the law-making power is constitutionally prohibited to enact.

In the light of what has preceded, the conclusions hereinbefore expressed would seem to be self-evident, or at least to be in no need of any further direct argumentative support. It may be, however, that some comment is necessary to show the bearing, upon these propositions, of the power, in libel cases, sometimes exercised by jurors, to be judges of the law as well as of the fact.

Our acquaintance with the law of evolution enables us to deduce some accurate knowledge of the order and development of events in our juridical history. Thus we know that the growing coherence of tribal and inter-community life was necessarily expressed in rules of conduct increasing in complexity, number, and definiteness of statement, necessitating and accompanying an unfolding differentiation of the functions of the court from those of other officials, and the development of expertness in legal lore, eventually resulting in the differentiation of the functions of judge and jury. Thus we came to a definite conception of the right to enjoy "liberty under law," as distinguished from liberty by permission under despotism. The former affords at least to every person the protection of precisely stated, and knowable, rules of conduct, the observance of which insures absolute freedom from judicial penalties. This conception of *liberty under law* was crystallized into the constitutional guarantees of "due process of law," the inhibition against *ex post facto* laws, and the separate lodgment and limitation of the legislative authority.

The most conspicuous instance of judicial atavism is in cases of criminal libel, where the jury is authorized to determine the law as well as the facts. The immediate purpose here is critically to inquire into the origin, justification, and constitutional bearing of this anomaly in our jurisprudence. So far as my researches have informed me, there is not a single judicial opinion wherein the considerations which seem to me most important, and herein to be urged, were brought to the attention of the court, or considered on judicial initiative. More than any other one man, Thomas Erskine is responsible for bringing about that change of criminal procedure by virtue of which, in libel cases only, jurors became judges of the law as well as of the facts. In order that we may rightly appreciate the bearing of this anomaly of the law upon our own constitutional problems, we must study his motives, his arguments, the judicial reply, and the final outcome of the issue, by the passage of the Fox Libel Law. In the famous case of the Dean of St. Asaph, the final court-issue was made, and Erskine's motives were laid bare and his patient research and great intellectual acumen produced what probably is the best arguments that could be made in support of his contention. It is these that we will now consider critically, in relation to their proper influence upon present issues.

When we remember the history of the infamous Star Chamber court, and the other outraging judges who were so servile in the lawless execution of the will of their tyrannous royal master, we are not astonished that Erskine should have found his desire for making jurors judges of law in his reflections upon "the danger which has often attended the liberty of the press in former times, from the arbitrary, dependent judges, raised to their situations without abilities or worth, in proportion to their servility to [royal] power."[1] "No man in the least acquainted with the history of nations, or of his own country, can refuse to acknowledge, that if the administration of criminal justice were left in the hands of the Crown, or its deputies, no greater freedom could possibly exist than government might choose to tolerate from the convenience or policy of the day."[2] In the United States, our judiciary has never been servile to an appointing power in such a manner as, *on that account,* to make it specially dangerous to liberty of speech, nor so as to make it specially desirable to invest juries, in cases of criminal libel, with authority to overrule the judges in matters of law. This motive, therefore, does not now exist for desiring to maintain an anomaly in our judicial procedure, though from an habitual attachment to forms, rather than an understanding of the reasons for them, we have in practise

[1]Erskine's Speeches, Edition 1810, V. I, p. 154.
[2]Erskine's Speeches, Edition 1810, V. I, p. 273.

continued the procedure for which Erskine so ably contended, long after the reason for the anomaly has ceased to exist.

To Erskine's mind no other practical remedy could have presented itself for restraining the arbitrary power of a judiciary that was always servile to royal tyrants, no other means to check their proneness to extend constructive treason by judicial legislation, and the consequent lawless abridgment of freedom of speech. In the United States there are other available means of subjecting courts to a reign of law, and of preserving freedom of speech as the condition of all other liberties. Frequent elections and legislative control, under our suffrage system, are quite as effective in checking judicial tyranny as a jury could possibly be. This reason for perpetuating an anomaly also fails, under present conditions. No other reasons being suggested by Erskine, nor by observation, we may proceed to consider his legal argument.

Erskine's first reason, offered in support of his anomalous proposition that jurors were the rightful judges of the law as well as of the fact, was founded upon ancient precedent. He insisted that "it is but as yesterday, when compared with the ages of the law itself, that judges * * * * have sought to fasten a limitation upon the right and privileges of jurors, totally unknown in the ancient times," and by retracing far enough the juridical history, he could find precedents to uphold his contention.

But the answer to this argument was ready at hand in the fact that this simple judicial method had long been outgrown. As early as A. D. 1174, Henry divided the Kingdom into six districts and assigned three itinerant judges,[3] and the differentiation of the functons of judge and the jury, at least as early as the reign of Elizabeth, had been crystallized into the maxim, *"Ad quaestionem facti respondent juratores, ad questionem juris respondent judices."*[4] Mr. Justice Buller said the contention of Mr. Erskine had been completely abandoned by all the profession except by Mr. Erskine. He added: "I do not know of any one question in which the law is more thoroughly settled."[5] Lord Mansfield had already expressed his conviction that such a contention was "perfectly frivolous," and that it was strange he should be contesting points now, that the

---

3Debates on the Grand Remonstrance, p. 9.
4Erskine's Speeches, Edition 1810, V. I, p. 221.
5Erskine's Speeches, Edition 1810, V. I, p. 218.

greatest lawyers in the court had submitted to for years before he was born."[6]

After Erskine had harked back to the time of the Saxon era when "the whole administration of justice, criminal and civil, was in the hands of the people, without the control or intervention of any judicial authority, delegated to fixed magistrates by the crown,"[7] he could not but acknowledge that the evolutionary processes had wrought changes. He said: "When the civilization and commerce of the nation had introduced more intricate questions of justice, * * * * the rules of property in a cultivated state of society became by degrees beyond the compass of the unlettered multitude, and in certain well known restrictions undoubtedly fell to the judges; yet more perhaps from necessity than by consent."[8] But he argued that these products of evolution should not be acknowledged as attaching to criminal trials, and be it observed that in this respect he recognized no difference in principal between cases of criminal libel and other criminal trials. His argument ran thus: "In a question of property between private individuals, the Crown can have no possible interest in preserving the one to the other, but it may have an interest in crushing both of them together, in defiance to every principle of humanity and justice, if they should put themselves forward in a contention for public liberty, against a government seeking to emancipate itself from the dominion of the laws."[9] —"Where is the analogy between ordinary civil trials, between man and man, where Judges can rarely have an interest, and great State prosecutions, where power and freedom are weighing against each other, the balance being suspended by the servants of the executive Magistrate?"[10]

It will be observed that this is an argument which might be given great weight if addressed to a body vested with legislative discretion, and exhibits to us the motive of Erskine, rather than the actual practise and state of the juridical evolution, as fixed by precedent.

However, Erskine was not content with this alone. With great intellectual acumen he undertook to show that many of the judicial opinions which were in *seeming* conflict with

6Erskine's Speeches, Edition 1810, V. I, pp. 211-212.
7Erskine's Speeches, Edition 1810, V. I, p. 270.
8Erskine's Speeches, Edition 1810, V. I, p. 272.
9Erskine's Speeches, Edition 1810, V. I, p. 273.
10Erskine's Speeches, Edition 1810, V. I, p. 254.

his theory were in fact quite consistent therewith, but he had to admit that against his contention there existed "undoubtedly the sanction of several modern cases," and he added, "I wish, therefore, to be distinctly understood that I partly found my motion for a new trial in opposition to these decisions."[11] The court, however, followed the precedent.

One more of Erskine's arguments must be mentioned. He contended that: "A verdict on an indictment, upon the general issue, Not Guilty, universally and unavoidably involves a judgment of law as well as of fact, because the charge comprehends both and the verdict is co-extensive with it."[12]

Because the court can not hold an inquisition on the mental processes of jurors it follows, in most cases, and especially where intent is an element of crime, that a verdict on the general issue inextricably involves questions of law, as to which it is within the power of jurors to ignore the instructions of the court and with impunity. Erskine argued that because of the existence of this *power* the court should acknowledge a claim of *authority* in the jury to rejudge the law, as a matter of admitted right.

The court, however, held that the unavoidable *power* of jurors to ignore the law, as expounded by the judge, was no reason for admitting a claim of such *authority* as rightly vested in them. Erskine had argued that "the constitution never intended to invest judges with a discretion which cannot be tried and measured by the plain and palpable standard of law."[13] In its decision, overruling Mr. Erskine's argument, the court applied the same limitation to the discretion of jurors. Both positions are unquestionably correct from the viewpoint of all who believe in *liberty under law*. The opinion of the court in part reads as follows: "Miserable is the condition of individuals, dangerous is the condition of the State, *if there is no certain law,* or, which is the same thing, no certain administration of law to protect individuals, or to guard the State. * * * * What is contended for? That the law shall be in every particular cause what any twelve men, who shall happen to be the jury, shall be inclined to think, liable to no review, and subject to no control, under all the bias of interest in this town, when thousands more or less

11Erskine's Speeches, Edition 1810, V. I, p. 298.
12Erskine's Speeches, Edition 1810, V. I, p. 309.
13Erskine's Speeches, Edition 1810, V. I, p. 331.

are concerned in the publication of newspapers, paragraphs, and pamphlets. Under such an administration of law, *no man could tell, no counsel could advise, whether a paper was or was not punishable.*"[14]

Thus we see that certainty in the criteria of guilt was even then held to be an essential to the existence of "law" and of "due process of law,"[15] though unfortunately this essential had not been consistently demanded. Thus, to the end of promoting certainty and uniformity as indispensable to the existence of law, do we find it to be the established practise long before the American Revolution that courts, and not jurors, are the expositors of the law and that in all criminal cases, including those of libel, both court and jury should be precluded from creating the criteria of guilt. However, under the special conditions existing in England, and which conditions were abolished by our American Constitutions, there was an urgent necessity for curtailing the power of courts in the matter of "interpreting" the inexcusably vague "law" of libel. To give to juries a right to overrule the judges' conception of the law seemed, and was, the only practical attainable relief under then existing British conditions. Accordingly the agitation continued, along the lines mapped out by Erskine, until in 1792 the Fox Libel Act was passed, which in all cases of criminal libel gave English juries authority to be judges of both the law and fact.

From the foregoing review, it must be apparent that neither on principles of juridical philosophy nor on precedent, can it be said that at the time of the American Revolution English juries had acknowledged authority to be judges of libel-law. It follows that Fox's libel law was not merely declaratory, but a distinct atavic innovation, and accordingly it has been held that this practise never became a part of the common law of the colonies.[16] Even if this were otherwise, it would have no application to our present obscenity laws, because the circulation of obscene literature was not a common-law offense.[17] Even though not yet universally admitted, at least as according to precedent and right reason,

[14] Erskine's Speeches, Edition 1810, V. I, pp. 379-380.

[15] In the "Grand Remonstrance" of 1641, addressed by the Long Parliament to the King, one of the complaints was that the rules of common law which had survived through centuries of comparative barbarism, had lost their certainty. Debates on the Grand Remonstrance, p. 236.

[16] Negley *vs.* Farroud, 60 Md. 178-180; Com. *vs.* Blauding, 20 Mass. (3 Pick) 306.

[17] "Obscene Literature at Common Law." *Albany Law Journal*, May, 1907.

the following principle of English constitutional law as stated by De Lolme in 1773, was adopted into our American Constitutions as a natural limitation necessary to preclude judicial despotism, and is an essential element of our "due process of law," and in all cases precludes the *ex post facto* creation of criteria of guilt, even by juries.

De Lolme's pre-revolutionary statement of the principle of the English Constitution now under consideration, is as follows:

"The judicial power ought, therefore, absolutely to reside in a subordinate and dependent body—dependent, not in its particular acts, with regard to which it ought to be a sanctuary, but in its rules and in its forms, which the legislative authority must prescribe. * * * * The courts and their different forms must be such as to inspire respect, but never terror; and the cases ought to be so accurately ascertained, the limits so clearly marked, that neither the executive power, nor the judges, may ever hope to transgress them with impunity.[18]

CONCLUSION.

The foregoing discussion, and the discussions and authorities cited, justify the following conclusions: At the time of the separation of the American Colonies, there was no such crime as "obscene libel" distinct from blasphemy, nor had jurors in any libel case the authority to be judges of the law as well as of the facts. Under the common-law and "due process of law," neither judges nor jurors could be allowed to create the criteria of guilt, which must always be precisely defined by the legislative authority, before the act to which it is applied. It would be beyond the constitutional authority for juries to penalize acts not clearly within some prior statutory definition of crime, or for them to create such definition where the legislature had failed to complete that task, as in the case of "obscenity" laws. Although the legislature might perhaps authorize the jury to acquit, even where conduct is clearly within a precisely stated legislative test of criminality, yet the legislative department can not create, nor directly or indirectly authorize court or jury to create *ex post facto* standards of guilt, and the attempt to confer, upon

[18]De Lolme. The Constitution of England, pp. 121-122, Bohn Edition. First published in Holland, 1773, and the first English edition published in 1775.

courts or juries, such prohibited legislative discretion, is unconstitutional. Accordingly all laws against "obscene" literature or art are, because the statutes do not prescribe the standards of criminality, attempts to delegate to juries the legislative authority to create *ex post facto* criteria of guilt, and, therefore, are void.

TABLE OF CASES ARISING UNDER "OBSCENITY" AND KINDRED STATUTES

U. S. vs. Durant, 46 F. R. 753
U. S. vs. Grimm, 50 F. R. 528
U. S. vs. Martin, 50 F. R. 918
U. S. vs. Harman, 50 F. R. 921
U. S. vs. Males, 51 F. R. 41
U. S. vs. Wilson, 58 F. R. 768
U. S. vs. Andrews, 58 F. R. 861
U. S. vs. Warner, 59 F. R. 355
U. S. vs. Adams, 59 F. R. 664-676-677
U. S. vs. Jarvis, 59 F. R. 357
U. S. vs. Andrews, 59 F. R. 861
U. S. vs. Nathan, 61 F. R. 936
U. S. vs. Ling, 61 F. R. 1001
U. S. vs. Reed, 73 F. R. 289
U. S. vs. Lamkin, 73 F. R. 459-463
U. S. vs. Janes, 74 F. R. 545
U. S. vs. Brazeau, 78 F. R. 464
U. S. vs. Timmons, 85 F. R. 204 ; 30 C. C. A. 79, and notes
Saffer vs. U. S. 31 C. C. A. I.; 87 F. R. 329
U. S. vs. Tubbs, 94 F. R. 356
U. S. vs. Clifford, 104 F. R 296
U. S. vs. DeGignac, 113 F. R. 197; C. C. A.
Konda vs. U.S. 116 F. R. 91
U. S. vs. Harris, 122 F. R. 551
U. S. vs. Wyatt, 122 F. R. 316
Harvey vs. U. S. 127 Fed. 357
U. S. vs. Moore, 129 F. R. 159
U. S. vs. Wroblenski, 118 F. R. 496
U. S. vs. Wroblenski, 129 F. R. 162
U. S. vs. Coleman, 131 F. R. 151-152 (N. Y).
U. S. vs. Pupke, 133 F. R. 243 (Prev.).
(U. S. vs. Sherman—see Comstock's Brief 33)
Burton vs. U. S. 142 F. R. 57 C. C. A.
Demoli vs. U. S. 144 Fed. 363 C. C. A.
Rinker vs. U. S. 151 Fed. R. 755
Hanson vs. U. S. 157 F. R. 749
Shepard vs. U. S. 160 F. R. 584
U. S. vs. Macfadden, 165 F. R. 51
Knowles vs. U. S. 170 F. R. 409

ALABAMA
Henderson vs. State, 63 Ala. 193

CALIFORNIA
Peop. vs. Zuell, 82 Pac. 1128

CONNECTICUT
Knowles vs. Conn. (1808) 3 Day 103

GEORGIA
Dillard vs. State, 41 Ga. 279
Montross vs. State, 72 Ga. 261
Brigman vs. State, 123 Ga. 505 ; 51 S. E. Rep 504
State vs. Kelly, 55 S. E. Rep 482
Redd vs. State, 67 S. E. 709

ILLINOIS
People vs. McNair, 89 Ill. 441. Cent. Law J. 235
Fuller vs. People, 92 Ill. 182

INDIANA
McJunkin vs. State, 10 Ind. (1858)
Ardery vs. State, 56 Ind. 328
Thomas vs. State, 2 N. E. Rep. 808 ; 103 Ind. 419

MASSACHUSETTS
People vs. Holmes, 17 Mass. 336 (1821)
People vs. Tarbox, 1. Cush, 66
Com. vs. Kneeland, 20 Pick. 206
Com. vs. Dejardin, 126 Mass. 46
Com. vs. Wright, 139 Mass. 382. I. N. E. Rep. 411
Com. vs. McCance, 164 Mass. 162; 29 L. R. A. 61.
Com. vs. Buckley, 200 Mass. 346

MICHIGAN
Peop. vs. Giradin 1 Mich, 90
Peop. vs. Harris, 13 Detroit Legal News ; 107 N. W. 715

MISSOURI
State vs. Appling (1857) 4 Jones' Mo. R. 315
Williams vs. State, 4 Mo. 480
Edgar vs. McCutchan, 9 Mo. 768

NEW JERSEY
Larison vs. State, 49 N. J. L. 256. 60 Am. Rep. 606
State vs. Goldstein, 72 N. J. Law 336-62 Atl. Rep. 10c6
State vs. Hill, 73 N. J. Law 77 ; 62 Atl. R. 936

NEW YORK
People vs. Muller, 32 Hun. 209-96. N. Y. 408-48. A. Rep. 635.
People vs. Justice of Special Sessions, 10 Hun. 224
People vs. Hallenbeck, 52 How. Pr. 502
People vs. Daniley, 63 Hun. 579
Matter of Worthington, Co., 62 St. Rep. 115; 30 N. Y. Sup. 361; (24 L. R. 110 note)
People vs. Jake Berry, 1. N. Y. Crim. R. 43
People vs. Eastman, Law Jour. June 7, 1907. 188 N. Y. 478
People vs. Daly, N. Y. Law Jour. July 9, 1907, and June 17, 1907
St. Hubert's Guild vs. Quinn, 18 N. Y. Sup. 582.

NORTH CAROLINA.

State vs. Toole, 106 N. C. 736 ; 11 S. E. Rep. 168.

OHIO

State vs. Zurhorst, 79 N. E. 238

PENNSYLVANIA

Com. vs. Sharpless, 2 Searg. & R. 91

Com. vs. Landis, 8 Phila. 453

Barker vs. Com. (1852) 19 Pa. R. 412

RHODE ISLAND

State vs. Smith, 17 R. I. 371

SOUTH CAROLINA

Phalen vs. State Va., 8 Howard, 168 (S. C.)

Union Co. vs. Landing Co. 4 S. C. 652

TENNESSEE

Peel or Bell vs. State, (1851) 1 Swan's Tenn. R. 42.

Brooks vs. State (1831) 2 Yerg. 482-483

Nolin vs. Mayor, 4 Yerg. (12 Tenn.) 163

State vs. Pennington, 5 Lea, 506.

TEXAS

State vs. Hanson, 23 Tex. Cr. App. 232

Smith vs State, 24 Tex. Cr. App. 1

Griffin vs. State, 43 Tex. Cr. App. 428

Huffman vs. State, 49 Tex. Cr. Rep. 319 ; 92. S. W. Rep. 419

VERMONT

State vs. Brown, 1 Williams (27 Vermont) 619

State vs. Bacon, 41 Vt. 526.

INDEX.